Created and Directed by Hans Höfer

INSIGHT GUIDES

SCOTLAND

Edited and Produced by Brian Bell

Principal Photography: Douglas Corrance

Updated by Marcus Brooke

LICATIONS

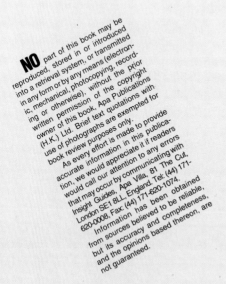
SCOTLAND

Third Edition (Reprint)
© **1995 APA PUBLICATIONS (HK) LTD**
All Rights Reserved
Printed in Singapore by Höfer Press Pte. Ltd

Distributed in the United States by:	Distributed in Canada by:	Distributed in the UK & Ireland by:	Worldwide distribution enquiries:
Houghton Mifflin Company	**Thomas Allen & Son**	**GeoCenter International UK Ltd**	**Höfer Communications Pte Ltd**
222 Berkeley Street	390 Steelcase Road East	The Viables Center, Harrow Way	38 Joo Koon Road
Boston, Massachusetts 02116-3764	Markham, Ontario L3R 1G2	Basingstoke, Hampshire RG22 4BJ	Singapore 2262
ISBN: 0-395-66191-9	ISBN: 0-395-66191-9	ISBN: 9-62421-066-7	ISBN: 9-62421-066-7

ABOUT THIS BOOK

Robert Louis Stevenson, the Edinburgh author of *Treasure Island* and *Dr Jekyll and Mr Hyde,* would not have been popular with the Scottish Tourist Board. "For all who love shelter and the blessings of the sun," he wrote, "who hate dark weather and perpetual tilting against squalls, there could scarcely be found a more unhomely and harassing place of residence." Still, Edinburgh and Scotland continue to enchant visitors. Emulating Stevenson's honesty, *Insight Guide: Scotland* paints a realistic portrait of Scotland today.

This latest, completely updated edition has been supervised by the book's original project editor, **Brian Bell**, who is now editorial director in charge of Apa Publications' London office, which has helped spearhead the phenomenal expansion of the series. A journalist with wide experience in newspapers and magazines, Bell was attracted to Apa's philosophy that a country's warts should not be omitted from a guidebook; they can be as interesting as its beauty spots and make it more enticing to the adventurous traveller. As a Northern Irishman with Scottish Presbyterian antecedents, he was well-placed to assemble an authoritative team of writers and photographers who would provide a true insight into one of the most alluring yet misunderstood regions of the British Isles.

The Writers

Bell turned first to **George Rosie**, one of the guide's leading contributors, who began his career in Dundee with D.C. Thomson, a company that turns out newspapers and children's comics. Rosie moved to London and joined the *Sunday Times* in 1974, but later returned to Scotland to write about it from the inside for for newspapers and TV.

"In many ways," says Rosie, "Scotland is the most infuriating place in Europe – a slightly dotty 'nearly country' with its own system of law, education, established church and civil service unsupervised by any elected assembly and with no politics of its own. There are times when its very core seems to consist of a mush of bad history and sentimental song. But then I find myself on a snow-battered ridge on the Cairngorm Mountains, or helicoptering out to a North Sea oil platform, or lurching across the Minch in a fishing boat, or being dazzled by some benign and subtle point of Scots law, and I suddenly realise that no other part of the UK – not even London itself – has so much to offer."

Julie Davidson, who wrote five of the "Places" chapters, is another Scottish journalist who has made her mark in Britain's national media. She thinks it's ideal to be able to earn part of her income in London without having to live there and cannot imagine living anywhere else other than Scotland.

One man who has done more than most to fight the myths is the author of the "Highlanders and Lowlanders" chapter, **Christopher Smout**, whose masterly two-volume *History of the Scottish People* appealed equally to both academic and general readers. Although English by birth, he has lived in Scotland since 1959 and is Professor of Scottish History at the University of St Andrews. "Scotland still seems to me the most beautiful country in Europe," he says, "and the Scots among the kindest people. In 30 years, the country has become rather more prosperous, much more unified by good roads,

Bell

Rosie

Davidson

Smout

May

gained a flashy Glasgow and lost a certain amount of solid distinctiveness."

Yet many Scots choose to live elsewhere. **Naomi May**, who wrote the chapter on religion, was born in Glasgow, grew up in the southwest county of Renfrewshire and now lives in London. A novelist and artist, she recalls that her favourite subject at school, Scottish history, had all the right ingredients: feuds, murder, revenge, intrigue and fierce defiance of the Sassenachs (English).

Marcus Brooke, who contributed several chapters and a selection of photographs, as well as a revised and much expanded Travel Tips section for this edition, claims that Scotland is the most beautiful country in the world – except for its weather. Since 1964, armed with typewriter and cameras, he has travelled the world pursuing his interest in archaeology and anthropology and contributing to many newspapers and magazines. He returns frequently to his native Glasgow.

There's a less dour side to the Scottish character, of course, brought out in the "Song and Dance" chapter by **Alastair Clark**. Not only has he written a regular music column for *The Scotsman* for the past 20 years, but he is also an accomplished musician.

Conrad Wilson, author of the food chapter, writes about food and wine for *The Scotsman,* and is also the paper's music critic.

Stuart Ridsdale, who explored the Borders for this guide, could be called a near-Scot; recent generations of his family have hailed from Yorkshire in England, earlier antecedents can be found in the tiny Northumberland village of Ridsdale.

Roland Collins, another contributor to the "Places" section, did the next best thing to being born north of the border: he married a Scot. After a long career in advertising, he devotes time to his painting and photography. Seen through his eyes, "watering from peat smoke," Scotland's rugged individuality is the natural child of the largely inhospitable Highlands and a punishing climate.

Dymphna Byrne, a travel journalist who has written books on camping and on Israel, became interested in the Hebridean islands during camping holidays on mainland Scotland with her husband and three sons.

Cowan Ervine, who wrote the panel on Scottish law, is a Northern Irishman who teaches law at the University of Perth.

The Photographs

The photographs for *Insight Guide: Scotland* came from many sources, and were ably assembled by **Judy Lehane**, a London-based Scot and the author of a book on the Hebridean island of Eigg. But one name dominates the credit list: **Douglas Corrance**, an Edinburgh-based photographer now in demand internationally. His career began on an Inverness newspaper, and he spent 11 years as the Scottish Tourist Board's principal photographer. He has since published several collections of his photography, and his work appears in Insight Guides to Glasgow, Edinburgh, New York and the Côte d'Azur.

Should auld acquaintance be forgot, Apa Publications would like to raise a glass to the many people who helped in the compilation of this guide. Especially valuable assistance came from **Caledonian MacBrayne, Eddie Holmes** of the Scottish Tourist Board, **Libby Weir Breen** of the Shetland Tourist Organisation, and **Jane Johnson** of the Oban, Mull and District Tourist Board. The book was indexed by **John Goulding**.

Brooke   *Wilson*   *Collins*   *Bryne*   *Corrance*

CONTENTS

History

Features

Places

Maps

TRAVEL TIPS

Compiled by Marcus Brooke

**For detailed information,
see page 305**

THE SCOTTISH CHARACTER

A native of Scotland, it has been said, considers himself a Scot before he thinks of himself as a human being, thus establishing a clear order of excellence. This attitude, naturally enough, wins him few popularity points from the rest of the human race and none at all from his nearest neighbour, England. Indeed, English literature is so peppered with anti-Scots aphorisms that the cumulative impression given amounts to national defamation.

"I have been trying all my life to like Scotchmen," wrote the essayist Charles Lamb, "and am obliged to desist from the experiment in despair." P.G. Wodehouse was no kinder: "It is never difficult," he wrote, "to distinguish between a Scotsman with a grievance and a ray of sunshine." And Dr Samuel Johnson, whose tour of the Hebrides in 1773 was immortalised by his Scottish biographer James Boswell, produced the most enduring maxim: "The noblest prospect that a Scotchman ever sees is the high road that leads him to England."

Shotgun marriage: It is a road that many have taken: an estimated 20 million Scots, one of the most inventive peoples on earth, are scattered throughout every continent – four times as many as live in Scotland itself. Yet an unease towards the English, a suspicion that they are his social superiors, has for centuries blighted the Scots psyche. The union of the two countries in 1707, after centuries of sporadic hostility, was regarded by most Scots as a shotgun marriage and more than 280 years have scarcely diluted the differences in outlook and attitude between the ill-matched partners.

In 1987, for instance, Margaret Thatcher led Britain's Conservative Party to a third successive election victory, winning a commanding number of constituencies in the south of England particularly; yet in Scotland, where she was seen as an unsympathetic English figure, she won fewer than one in

four of the votes cast and held only 10 of the 72 Scottish seats in the House of Commons. It was a devastating rejection and talk began once again of giving Scotland back its separate parliament. Yet, as so often before, the alienation failed to find a political focus. People recalled the frustratingly indecisive result of a 1979 referendum which asked the Scots whether they really wanted a devolved government: a third said yes, a third said no, and the remaining third didn't bother to vote. In the 1992 general election, the Scots again

confounded the pundits: although it had been predicted that the Conservatives would be driven from Scotland, they actually increased their vote marginally.

Perhaps they can't agree on a solution to their age-old problems, but the Scots are unanimous in identifying who has caused them: England. It is an old tune, often played. When the future Pope Pius II visited the country in the 15th century, he concluded: "Nothing pleases the Scots more than abuse of the English."

In that respect, the Scots resemble England's other close neighbours, the French, with whom they have intimate historical

Preceding pages: jazz at the Edinburgh Festival; Scottish thistle; red deer; Edinburgh Castle from Princes Street Gardens; standing by at Orkney airport. Left, on guard at Blackness Castle. Right, stall holder in Paddy's Market, Glasgow.

connections. Both share an outspokenness, which the English mistake for rudeness. Both are proud peoples, a characteristic which, in the case of the Scots, the English translate as ingratitude. "You Scots," the playwright J.M. Barrie once had one of his characters say, "are such a mixture of the practical and the emotional that you escape out of an Englishman's hand like a trout." Barrie, the creator of Peter Pan, was a Scot himself and often cast a cynical eye over his fellow countrymen. "There are few more impressive sights in the world," he declared, "than a Scotsman on the make."

It is noticeable that the butt of most of these waspish epigrams is the Scots *man*.

directly in touch with their God. No man was deemed inherently better than the next – and that included the clergy, who were made directly answerable to their congregations. This democratic tradition, allied with a taste for argument born of theological wrangling, runs deep and has led more than one English politician to brand troublesome Glasgow shipyard workers, for example, as Communists. Some might have been; but most were simply exercising their right to be individualists. It was an attitude that would allow a riveter to regard himself as being every bit as good as the shipyard boss and whenever necessary, to remind the boss of that fact. Deference? What's that?

Until recently, women, though no less strong in character, played a subsidiary role in the country's public affairs. It was very much a man's world. Thus, although Scottish law introduced desertion as grounds for divorce in 1573 (364 years before England got around to doing so), it retained a robust, Calvinistic view about what wives ought to put up with.

Certainly, the Calvinist tradition is central to the Scots character. While England absorbed the Reformation with a series of cunning compromises, Scotland underwent a revolution, replacing the panoply of Roman Catholicism with an austere Presbyterianism designed to put the ordinary people

In many other ways, too, the Scots character is a confusing one. It combines dourness and humour, meanness and generosity, arrogance and tolerance, cantankerousness and chivalry, sentimentality and hard-headedness. One aspect of these contradictions is caught by a *Punch* cartoon showing a hitchhiker trying to entice passing motorists with a sign reading "Glasgow – or else!" On the positive side, a bad climate and a poor soil forged an immensely practical people. But there was a price to be paid: these disadvantages encouraged frugality and a deep-seated pessimism. "It could be worse" comes easily to the lips of the most underprivileged.

The situation is redeemed by laughter. Scottish humour is subtle and sardonic and, in the hands of someone as verbally inventive as the Glasgow-born comedian Billy Connolly, can leave reality far behind with a series of outrageously surreal non-sequiturs. It has also been used, over the years, to cement many a Scottish stereotype. "My father was an Aberdonian," the veteran comedian Chic Murray would say, "and a more generous man you couldn't wish to meet. I have a gold watch that belonged to my father, he sold it to me on his death bed... so I wrote him a cheque."

Alcohol features prominently in Scottish jokes, as it does in many aspects of the

Experience suggests that the worst of them could be taken by the Red Army in three days, a day-and-a-half if tactical nuclear weapons were used."

Like the Irish, the Scots have realised that there's money to be made from conforming to a stereotyped image, however bogus it may be. Although few in Scotland ever eat haggis (once described as looking like a castrated bagpipe), it is offered to tourists as the national dish. Heads of ancient Scottish clans, living in houses large enough to generate cashflow problems, have opened their homes to tour groups of affluent Americans. Others have opened "clan shops" retailing an astonishing variety of tartan artefacts, in-

country's life. Until recently the single-minded aim of Scottish pubs was to enable their clientele to get drunk as fast as possible, a purpose reflected in their decor. "Some of them," wrote the journalist Hugh McIlvanney, "are so bare that anyone who wants to drink in sophisticated surroundings takes his glass into the lavatory." Matters have improved, though some hostelries should still be approached with caution. "There is," wrote McIlvanney, "a relentless inclination to exaggerate the toughness of Glasgow pubs.

Left, a pub in Jedburgh. **Above**, comedian Billy Connolly in his hairy heyday.

cluding Hairy Haggisburger soft toys. Still others have taken to appearing in Japanese TV commercials extolling their "family brand" of whisky. The cult of the kilt – based, someone mused, on the self-deception that male knees are an erogenous zone – is a huge commercial success.

But the image obscures the real Scotland. It's worth lingering long enough to draw back the tartan curtain and get to know one of Europe's most complex peoples. There's no guarantee that the more innocent tourists won't have the wool pulled over their eyes; but, if it's any consolation to them, it's sure to be best-quality Scottish wool.

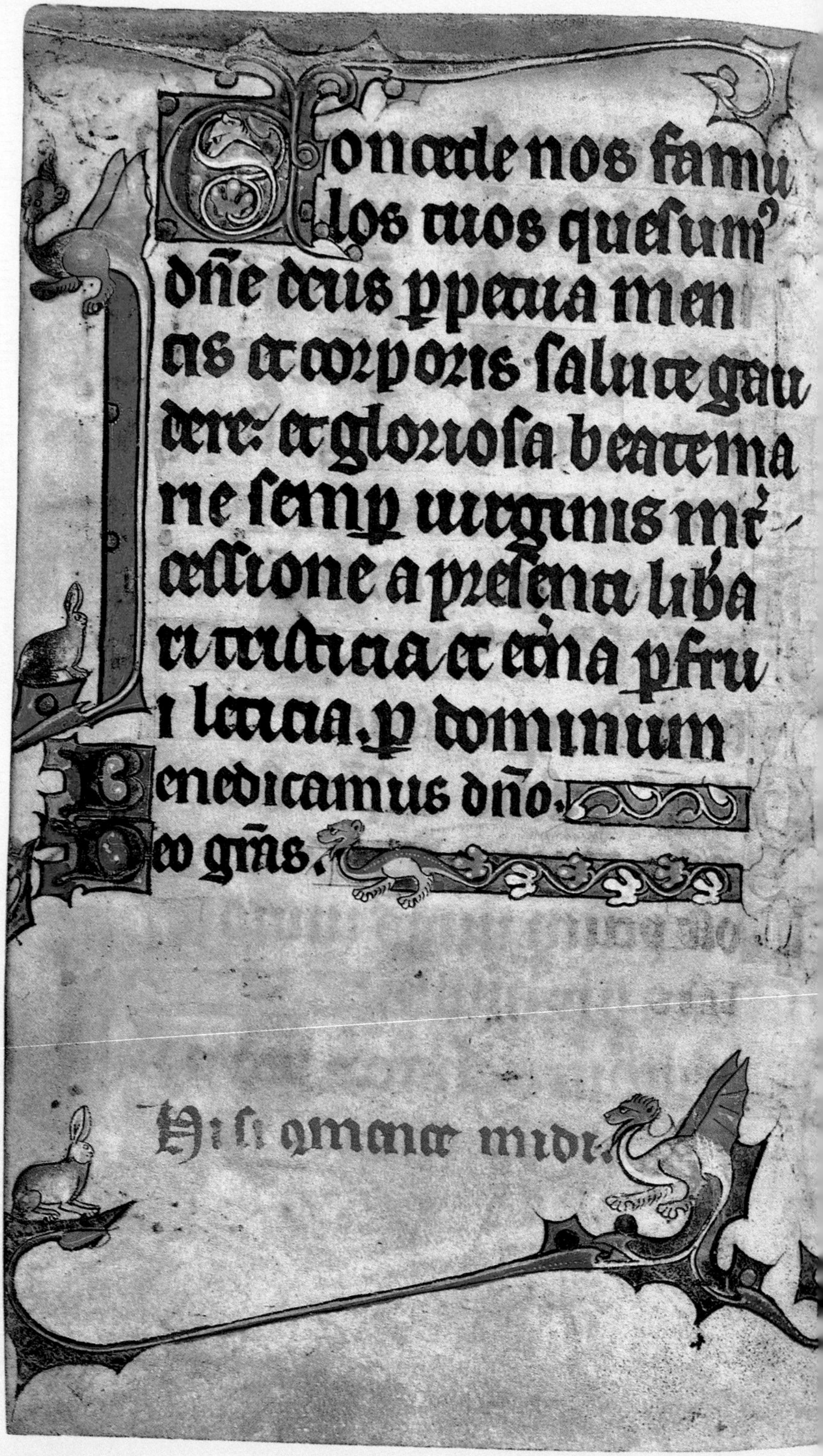

oncede nos famu
los tuos quesum̄
dñe deus ppetua men
tis et corporis salute gau
dere: et gloriosa beate ma
rie semp̄ uirginis in̄
tcessione a presenti libe
ri tristicia et eterna pfru
i leticia. p̄ dominium

Benedicamus dño.
Deo gr̄as.

Hic si qmenie midi⁊

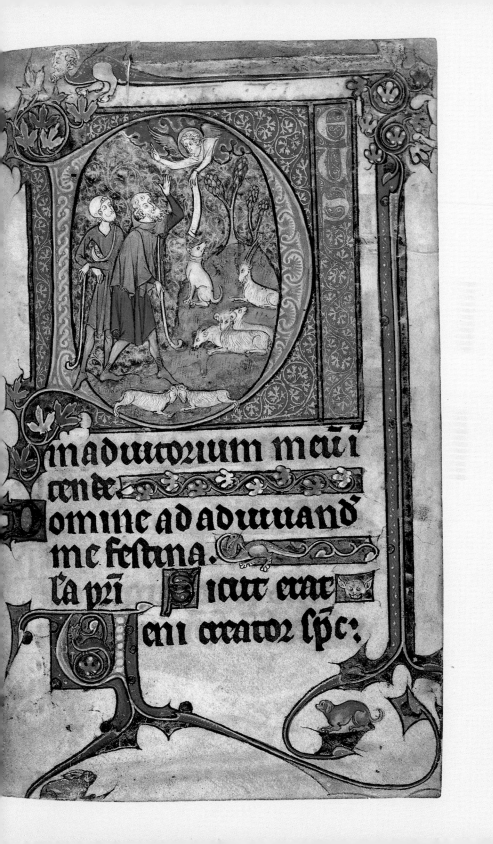

ma dniitozium meii i
cendie
Domine ad adiunand
me festina.
la pri   S init erat
eni creator spc;

BEGINNINGS

On a bleak, windswept moor three witches crouch round a bubbling cauldron, muttering oaths and prophesying doom. A king is brutally stabbed to death and his killer, consumed by vaulting ambition, takes the throne, only to be murdered himself soon afterwards. "Fair is foul, and foul is fair."

To many people, these images from Shakespeare's *Macbeth* are their first introduction to early Scottish history. But of course, the Scots will tell you, Shakespeare was English and, as usual, the English got it wrong. There is perhaps some truth to the tale, they admit – Macbeth, who reckoned he had a better hereditary claim to the throne than its occupant, did kill Duncan in 1040 – but thereafter he ruled well for 17 years and kept the country relatively prosperous.

Power games: Where Shakespeare undeniably showed his genius, however, was in managing to heighten the narrative of a history that was already (and remained) melodramatic beyond belief. Scotland's story was for centuries little more than the biographies of ruthlessly ambitious families jostling for power, gaining it and losing it through accidents of royal marriages, unexpected deaths and lack of fertility.

A successful king needed cunning as well as determination, an ability to judge just how far he could push powerful barons without being toppled from his throne in the process. Future marriage contracts were routinely made between royal infants and, when premature death brought a succession of kings to the throne as children, the land's leading families fought for advancement by trying to gain control over the young rulers, occasionally by kidnapping them.

Summarise some of the stories and they seem more histrionic than historical. A sexy young widow returns from the French court to occupy the throne of Scotland, lays claim to the throne of England, conducts a series of passionate affairs, marries her lover a few weeks after he has allegedly murdered her second husband, loses the throne, is incar-

Preceding pages: *The Annunciation to the Shepherds,* from the early 14th-century Murthly Book of Hours. **Left,** Romans building Hadrian's Wall.

cerated for 19 years by her cousin, the Queen of England, and is then, on a pretext, beheaded. No soap-opera scriptwriter today would dare to invent as outrageous a plot as the true-life story of Mary Queen of Scots.

Nameless people: Our earliest knowledge of Scotland dates back more than 6,000 years, when the cold, wet climate and the barren landscape would seem familiar enough to a time-traveller from the present day. Then the region was inhabited by nameless hunters and fishermen.

Later, the mysterious Beaker People from Holland and the Rhineland settled here, as they did in Ireland, leaving as a memorial only a few tantalising pots. Were the eerie

natives "painted men", encountered fearsome opposition. An early Scots leader, called Calgacus by the Romans, rallied 30,000 men – a remarkable force but no match for the Roman war machine. Even so, the Romans respected their enemy's ability enough for the historian Tacitus to feel able to attribute to Calgacus the anti-Roman sentiment: "They make a wilderness and call it peace."

Soon, however, the "barbarians" began to perfect guerrilla tactics. In the year 118, for instance, the Ninth Legion marched north to quell yet another rebellion and was never seen again. Was it really worth all this trouble, the Romans wondered, to subdue such barbarians? Hadrian's answer, as emperor,

Standing Stones of Callanish, on the island of Lewis, built by them as a primitive observatory? Nobody can be certain. Celtic tribes, driven by their enemies to the outer fringes of Europe, settled in Scotland, as they did in Ireland, Cornwall, Wales and Brittany, and mastered iron implements. The blueprint for a tribal society was in place.

It was the Romans who gave it coherence. The desire of Emperor Vespasian in AD 80 to forge northwards from an already subjugated southern Britain towards the Grampian Mountains and the dense forests of central Scotland united the tribes in opposition. To their surprise, the Romans, who called the

was no. He built a fortified wall that stretched for 73 miles (117 km) across the north of England, isolating the savages. A successor, Antoninus, tried to push back the boundaries in 142 by erecting a fortified wall between the Rivers Forth and the Clyde. But it was never an effective exercise. The Roman Empire fell without ever conquering these troublesome natives and Scottish life carried on without the more lasting benefits of Roman civilisation, such as good roads. A complex clan system evolved, consisting of large families bound by blood ties.

Europe's Dark Ages enveloped the region. What records remain portray raiders riding south to plunder and pillage. True Scots were born in the 6th century when Gaels migrated from the north of Ireland, inaugurating an epoch in which beautifully drawn manuscripts and brilliant metalwork illuminated the cultural darkness.

As with much of Western Europe, Scotland's history at this time was a catalogue of invasions. The most relentless aggressors were the Vikings, who arrived in the 9th century in their Scandinavian longships to loot the monasteries which had been founded by early Christian missionaries such as St Ninian and St Columba.

Eventually, in 843, the warring Picts, a fierce Celtic race who dominated the south-

to William the Conqueror in 1066 drove many English lords northwards, turning the Lowlands of Scotland into an aristocratic refugee camp. Scotland's king, Malcolm, married one of the refugees, Margaret, a Hungarian-born Christian reformer. She drew her standards from England and, some believe, gave Scots their eternal inferiority complex by forcing them to measure themselves constantly against the English.

Partly to please her, Malcolm invaded England twice. During the second incursion, he lost his life. This gave William Rufus, the Conqueror's son and successor, an opportunity to involve himself in Scottish affairs by securing the northern throne for Malcolm's

west, and united with the Scots under Kenneth MacAlpine, the astute ruler of the west coast Kingdom of Dalriada. But Edinburgh wasn't brought under the king's influence until 962 and the Angles, a Teutonic people who controlled the south of the country, were not subjugated until 1018. Feuding for power was continuous. It was in this period that Macbeth murdered his rival, Duncan, and was killed in turn by Duncan's son.

Norman conquest: The collapse of England

Left, Roman panel from Glasgow University's Hunterian Museum. Above, William Wallace rallies the Scots against the English.

eldest son, Edgar, the first of a series of weak kings. A successor, David I, having been brought up in England, gave many estates to his Norman friends. Also, he did nothing to stop English replacing Gaelic and he introduced feudalism into the Lowlands.

But true feudalism never really took root. French knights, accustomed to deference, were surprised to find, when they rode through a field of crops, that the impertinent Scottish peasants would demand compensation. Although the Normans greatly influenced architecture and language, they in no sense conquered the country. Instead, they helped create a social division that was to dominate

Scotland's history: the Lowlands were controlled by noblemen who spoke the same Norman French and subscribed to the same values as England's ruling class, while the Highlands remained untamed, under the influence of independent-minded Gaelic speakers, and the islands were loyal, more or less, to Norway.

The Highland clans, indeed, were virtually independent kingdoms, whose chiefs, under the old patriarchal system, had the power of life and death over their people. Feuds between clans were frequent and bloody, provoking one visiting scholar to pronounce: "The Scots are not industrious and the people are poor. They spend all their

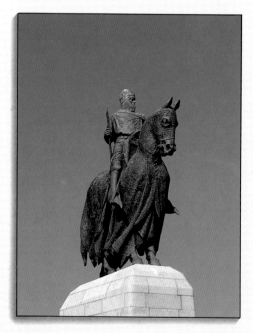

time in wars and, when there is no war, they fight one another."

Over the next three centuries the border with England was to be constantly redefined. The seaport of Berwick-upon-Tweed, now the most northerly town in England, was to change hands 13 times. In the 1160s the Scots turned to French sympathisers for help, concluding what came to be known as the Auld Alliance. In later years the pact would have a profound influence on Scottish life, but on this occasion it was no match for England's might.

After a comparatively peaceful interlude, England's insidious interference provoked a serious backlash in 1297. William Wallace, a violent youth from Elderslie, became an outlaw after a scuffle with English soldiers in which a girl (some think she was his wife) who helped him escape was killed by the Sheriff of Lanark. Wallace returned to kill the Sheriff, but didn't stop there; soon he had raised enough of an army to drive back the English forces, making him for some months master of southern Scotland. But he wasn't supported by the nobles, who considered him low-born, and, after being defeated at Falkirk by England's Edward I (the "Hammer of the Scots"), he met his expected fate by being hanged, drawn and quartered. His quarters were sent to Newcastle, Berwick, Sterling and Perth.

Bruce's victory: The next challenger, Robert the Bruce, who was descended from the Norman de Brus family, got further as a freedom fighter – as far as the throne itself, in fact, though he didn't sit on it long. During a year's exile on Rathlin Island, off the coast of Ireland, he is said to have been inspired by the persistence of a spider in a cave and he returned to Scotland to win a series of victories. Soon the French recognised him as King of Scotland and the Roman Catholic Church gave him its backing.

England's new king, Edward II, although he had little stomach for Scottish affairs, could not ignore the challenge and, in 1314, the two forces collided at Bannockburn, south of Stirling. Bruce's chances looked slim: he was pitching only 6,000 men against 20,000 English. But he was shrewd enough to hold the high ground, forcing the English into the wet marshes, and he won.

Because the Pope did not recognise the new monarch, Bruce's subjects successfully petitioned Rome, and the Declaration of Arbroath in 1320 confirmed him as King.

Like the Romans, England's Edward III decided that Scotland was more trouble than it was worth and in 1328 granted it independence. He recognised Bruce as king and, cementing the treaty in the customary manner, married his young sister to Bruce's baby son. Peace had been achieved at last between two of the most rancorous of neighbours. It seemed too good to be true – and it was.

<u>Left</u>, Robert the Bruce's statue in Stirling. <u>Right</u>, Bruce kills Sir Henry de Bohun in single combat at Bannockburn.

Bruce brought his axe crashing down upon the head of Bohun

Robert Bruce sends a defiance to Edward III.

The outbreak in 1339 of the intermittent Hundred Years' War between England and France kept Edward III's mind off Scotland. He failed, therefore, to appreciate the significance of a pact concluded in 1326 between France and Scotland by Robert the Bruce. Yet the Auld Alliance, as the pact came to be known, was to keep English ambitions at bay for centuries and at one point almost resulted in Scotland becoming a province of France.

Principal beneficiaries of the deal were the kings of the Stewart (or Stuart) family. Taking their name from their function as High Stewarts to the king, they were descended from the Fitzalans, Normans who came to England with William the Conqueror in 1066.

When the Bruce family failed to produce a male heir, the crown passed in 1371 to the Stewarts because Marjorie, Robert the Bruce's daughter, had married Walter Fitzalan. The first of the Stewarts, Robert II, faced a problem that was to plague his successors: he had constantly to look over his shoulder at England, yet he could never ignore another threat to his power – his own dissident barons and warring chieftains.

Stabbed to death: His son, Robert III, trusted these ambitious men so little that he sent his oldest son, James, to France for safety. But the ship carrying him was waylaid and young James fell into the hands of England's Henry IV. He grew up in the English court and didn't return to Scotland (as James I) until 1422, at the age of 29. His friendliness with the English was soon strained to breaking point, however, and he renewed the Auld Alliance, siding with France's Charles VII and Joan of Arc against the English. But soon James was murdered, stabbed to death before his wife by his uncle, a cousin and another noble.

His son, James II, succeeded at the age of six, setting another Stewart pattern: monarchs who came to the throne as minors, creating what has been called an infantile paralysis of the power structure. In 1460 James, fighting to recapture Roxburgh from the English, died when one of his own siege

guns exploded. James III, another boy king, succeeded. He had time to marry a Danish princess (in the process bringing the Norse islands of Orkney and Shetland into the realm) before he was locked in Edinburgh Castle by the scheming barons and replaced by his more malleable younger brother. The arrangement didn't last and soon James's son, James IV, was crowned king, aged 15.

This latest James cemented relations with England in 1503 by marrying Margaret Tudor, the 12-year-old daughter of Henry VII,

ous aues bien
ouy recordes de
treues entre les
anglois z lee–

the Welsh warrior who had usurped the English throne 18 years before. The harmony was short-lived: the French talked James into attacking England and he was killed at the battle of Flodden Hill. It was Scotland's worst-ever defeat at English hands, wiping out the cream of a generation, and some argue that the country never recovered from the blow. James's heir, predictably, was also called James and was just over a year old. The power-brokers could continue plotting.

James V entered legend by posing as a commoner to find out how his people really lived. He also carried on the unceasing battle against the cattle rustlers who controlled the

Left, Robert Bruce meets with Edward III. Right, Edward III takes Berwick in 1333.

border area. Torn between the French connection and the ambitions of England's Henry VIII who tried to enrol him in his anti-Catholic campaign, James declared his loyalties by marrying two Frenchwomen in succession. Life expectation was short, however, for kings as well as for peasants, and James V died in 1542 just as his second queen, Marie de Guise, gave birth to a daughter. At less than a week old, the infant was proclaimed Mary Queen of Scots.

Ever an opportunist, Henry VIII despatched an invasion force which reduced Edinburgh, apart from its castle, to rubble. It was known as a "Rough Wooing" and left hatred that would last for centuries. The immediate question was: should Scotland ally itself with Catholic France or Protestant England? In the ensuing tug-of-war between the English and the French, the infant Mary was taken to France for safety and, when 15, married the French Dauphin. The Auld Alliance seemed to have taken on a new life. "France and Scotland are now one country," declared Henry II of France, rather prematurely, and Mary made a will bequeathing Scotland to France if she died childless.

When the King of France died in 1558, Mary, still only 16, ascended the throne with her husband. Her ambitions, though, didn't end there: she later declared herself Queen of England as well, basing her claim on the Catholic assumption that England's new queen, Elizabeth I, was illegitimate because her father, the much married Henry VIII, had been a heretic.

Forged in fire: This bid for power set alarm bells ringing among Protestants. Their faith had been forged in fire, with early preachers such as George Wishart burned at the stake, and it contained little room for compromise.

The Protestants' visionary was John Knox, a magnetic speaker and former priest whose aim, inspired by Calvinism, was to drive Catholicism out of Scotland completely. His followers had burgeoned into a popular movement, pledging themselves by signing the

First Covenant to "forsake and renounce the congregation of Satan", and carrying Calvin's doctrines to extremes by completely outlawing the Latin Mass throughout Scotland.

Mary Queen of Scots (who preferred the "Stuart" spelling of her dynastic name) shared none of the austere values of Knox's brethren. When her husband died in 1560, she returned to Scotland, a vivacious, wilful and sexy woman. It was hard to remember that she was still a teenager – except when it came to her judgement in choosing men. She married a Catholic, Henry Darnley, who was by contemporary accounts an arrogant, pompous and effeminate idler, and soon she began spending more and more time with her secretary David Rizzio, an Italian. When Rizzio was stabbed to death in front of her, Darnley was presumed to be responsible, but who could prove it? Mary appeared to turn back to Darnley and, a few months later, gave birth to a son. Immediately afterwards, however, Darnley himself was murdered, his strangled remains found in a building reduced to rubble by an explosion. Mary and her current favourite, James Hepburn, Earl of Bothwell, were presumed responsible – but again, who could prove it?

Bothwell, a Protestant, quickly divorced his wife and, with few fanfares, became Mary's third husband, three months after

reach France, then threw herself on the mercy of her cousin, Elizabeth I. Her previous claim to the English throne, however, had not been forgotten. Elizabeth, adopting the motto "strike or be stricken", offered her the bleak hospitality of various mansions, in which she remained a prisoner for the next 20 years. In 1587 she was convicted, on somewhat flimsy evidence, of plotting Elizabeth's death and was beheaded at Fotheringay Castle.

Her son, by this time secure on the Scottish throne, made little more than a token protest. Because Elizabeth, the Virgin Queen, had no heir, James had his sights set on a far greater prize than Scotland could offer: the throne of England. On 27 March 1603, he learned that

Darnley's death. Few writers of fiction would have dared concoct such an audacious scenario, but even Mary had gone too far this time. Protestant Scotland forced its Catholic queen, still only 24, to abdicate, locking her in an island castle on Loch Leven. Bothwell fled to Norway, where he died in exile. And so, in 1567, another infant king came to the throne: Mary's son, James VI.

Still fact rivalled fiction. Mary escaped from Loch Leven, tried unsuccessfully to

Left, Robert Herdman's portrait of the execution of Mary Queen of Scots. **Above**, Scottish border raiders; and James I.

the prize was his. On hearing of Elizabeth's death, he set out for London, and was to set foot in Scotland only once more in his life.

Final slight: Scots have speculated ever since about how differently history would have turned out had James VI of Scotland made Edinburgh rather than London his base when he became James I of England. But he was more in sympathy with the divine right of kings than with the notions of the ultra-democratic Presbyterians, who were demanding a strong say in civil affairs. Also, James was no John Knox: London was a warmer, drier, more comfortable place and offered a rather wider selection of civilised entertainment. And, as he wrote, ruling from a distance of 400 miles was so much easier.

His son Charles succeeded to the throne in 1625, not knowing Scotland at all. Without, therefore, realising the consequences, the absentee king tried to harmonise the forms of church service between the two countries. The Scots would have none of it: religious riots broke out and one bishop is said to have conducted his service with two loaded pistols placed in front of him. A National Covenant was organised, pledging faith to "the true religion" and affirming the unassailable authority in spiritual matters of the powerful General Assembly of the Church of Scotland. Armed conflict soon followed: in 1639

supporters of the king. Charles, becoming desperate, tried to gain the Scots' support by promising a three-year trial for Presbyterianism in England. But his time had run out: he was beheaded on 30 January 1649.

Charles's execution came as a terrible shock north of the border. How dare England kill the king of Scotland without consulting the Scots! Many turned to Charles's 18-year-old son, who had undertaken not to oppose Presbyterianism, and he was proclaimed Charles II in Edinburgh. But Cromwell won a decisive victory at the Battle of Dunbar and turned Scotland into an occupied country, abolishing its separate parliament.

Rotten judgement: By the time the monar-

the Scots invaded northern England, forcing Charles to negotiate.

Soon the king's luck ran out in England too. Needing money, he unwisely called together his parliament for the first time in 10 years. A power struggle ensued, leading swiftly to civil war. At first the Scottish Covenanters (so named because of their support for the National Covenant of 1638) backed Parliament and the Roundhead forces of Oliver Cromwell; their hope was that a victorious Parliament would introduce compulsory Presbyterianism in English and Irish churches as well as in Scotland. Soon the Roundheads began to outpace the Cavalier

chy was restored in 1660, Charles II had lost interest in Scotland's religious aspirations and removed much of the Presbyterian church's power. Violent intolerance stalked the land during his reign and the 1680s became known as the Killing Time. Secret groups of Covenanters began holding services in the open air. Their risk increased when, after Charles died of apoplexy in 1685, his brother James, a Catholic, became king. With the rotten judgement that dogged the Stewart line, James II imposed the death penalty for worshipping as a Covenanter. His power base in London soon crumbled, however, and in 1689 he was deposed in favour of his Protestant nephew and son-in-law, William of Orange.

Some Scots, mostly Highlanders, remained true to James. The Jacobites, as they were called, rose under Graham of Claverhouse and almost annihilated William's army in a fierce battle at Killiecrankie in 1689. However, Claverhouse was killed, leaving the Jacobites leaderless; most of them lost heart and returned to the Highlands.

Determined to exert his authority over the Scots, William demanded that every clan leader swear an oath of loyalty to him. Partly because of bad weather, partly through a misunderstanding of where the swearing would take place, one chieftain, the head of

Scotland's bloodstained history. The barbarity of the massacre produced a public outcry, not so much because of the number killed but because of the abuse of hospitality.

Queen Anne, the second daughter of James II, succeeded William in 1702. Although she had given birth to 17 children, none had survived and the English establishment was determined to keep both thrones out of Stewart hands. They turned to Sophie of Hanover, a granddaughter of James VI/James I. If the Scots would agree to accept a Hanoverian line of succession, much needed trade concessions would be granted. There was just one other condition: England and Scotland should unite under one parliament.

the Clan MacDonald, took his oath several days after the king's deadline. Here was a chance to make an example of a prominent leader. Members of the Campbell clan, old enemies of the MacDonalds, were ordered to lodge with the MacDonalds at their home in Glencoe, get to know them and then, having won their confidence, put every MacDonald younger than 70 to the sword. The Campbells were only too pleased to carry out their commission and the Massacre of Glencoe in 1692 remains one of the bloodiest dates in

Left, Scottish Covenanters meet in Edinburgh. **Above**, grief after the Massacre of Glencoe.

As so often before, riots broke out in Edinburgh and elsewhere. But the opposition was fragmented and, in 1707, a Treaty of Union incorporated the Scottish parliament into the Westminster parliament to create the United Kingdom. Unknown to the signatories, the foundation of the British Empire was being laid. To the politicians in London, the fact that Scotland had ceased to exist forever as a separate nation would have seemed a small price to pay for such future glory. But many Scots took a different view: "We are bought and sold for English gold," they sang. Like so many Scottish songs, it was a lament.

The ink was hardly dry on the Treaty of Union of 1707 when the Scots began to smart under the new constitutional arrangements. The idea of a union with England had never been popular with the working classes, most of whom saw it (rightly) as a sell-out by the aristocracy to the "Auld Enemy". Scotland's businessmen were outraged by the imposition of hefty, English-style excise duties on many goods and the high-handed Government bureaucracy that went with them. The aristocracy who had supported the Union resented Westminster's peremptory abolition of Scotland's privy council. And everybody hated the new tax on French claret, then the Scotsman's favourite tipple. Even the hardline Cameronians – the fiercest of Protestants – roundly disliked the Union in the early years of the 18th century.

All of which was compounded by the Jacobitism (support for the Stuarts) which haunted many parts of Scotland, particularly among the Episcopalians of Aberdeenshire, Angus and Perthshire, and among the Catholic clans (such as the MacDonalds) of the Western Highlands. And many Whigs who loathed the Stuart dynasty were hedging their bets. No one in Scotland (or in England, for that matter) had forgotten the Restoration of 1660 when the Stuart kings had come back from the dead. It had happened once; it could happen again.

And, given that one of the main planks of Jacobitism was the repeal of the Union, it was hardly surprising that the Stuart kings cast a long shadow over Scotland in the first half of the 18th century. In fact, within a year of the Treaty of Union being signed, the first Jacobite insurgency was under way, helped by a French regime ever anxious to discomfit the power of the English.

In January 1708 a flotilla of French privateers commanded by Comte Claude de Forbin battered its way through the North Sea gales carrying the 19-year-old James Stuart, the self-styled James VIII and III. After a brief

sojourn in the Firth of Forth near the coast of Fife the French privateers were chased round the top of Scotland and out into the Atlantic by English warships, Many of the French vessels foundered on their way back to France, although James survived to go on plotting. On dry land, the uprising of 1708 was confined to a few East Stirlingshire lairds who marched up and down with a handful of men. They were quickly rounded up, and in November 1708 five of the ringleaders were tried in Edinburgh for treason. The verdict on all five was "not proven" and they were set free.

Shocked by this display of Scottish leniency, the British Parliament passed the Treason Act of 1708 which brought Scotland into line with England. Until 1708 Scottish traitors could expect to be executed and have their estates forfeited, although their families continued to have a claim on their goods. After the Treason Act of 1708 traitors could expect to be hanged, taken down alive, disembowelled while still conscious, and then "quartered" into four pieces.

The next Jacobite uprising, in 1715, was a much more serious affair, if only because it

Preceding pages, David Morier's portrayal of Culloden, painted in 1746. **Left,** the Young Chevalier, Prince Charles Edward Stuart. **Right,** history recalled today in Greenock.

found some support in the North of England. Many historians take the view that the '15 was the only insurgency which the Jacobites *might* have won. Disaffection in Scotland with the Union was widespread, the Hanoverians had not totally secured their grip on Britain, there were loud pro-Stuart mutterings in England, and much of Britain had been stripped of its military.

An odd outcome: But the insurrection was led by the Earl of Mar, a military incompetent known as "Bobbing John", whose support came mainly from the clans of the Central and Eastern Highlands. Clan Campbell – the staunchest of Whigs – was the spearhead of the Hanoverian forces. When the two sides

much. The insurrection of 1715 quickly ran out of steam. The Pretender himself did not arrive in Scotland until the end of December and the forces he brought with him were too little, and too late. He then did his cause no good by stealing away at night (along with "Bobbing John" and a few others), leaving his followers to the wrath of the Whigs. The Duke of Argyll was sacked as commander of the government forces for fear he would be too lenient. Dozens of rebels – especially the English ones – were hanged, drawn and quartered, and hundreds were deported.

Not that the débâcle of 1715 stopped the Stuarts trying again. In 1719 it was the Spaniards who decided to try to queer the

clashed at Sheriffmuir near Stirling on 13 November, Mar's Jacobite army had a four-to-one advantage over the tiny Hanoverian force commanded by "Red John of the Battles" (as the Duke of Argyll was known). But, instead of pressing his huge advantage, Mar withdrew his Highland army after an inconclusive clash, during which John Gordon of Glenbuchat, recalling Claverhouse, cried out in despair: "Oh, for an hour of Dundee!". The Duke of Argyll was puzzled but delighted. "By this Battle," one contemporary wrote, "the Heart of the Rebellion was broke."

Which was a slight exaggeration, but not

Hanoverian pitch by backing the Jacobites. Again it was a fiasco. In March 1719 a little force of 307 Spanish soldiers sailed into Loch Alsh where they joined up with a few hundred Murrays, Mackenzies and Mackintoshes. This Spanish-Jacobite stage army was easily routed in the steep pass of Glenshiel by a British unit which swooped down from Inverness to pound the Jacobite positions with their mortars. The Highlanders (as was their wont) simply vanished into the mist and snow of Kintail, leaving the wretched Spaniards in their gold-on-white uniforms to wander about the sub-arctic landscape before surrendering to the British troops. (There is still a niche high up in the Kintail mountains called Bealach-na-Spainnteach – The Pass of the Spaniards.)

But it was the insurrection of 1745, "so glorious an enterprise", led by Charles Edward Stuart (Bonnie Prince Charlie), which shook Britain, despite the fact that by then the Hanoverian regime was well dug in. The Government's grip on the turbulent parts of Scotland had never seemed firmer. There were military depots at Fort William, Fort Augustus and Fort George and an effective Highland militia (later known as the Black Watch) had been raised. General Wade had thrown a network of military roads and bridges across the Highlands. Logically Scotland, hardly any cavalry or artillery, and Clan Campbell was no longer an effective fighting force. The result was that Bonnie Prince Charlie and his ragtag army of MacDonalds, Camerons, Mackintoshes, Robertsons, McGregors, Macphersons and Gordons, plus some lowland cavalry and a stiffening of Franco-Irish mercenaries, was able to walk into Edinburgh and set up a "royal court" in Holyrood Palace.

In September the Young Pretender sallied out of Edinburgh and wrecked General John Copy's panicky Hanoverian army near Prestonpans, and then marched across the border into England, causing much fluttering among Whigdom's fainter hearts. But

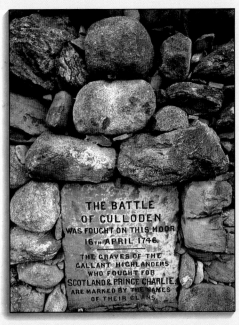

Charles, the Young Pretender, should never have been allowed to set foot out of the Highlands after he raised his standard at Glenfinnan in August 1745.

But having set up a military "infrastructure" in the Highlands, the British Government had neglected it. The Independent Companies (the Black Watch) had been shunted out to the West Indies, there were fewer than 4,000 (mostly green) troops in the whole of

Left, Culloden's victor, the Duke of Cumberland. **Above left**, Prince Charlie's much romanticised farewell in 1746 to Flora MacDonald. **Above right**, Culloden remembered.

Stuart's success was an illusion. There was precious little support for his cause in the Lowlands of Scotland. Few Jacobite troops had been raised in Edinburgh, and Glasgow and the southwest were openly hostile. Some men had been drummed up in Manchester, but there was no serious support from the Roman Catholic families of northern England. Charles got as far as Derby and then fled back to Scotland with two powerful Hanoverian armies hot on his heels.

After winning a rearguard action at Clifton, near Penrith, and what has been described as a "lucky victory" at Falkirk in January 1746, the Jacobite army was cut to pieces by the

Duke of Cumberland's artillery on Drummossie Moor, Culloden, near Inverness on 16 April 1746. It was the last great pitched battle on the soil of mainland Britain. It was also the end of the Gaelic clan system which had survived in the mountains of Scotland long after it had disappeared from Ireland. The day when an upland chieftain could drum up a "tail" of trained swordsmen for cattle raids into the Lowlands were over.

Following his post-Culloden "flight across the heather", Charles, disguised as a woman servant, was sheltered on the Isle of Skye by Flora MacDonald, thus giving birth to one of Scotland's abiding romantic tales. He was then plucked off the Scottish coast by a French privateer and taken into exile, drunkenness and despair in France and Italy. A few dozen of the more prominent Jacobites were hauled off to Carlisle and Newcastle where they were tried, and some of them hanged. The estates of the gentry who had "come out" in the '45 were confiscated by the Crown. And for some time the Highlands were harried mercilessly by the Duke of Cumberland's troopers (the fiercest of whom were probably Lowland Scots).

In an effort to subdue the Highlands, the government in London passed the Disarming Act of 1746 which not only banned the carrying of claymores, targes, dirks and muskets, but also the wearing of tartans and the playing of bagpipes. It was a nasty piece of legislation, but never much of a success. The British Government also took the opportunity to abolish Scotland's inefficient and often corrupt system of "Courts of Regality" by which the aristocracy (and not just the Highland variety) dispensed justice, collected fines, and wielded powers of life and wealth.

Age of enlightenment: It is one of the minor paradoxes of 18th-century European history that, while Scotland was being racked by dynastic convulsions which were 17th-century in origin, the country was transforming itself into one of the most forward-looking societies in the world. Scotland began to wake up in the first half of the 18th century. By about 1740 the intellectual, scientific and mercantile phenomenon which became known as the Scottish Enlightenment was well under way, although it didn't reach its peak until the end of the century.

Whatever created it, the Scottish Enlight-

enment was an extraordinary explosion of creativity and energy. And while, in retrospect at least, the period was dominated by David Hume the philosopher and Adam Smith the economist, there were many others such as William Robertson, Adam Ferguson, William Cullen, and the Adam brothers. Through the multi-faceted talents of its literati, Scotland in general and Edinburgh in particular became one of the intellectual power-houses of Western Europe. "I may truly say that it is not easy to conceive a university where industry was more general," wrote Sir James Mackintosh about Edinburgh University in 1780s, "where reading was more fashionable, where indolence and ig-

norance were more disreputable."

Not that the Enlightenment was confined to the salons of Edinburgh. Commerce and industry also thrived. "The same age, which produces great philosophers and politicians, renowned generals and poets, usually abounds with skilled weavers and ship-carpenters," David Hume wrote in 1752. "We cannot reasonably expect that a piece of woollen cloth will be brought to perfection in a nation which is ignorant of astronomy, or where ethics are neglected. The spirit of the age affects all the arts."

In the late 18th century Scotland was in the throes of industrialisation. By 1760 the famous Carron Ironworks in Falkirk was churning out high-grade ordnance for the British military. By 1780 hundreds of tons of goods were being shuttled between Edinburgh and Glasgow along the Forth-Clyde canal. The Turnpike Act of 1751 improved the road system dramatically and created a brisk demand for carriages and stage coaches. In 1738 Scotland's share of the tobacco trade (based in Glasgow) was 10 percent; by 1769 it was more than 52 percent. There was a huge upsurge of activity in many trades: carpet weaving, upholstery, glass making, china and pottery manufacture, linen, soap, distilling and brewing.

The 18th century changed Scotland from late 18th and early 19th century probably owed more to the "improving" attitudes triggered by the Enlightenment than to the greed of the lairds (although that played its part). By the end of the century every Scottish landowner worth his salt was determined to improve his estate. Agricultural improvement was not only profitable, it was extremely fashionable. And the idea quickly spread from the landowners to their tenant farmers.

Nor was the enthusiasm confined to the plump farms of the Lowlands. The gentry of the Highlands – the clan chiefs – were also caught up in the drive to improve their lands. The enterprising Sir John Sinclair, for exam-

Ladys Magazine.

A View of Glasgow.

one of the poorest countries in Europe to a state of middling affluence. The urban bourgeoisie grew in power and prosperity, especially in Edinburgh and Glasgow. It has been calculated that between 1700 and 1800 the money generated within Scotland increased by a factor of more than 50, while the population stayed more or less static (at around 1½ million).

The Clearances: But the Enlightenment and all that went with it had some woeful side-effects. The Highland "Clearances" of the

Left, a Skye crofter. **Above**, Glasgow in the 18th century.

ple, pointed out that, while the Highlands were capable of producing from £200,000 to £300,000 worth of black cattle every year, "the same ground will produce twice as much mutton and there is wool into the bargain."

The argument proved irresistible. Sheep – particularly Cheviots – and their Lowland shepherds began to flood into the glens and straths of the Highlands, displacing the Highland "tacksmen" and their families. The worst of the Clearances – or at least the most notorious – took place on the huge estates of the Countess of Sutherland and her rich, English-born husband, the Marquis of Stafford. Although Stafford spent huge sums of money building roads, harbours and fish-curing sheds (for very little profit) his estate managers evicted tenants with real ruthlessness. It was a pattern which was repeated all over Highland Scotland at the beginning of the 19th century, and then again later when people were displaced by the red deer of the "sporting" estates. The Highland Clearances remain a painful memory in Scotland.

Radicals and reactionaries: As the industrial economy of Lowland Scotland burgeoned at the end of the 18th century, it sucked in thousands of immigrant workers from all over Scotland and Ireland. The clamour for democracy grew. Some of it was fuelled by

Scotland was relentless. According to the 19th-century judge Lord Cockburn, "Who steered upon him (*Dundas*) was safe; who disregarded his light was wrecked."

But nothing could stop the spread of libertarian ideas in an increasingly industrialised workforce. The ideas contained in Tom Paine's *Rights of Man* spread like wildfire in the Scotland of the 1790s. The cobblers, weavers and spinners proved the most vociferous democrats, but there was also unrest among farmworkers, and among seamen and soldiers in the Highland regiments. Throughout the 1790s a number of radical "one man, one vote" organisations sprang up, such as the Scottish Friends of the People and the

the ideas of the American and French revolutions, but much of the unrest was a reaction to Scotland's hopelessly inadequate electoral system. At the end of the 18th century there were only 4,500 voters in the whole of Scotland and only 2,600 voters in the 33 rural countries.

And for almost 40 years Scotland was dominated by the powerful machine politician Henry Dundas, the First Viscount Melville, universally known as "King Harry the Ninth". As Solicitor General, Lord Advocate, Home Secretary, Secretary for War and then First Lord of the Admiralty, Dundas wielded awesome power. And his grip on

United Scotsmen (a quasi-nationalist group which modelled itself on the United Irishmen of Wolfe Tone).

But the brooding figure of Dundas was more than a match for the radicals. Every organisation which raised its head was swiftly infiltrated by police spies and *agents provocateurs*. Ringleaders (such as the advocate Thomas Muir) were framed, arrested, tried and deported. Some, such as Robert Watt who led the "Pike Plot" of 1794, were hanged. Meetings were broken up by dragoons, riots

Festive fun: a 19th-century poster, now in Glasgow's People's Palace.

46

were put down by musket-fire, the Scottish universities were racked by witchhunts.

Although Dundas himself was discredited in 1806, after being impeached for embezzlement, and died in 1811, the anti-Radical paranoia of the Scottish ruling class lingered. Establishment panic reached a peak in 1820 when the so-called Scottish Insurrection ended in the legally-corrupt trial of weavers James Wilson, John Baird, Andrew Hardie and 21 other workmen. A special (English) Court of Oyer and Terminer was set up in Glasgow to hear the case, and Wilson, Baird and Hardie were sentenced to be hanged, beheaded and quartered. They were spared the latter part of the sentence.

Reform and disruption: By the 1820s most of Scotland (and indeed Britain) was weary of the political and constitutional corruption under which the country laboured. In 1823 Lord Archibald Hamilton pointed out the electoral absurdity of rural Scotland. "I have the right to vote in five counties in Scotland, in not one of which do I possess an acre of land," he said, "and I have no doubt that if I took the trouble I might have a vote for every county in that kingdom." Hamilton's motion calling for parliamentary reform was defeated by only 35 votes.

But nine years later, in 1832, the Reform Bill passed into law, giving Scotland 30 rural constituencies, 23 burgh constituencies and a voting population of 65,000 (compared to a previous 4,500). Even this limited extension of the franchise – to male householders whose property had a rentable value of £10 or more – generated much wailing and gnashing of teeth among Scottish Tories.

No sooner had the controversy over electoral reform subsided than it was replaced by the row between the "moderates" and the "evangelicals" within the Church of Scotland. "Scotland," Lord Palmerston noted at the time, "is aflame about the church question." But this was no genteel falling-out among theologians. It was a brutal and bruising affair which dominated political life in Scotland for 10 years and raised all kinds of constitutional questions.

At the heart of the argument was the Patronage Act of 1712 which gave Scots lairds the same right English squires had to appoint, or "intrude" clergy on local congregations. Ever since it was passed, the Church of Scotland had argued (rightly) that the Patronage Act was a flagrant and illegal violation of the Revolution Settlement of 1690 and the Treaty of Union of 1707, both of which guaranteed the independence of the Church of Scotland.

But the pleas fell on deaf ears. The English-dominated parliament could see no fault in a system which enabled Anglicised landowners to appoint like-minded clergymen. Patronage was seen by the Anglo-Scottish establishment as a useful instrument of political control and social progress. The issue came to a head in May 1843 when the evangelicals, led by Dr Thomas Chalmers, marched out of the annual General Assembly of the Church of Scotland in Edinburgh to form the Free Church of Scotland.

Chalmers, theologian, astronomer and brilliant organiser, defended the Free Church against bitter enemies. His final triumph, in 1847, was to persuade the London parliament that it was folly to allow the aristocracy to refuse the Free Church land on which to build churches and schools. A few days after giving evidence, Chalmers died in Edinburgh.

The rebellion of the evangelicals was brilliantly planned, well funded and took the British establishment completely by surprise. Four hundred teachers left the kirk and, within 10 years of the Disruption, the Free Church had built more than 800 churches, 700 manses, three large theological colleges and 600 schools, and brought about a huge extension of education. After 1847, state aid had to be given to the Free as well as to the established Church schools, and in 1861 the established Church lost its legal powers over Scotland's parish school system. This prepared the ground for the Education Act of 1872 which set up a national system under the Scottish Educational Department. And, although it ran into some vicious opposition from landowners, especially in the Highlands, the Free Church prevailed.

In fact, it can be argued that the Disruption was the only rebellion in 18th- or 19th-century British history that succeeded. Chalmers and his supporters had challenged both the pervasive influence of the Anglo-Scottish aristocracy and the power of the British Parliament, and won. The Patronage Act of 1712 was finally repealed in 1874, and the Free Church re-merged with the Church of Scotland in 1929, the two becoming the United Established Church of Scotland.

During the Victorian and Edwardian eras, Scotland, like most of Europe, became urbanised and industrialised. Steelworks, ironworks, shipyards, coal mines, shale-oil refineries, textile factories, engineering shops, canals and of course railways proliferated all over 19th-century Scotland. The process was concentrated in Scotland's "central belt" (the stretch of low-lying land between Edinburgh and Glasgow) but there were important "outliers" like Aberdeen, Dundee, Ayrshire and the mill-towns of the Scottish borders. A few (very small) industrial ventures found their way deep into the Highlands or onto a few small islands.

It was a process which dragged in its wake profound social, cultural and demographic change. The booming industries brought thousands of work-seeking immigrants flocking into lowland Scotland. Most came from the Highlands and Ireland, and many nursed an ancient distaste for the British establishment which translated itself into left-wing radicalism. Scots of Irish descent are still the main prop of the Labour Party in Scotland. The immigrants were also largely Roman Catholic, which did something to loosen the grip of the Presbyterian churches on Scottish life.

Huge metropolis: Industry transformed the city of Glasgow and the River Clyde. From being an amiable 18th-century backwater (the name is corrupt Gaelic for "the dear green place"), Glasgow became the Second City of the Empire, the Victorian city *par excellence*. Between 1740 and 1840 its population leapt from 17,000 to 200,000 and then doubled to 400,000 by 1870. The small Georgian city became a huge industrial metropolis built on the kind of rectangular grid common in the United States, with industrial princes living in splendour while Highland, Irish, Italian and Jewish immigrants swarmed in the noisome slums.

In many ways 19th-century Glasgow had more in common with Chicago or New York than with any city in Britain. Working-class conditions were appalling. Rickets, cholera, smallpox, tuberculosis, diphtheria and alcoholism were rampant. The streets were unclean and distinctly unsafe. Violence was endemic as Highlanders and Irishmen clashed in the stews and whisky dens, while Orangemen from Ulster were used as violent and murderous strike-breakers. The city hangman was never short of work.

But there was no denying Glasgow's enormous industrial vitality. By the middle of the

century the city was peppered with more than 100 textile mills (an industry which by that time employed more than 400,000 Scots). There were ironworks at Tollcross, Coatbridge and Monklands, productive coal mines all over Lanarkshire and the River Clyde was lined with boiler makers, marine-engineering shops, and world-class shipyards. For generations the label "Clyde built" was synonymous with industrial quality.

According to the historian T.C. Smout, by 1913 Glasgow and the surrounding area was making "one-fifth of the steel, one-third of the shipping tonnage, one-half of the marine-engine horsepower, one-third of the railway

Preceding pages: the elegant Edinburgh residence of Scotland's Secretary of State. **Left**, *First Steamboat on the Clyde*, painted by John Knox. **Right**, slum dwellers in Glasgow's Gorbals.

locomotives and rolling stock, and most of the sewing machines in the United Kingdom".

Nor was industry confined to Glasgow and its environs. The Tayside city of Dundee forged close links with India and became the biggest jute-manufacturing centre in Britain. The Carron Ironworks at Falkirk was Europe's largest producer of artillery by the year 1800. In West Lothian a thriving industry was built up to extract oil from shale (a process discovered by James "Paraffin" Young). Scotland's east-coast fisheries flourished, and by the end of the century the town of Wick in Caithness became Europe's biggest herring port.

As well as producing large quantities of Dundee jute man Robert Fleming set up the Scottish American Investment Trust to channel money into American cattle ranches, fruit farms, mining companies and railways, mainly in Arizona, Nevada and Texas. The biggest cattle ranch in the USA – Matador Land & Cattle Company – was run from Dundee until 1951. The outlaw Butch Cassidy once worked for a cattle company operated from the fastidious New Town of Edinburgh.

But investment was a two-way process. By the end of the 19th century, Scotland, with its educated workforce and proximity to European markets, was attracting inward investment. The American-funded North British Rubber Company moved into Edin-

books, biscuits and bureaucrats, Edinburgh was a centre of the British brewing industry; at one stage there were more than 40 breweries within the city boundaries. And, in the latter part of the 19th century, the Scotch whisky industry boomed, thanks to the devastation of the French vineyards in the 1880s by phylloxera which almost wrecked the thriving cognac industry.

Cowboy connection: Inevitably, this growth of industry generated huge amounts of cash. Both Edinburgh and Dundee became centres for the investment trusts which sunk large quantities of cash into ventures all over the world, and particularly the USA. In 1873 the burgh in 1857. In 1884 the Singer Company built one of the biggest factories in the world at Clydebank to manufacture mass-produced sewing machines. It was the start of a 100-year trend which has done much to undermine the Scottish economy's independence.

Despite the enthusiasm of Queen Victoria and the British gentry for the Highlands, the direst poverty stalked upland Scotland. Land reform was desperately needed. Following an outburst of rioting in Skye in 1882 and the formation of the Highland Land League in 1884, Gladstone's Liberal government passed the Crofters (Scotland) Holdings Act of 1886 which gave crofters fair rents, security of tenure, and the right to pass their croft on to their families. But it was Lord Salisbury's Conservative government who put the Scottish Secretary in the British cabinet, and established the Scottish Office in Edinburgh and London in 1886.

By the end of the 19th century the huge majority of the Scottish population was urban, industrialised, and concentrated in the towns and cities of the Lowlands. And urban Scotland proved a fertile breeding ground for the British Left. The Scottish Labour Party (SLP) was founded in 1888, although it soon merged with the Independent Labour Party (ILP), which in turn played a big part in the formation of the (British) Labour Party.

of left-wing leaders like Keir Hardie and John Maclean. With less than 10 percent of the British population, the Scots made up almost 15 percent of the British Army. And when the butcher's bill was added up after the war it was found that more than 20 percent of all the Britons killed were Scots.

They came from every corner of Scotland. The Royal Scots – which recruits in and around Edinburgh – raised no fewer than 35 battalions. Enough Glaswegians joined the Highland Light Infantry (HLI) to form 26 battalions. The Cameronians – the descendents of the Protestant zealots of the 17th century – raised 27 battalions. The Gordon Highlanders raised 21 from the area around

Britain's first Labour MP, Keir Hardie, was a Scot, as was Ramsay MacDonald, Britain's first Labour prime minister.

The Great War: When World War I broke out in 1914 the Scots flocked to the British colours with an extraordinary enthusiasm. Like Ireland, Scotland provided the British Army with a disproportionate number of soldiers. Like the Irish, the Scots suspended their radicalism and trooped into the forces to fight for King and Empire, to the despair

<u>Left</u>, **herring drifters near the port of Peterhead.**
<u>Above</u>, **Labour Party leader Ramsay MacDonald with his son and daughter in 1929.**

Aberdeen. The sparsely populated Highlands produced 19 battalions of Seaforth Highlanders and 13 of Cameron Highlanders. The Hebrides, Orkney and Shetland proved rich recruiting ground for the Royal Navy and the Merchant Marine.

In addition to which, the shipyards of the Clyde and the engineering shops of West Central Scotland were producing more tanks, shells, warships, explosives and fieldguns than any comparable part of Britain. That explains why the British Government took such a dim view of the strikes and industrial disputes which hit the Clyde between 1915 and 1919 and led to the area being dubbed

LAYING DOWN THE LAW

One curious feature of the Scottish legal system is Not Proven – "that bastard verdict", as Sir Walter Scott called it. At the end of a criminal trial the verdict can be "guilty" or "not guilty", as in England, *or* the jury may find the charge "not proven". It's an option that reflects Scots logic and refusal to compromise by assuming a person innocent until proved guilty, though it does confer a stigma on the accused.

The jargon of Scots lawyers is distinctive, too. If you embark on litigation you are a "pursuer". You sue a "defender". "Law Burrows" (nothing to do with rabbits) is a way of asking the courts

to prevent someone harassing you. If you disagree too outspokenly with a judge's decision, you may be accused of "murmuring the judge".

Though few outsiders realise it, the Scots have maintained a distinctive legal system despite three centuries of political union with the rest of the UK. It is unique in being a legal system lacking its own legislature. Since the 1707 Act of Union abolished the Scottish parliament, the UK parliament in London has made laws for the country.

Scottish law is quite different in origin from that of England and those countries (such as the US and many Commonwealth nations) to which the English system has been exported, and is closer to the legal systems of South Africa, Sri Lanka,

Louisiana and Quebec. It was developed from Roman Law and owes much more to continental legal systems than does that of England – thanks partly to the custom of Scottish lawyers, during the 17th and 18th centuries, studying in France, Holland or Germany. Solicitors, the general practitioners of the law, regard themselves as men of affairs, with a wider role than lawyers in some countries have adopted. Advocates, who are based in Parliament House in Edinburgh and to whom a solicitor will turn for expert advice, also refuse to become too narrowly specialised. This is important if they wish to become Sheriffs, as the judges of the local courts are called.

Some practitioners have demonstrated outstanding talents beyond the confines of the law. Sir Walter Scott was, for most of his life, a practising lawyer. In Selkirk, near the palatial house he built at Abbotsford, can be seen the courtroom where he presided as Sheriff. Robert Louis Stevenson qualified as an advocate, the equivalent of the English barrister, though he quickly deserted the law for literature.

Inevitably, English law has had its influence. Much modern legislation, especially commercial law, has tended to be copied from England. The traffic, however, hasn't been all one-way. In Scottish criminal trials, the jury of 15 has always been allowed to reach a majority verdict, a procedure only recently adopted by England. The English have recently introduced a prosecution service, independent of the police, similar to that which operates in Scotland. Some in England would also like to import the "110-day rule": this requires a prisoner on remand to be released if his trial doesn't take place within 110 days of his imprisonment. More controversially, Scottish judges have power in criminal cases to create new crimes – a power they use sparingly.

Many in England envy the Scottish system of house purchase. Most of the legal and estate agency work is done by solicitors and seems to be completed far faster than in England. Scottish laws on Sunday trading are more liberal, and divorce was available in Scotland several centuries before it was south of the border.

Along with the kirk, the separateness of the Scottish legal system plays a vital part in establishing a sense of national identity. That's why many Scots lawyers resent the failure of Westminster to have proper regard to the fact that the law is different in Scotland. Whether it's *better* is a separate question; the best verdict in this case may be "not proven". ∎

"Red Clydeside". When Glasgow workers struck for a 40-hour week in January 1919 the Secretary of State for Scotland panicked and called in the military.

Glaswegians watched open-mouthed as thousands of armed troops backed by tanks poured onto the streets of Glasgow to nip the Red Revolution in the bud. And at a huge rally in George Square on 31 January 1919, the police baton-charged the crowd.

The hungry years: The 1920s and 1930s were sour years for Scotland. The great "traditional" industries of shipbuilding, steel-making, coal-mining and heavy engineering which towered over the Scottish economy went into a decline from which they have

State for Scotland, wrote a memo to the Cabinet pointing out that "the social condition of Scotland is indicated by the fact that 23 percent of its population live in conditions of gross overcrowding, compared with 4 percent in England... Maternal mortality is half as high again as in England. In proportion to the population twice as many cases of pneumonia and scarlet fever were notified... while the diphtheria figure was higher by a third."

Most of urban Scotland saw its salvation in the newly-formed Labour Party, which not only promised a better life but also a measure of Home Rule. Support for the Labour Party had showed early. At the General

never recovered. The Scotch whisky industry reeled from the body-blow of American prohibition.

The new light engineering industries – cars, electrics and machine tools – stayed stubbornly south of the border. Unemployment soared to almost three in 10 of the workforce and Scots boarded the emigrant ships in droves. An estimated 400,000 Scots (10 percent of the population) emigrated between 1921 and 1931.

In 1937 Walter Elliot, the Secretary of

Above, the Hungry Thirties: Glasgow kids keep smiling despite the poverty.

Election of 1922 an electoral pattern was set which has remained (with one exception) ever since: England went Conservative even if Scotland voted Labour.

But the 1920s and 1930s also saw revival of a kind of left-wing cultural nationalism, which owed a lot to the poetry of Hugh MacDiarmid, the writing of Lewis Grassic Gibbon and the enthusiasms of upper-crust nationalists like Ruaridh Erskine of Marr and R.B. Cunninghame-Graham. From the Scottish literary renaissance of the inter-war years the nationalist movement grew increasingly more political. In 1934 the small (but right-wing) Scottish Party merged with the National Party of Scotland to form the Scottish National Party (SNP).

The world at war: It wasn't until World War II loomed that the Scottish economy began to climb out of the doldrums. And when war broke out in September 1939 the Clydeside shipyards moved into high gear to build warships like the *Duke of York*, *Howe*, *Indefatigible* and *Vanguard*, while the engineering firms began pumping out small arms, bayonets, explosives and ammunition. The Rolls-Royce factory at Hillington near Glasgow produced Merlin engines for the RAF's Spitfires. Clydeside became one of Britain's most important war-time regions.

The point wasn't missed by the Germans. On 13 and 14 March 1941, hundreds of German bombers, operating at the limit of their range, devastated Clydeside. More than 1,000 people were killed (528 in the town of Clydebank) and another 1,500 injured. It was a fearsome raid and shocked many who had thought Scotland out of the firing line. But it was nothing compared to the pounding inflicted on London and the cities of southern Britain, and did no permanent damage to Clydeside's contribution to the war effort.

The postwar period: War killed more than 58,000 Scots (compared to the 148,000 who had lost their lives in World War I) but had the effect of galvanising the Scottish economy for a couple of decades. And there's no doubt that the Labour Government which came to power in 1945 worked major improvements on Scottish life.

The National Health Service proved an effective instrument against such plagues as infant mortality, tuberculosis, rickets, and scarlet fever. Housing conditions improved in leaps and bounds as the worst of the city slums were pulled down and replaced by roomy (although often badly-built) council houses. Semi-rural new towns like East Kilbride, Glenrothes, Cumbernauld, Irvine and Livingston were established in key locations throughout central Scotland.

What went largely unnoticed in the postwar euphoria was that the Labour Government's policy of nationalising the coal mines and the railways was stripping Scotland of much of its decision-making powers, and therefore management jobs. The process continued through the 1960s and 1970s when the steel, shipbuilding and aerospace industries were also "taken into public ownership".

This haemorrhage of economic power and influence has been compounded by Scottish companies being sold to English and foreign predators. In 1988 British Caledonian, originally a Scotland-based airline, was swallowed up by British Airways. To an alarming extent, Scotland's economy now has a "branch factory" status.

English enthusiasm for Labour's experiment flagged and in 1951 Sir Winston Churchill was returned to power. Scotland, of course, continued to vote Labour (although in the general election of 1955 the Conservatives won 36 of Scotland's 71 seats, the only time they have had a majority north of the border). And, while Home Rule for Scotland was off the political agenda Scottish nationalism refused to go away.

In the late 1940s two-thirds of the Scottish electorate signed a "national covenant" demanding home rule. In 1951 a squad of young nationalists outraged the British establishment by whisking the Stone of Destiny out of Westminster Abbey, and hiding it in Scotland. And in 1953 the British establishment outraged Scottish sentiment by insisting on the title of Queen Elizabeth II for the new queen, despite the fact that the Scots had never had a Queen Elizabeth I.

But while Scotland did reasonably well out of the Conservative-led "New Elizabethan Age" of the 1950s and early 1960s, the old structural faults soon began to reappear. By the late 1950s the well-equipped Japanese and German shipyards were snatching orders from under the noses of the Clyde, the Scottish coalfields were proving woefully inefficient and Scotland's steel works and heavy engineering firms were losing their grip on their markets.

And, although the Conservative government did fund a new steel mill at Ravenscraig, near Motherwell, and entice Rootes to set up a car plant at Linwood and the British Motor Corporation to start making trucks at Bathgate, it was all done under duress and all these projects have been abandoned. Scotland's distance from the market-place continued to be a crippling disadvantage. The Midlands and south of England remained the engine-room of the British economy. The drift of Scots to the south continued.

The impact of oil: Although the Scots voted heavily for the Labour Party in the general elections of 1964 and 1966, Labour's complacency was jolted in November 1967 when Mrs Winnie Ewing of the SNP snatched the Hamilton by-election from the Labour Party. Although Ewing lost her seat at the 1970 general election, her success marked the start of an upsurge in Scottish nationalism that preoccupied Scottish – and, to some extent, British – politics for a decade.

When Harold Wilson's Labour government ran out of steam in 1970 it was replaced by the Conservative regime of Edward Heath – although, once again, the Scots voted overwhelmingly Labour. But in the early 1970s Scotland got lucky. The oil companies struck big quantities of oil. All round Scotland engineering firms and land speculators be-

1974 and took more than 20 percent of the Scottish vote. In October 1974 they did even better, cutting a swathe through both parties to take 11 seats and more than 30 percent of the Scottish vote. It looked as if one more push by the SNP would see the United Kingdom dissolved, and the hard-pressed British economy cut off from the oil revenues it so badly needed. The 1970s also saw a flurry of bomb attacks on oil pipelines and electricity pylons by nationalist extremists (some of whom had links with Ireland's IRA).

The Labour government responded to the nationalists' political threat with a constitutional defence. It offered Scotland a directly-elected assembly with substantial (although

gan snapping up sites on which to build platform yards, rig repair bases, airports, oil refineries and petrochemical works. Nothing like it had been seen since the industrial revolution. A new sense of optimism pervaded Scotland.

The SNP was quick to take advantage of the mood. Running on a campaign slogan of "It's Scotland's Oil", the SNP won seven seats in the general election of February

Contrasts of modern Scotland: a Hebridean weaver using a traditional handloom to make Harris tweed; and youths in East Kilbride, soaking in the sun.

strictly limited) powers. The government even purchased and renovated the old Royal High School in Edinburgh, which would become the home of the new assembly, but sold it in 1994. The whole package was to go ahead if the Scottish people voted "yes" in a national referendum.

At which point Westminster changed the rules. At the instigation of Labour MP George Cunningham, Parliament decided that a simple majority was not good enough, and that devolution would go ahead only if more than 40 percent of the Scottish electorate voted in favour. It was an impossible condition. Predictably the Scots failed to vote yes by a big majority in the referendum of March 1979 (although they *did* vote yes) and the Scotland Bill lapsed. Shortly afterwards, the 11 SNP members joined a vote of censure against the Labour government – which fell by one vote. In the ensuing general election, Margaret Thatcher was voted into power and promptly made it plain that any form of Home Rule for Scotland was out of the question.

The Thatcher years: The Devolution débâcle produced a genuine crisis of confidence among Scotland's political classes. Support for the SNP slumped, the Alliance could do nothing. And the Labour Party, armed with the majority of the Scottish vote, could only watch helplessly as the aluminium smelter at

Invergordon, the steel mill at Gartcosh, the car works at Linwood, the pulp mill at Fort William, the truck plant at Bathgate and much of the Scottish coalfield perished in the economic blizzard of the 1980s. Even the energetic and well-founded Scottish Development Agency could do little to protect the Scottish economy. Unemployment climbed to more than 300,000, and the electronics industry's much vaunted "Silicon Glen" proved far too small to take up the slack.

So the political triumph of Thatcherism in Britain found no echoes in Scotland. At the general election of June 1987 the pattern which first emerged in 1922 repeated itself;

England voted Tory and Scotland voted Labour. Out of 72 Scottish MPs 50 were Labour and only 10 were Conservative. This immediately raised the argument that the then Scottish Secretary, Malcolm Rifkind, was an English governor-general with "no mandate" to govern Scotland. Rifkind's response was that the 85 percent of the Scottish electorate who voted for "British" parties were voting for the sovereignty of Westminster and therefore had to accept Westminster's rules.

At the end of 1987 the Labour Party tabled yet another Devolution Bill which was promptly thrown out by English MPs to the jeers of the SNP who claimed that Labour's "Feeble Fifty" could do nothing if they were prepared to play the Westminster game. The SNP resurrected the old quip that "a shiver ran along the Scottish Labour benches looking for a spine to run up".

In Britain's 1992 general election, even though Mrs Thatcher had been replaced as Tory leader by the more emollient John Major, many pundits predicted that the Tories would be all but wiped out north of the border. Surprisingly, despite a background of continuing job losses, they did better than forecast, marginally increasing their vote. In tough economic times, it seemed as if many Scots preferred the devil they knew.

One consequence of Labour's defeat, however, was that the party elected a new leader at national level: John Smith, a cautious Edinburgh lawyer. Many saw him as Britain's next prime minister, but he died of a heart attack in 1994.

Meanwhile, nationalism remains the question mark hanging over Scotland's future. Scots have now been members of the United Kingdom for more than 280 years, and Scottish history is deeply enmeshed with that of Britain. Yet a powerful undertow of resentment keeps breaking the surface: the Jacobite insurgencies of 1708, 1715 and 1745; the radical "rebellion" of 1820; the Disruption in the Church of Scotland in 1843; the formation of the SNP in the 1930s; the startling upsurge of nationalism in the 1970s. But will it ever surge strongly enough to threaten the Treaty of Union of 1707?

Left, Scottish politician John Smith, tipped before his death as the UK's next prime minister. Right, the Rev. Alan Cameron, who busked for many years outside the Scottish National Gallery.

The division between the Highlander and the Lowlander was one of the most ancient and fundamental in Scotland's history. "The people of the coast," said John of Fordun, the Lowland Aberdeenshire chronicler, writing in 1380, "are of domestic and civilised habits, trusty, patient and urbane, decent in their attire, affable and peaceful.... The Highlanders and people of the islands, on the other hand, are a savage and untamed nation, rude and independent, given to rapine, easy-living, of a docile and warm disposition, comely in person but unsightly in dress, hostile to the English people and language and, owing to diversity of speech, even to their own nation, and exceedingly cruel."

The division was seen to be based on what Fordun called "the diversity of their speech": the Lowlanders spoke Scots, a version of Middle English, the Highlanders spoke Gaelic. The line between the two languages broadly coincided with the line of the hills. North of the Highland fault running from just above Dumbarton to just above Stonehaven, and west of the plains of Aberdeenshire and the Moray Firth, Gaelic was spoken. Outside that area, Scots was spoken, except in the northern isles of Orkney and Shetland, where a kind of Norse was spoken, and perhaps in a few pockets of the southwest where another form of Gaelic may have lingered until late in the Middle Ages.

Four hundred years later, things hadn't changed that much. When Dorothy and William Wordsworth made a brief trip into the Loch Lomondside, within 20 miles (32 km) of Glasgow, and when Patrick Sellar, the Lowland sheep-farmer, wrote to his employer, the Countess of Sutherland, about the nature of the people over whom he was appointed as estate manager, John of Fordun would have recognised the tone. Sellar spoke of "the absence of every principle of truth and candour from a population of several hundred thousand souls." He compared these "aborigines of Britain" with the "aborigines of America", the Red Indians: "both live in

turf cabins in common with the brutes: both are singular for patience, courage, cunning and address. Both are most virtuous where least in contact with men in civilised State, and both are fast sinking under the baneful effects of ardent spirits."

Then, in the 19th century, a startling turnabout occurred. Many Scots began to adopt as their national symbols the very trappings of the despised Highland minority – the kilt and the tartan, the bagpipe and the bonnet, the eagle's feather and the dried sprig of

heather: it blended into a kitsch everyone across the world can recognise. As recently as the late 1980s, when the American broadcasting networks wished to devote a minute of their national news bulletins to the question of why Scotland felt unsympathetic to the policies of Britain's then prime minister, Margaret Thatcher, they chose to use 30 seconds setting the scene with men with hairy knees throwing pine trees about at a Highland gathering: how else could the great American people identify a Scot?

The fact that most Scots would not be seen dead in a kilt or dream of attending anything as outlandish as the Highland games is not

Preceding pages: Glasgow football crowd; an Arinacrinachd weaver. **Left**, bagpipers at Glencoe. **Right**, starting young at Glenfinnan.

very relevant. The adoption of these public symbols has something to do with the campaigns of Sir Walter Scott to romanticise the Highlanders, something to do with the charismatic powers of the Glasgow Police Band, which in Victorian days was largely recruited from Highlanders, and something to do with a music hall that loved a stereotype. The mask stuck.

Rich wives: At the same time, ironically, true Highland society was in a state of collapse. Ever since the 17th century its distinctive character and Gaelic culture had been eroded by the steady spread of hostile government power, the march of commercial forces tying Scotland together as one mar-

more. Simultaneously, Gaelic began a catastrophic decline, from being universally the language of the Highland area to being the language, as it is today, only of the Outer Hebrides and a few other communities, mainly on islands, in the extreme west.

So the Highland-Lowland division today has a rather different meaning from what it had in the past. It is certainly not any longer the most obvious or important division, ethnically and culturally, among the Scottish people as a whole. The Lowlanders themselves were never uniform: the folk of Aberdeenshire spoke "Doric", a dialect of their own, very different in vocabulary and intonation from, say, the folk of Lothian or

ket, and the Lowlandisation of the clan chiefs as they sought wives with better dowries than the mountains could provide. The failure of the Jacobite risings in 1715 and 1745 was important, but the transformation would have come about anyway, for other perfectly mundane reasons.

By 1800 Highland landowners wanted their estates to produce as much cash as possible as quickly as possible, just as landowners did elsewhere in Scotland. In the course of the next 50 years they cleared most of the land surface of peasant farms, which paid little rent, in order to accommodate the Lowlander and his sheep, which paid a good deal

Galloway. In the 19th century this sort of regionalism was greatly compounded and complicated by the immigration of the Irish, about two-thirds of them Catholic and one-third Protestant.

The Catholic Irish, oppressed by poverty and the sectarianism that accompanied their movement, crowded into distinct areas – Glasgow and Dundee among the cities, and the small mining or iron-working towns of Lanarkshire, Lothian and Fife. Today, especially in the west, it is the Catholic-Protestant division that continues to have most meaning in people's lives. The Catholics are, overall, still a minority in Scotland, but their church now has more attenders on Sundays than any Protestant denomination – even the Church of Scotland itself. Intermarriage between the two communities has dissolved animosities in the past half-century, but even today politicians deal cautiously with anything that touches, for example, on the right of Scottish Catholics to have their own state-aided schools.

Being a "Lowlander" has less meaning than having a religious affiliation, or coming from Edinburgh rather than Glasgow, or even than backing a certain football team. (Sports allegiances are a subtle blend of the regional and the religious. Celtic, for example, is Glasgow Catholic and Rangers is Glasgow

with the prefix "Mac" or theoretically belong to some clan like Grant or Gunn, Murray or Munro; but, apart perhaps from a greater fondness for dressing in tartan and doing Highland reels at party time, there is little that is distinctive about being a Highlander in most communities that lie beyond the geological Highland line.

In the west, however, in the Inner and Outer Hebrides and along the extremities of the mainland coast from Argyll to Sutherland, the ancient significance and meaning of being a Highlander is very much alive. Not all these communities necessarily or predominantly speak Gaelic rather than English, though in the Western Isles the power of

Protestant, but Aberdeen United has no sectarian overtone, though an obvious regional one.)

Being a "Highlander" has an uncertain and ambiguous meaning over most of the area covered today by Highland and Grampian Region. The citizens of Pitlochry or Inverness don't, for the most part, speak Gaelic, are mostly ordinary lukewarm Protestants, and enjoy a lifestyle and a culture not obviously very different form that of the citizens of Perth or Aberdeen. They may have a name

Left, sheep drovers in the 19th century. **Above**, assessing the form at the Braemar Gathering.

the language is much less dimmed than elsewhere. All of them are, however, historically "crofting communities": that is, they are the relics of a traditional peasantry who, thanks to a campaign of direct action in the 1880s, won from the British parliament the right to live under the same kind of privileged land-law as their brethren in Ireland. The Crofters Holding Act in 1886 conferred on the crofting inhabitants of these areas security of tenure, the right to hand on their holdings to heirs, and a rent which was fixed not by the whim of the estate manager but by the arbitration of a Land Court sitting in Edinburgh.

Crofting is still largely the economic

foundation of these communities. It can best be described as small-scale farming that involves individual use of arable land and some communal use of the grazing on the hill and moor. Very often, crofting is (or was) combined with some other activity, such as fishing or weaving, especially on the islands of Harris and Lewis.

Today, inevitably, it involves regulation and subsidy on a massive scale, and the crofter becomes an expert in milking the grants available from the European Community, the Nature Conservancy, Highland and Island Enterprise, the Department of Agriculture and Fisheries, and anyone else who looks good for a touch. Old animosities are

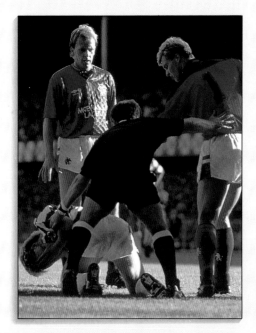

sometimes rekindled when the Lowlander considers the Highlander's expertise in living off the hand-outs of the taxpayer, and the Highlander in return resents the indifference of Edinburgh and London towards the real problems of living in remote communities.

The real thing: But the Highland way of life in these areas goes beyond the details of economic existence, and can best be understood in Scotland by a journey to the Outer Hebrides. In Lewis the visitor encounters the Protestant version of a Gaelic culture dominated, especially on Sundays, by grim Calvinist churches known to outsiders as the "Wee Frees". Jesus may have walked on

water, but if he had dared walk on the glorious beaches of Harris or Lewis on a Sunday he would have been ostracised. In Barra and South Uist the tourist finds the Catholic version, implanted by the 17th-century Counter-Reformation and not involving such denial of life's pleasures.

There are those who would argue that the Highland way of life exists in a still purer form in the Canadian Maritimes, especially in the Catholic Gaelic-speaking communities of Cape Breton Island, who trace their origins directly to the evictions and migrations that followed the 1745 Rebellion and the Clearances of the 19th century.

Wherever it survives, irrespective of religious background, the Gaelic tradition in many respects defies the dominant world outside, though the values of that world intrude even on its remotest fastnesses. In some ways, the Gaelic Highlander is indeed aboriginal, as Patrick Sellar said, though he only meant it as an insult. The Highlander is often unmodern in priorities, is materialistic yet with little sense of individual ambition, attaches little importance to clock-watching; indeed, the word *mañana* might spring automatically to many people's lips. Gaelic society is supportive of its members, has an abiding sense of kinship and an unembarrassed love of a song and a story, as it has an unembarrassed love of drink.

With every passing year it appears superficially less likely that its distinctiveness can survive another generation, but its efforts to survive become more, not less, determined as the 21st century approaches. The recent creation of a unified local government authority, the Western Isles Council, which conducts its business in Gaelic, has given a remarkable new confidence and ability to deal with modern political society. It is perhaps unlikely that any Ayatollah will arise in Stornoway, but the Highland way of life is far from finished on the islands.

On the other hand, elsewhere in Scotland, John of Fordun and Patrick Sellar have really had the last word. It is their Anglicised Lowland Scotland that now runs from the Mull of Galloway to John o' Groats. The tartan and the bagpipe ought not to fool the visitor: it does not fool the Scot, though he enjoys the pretence of it all.

Above, everyday aggro at a football game.

SCOTS IDIOMS

There are moments in the lives of all Scots – however educated, however discouraged by school or station from expressing themselves in the vernacular – when they will reach into some race memory of language and produce the only word for the occasion.

The Scots idiom tends to operate at two ends of a spectrum: from abusive to affectionate. So the word for the occasion might well be *nyaff*. There are few Scots alive who don't know the meaning of the insult *nyaff* – invariably *"wee nyaff"* – and there are few Scots alive who don't have difficulty telling you. Like all the best words in the Scots tongue, there is no single English word which serves as translation. The most that can be done for *nyaff* is to say it describes a person who is irritating rather than infuriating, whose capacity to annoy and inspire contempt is just about in scale with his diminutive size, and the cockiness that goes with it.

The long historical partnership between Scotland and France has certainly left its mark on the Scots tongue. Scottish cooks use "ashets" as ovenware – a word which derives from *assiette*, meaning plate – while the adjective "douce", meaning gentle and sweet-natured, is a direct import of the French *douce*, meaning much the same thing. But the most satisfying Scots words – resounding epithets like *bauchle* (a small, usually old and often misshapen person) and evocative adjectives like *shiplit* (sickly-looking) and *wabbit* (weak and fatigued) – belong to that tongue which came under threat in the early 17th century when King James VI moved to London to become James I of England.

Until then, the Lowland Scots (as opposed to Gaelic-speaking Highlanders) whose racial inheritance was part-Celtic and part-Teutonic spoke their own version of a northern dialect of English, and "Scots" was the language of the nobility, the bourgeoisie and the peasants. But when king and court departed south, educated and aristocratic Scots adopted the English of the "élite", and the Scots tongue received a blow from which it has never recovered.

Yet what could be more expressive than a mother saying of her child, "The bairn's a wee bit wabbit today"? What could be more colourful than the remark that the newspaper vendor on the

Sales patter at Glasgow's Barras street market.

corner is "a shilpit wee bauchle"? The words themselves almost speak their meaning, even to non-Scots, and they are beginning to creep back into the vocabulary of the middle-class.

The dialects of Glasgow and Scotland's urban west have been much influenced by the mass infusions of Gaelic and Irish from their immigrant populations from the Highlands and Ireland, but Glasgow's legendary "patter" has an idiom all its own, still evolving and still vitally conscious of every subtle shift in the city's preoccupations. Glasgow slang specialises in abuse which can be affectionate or aggressive. A *bampot* is a harmless idiot; *heidbanger* is a dangerous idiot.

Predictably, there is a rich seam of Glasgow vernacular connected with drink. If you are drunk

you might be *steamin'*, *stotious*, *wellied*, *miraculous* or *paralytic*. If you are drinking you might be consuming a *wee goldie* (whisky) or a *nippy sweetie* (any form of spirits). And if you are penniless you might have to resort to *electric soup*, the hazardous mixture of meths and cheap wine drunk by down-and-outs.

If a Glaswegian calls you *gallus*, it is a compliment. The best translation in contemporary idiom is probably streetwise, although it covers a range of values from cocky and flashy to bold and nonchalant. The word derives from gallows, indicating that you were the kind of person destined to end up on them. In Glasgow that wasn't always a reason for disapproval. ■

When Sunday was still solemnly observed as the Lord's Day, a young minister was asked to preach to George V at at his Highland palace, Balmoral. Nervous at such an honour, the minister enquired: "What would the King like the sermon to be about?" His Majesty replied: "About five minutes."

What he was dreading, of course, was an interminable exhortation to high moral endeavour. Until recent times the Sabbath was a day when profane activity ceased. The intervals between services were spent in prayer or with improving books. The most devout drew down their window-blinds. Woe to the golfer, the wife who cooked, the child who fidgeted in the kirk (*church*), the boy who whistled on the way home! The Presbyterian ethic is strict and challenging – well-suited to promote survival in a poor country with a harsh climate. Whether the kirk has shaped the Scots or the Scots their kirk, it is impossible to understand Scottish character and attitude without taking into account the austere religious background.

The Scots worship God, their Maker, in a plain dwelling dominated by a pulpit. There are no idolatrous statues or other Papist frumperies such as stained glass, holy pictures, gorgeous surplices or altar hangings. The clergy are attired in sober black and a sparingly used Communion table replaces the altar. The appeal is to the conscience and to the intellect, with the minister's address based on a text from the Bible, the only source of truth. To avoid "vain repetitions", there's no liturgy, or even such set forms as the Lord's Prayer and the Apostles' Creed. Prayers, sometimes prolonged like the sermon, are *extempore*. The one concession to the senses is the singing of hymns and a psalm.

The reason for this lack of "outer show" is that ritual is thought irrelevant; what matters is the relation of the individual soul to his or her Maker. Hence the emphasis on self-reliance and personal integrity. With honesty a prime virtue, the Roman Catholic

practice of currying divine favour through bribing the saints is despised as devious. Presbyterians bow their heads in prayer, but feel no need to grovel on their knees; they talk to God directly. This directness characterises all other dealings, and strangers may be disconcerted by the forthright expression of opinion, prejudice, liking or disapproval.

Rigorously democratic, the Church of Scotland is without bishops or hierarchy. In most other churches, the "man in the pew" has no say in the appointment of clergy, who

are imposed from above. The Scots minister, however, is chosen by the congregation, whose elders, having searched far and wide for a suitable incumbent, will invite him to test his worth by a trial sermon. Where other churches' cardinals and archbishops hold office for life, the kirk's leader, the Moderator, is elected for one year only.

The kirk is also a symbol of national independence. At its General Assembly the Sassenach (English) Queen or her representative, the Lord High Commissioner, is invited as a courtesy but may not take part in the debates. These are much publicised by the media, since, as there is no Scottish

Preceding pages, Presbyterian minister. **Left**, Scottish Presbyterians in the 17th century worship in defiance of the law. **Right**, reformer John Knox.

Parliament, politics and economics are discussed along with matters clerical, and a report submitted to the Government of the day. The General Assembly, which meets once a year for a week in Edinburgh, is attended by ministers and elders from almost every kirk in the land, its deliberations observed (sometimes critically) by laymen in the public gallery.

The belief that all are equal in the eyes of the Lord has produced a people more obedient to the dictates of conscience than to rank or worldly status. The humble shepherd, who roves the mountains in communion with the Almighty, will stomach no affront from his so-called "betters". This has nothing to do

astonishing number of innovative thinkers in many diverse fields.

The academic excellence, of which the Scots are so proud, owes its merit to John Knox, who insisted that every child, however poor, must attend a school supervised by the kirk. By the early 1700s Scotland was almost unique in having universal education.

Knox's concern, however, was more spiritual than scholastic: the new-born babe is not innocent but "ignorant of all godliness", his life thereafter being a thorny and arduous pilgrimage from moral ignorance at birth towards knowledge of the Lord. With the help of the *tawse* (a strap), children were brought up as slaves to the "work ethic",

with modern egalitarianism: the novels of Sir Walter Scott, set long ago in feudal times, abound with scenes where servants defy their masters on points of principle. Even the Lord's anointed are not exempt: though a minister has no qualms about berating sinners from the pulpit, they in turn will take issue with him over errors in his sermon.

Cut and thrust: Unlike the English, who avoid confrontation, the average Scot has an aggressive zest for argument, preferably "philosophical". At its worst this fosters a contentious pedantry, at its best moral courage and the independence of mind which, from a tiny population, has engendered an

sober, frugal, compulsively industrious. Even today, a popular theme for sermons is the mountain climber who strains every muscle to reach the summit only to find he's not in heaven, as he'd foolishly thought, but facing a peak still higher. No respite "here below", no end to a man's striving.

Values are positive: duty, discipline, the serious pursuit of worthwhile achievement and a role of benefit to the social good. Hard-headed and purposeful, there's no time to waste on frivolous poetics. Scotland has pro-

Above, Sunday morning congregation in Stornoway in the Outer Hebrides.

duced philosophers like David Hume, the economist Adam Smith, Watt, Telford and Macadam, whose roads revolutionised public transport; lawyers, doctors, scientists, engineers and radical politicians in search of Utopia – Knox's Godly Commonwealth in secular translation. And, although the General Assembly of 1796 declared that "to spread the Gospel seems highly preposterous, in so far as it anticipates, nay reverses, the order of Nature," yet Scotland would give the world, especially Africa, more Protestant missionaries – such as David Livingstone, John Phillip, Robert Moffat, Mary Slessor – than any other European country.

Balance sheet: With the pressure to achieve so relentless, there's short shrift for the idle. Religious imagery is businesslike: at the Last Day people go to their *reckoning* to settle *accounts* with their Maker; its not sins or trespasses for which pardon is implored but, "Forgive us our *debts* as we forgive our *debtors*." In a land where it's a struggle to survive, the weakest, who go to the wall, have *earned* their just deserts.

"Fear of the Lord is the beginning of wisdom." Understandably so, since the Ultimate Judge, equally precise, has no truck with back-sliders. Some years ago the *Glasgow Herald* published a sermon from a minister famous for "broadsides" from the pulpit. Castigating those in kirk for false motives – the farmer praising God for a rich harvest, the vain female showing off her new bonnet – he gave an awful warning of repentance too late. "Once the account is examined and the balance found wanting, ye'll writhe in Hell, the eternal flames having a scald at your feet. Then ye'll fall on your knees and cry, 'Lord, Lord, we didna ken (*know*)'. But the Lord will look down, from His infinite mercy, and He'll say 'Well, ye ken now'."

Because divine chastisement is ever-imminent, it's not surprising the Scot is canny (*cautious*) and that, when his fortunes prosper, the most he will permit himself to say is: "I can't complain." There's nothing meek and mild about the masculine virtues pleasing to God the Father, the Old Testament God of Wrath, who sets the tone for those in command, especially in the family. Some of the most powerful Scottish novels, such as Stevenson's *Weir of Hermiston*, show the terrifying impact of stern fathers on weak or hyper-sensitive sons.

With one slip from the "strait and narrow" leading to instant perdition, it's said the Scots have a split personality: Jekyll and Hyde. God's Elect are teetotal, but alcoholism is "the curse of Scotland"; while it's almost unheard of for a kirk member to go to prison, Glaswegians proudly boast the busiest criminal court in Europe. It would seem, therefore, that the unofficial influence of the kirk is defiance of all it stands for.

Its ministers have, at all times, lashed "the filthy sins of adultery and fornication" and the taboo on the flesh is so intense that, even in the nursery, mothers, fearing to "spare the rod and spoil the child", economise on caresses. Yet the poet Robert Burns, a flamboyant boozer and wencher, is a national hero, the toasting of whose "immortal memory" provides an annual excuse for unseemly revels. Visitors to puritan Scotland may be puzzled by the enthusiasm for his blasphemous exaltation of sensual delights. But perhaps, if paradoxically, Burns' anarchic *joie de vivre* also stems from the teaching of the kirk, to whose first demand, "What is the chief end of man?" the correct response is: "To glorify God and *enjoy* Him forever."

Though the kirk's faithful have declined – today fewer than one in five are regular communicants – its traditions die hard. Fire and brimstone sermons may be a thing of the past and it's only in some of the outer isles that the Sabbath is kept holy. Sunday is a day, as elsewhere, for sport, idle leisure or washing the car; even Christmas, once by-passed as Papist, is now approved for uniting the family clan. The kirk, however, remains important both in politics, through the General Assembly, and socially as the principal dispenser of charitable aid to the poor and afflicted in this Vale of Tears.

More significant, though, than its public function is an enduring impact on the moulding of character. Scots are still brought up to be thrifty, upright and hard-working, while those who rebel put an energy into their pleasures that can often seem self-destructive. There's success or failure, no limbo in between. Nothing is done by halves and, however secularised the goal, the spur remains: a punitive drive to scale impossible heights. For the individual who fails to appease, if not his Maker, his own expectations, the jaws of Hell still gape for those found "wanting".

When the English social scientist Havelock Ellis produced his *Study of British Genius* (based on an analysis of the *Dictionary of National Biography*) he came up with the fact that there were far more Scots on his list than there should have been. With only 10 percent of the British population, the Scots had produced 15.4 percent of Britain's geniuses. And when he delved deeper into the "men of Science" category he discovered that the Scots made up almost 20 percent of Britain's eminent scientists and engineers.

Not only that, but the Scots-born geniuses tended to be peculiarly influential. Many of them were great original scientists like Black, Hutton, Kelvin, Ramsay and Clerk Maxwell whose work ramified in every direction. Others were important philosophers like the sceptic David Hume, or the economist Adam Smith whose words, according to one biographer, have been "proclaimed by the agitator, conned by the statesmen and printed in a thousand statutes".

Great Scots: Scotland, like Ireland, produced a long string of great military men such as Patrick Gordon (Tsar Peter the Great's right-hand man), James Keith, David Leslie and John Paul Jones. There are also great explorers such as David Livingstone, Mungo Park, David Bruce and John Muir, and accomplished financiers like John Law who founded the National Bank of France and William Paterson who set up the Bank of England. Andrew Carnegie, also a Scot, ruthlessly put together one of the biggest industrial empires America has ever seen, sold it when it was at its peak, then gave much of his money away on the fine Presbyterian basis that "the man who dies rich dies disgraced".

Just why a small, obscure, impoverished country on the edge of Europe should produce such a galaxy of talent is one of the conundrums of European history. As nothing in Scotland's brutal medieval history hints at the riches to come, most historians have concluded that Scotland was galvanised in the 16th and 17th centuries by the intellec-

Right, Eureka! A popular version of how James Watt discovered steam power.

tual dynamics of the Protestant Reformation. This is a plausible theory. Not only did the Reformation produce powerful and challenging figures such as John Knox and his successor Andrew Melville, but it created a church which reformed Scotland's existing universities (Glasgow and St Andrews), set up two new ones (Edinburgh and Aberdeen), and tried to make sure that every parish in Scotland had its own school.

When Thomas Carlyle tried to explain the proliferation of genius in 18th- and 19th-century Scotland, he found "Knox and the Reformation acting in the heart's core of every one of these persona and phenomena." This is a large claim, and overlooks the well-

It was a sceptical, questioning, intellectually-charged atmosphere in which talent thrived. And, interestingly, that talent didn't fall foul of established religion: few Scots had a problem squaring their faith with their intellectual curiosity. An extraordinary number of Scotland's ablest and most radical thinkers were "sons of the manse"—that is, born into clergy homes. This meant that, in 1816, when Anglo-Catholics were squabbling over the precise date of the Creation, the Presbyterian intellectual Thomas Chalmers could ask: "Why suppose that this little spot (the planet earth) should be the exclusive abode of life and intelligence?"

And nothing thrived more than the science

run network of primary schools inherited from the Roman Catholic authorities.

But, whatever the reason, 18th-century Scotland produced an astonishing number of talents. As well as David Hume and his friend Adam Smith, Scottish society was studded with able men like Adam Ferguson, who fathered sociology, William Robertson, one of the finest historians of his age, and the teacher Dugald Stewart. There were also gifted eccentrics like the high-court judge Lord James Monboddo who ran into a barrage of ridicule by daring to suggest (100 years before Darwin) that men and apes might, somehow, be related.

of medicine. In the late 18th and early 19th centuries Edinburgh and Glasgow became two of the most important medical centres in Europe and produced physicians such as William Cullen, John and William Hunter (who revolutionised surgery and gynaecology in London), the three-generation Munro dynasty, Andrew Duncan (who set up the first "humane" lunatic asylums), Robert Liston and James Young Simpson (who discovered the blessings of chloroform). It was a Scot, Alexander Fleming, who, in 1929, hit on penicillin, the most effective antibiotic ever devised.

While Scotland has never produced a classical composer of any note, or a painter to compare with Rembrandt or Michelangelo, the reputation of 19th-century portraitists like Raeburn, Wilkie and Ramsay are now being upgraded. But in the Adam family (father William and sons Robert, John and James), Scotland threw up a dynasty of architectural genius which was highly influential. (One of the scandals of modern Scotland is the number of Adam-designed buildings which are collapsing into ruin.)

Scotland has three international class writers in Robert Burns (1759–96). Walter Scott (1771–1832) and Robert Louis Stevenson (1850–84), but the ranks of the Scottish literati are modest. Certainly, they can't com-

Nasmyth, who dreamed up the steam hammer; James "Paraffin" Young, who first extracted oil from shale; Alexander Graham Bell, who invented the telephone; and John Logie Baird, father of television. More important in world terms were Scotland's "pure" scientists such as John Napier who invented logarithms: Joseph Black, who described the formation of carbon dioxide; James Hutton, Roderick Murchison and Charles Lyell, who by their efforts created modern geology; and Lord Kelvin (an Ulster Scot), who devised, among much else, the second law of thermodynamics and whose name is remembered (like that of Fahrenheit and Celcius) as a unit of temperature.

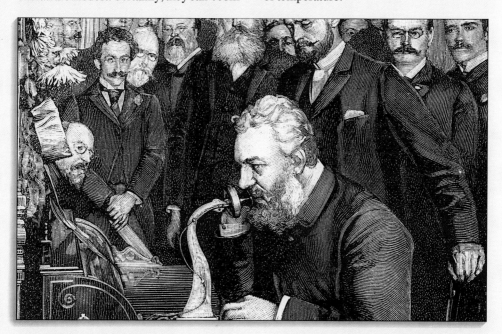

pare with the word-spinning talent produced by the Anglo-Irish culture of Joyce, Yeats, Synge, Shaw and O'Casey.

However, the number of technologists born in Scotland in truly remarkable: James Watt, who improved the steam engine beyond measure; the civil engineer Thomas Telford; John Dunlop, who invented the pneumatic tyre; John Macadam, who gave his name to the metalled road; Charles MacIntosh, who did the same to waterproofed fabric; James

Left, an 1827 view of engineer John Macadam. **Above**, Alexander Graham Bell, inventor of the telephone.

Then there's the Scotsman who is said to have virtually invented the modern world: James Clerk Maxwell, the 19th-century physicist who uncovered the laws of electrodynamics which underlie just about everything we know of electricity, electronics and nuclear physics. Albert Einstein described Clerk Maxwell's work as a "change in the conception of reality" which was the "most fruitful that physics has experienced since the time of Newton". And Max Planck, the German physicist, said Clerk Maxwell was among the small band who are "divinely blest, and radiate an influence far beyond the border of their land".

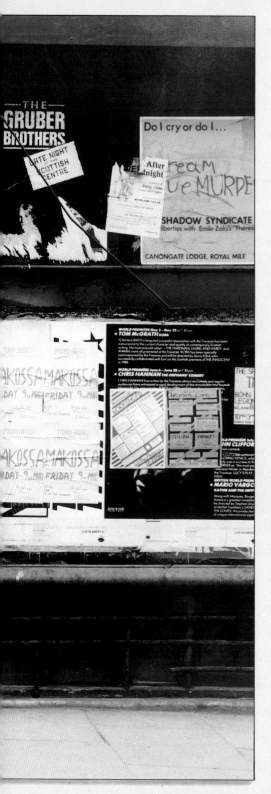

THE GREAT TARTAN MONSTER

When it comes to selling drink, the Mackinnons of Edinburgh (and formerly of Skye) are no slouches. In fact their family company, the Drambuie Liqueur Co. Ltd, is one of the most successful companies in Scotland, and demand for their sweet-tasting liqueur has boomed even at those times when the sales of "conventional" whiskies have been crashing through the floor.

And it has all been done on the coat-tails of that great loser, Bonnie Prince Charlie. Not only does Drambuie claim to be based on a "secret" recipe given to the Mackinnon family by the prince himself, but the Stuart's kilted portrait adorns every bottle. And the conference room in Drambuie's Edinburgh HQ is an exact replica of the 18-century French frigate which sailed the Prince into exile (not to mention drunkenness and despair) in France and Italy.

But, thanks to Bonnie Prince Charlie, the Mackinnons are now turning over more than £23 million a year and paying themselves huge salaries. "The drink itself may be nothing famous," says one Edinburgh expert, "but the marketing has been superb." The Jacobite rising of 1745–46 was a major disaster for the Stuarts, but it has been good news for the Mackinnons.

The success of Drambuie – "the Prince's Dram" – is tartanry in action. The Mackinnon millions are yet another tribute to that *mélange* of chequered cloth, strident music, mawkish song and bad history which has stalked Scotland for generations and refuses to go away. Tartan tea-towels and tartan tea-cosies; tartan pencils and tartan postcards; tartan golf club covers and a wide assortment of comestibles packaged in tartan – all are eagerly purchased.

Tartanry is a vigorous subculture which, by some alchemy, manages to lump together Bonnie Prince Charlie, John Knox, pipe bands, Queen Victoria, Rob Roy, Harry Lauder, Mary Queen of Scots, Edinburgh Castle and the White Heather Club dancers. It is a cultural phenomenon which has defied

Left, ancient and modern: tartan adapts itself to the punk look.

every attempt by the Caledonian intelligentsia to understand it or explain it away.

Fun or frightful?: Many resent the fact that this debased and often silly version of Gaeldom has come to represent the culture of Adam Smith, David Hume, Robert Burns and James Clerk Maxwell. Others regard tartanry as a harmless effervescence which has kept alive a sense of difference in the Scottish people that may yet prove politically decisive. Even more think it is wonderful and buy Andy Stewart records.

But it certainly demands elaborate and expensive tribute. A full set of Highland "evening wear" consisting of worsted kilt, Prince Charlie Coatee, silver-mounted

despised and oppressed it. Right into the 19th century there was nothing fashionable (or even respectable) about Highlanders. They were about as popular in 18th-century Britain as the IRA is now. Their kilts, tartans and bagpipes were hopelessly associated in the public mind with the Jacobite assaults on the Hanoverian ascendancy in 1715, 1719 and 1745. In fact, in 1746 the whole caboodle – bagpipes and all – was banned by the British Government "under pain of death" and remained banned until 1782.

But, with the Jacobite menace safely out of the way, the élites of Hanoverian Britain began to wax romantic over the Highland clans. The bogus "Ossian" sagas of James

sporran, lace jabots and cuffs, ghillie shoes, chequered hose and *sgian dubh* can cost up to £1,000. Even a "day wear" outfit of a kilt in "hunting" tartan, Argyle Jacket, leather sporran and civilian brogues will set the wearer back £350.

Of course, none of this applies to the Highlanders who actually live in the Highlands. As anyone who knows the area will confirm, the day dress of the Highland crofter or shepherd consists of boiler suit, wellington boots and cloth cap. For important evening occasions he takes off his cap.

Tartanry could be regarded as Gaeldom's unwitting revenge on the country which once

Macpherson became the toast of Europe (Napoleon loved them) while Sir Walter Scott's romantic novels became runaway best sellers. And it was Scott who orchestrated the first-ever outburst of tartan fervour: King George IV's state visit to Edinburgh in 1822. Determined to make the occasion high romance, Scott wheeled into Edinburgh dozens of petty Highland chieftains and their tartan-clad "tails" and gave them pride of place in the processions. The huge 20-stone (127-kg) frame of George IV himself was draped in swathes of Royal Stewart tartan over flesh-coloured tights.

"Sir Walter Scott has ridiculously made us

appear to be a nation of Highlanders," grumbled one Edinburgh citizen at this display of tartan power, "and the bagpipe and the tartan are the order of the day."

And Scott's own son-in-law, John Lockhart, pointed out that the same gentry strutting around Edinburgh in their Highland finery were the very people who were ousting their own clansfolk to make way for sheep. "It almost seems as if there was a cruel mockery in giving such prominence to their pretentions," Lockhart wrote.

But there was no stopping the tartan bandwagon. "We are like to be torn to pieces for tartan" wrote an Edinburgh merchant to the weaving firm of William Wilson and Son of

manuscript which described hundreds of hitherto unknown tartans.

But the real clincher came in 1858 when Queen Victoria and Prince Albert bought Balmoral Castle as a summer residence and furnished it almost entirely with specially-designed (by Albert) "Balmoral" tartan. After that, the English mania for Highland Scotland knew no bounds. Every Lancashire industrialist and City of London financier had to have his shooting lodge in the mountains, while every family name in Scotland was converted into a "clan" complete with its own tartan.

All of which was helped along by the stirring performances of the Highland regi-

Bannockburn in the wake of George IV's visit. "The demand is so great that we cannot supply our customers." Wilson took the hint and installed 40 extra looms.

The tartan business got another boost when a couple of amiable English eccentrics known as the "Sobieski Stuarts" (born Charles and John Allen) popped up, claiming to be the direct descendents of Bonnie Prince Charlie and his wife Louisa of Stolberg. They also claimed to have an "ancient" (i.e. fake)

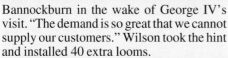

Left, Sir Walter Scott and friends, who helped create the romantic Highland image. **Above**, more modern manifestations of tartanry.

ments in the Crimean War and the Indian Mutiny. In their "Government" tartans (essentially variations on the Black Watch), red coats and feathered bonnets, the Highland battalions were an awesome sight.

By 1881 the British military were so besotted with tartanry that the War Office ordered all Scotland's Lowland regiments to don tartan trousers and short Highland-style doublets. Venerable Lowland regiments like the Royal Scots and the Royal Scots Fusiliers were outraged and protested that their military tradition was both older and a lot more distinguished than that of the Highlanders. But their pleas fell on deaf ears. Only the

Scots Guards, as members of the élite Brigade of Guards, were granted the right *not* to wear tartan on their uniforms.

The military victory of tartanry is now complete. Every Scottish regiment (including the Scots Guards) has its pipes and drums, all of whom dress in full Victorian-Highland paraphernalia of dress tartan, silver-buttoned doublets, feather bonnets and horsehair sporrans. And Edinburgh Castle, which resisted every foray of Bonnie Prince Charlie's Highland raiders, is now home of the British Army's school of piping, and the centre of that triumph of Highland-military kitsch, the annual Edinburgh Military Tattoo.

Marauding bands: Not that the cult of the hard-line Protestants are happy to swathe themselves in the tartans of the Jacobite clans, most of whom were Catholic or Episcopalian. On the other side of the Irish fence, the saffron-kilted pipers of Ireland have abandoned their melodic "Brian Boru" pipes for the Great Highland Bagpipe.

Another (somewhat quieter) arm of tartan imperialism is the Royal Scottish Country Dance Society (RSCDS) which is run from Edinburgh and which, at the last count, had more than 26,000 members prancing and leaping around ballrooms all over the world. This may be understandable in Scot-infested corners of the globe like the United States, Canada and New Zealand but it isn't so

Highland bagpipe is confined to the military. Far from it. According to the Royal Scottish Pipe Band Association (RSPBA), there are now more than 400 pipe-bands alive and wailing in the UK alone, with hundreds more all over the world. Every year the bands flock to the one or other of the RSPBA's five championships. The biggest prize is the World Pipe Band Championship which used invariably to be won by a Scottish band, but which in 1987 went to the 75th Fraser Highlanders from Canada and, in 1992 and 1993, to the Field-Marshall Montgomery Band from Northern Ireland. Eighty of the RSPBA's member bands are in Northern Ireland, where

explicable in France, Holland, Sweden, Kenya or Japan. Just why the sensible citizens of Paris, The Hague, Gothenburg, Nairobi and Tokyo should want to trick themselves out in tartan to skip around in strict tempo to tunes like "The Wee Cooper O'Fife", "The Duke of Perth", "Cadgers in the Canongate" or "Deuks Dang Ower My Daddie" is a deep and abiding mystery.

It may have something to do with Scottish country dancing's royal and aristocratic connections. The Queen herself is patron of the RSCDS and the Royal prefix was granted by her father King George VI just before he died in 1952. Other exalted members include the

Earl of Mansfield (who is President of the RSCDS) the Duke of Atholl, Lord Glenconner and Sir Donald Cameron of Lochiel.

But it seems unlikely that the Royal laying on of hands will ever extend to the crowd of kilted warblers, accordion players, comics and fiddlers who make their living entertaining Scotland (and the Scottish diaspora). Usually showbiz tartanry finds its own niche, but occasionally, as in the case of the Bay City Rollers or the fearsome Jesse Rae (half-Highlander, half-Viking), it escapes into the mainstream of pop culture. Interestingly, none of the newer breed of Gaelic-speaking folk-rock bands such as Runrig or Ossian has ever been seen near a scrap of tartan.

mates there are about 100 such games held in Scotland every year. Most attract crowds of up to 5,000, although the Braemar Gathering (with the Royal Family in attendance), can easily pull in more than 20,000.

But even Braemar cannot compete with the 40,000 or 50,000-strong crowds who flock to watch the big Highland games in the USA. The event at Grandfather Mountain in North Carolina is now the biggest of its kind on earth. American tartanry buffs are very keen on "clan gatherings" in which they get togged up in a kind of "Sword of Zorro" version of Highland dress, and march past their "chief" brandishing their broadswords.

But perhaps the daftest manifestation of

Olympic efforts: Yet another manifestation of tartanry is the Highland games circuit. Every year between May and September villages and towns the length of Scotland (plus a few in England) stage a kind of Caledonian olympics in which brawny, kilted figures toss the caber, putt the shot and throw the hammer while squads of little girls in velvets and tartans dance their hearts out to the sound of bagpipes. Andrew Rettie of the Scottish Highland Games Association (which has not yet acquired a "Royal" prefix) esti-

<u>Left</u>, members of the Royal Family attending the Braemar Games. <u>Above</u>, a sheaf of tartans.

competitive tartanry is "haggis-hurling", an event dreamed up in 1977 by an Edinburgh public relations man, Robin Dunseath, as "a bit of an upmarket joke". To Dunseath's utter astonishment the "ancient" sport of haggis-hurling took off and has gone from strength to strength. Dunseath (an Irishman) now despatches his "How To Run a Haggis Hurl" kits all over the globe. The world record is held by Stewart Pettigrew of Saltcoats who hurled a 1½-lb (680-gm) "competition" haggis more than 181 ft (55 metres). It has been a golden decade for the sport's "official" haggis makers, Dalzell & McIntosh of Stockbridge in Edinburgh.

In spite of its puritanism and thunderings from the kirk against "vain outer show", Scotland is unique among the British provinces in having a distinctive painterly tradition. The art of Protestant northern Europe tends to be tormented and morbid and, given a Calvinist shadow of guilt and sin, one would expect Scottish painting to be gloomily angst-ridden. Instead, as if in defiance of all that the kirk represents, it is extroverted, joyful, flamboyant, robust – much more sensuous (even if less complex) than English art with its inhibiting deference to the rules of good taste.

It's significant that young Scottish artists have mostly by-passed the Sassenach (English) capital to study abroad, those from Edinburgh in Rome, the Glaswegians a century later in pleasure-loving Paris. Growth of the arts in Scotland is linked to the relative importance of its two major cities, and the rivalry between them (culture versus commerce) has resulted in aesthetic dualism: where Edinburgh's painters are rational and decorous, raw but dynamic Glasgow has produced exuberant rebels.

The Enlightenment: Before the 18th century, Scottish art scarcely existed. There was no patronage from the kirk, which forbade idolatrous images, or from the embattled aristocracy. In a country physically laid waste by the Covenanter wars and mentally stifled by religious fanaticism, painters were despised as menial craftsmen.

The return of peace and prosperity, however, gave rise to a remarkable intellectual flowering, the Edinburgh Enlightenment, which lasted, roughly, from 1720 until 1830 and caused the city to be dubbed the "Athens of the North". The rejection of theology for secular thought was accompanied by a new enthusiasm for the world and its appearance, the brothers Adam evolving a style in architecture and design which was adopted all over Europe and has remained to this day the classic model of elegance and grace.

Preceding pages, Wilkie's *Pitlessie Fair*. **Left**, Raeburn's perennially popular Rev. Robert Walker skating on Duddingston Loch. **Right**, Ramsay's portrait of David Hume.

A need arose, meanwhile, for portraits to commemorate the city's celebrated sons. Though the earliest portrait painters, Smibert and Aikman, achieved modest recognition as artists not craftsmen, Allan Ramsay, son of a poet and friend of the philosopher David Hume, expected to be treated as an equal by the intellectual establishment, many of whose members he immortalised with his brush.

Considering the visual austerity of his background – Edinburgh had no galleries, no art school and only a few enlightened collec-

tors – Ramsay's rise to fame is astonishing. Leaving home to study in Italy, he returned to London in 1739 and was an instant success, finally ending up as court painter (in preference to Reynolds) to George III. Despite his classical training, Ramsay cast aside impersonal idealism for "natural portraiture", concentrating on light, space and atmosphere and the meticulous rendering of tactile detail: ribbons, cuffs, the curl of a wig, the bloom on a young girl's cheek. Above all, he was interested in the character of his sitters, combining formal dignity with intimacy and charm. The refined distinction of his best work, such as the portraits of his two wives, has earned him an honourable position in the history not just of Scottish but of British art.

His achievement was rivalled in the next generation by Sir Henry Raeburn, knighted in 1822 by George IV and made King's Limner (*painter*) for Scotland. Raeburn also studied in Italy and his *oeuvre*, like Ramsay's, was confined to portraiture with an emphasis on individual character, the fiddler Neil Gow or a homely matron receiving the same attention as a scholar or fashionable beauty. But his style is broader and more painterly, the poses more dramatic: Judge Eldin looking fierce in his study, the Clerks of Penicuik romantically strolling, the Rev. Robert Walker taking a turn on the ice.

Pitlessie Fair (painted at 19) was the start of a career which earned him a knighthood and outstanding popularity, his "low-life" comedies, like *The Penny Wedding* creating a taste for such subjects that persisted throughout the Victorian era.

Although no one equalled Raeburn or Wilkie, there was a new public interest in the arts, which continued to flourish in Edinburgh during the 19th century. Notable in landscape are David Roberts with his views of the Holy Land and, later, William McTaggart, "the Scottish Impressionist". The academic mainstream, however, was confined to historical melodrama, sentimental cottagers and grandiose visions of the High-

Raeburn was the first Scottish painter of national renown to have remained in his native Edinburgh and, in doing so, he established the arts in Scotland and their acceptance by the public. Interested prestige led to ventures in other *genres*, especially landscape. Though Alexander Nasmyth painted an italianate Scotland, gilded and serene, the choice of local vistas rather than a classical idyll in the manner of Claude was startling in its novelty.

Equally novel was David Allan's transfer of the pastoral tradition of nymphs and shepherds into scenes from Scottish rural life. He was followed by David Wilkie whose

lands as inspired by Sir Walter Scott.

The Glasgow Boys: The 1880s saw a new departure when a group of students, nicknamed the Glasgow Boys, united in protest against Edinburgh's stranglehold on the arts. Due to rapid industrial expansion Glasgow had grown from a provincial town into "the second city of the empire" and, in contrast to 18th-century Edinburgh, there were galleries, an art school and lavish collectors among the new rich (one of whom was William Burrell) who were anxious to buy status through cultural patronage.

Initially, though, the Glasgow Boys scandalised their fellow citizens. Rejecting the turgid subjects and treacly varnish of the academic "glue-pots", they abandoned their studios to paint in the open air, choosing earthy, peasant themes that lacked "message" or moral and gave offence to the genteel. The public, devoted to gain, godliness and grand pianos (whose legs were prudishly veiled) was both affronted and bemused by Crawhall's lyrical cows, the voluptuous cabbages tended by James Guthrie's farm hands, the indecent brilliance of the rhubarb on Macgregor's *Vegetable Stall*.

Influenced by Whistler and the European Realists, most of the Glasgow Boys left Scotland in disgust to study in Paris – where they were subsequently acclaimed. This suc-

latterly, as doctrinaire as the hated "glue-pots", the Glasgow Boys had an important influence on younger artists, giving them the courage to experiment through their flamboyant handling of paint and colour. Oppressed by the Calvinism, philistinism and drabness of Scottish life, rebels of the next generation, led by Peploe, Cadell, Hunter and Fergusson, again fled to Paris where they were intoxicated by the decorative art of Matisse and the Fauves (wild beasts). Discarding conventional realism, they flattened form and perspective into dancing, linear rhythm, with colour an expression of a pagan *joie de vivre*. The Fauves' English imitators were never as uninhibited as the Scots, who

cess abroad tickled civic pride (what Edinburgh artist could compete?) and the canny burghers, who had once been so hostile, began to pay high prices for their pictures, Sadly, the Glasgow Boys now lost their freshness and became respectable: Lavery a fashionable portrait painter, Guthrie a conservative president of the Royal Scottish Academy, while Hornel retreated into orientalism. Today, there is a revival of interest – and investment.

New experiments: Although they became,

Left, **Lorimer's *Ordination of the Elders*. Above**, **MacGregor's *Vegetable Stall*.**

sold well both in Paris and London.

As with the Glasgow Boys, fame abroad brought the Scottish Colourists belated success at home. Peploe and Hunter returned to paint a Scotland brightened by gallic sunshine and the witty Cadell to transform Glasgow housewives into flappers of the Jazz Age.

A gloomier fate, though, awaited the architect and designer Charles Rennie Mackintosh, who is by far the most important figure of this period and, as an originator of *art nouveau*, has an international standing. Glasgow School of Art, his architectural masterpiece, is one of the city's most remarkable buildings and the Glasgow Style he initiated in furniture and the decorative arts is now admired the world over. Yet in his day "Toshie" was dismissed as a drunken eccentric and was such a failure professionally that he abandoned architecture and a public which had mocked him to paint watercolours in France. These watercolours, nonetheless, have a refinement of sensibility that is rare in Scottish art: hauntingly poetic, mysterious and exquisite.

Modern times: From the 1930s, Scottish painters have performed creditably, though landscape (the Scots have an unbounded pride in their lochs and glens) has tended to predominate. In a country where intellectual achievement allied to public service is so

highly esteemed, it's curious that the arts in Scotland have mostly been devoted to expressing simple emotion and visual pleasure, avoiding politics, social comment or even a cerebral interest in stylistic experiment. In the 1950s, Colquhuon and MacBryde adopted Cubism not for formal reasons but as a means of conveying romantic melancholia.

Since World War II, while modern trends have been pursued with characteristic vigour, there's been a loss of optimism and sparkle. More poignant than the Modernists is Joan Eardley, who turned her back on artistic fashion to paint urchins in the Glasgow back streets, then, after settling in a remote fishing village in the northeast, somberly elemental landscapes.

John Bellany, the son of a fisherman, is unusual in that he has the tormented vision one might expect, but rarely finds, among artists brought up under Calvinism. Overwhelmed, after a visit to Buchenwald, by human wickedness, he gave up modish abstracts to return to figurative art of a tragic, often nightmarish monumentality. Later, after liver failure, confrontation with death and a last-minute reprieve, he unleashed intense energy with a prolific output of superb, lyrical autobiographical canvasses.

Another post-war change is that German Expressionism, with its energy and gloom, has replaced the hedonistic influence of the French, especially in recent times when Glasgow School of Art has produced a new group of rebels. Known (unofficially) as the Glasgow Wild Boys, they have also rejected Modernism for gigantic narrative pictures with literary, political or symbolist undertones. The most successful, Adrian Wiszniewski and Stephen Campbell, have been rapturously received in New York.

Wiszniewski, a Pole born in Scotland, has adapted Slavic folk art to express nostalgia for the past, disenchantment with the present. Campbell, combining macho brutalism with whimsy, draws his inspiration from P.G. Wodehouse and Bram Stoker. Although affecting social "concern" and apparently doom-laden, the most striking quality of these young painters is anarchic ebullience.

Other brilliant Glasgow graduates include Stephen Conroy, Peter Howson, Mario Rossi, Craig Mulholland and Steven Campbell, who, with the exception of Howson, are all from in and around Glasgow. Women have also announced their presence. Allison Watt, Lesley Banks and Jenny Saville are graduates of Glasgow. Watt earned notoriety for her painting of the Queen Mother with a teacup on her head, and Saville's oils scarcely flatter women. Banks's canvasses are surrealistic.

Painting in Scotland retains an almost aggressive vitality, with self-confidence boosted by superb municipal collections, notably the Burrell, which has replaced Edinburgh Castle (scoring for Glasgow) as Scotland's principal tourist attraction.

Left, James Guthrie's *Hind's Daughter*. **Right**, Joan Eardley's *Street Kids*.

The days when Billy Connolly, the Glasgow comedian, could dismiss Scottish folk music as four Aran sweaters singing "the Wild Rover" are, thankfully, over. It's not just that the performers have ditched their woolly jerseys in favour of tee-shirts and jeans; the sound of Scottish music has changed dramatically in the past 25 years – and that's *before* you take into account the insidious influence of the phenomenally successful Scottish pop groups such as Wet Wet Wet, Big Country and Simple Minds.

Nothing has been more dramatic than the forging of an alliance between two previously alien schools. On the one hand: the inheritor of the bagpipe tradition, regarded until then as a musical law unto themselves, reared on raw, warrior iron, nurtured on centuries of exclusivity. On the other hand: the freebooting young adventurers of the folk-music revival, ready to play and sing anything that had its roots embedded somewhere in Celtic culture.

Pipers who joined folk groups were regarded as renegades by the piping fraternity – all those years of training in the supreme art going to waste! But for folk musicians, the bagpipe provided much needed instrumental beef in an increasingly noisy market-place.

Whether the piping Establishment has benefited is debatable. They are a gritty, stubborn lot, much given to internecine warfare over the etiquette and mystique of piping disciplines which have been handed down like family heirlooms through the generations. Discipline still rules at the sponsored competitions, where pipers from all over the world challenge each other at what in the Gaelic is called *pìobaireached* (pibroch).

Just to confuse the uninitiated, *piobaireachd* has another title, *ceòl mór* (Great Music). This is a truly classical music, built to complex, grandiloquent proportions and actually playable only after years of study and practice. Those who *can* play it do so by memory, in the manner of the great Indian raga players. The pipe music that most of us are familiar with – stretching from "Mull of Kintyre" to reels, marches, jigs and strathspeys – is referred to by the classicists as *ceòl beag* (Small Music).

Great or Small, much of it has survived thanks to patronage rather than household popularity. The earliest royal families in Scotland are credited with having a piper, or several, on their books, and no upwardly mobile landlord of ancient times could afford to be without his piper. But it was in the warring Highland clan system that the pipes flourished, both on the domestic scene and

battle ground. The blood-tingling quality of the Great Highland Bagpipe, with its three resonant drones, was quickly recognised by the early Scottish regiments, and the military connection remains to this day. Even now, the Scots still use the pipes to soften up the English at soccer and rugby internationals. Sometimes it seems to work.

With the pipes pouring forth on every big public occasion, there's no serious dispute about their role as bearers of the country's national music. But piping can offer nothing to compare with the phenomenal resurgence of Scots fiddle music, which had thrived only in geographical pockets until the folk

Preceding pages, Shetland musicians. **Left**, an Orange parade, Glasgow. **Right**, local ceilidh.

music revival got its full head of steam in the 1960s. Today, it's reckoned that there are more fiddlers in Scotland than ever before.

The fiddle has been part of Scottish music for more than 500 years – King James IV had "fithelaris" on his payroll in the 15th century. As a vehicle for dance music it left the pipes standing. The fiddle reached its Golden Age in the 18th century, when Scots musicians sailed to Italy to study and brought back not only the tricks of the classical trade but, perhaps more significantly, a steady supply of exquisite violins, which were soon copied by enterprising local craftsmen.

At the same time, the dancing craze had begun. Country fiddlers found their robust

trained, and technically virtuosic, the "King of the Strathspey" won international acclaim, and the arrival of recording in the later part of his career helped to spread the message – even as far as fiddle-packed Shetland, which had until then resolutely stuck to its own Norse-tinged style. (From Shetland comes the fiddling giant of the present day, Aly Bain – a sort of contemporary Niel Gow and Scott Skinner rolled into one.)

Another traditional instrument that has become increasingly popular is the *clarsach*, or Scots harp, which first appeared in 8th-century Pictish stone carvings. Some of the great *clarsach* music came from Ruaridh Dall Morrison (the Blind Harper) in the 17th

jigs and reels much in demand at posh balls and parties, and the first major collections of Scots fiddle tunes were published, making the music widely accessible. The Golden Age produced its golden boy – Niel Gow, a prolific composer and, by every account, an extraordinary gifted player.

By the early 19th century, though, high society, as fickle as ever, had turned its fancy to the new polkas and waltzes that were flooding in from Europe. The rural fiddlers played on regardless, and it was the Aberdeenshire village of Banchory that produced the most famous Scots fiddler of all – James Scott Skinner, born in 1843. Classically

century. Much smaller than the modern concert harp, the *clarsach* had become virtually extinct until it was revived in the early 1970s by Alison Kinnaird and other young enthusiasts. Now it finds a place in folk bands and there is a thriving Clarsach Society.

If the fiddle and the *clarsach* have fought their way back into the mainstream of Scottish culture, they were both a long way behind folksong in doing so. The classic narrative ballads and pawky bothy (*a Gaelic word meaning "hut"*) ballads had survived largely

Above, sword dance at the Royal Scottish Country Dance Society's Edinburgh headquarters.

in the hands of farm workers and the travelling folk (the tinkers) of Perthshire and the northeast. The advent of the tape recorder has enabled collectors like Hamish Henderson to bring their songs to the ears of the young urban folk revivalists. It was Henderson who discovered Jeannie Robertson, a magnificent traditional singer living in obscurity in Aberdeen. She was the Bessie Smith of Scottish folksong, and her influence soon showed itself in the folk clubs that sprang up all over Scotland.

The folk clubs served, too, as spawning grounds for new songwriting, especially of the polemical brand, producing some of the best songs since Robert Burns. Burns is credited with more than 300 songs, many of them set to traditional fiddle tunes, and you can still hear them in all sorts of venues.

Many of the early folk clubs are still in existence – notably those in Edinburgh, Aberdeen, Kirkcaldy, Stirling and St Andrews. The visitor should inquire about folk clubs in the vicinity. Sadly, the type of *ceilidh* that is laid on for tourists tends to be neither traditional nor contemporary but caught in a time-warp of kilt, haggis and musical mediocrity. In the Gaelic, *ceilidh* means a gathering. The Gaelic-speaking community, now mostly confined to the west Highlands and islands, holds its great gathering, the National Mod, in different parts of Scotland every year. There, you can sample some beautiful singing as young and old compete for much-coveted prizes.

Even the folk scene finds competitions stimulating. Since the 1960s there has been a steady growth in the number of folk festivals. From Easter until autumn, there's hardly a weekend when there isn't a folk festival somewhere in Scotland. In cities like Edinburgh and Glasgow, the festivals are among the biggest of their kind in the world; Edinburgh's lasts for 10 days. But there's nothing to beat the smaller traditional folk festivals in rural areas, where the atmosphere is friendlier and the talent tends to be local rather than imported. Among the best events are those at Keith (June), Auchtermuchty (August) and Kirriemuir (September). Orkney (May) is also famous for its annual celebrations of traditional music.

Every folk festival has its unofficial "fringe": invariably located in the bars serving the best whisky in town. Many a pub session can excel the finest organised *ceilidh* or competition. Away from the festivals, Scottish pub sessions can be disappointing affairs. It's perhaps a hangover from the days when music was banned in licensed premises.

As for dancing, well, you are unlikely to find it in the pub for reasons of space, if nothing else. The cunning Irish centuries ago devised a way of dancing in tight cottage corners: they keep their arms rigid at the sides of the body. For the Scots, dancing is reserved for the village hall or the ballroom. Many of the traditional dances, including the famous Highland Fling, call for the raising of the arms to depict the antlers of the red deer – splendidly symbolic but treacherous at close quarters. Popular formations like the Eightsome Reel and the Dashing White Sergeant also involve much hectic birling among large groups.

Like the accordion-pumped music which fires these breath-sucking scenes, Scottish dancing has its more rarified moments. There are country dance societies in various districts, and when the members get together they dance with the kind of practised precision that must have been essential at the earliest Caledonian Balls.

It's good fun to go along to a village hop – usually advertised as a *ceilidh* or ceilidh-dance – and trip the heavy fantastic. You don't have to know the steps: the locals will hurl you in the right directions and there will be time for a beer as the band move from "The Mason's Apron" to their idiosyncratic version of the latest Michael Jackson record.

As it happens, Scottish rock has begun to sit up and notice its Celtic heritage. The pre-eminent folk-rock band is Runrig, all-electronic but hitched musically to ancient Gaelic themes. In songwriting, too, folk music has made its mark in the rock venues. The leading singing songwriters – men such as Eric Bogle, Rab Noakes and the brilliant Dick Gaughan – have found eager new audiences there, and their influence can be clearly heard in the punkish protest music of groups like the Proclaimers.

Folk music in Scotland has its own poppy hybrids, beware of the Fiddle Rally – up to 100 deeply unhappy fiddlers, aged from 14 to 94, sawing away at "Largo's Fairy Dance" in wooden unison. And watch out for Billy Connolly's four Aran sweaters: they're not *entirely* extinct.

GAMES HIGHLANDERS PLAY

Highland Gatherings, which are sometimes described as "Oatmeal Olympics", are much more than three-ring circuses. As the Gathering gets going a trio of dancers are on one raised platform; a solitary piper is on another; a 40-man pipe band has the attention, if not of all eyes, at least of all ears; the "heavies" are tossing some unlikely object about; two men are engaged in some strange form of wrestling; a tug-o'-war is being audibly contested and an 880-yard (800-metres) race is in progress.

Track events are the least important part of these summer games – but don't tell the runners. The venue has been chosen for its scenic beauty rather than its "Tartan" track. At the Skye Games, milers literally become dizzy as they run round and round the track's meagre 130 yards (117 metres).

Everywhere the sound of pipes can be heard. It is not only the piper playing for the dancers; another solitary piper playing a mournful dirge in the individual piper's competition; or the 40-strong pipe band being judged in the arena. Around the arena, behind marquees, under trees, in any place which offers some slight protection to muffle the sound, those still to compete are busy rehearsing under the sharp ear of their leaders and coaches. It is amazing how the coach can stand in the centre of a circle of wailing pipes and immediately walk over to one set, incline his head towards them and tell their owner he is half-a-tone flat.

The solo pipers are undoubtedly the aristocrats of the Games and the highest honour – and the biggest prize – is awarded the pibroch winner. There are three competitions for solo pipers: pibrochs (classical melodies composed in honour of birthdays, weddings and the like); marches (military music); and strathspeys and reels (dance music). While playing a pibroch the piper marches slowly to and fro, not so much in time to the music, but in sympathy with the melody. On the other hand, when playing dance music, he remains in one position tapping his foot; and, understandably, when playing a march – for

Left, hammer throwing at a Highland meeting.
Right, tossing the caber.

who can resist the skirl of the pipes? – he strides up and down the platform.

Most dancers at Games are female, although, occasionally, a thorn appears among the roses. Seldom are any girls older than 18 and competitions are even held for three-and four-year-olds.

King Malcolm Canmore is credited with being responsible for one of the more famous dances seen at the Games. In 1054 he slew one of King Macbeth's chieftains and, crossing his own sword and that of the van-

quished chieftain, performed a *Gille Calum* (sword dance) before going into battle. The touching of either sword with the feet was considered an unfavourable omen.

The origin of the Highland fling is also curious. A grandfather was playing the pipes on the moors and having his young grandson dance to them. Two courting stags were clearly silhouetted against the horizon. The grandfather said to the lad: "Can ye nae raise yer hands like the horns of yon stags?" And so originated the Highland Fling. The dance is performed without travelling (that is to say, on one spot) and the reason is that the Scot, like the stag, does not run after his women: he expects them to come to him. A more mundane explanation for the dance being performed on one spot is that it was originally danced on a shield.

In the dance called *Sean Truibhas* – the Gaelic for old trews (*trousers*) – the performer's distaste for his garb is expressed. This dance originated after Culloden when the wearing of the kilt was proscribed.

One of the original aims of the Games was to select the ablest bodyguards for the king or chieftain, and this it perpetuated in today's heavy events. The objects used in these have evolved from what would be found in any rural community, such as a blacksmith's hammer or even a stone in the riverbed.

throws it up and, with luck, over the bar. A correct throw will just miss the thrower on its way down, while a bad throw is liable to cause untold mischief.

Caber tossing: The most unusual and spectacular event is tossing the caber, a straight, tapered pine-tree trunk shorn of it branches. It weighs about 125 lbs (57 kg) and is about 19 ft (six metres) long. The diameter at one end is about nine inches (23 cms) and at the other about five inches (13 cms). Two men struggle to carry the caber to a squatting competitor. They place it vertically with the narrow end in his cupped hands. The competitor gingerly rises and, with the foot of the caber resting against, and eight-ninth tower-

Hurling the hammer and putting the shot are similar, yet different, to these events as practised at the Olympics. At the "Oatmeal Olympics" the hammer has a wooden shaft rather than a chain and the weight of the shot varies. The 56-lb (25-kg) weight is thrown by holding, with one hand, a short chain attached to the weight; the length of weight and chain must not exceed 18 inches (45 cms). Then there is the tossing of the 56-lb (25-kg) weight. In this event it is not distance but height that counts. The competitor stands below and immediately in front of a bar and with his back to it. Then, holding the weight in one hand he swings it between his legs and

ing above, his shoulder, starts to run. This resembles the performance of an inebriate rather than an athlete.

Finally, at a suitably auspicious moment, the competitor stops dead, lets out an almighty roar, and thrusts his hands upwards. The wide end of the caber hits the ground; now is the moment of truth: will the quivering pole tumble backwards towards the hopeful competitor or will it attain the perpendicular and the turn over completely and fall away from him?

But why does an empty-handed, puffing judge trot alongside the competitor? Tossing the caber is judged not on distance but on style. An imaginary clockface is involved, and the athlete is presumed to be standing at the figure 6 when he makes his throw. A perfect throw lands at 12; a somewhat less perfect one at 11 or at 1 and so on. Naturally, the athlete will attempt, after throwing, to swivel his feet so that his throw appears perfect. Hence the puffing judge.

All this assumes that athletes will succeed in turning the caber end over end. Often all fail; when that happens, part of the caber is sawn off and they then try again.

Caber tossing is believed to have evolved from throwing tree trunks into the river after they have been felled. They would then float to the sawmill. It was important to throw the

How did the Games evolve? Some claim that they were first held in 1314 at Ceres in Fife when the Scottish bowmen returned victorious from Bannockburn. Others believe that it all began even earlier when King Malcolm organised a race up a mountain called Craig Choinich. The winner would receive a *baldric* (warrior's belt) and become Malcolm's foot-messenger.

A race up and down Craig Choinich is still a feature of the Braemar Games which is the highlight of the circuit. However, this isn't so much because of the calibre of the competition but because, since the time of Queen Victoria who revived the Games, they are invariably attended by the Royal Family.

trunks into the middle of the river or they would snag on the banks.

Colour codes: Colour is the keynote of the Games. All dancers and musicians are dressed in full Highland regalia, as are many of the judges and some spectators. Competitors in the heavy events all wear the kilt. The reds of the Stuarts, the greens of the Gordons and the blues of the Andersons all mingle with the green of the grass and the purple of the heather to produce a muted palette.

Two views of the Braemar Games: _left_, the judges deliberate; _above_, tug-o'-war team flexes its porridge-fed muscles.

Highland Games are very much in vogue and new venues are constantly announced. Currently, more than 100 Gatherings are held during the season which extends from the end of May until mid-September. In spite of the spectacular appeal of the great Gatherings (Braemar, Cowal, Oban), the visitor might find that the smaller meetings (Ceres, Uist in the Hebrides) are more enjoyable. These have an authentic ambience and competitors in the heavy events are certain to be good and true Scots and not professional intruders from foreign parts.

What's more, you may not even have to pay admission!

Those who imagine the Scots to be Calvinistic churls may be surprised to learn that the Scottish calendar is chock-a-block with local festivals. These are basically for the natives and are not mounted in order to attract the tourist. Indeed, at some, the tourist is scarcely welcome because his presence means that the service industries have to attend to his needs which doesn't leave them time to enjoy *their* festival.

Until the middle of this century Puritanical Scotland completely ignored Papish Christmas: offices, shops and factories all functioned as usual on 25 December. *The* great event on the Scottish calendar was the night of 31 December (Hogmanay) and New Year's Day (which indeed was called *Nollaig Bheag* – Little Christmas – in many parts of the Highlands). Traditionally, as the bells struck midnight, the crowds gathered around the focal points of towns would join hands and sing "Auld Lang Syne" and then whisky bottles would be passed around before all dispersed to go first-footing.

It is important that the first-foot (that is, the first person to cross a threshold in the new year) should be a dark-haired person who brings gifts of coal and salt which ensure that the house won't want for fire or food in the coming year. Also, the first-foot will normally carry a bottle of whisky.

Hot stuff: Fiery New Year processions which will drive out and ward off evil spirits have been held for centuries at Comrie, Burghead and Stonehaven. At the Comrie Flambeaux procession, locals walk through the town carrying burning torches; at Stonehaven, participants swing fireballs attached to a long wire and handle. Some suggest that the swing of fireballs is a mimetic attempt to lure back the sun from the heavens during the dark winter months.

The Burning of the Clavie at Burghead is held on the evening of 11 January. (This is when Hogmanay falls according to the Old Style calendar which was abandoned in 1752 but which still holds sway when deciding the

date of many celebrations.) The ceremony begins with the Clavie King lighting a tar-filled barrel which is then carried in procession through the town and from which firebrands are distributed. Finally, the Clavie is placed on the summit of Doorie Hill and allowed to burn for a time before being rolled down the hill. Fragments of the Clavie are treasured because they offer protection from the evil eye.

Much more recent in origin is the torchlight procession on Edinburgh's Princes

Street on 31 December; this marks the conclusion of a three-day Hogmanay extravaganza which includes carnival and funfair, and indoor and outdoor festivities. However, by far the greatest and most spectacular fire ceremony is Up-Helly-Aa, held at Lerwick in the remote island of Shetland on the last Tuesday in January. Casual visitors are not welcome at Up-Helly-Aa (compare the old Scots name for Twelfth Night, *Uphaliday*), at which the Shetlanders remember their Norse heritage: playing host would get in the way of their fun, so invitations are required. Up-Helly-Aa begins with the posting of "The Bill", a 10-ft (3-metre) high Proclamation at

Left, dressed up for the Galashiels Common Riding. **Right**, the climax of Lerwick's Up-Helly-Aa Viking festival.

the Market Cross and the displaying of a 30-ft (9-metre) model longship at the seafront.

Come evening, and with the Guizer Jarl magnificently dressed in Viking costume at the steering oar, the longship is dragged to the burning site. Team after team of guizers, each clad in glorious or grotesque garb and all carrying blazing torches, follow the ship. When the burning site is reached the "Galley Song" is sung; the Guizer Jarl leaves the longship; a bugle sounds; and hundreds of blazing torchs are hurled upon and consume the hull while the song changes to "The Norseman's Home". Celebrations continue all through the night.

At nearby Kirkwall, capital of Orkney, the "Ba' Game" leaves Australian Rules looking like a Sunday afternoon picnic. A good game lasts for several hours. If the harbour goal is reached it is obligatory to throw the ball into the water and several players – irrespective of their allegiance – dive in after it and finally sober up. The game is also held, although on a more modest scale, on Christmas Day. A similar "Ba' Game" is held at Jedburgh in the Borders early in February.

Burns Night (25 January) honours the birth of the national poet. In villages and cities throughout the land, Burns clubs and others toast the haggis (*see page 126*).

Evil spirits: A different kind of game can be

those who survived the Hogmanay celebrations gather on New Year's Day at the Mercat Cross for the "Ba' Game". Sides are taken: the Uppies who were born south of the Cathedral and the Doonies, born north of the Cathedral. The two teams attempt to carry a leather ball, about the size of a tennis ball, against all opposition, to their own end of the town. The waters of the harbour constitute the Doonies' goal and the crossroads at the opposite end is the Uppies' goal.

A giant scrum forms and the teams shove and shove, with the scrum becoming so torrid that steam rises from its centre. Infringements? What are *they*? Mayhem reigns and

seen at Lanark on 1 March. Then, the church bells peal out and the children of Lanark, armed with home-made weapons of paper balls on strings, race three times around the church, beating each other over the head as they go. After the race, town officials throw handfuls of coins for which the children scramble. Whuppity Scoorie is claimed by some to be a ridding of the town of evil spirits by scourging the precincts of the church. A somewhat more mundane explanation is that the festival represents the chasing away of winter and the welcoming of spring.

Above, the Galashiels Braw Lads gallop out.

About six weeks later, older children – students at St Andrews University – take part in the traditional Kate Kennedy pageant in which they play the parts of distinguished figures associated with the university or the town. Lady Kate, a niece of the founder of the university, was a great beauty to whom the students are said to have sworn everlasting allegiance. Women are banned from taking part in the procession and the role of Kate is always played by a first-year male student.

During the summer months, traditional fairs are held throughout the country. Until quite recently, farm employees who wished to change their jobs would seek out new employers at the Feeing Markets which were held at the end of each term. (The farming year was divided into three contractual terms.) These markets also attracted small stallholders eager to part the labourer from his term's wages. Such a market, enlivened with Highland dancing, country music and other entertainments, is still held in June at Stonehaven.

Later in the month, a similar fair is held at nearby Garmouth. However, the excuse for the Maggie Fair is that it commemorates the landing of the "merry monarch", Charles II, at nearby Kingston, after he had been proclaimed King of Scotland following the execution of his father King Charles I.

The first day of August is Lammas Day, or Lunasdal – the feast of the Sun God, Lugh – and was formerly an extremely popular day for local fairs. Such fairs are still held in August, although not on the first day, at St Andrews and neighbouring Inverkeithing.

Also at this time a bizarre ritual occurs on the day before the South Queensferry Ferry Fair. A man, clad head to toe in white flannel, is covered with an infinite number of burrs until he becomes a moving bush. Bedecked with flowers and carrying two staves, this strange creature makes his way from house to house receiving gifts. One theory for this strange practice equates the Burryman with the scapegoat of antiquity.

Fleet of foot: In late August, attention switches to the west coast where the ancient burgh of Irvine holds its Marymass Fair which dates from the 12th century. Horse races, very much a part of this fair, are said to be even older. These races are not only for ponies but also for Clydesdale cart-horses which, in spite of their great size (they weigh about one tonne) are remarkably fleet of foot. The fair's fame derives from the eponymous parish church yet an association with Mary Queen of Scots has arisen and the principal in the pageant is dressed as Mary Stuart. Celebrations continue for a week.

Throughout the early summer months the clippity clop of horses' hoofs is heard on the cobblestones of Border towns. The Riding of the Marches, first introduced in the Middle Ages, is the custom of checking the boundaries of common lands owned by the town. In some cases, the Riding also commemorates important local historical events which invariably involved warfare between the English and the Scots in the Middle Ages. The festivities often last for several days and are always stiff with protocol.

The Selkirk Gathering, held in June, is the oldest, the largest and the most emotional of the Ridings. It concludes with the Casting of the Colours which commemorates Scotland's humiliating defeat at the Battle of Flodden from which only one Selkirk warrior returned. At the "casting", flags are waved in proscribed patterns while the band plays a soulful melody.

Each town – including Annan, Dumfries, Duns, Galashiels, Jedburgh, Lanark (scarcely a Border town), Langholm and Lauder – has its own variations of the ceremonies; and all have other activities which include balls, concerts, pageants and sporting events. At Peebles the Riding incorporates the Beltane Fair which is the great Celtic festival of the sun and which marks the beginning of summer.

Aberdeen also has its Riding of the Marches but "horses" of a different kind are involved in a mid-August festival on the island of South Ronaldsay in Orkney. The "horses" are young boys or girls dressed in spectacular costumes. Pulling beautifully wrought miniature ploughs, often family heirlooms, and guided by boy ploughmen, these "horses" turn furrows on a sandy beach. Prizes are awarded for the best turned-out "horses" and for the straightest and most even furrows.

St Andrew's Day (30 November) is the country's national day, but is more or less ignored by most people. It does offer excuses for society types to dress in their finery, attend balls, toast the haggis once again, and imbibe unwise quantities of whisky. And so, inexorably, the festive year rushes headlong towards another Hogmanay.

THE LURE OF THE GREEN TURF

Visit the 19th hole at any of Scotland's 400 golf courses and you're almost certain to hear a heated argument, over a dram or two of whisky, as to where the game of golf originated. The discussion doesn't involve geography but rather topography: the "where" refers to *which* part of Scotland. All know that, in spite of the Dutch boasting of a few old paintings which depict the game, it all began in Scotland hundreds of years ago when a shepherd swinging with his stick at round stones hit one into a rabbit hole. Little did that rustic know the madness he was about to unleash when he murmured to his flock: "I wonder if I can do that again?"

Few courses have the characteristics of the quintessential Scottish course. Such a course, bordering the seashore, is called a links. It is on the links of Muirfield, St Andrews, Troon and Turnberry that the British Open – or "the Open" – is usually played.

The word links refers to that stretch of land which connects the beach with more stable inshore land, and a links course is a sandy, undulating terrain which borders the shore. One feature of such a course is its ridges and furrows which result in the ball nestling in an infinite variety of lies. Another feature is the wind which blows off the sea and which can suddenly whip up with enormous ferocity. A hole which, in the morning, was played with a driver and a 9-iron can, after lunch, demand a driver, a long 3-wood and a 6-iron.

Giant greens: Most golfers will immediately head for St Andrews. They will be surprised to find that the Old Course has two, rather than the customary four, short holes and has only 11 greens. Yet it is categorically an 18-hole course: seven greens are shared. This explains the enormous size of the greens, on which you can find yourself facing a putt of almost 100 yards (90 metres). Remember it is the homeward-bound player who has the right of way on these giant double greens.

At St Andrews the Old Course is flanked by the New on the seaward and by the Eden on the inland side. Tucked between the New and the white-caps of the North Sea is the

Right, St Andrews, a magnet for all golfers.

shorter Jubilee course. And then, in 1993, two additional course were squeezed in: the Strathtyrum is an 18-hole course of modest length while the Balgrove, originally built in 1972 and reconstructed in 1993, is a 9-hole beginners' layout. Don't be too distressed if you fail to obtain a starting time on the Old (two-thirds of starting times are allocated by ballot: contact the starter before 2pm on the day before you wish to play). The New is even more difficult.

Ancient as the Royal and Ancient Golf Club of St Andrews is, it must bow the knee to the Honorable Company of Edinburgh Golfers, which was formed in 1774 and which is generally accepted as the oldest golf club in the world. Its present Muirfield course which is at Gullane (pronounced *Gillun*), 13 miles (21 km) east of Edinburgh, is considered to be the ultimate test of golf.

The rough here is ferocious and if, on looking around, you fail to see your partner, don't panic and think he has been abducted by the "wee folk". He will merely be out of sight in one of the nearly 200 deep pot-bunkers which litter the course.

Not to worry if you can't play on Muirfield: the tiny village of Gullane is also the home of the three challenging Gullane courses (simply called 1, 2 and 3) and to Luffness New. The latter is "New" because, by Scotland's standards, it is just *that*, having been founded as recently as 1894.

Capital course: Back in the city of Edinburgh are more than a score of courses, two of which are home to very ancient clubs. The Royal Burgess Golfing Society claims to be even older than the Hon. Coy, while the neighbouring Bruntsfield Links Golfing Society is only a few years younger.

On the road from Gullane to Edinburgh you pass through Musselburgh where golf is known to have been played in 1672 and, most probably, even before that. Was this where Mary Queen of Scots was seen playing a few days after the murder of Lord Darnley, her second husband? Was Mary the world's first golf widow?

Glasgow, never outdone by Edinburgh, has nearly 30 courses. Outstanding among these are Killermont and Haggs Castle. The latter is less than 3 miles (5 km) from the city centre. While golfers thrill over birdies and eagles at Haggs their non-playing partners can enthuse over the renowned Burrell Col-

lection which is less than half-a-mile (1 km) away. Even closer to the Burrell is the excellent Pollok course. Further afield at Luss (23 miles/37 km northwest of the city) by the bonnie banks of Loch Lomond is a brand-new course designed by Tom Weiskopf. A second Jack Nicklaus course is a possibility and the Loch Lomond Golf Club may well become the best in Britain.

Troon, 30 miles (48 km) south of Glasgow and frequently the scene of the Open, is the kingpin in a series of nearly 30 courses bordering the Atlantic rollers. Here, without hardly ever stooping to pick up your ball, you can play for almost 30 miles (48 km). Troon itself has five courses. Then, to the north is Barassie with one and then Gailes with two courses. South of Troon are three courses at Prestwick – scene of the first Open in 1860 – and Ayr, also with three courses. Fifteen minutes further down the "course" are the exclusive Arran and Ailsa links of Turnberry. There's a much better chance of playing at Brunston Castle, a few miles to the southeast, where an excellent course – parkland rather than links – opened in 1992.

Golf widows will be delighted that Turnberry is a splendid spot from which to visit the Burns Country and Culzean Castle (pronounced *Cullane*), a magnificent 18th-century Robert Adam building with apartments gifted to General Dwight Eisenhower, a former frequenter of the Turnberry links.

Over on the east coast is another remarkable conglomerate of courses with St Andrews as its kingpin. About 30 miles to the north, across the Tay Bridge, are the three Carnoustie courses. The Medal course here, formerly scene of many Opens, has been called brutal, evil and monstrous. Then, 20 miles (32 km) south of St Andrews and strung, like a priceless necklace, along the north shore of the Firth of Forth, are the Elie, Leven, Lundin Links and Crail courses. The Crail course is claimed by golf-storians to be the seventh oldest in the world.

Other glittering gems are found in the northeast. Here are Balgownie and Murcar, two of Aberdeen's half-a-dozen courses; nearby Cruden Bay; Nairn, which is close to Inverness; and Dornoch, which stands in splendid isolation in the extreme northeast. The Balgownie and Cruden Bay clubs are both 200 years old and founders of the latter are probably turning in their graves at the new name of their club – the Cruden Bay Golf and Country Club.

Dornoch is, even for a Scottish course, under-played and may be Britain's most under-rated course. Authorities believe that this course, all of whose holes have a view of the sea, would be on the Open rota if it was closer to the main centres of population.

Down at the extreme southwest of the country is Machrihanish, another under-rated, under-played links which is far from the madding crowd. Its turf is so naturally perfect that "every ball is teed, wherever it is". And, if the views from here, which include Ireland and the Inner Hebrides, seduce you then you might wish to make your way over

the seas to Islay, which is renowned for both its whisky and its Machrie course.

Scotland, home of golf, also boasts some superb inland courses. Many *aficionados* consider the King's at Gleneagles to be the best inland course in Britain. Certainly, nowhere in the world can there be a championship course set in such dramatically beautiful scenery. Recently it was joined by the Monarch, the resort's newest course, which is from the drawing board of Jack Nicklaus and which has the flavour of an American rather than a Scottish course. These are just two of

Above, golf can sometimes be a risky business.

four courses which make up the Gleneagles complex. If these four aren't enough, a mere 30 miles (48 km) to the north is Blairgowrie with its fabled Rosemount course. Here, among parasol pines, larches, silver birch and evergreens, you'll come upon lost golf balls, partridges, pheasant and otter.

Soothing rain: Summer days in Scotland are long, and the eager beaver can tee off at 7am and play until 10pm – easily enough time for 54 holes unless you're prone to slice, hook or pull. The rough of gorse, broom, heather and whin is insatiable, and a great deal of time can be lost searching for balls. If you attempt 54 holes in a day, have no fear of tiring, for the turf on Scottish courses is very springy and a joy to walk upon and seldom, even on a summer's day, does the temperature reach 70°F (21°C). However, be prepared for light rain. The locals call it *brash* (a dialect word for light, soothing, pleasant rain) and you will soon find that you simply ignore it.

At many courses caddy cars are available. Caddies, however, are about as difficult to find as a haggis on the moors. If you can lay your hands on one of them (caddies, not haggis – you buy the latter in tins), you are in for a treat. The word, incidentally, comes from the French *cadet*, meaning a "young boy", and was used, especially in Edinburgh, to describe anyone who ran errands.

Club formalities: At the majority of courses no formal introduction is necessary: as a visitor, you just stroll up, pay your money, and play. Indeed, at some of the more remote country courses you merely deposit your money in the honour-box. Some clubs do ask that you be a member of another club. Others (certainly less than one in three) require an introduction by a member, although if you are an overseas visitor this formality is usually waived. And the better courses demand a valid handicap certificate which usually must be below 20 for men and 30 for ladies.

Note, however, that restrictions tighten up at weekends. And, joy of joys, at some courses to whose names you have thrilled – Carnoustie, St Andrews, for example – no introduction is needed. This doesn't mean you will gain entry to the clubhouse – for it, rather than the fairways and greens, is the holy of holies at a Scottish course. The reason: the clubhouse is the private domain of a particular club whose members happen to make use of the adjacent course.

It seems to be one of nature's iron laws that valuable assets fall into the hands of the already rich. Valuable *natural* assets are no exception. While Scotland, therefore, may have been blessed with more natural assets – red deer, salmon, grouse and sea trout – than most small European countries, they are owned by a handful of ultra-rich estate owners, many of whom live a long way from Scotland. This means that "field sports" such as deer stalking, salmon fishing and grouse shooting are touchy political issues, bound up with memories of the Highland Clearances and the ownership and use of the land.

While many (probably most) Scots accept that sporting estates are now essential to the economies of remote Highland areas, they are inclined to resent the fact that they are owned and exploited by local aristocrats, southern financiers or oil-rich Arabs. And there's growing unease about the hard-nosed line being taken by the newer proprietors, some of whom are trying to recoup their investment as fast as they can, often at the expense of local interests.

For example, when the North of Scotland Hydroelectricity Board (always known as "The Hydro") sold its fishing rights on the River Conon north of Inverness to City of London financier Peter Whitfield for a reputed £1.5 million, the deal had the effect of clearing the locals off the river: Whitfield immediately divided his fishing into beats which he sold on a weekly timeshare basis at prices of up to £15,000 a person per week. He found a ready market among rich southerners and Europeans, but none of the locals could afford that kind of money.

"That river used to be part of the local community," says one irate local angler. "Our people have fished it for generations. Now we've been elbowed off to make way for strangers."

The bitterness voiced over salmon fishing on the River Conon is echoed all over the Highlands. At the same time the Scottish Tourist Board and the Scottish Office relish

the idea of wealthy sportsmen from England and abroad spreading their cash in the hard-pressed economies of the uplands. But more and more sporting landlords (especially the newer ones) are alienating the Scottish public by trying to keep walkers, mountaineers and ramblers off their vast estates by littering the countryside with "Keep Out" signs (which are legally meaningless in Scotland).

"I suppose the trouble is that most sporting estates were started up for the private pleasure of the owner and a few of his guests,"

says David Hughes-Hallett of the Scottish Landowners Federation (SLF). "That makes them hard to defend politically. But these days are long gone. Nowadays most sporting estates are commercial ventures which have got to make money to cover their costs."

Of course, the health of Scotland's field sports depends heavily on the state of the ecology. This often leads to an uneasy alliance between left-wing environmentalists and Highland estate owners. Both groups fret constantly about the effects of acid rain, the damage caused by tributyle tin to salmon and sea trout and whether the rapid growth of tax-break forestry is polluting the water

Preceding pages, fishing holiday. **Left**, trophies from hunts in Brodick Castle, Arran. **Right**, a Highlands gamekeeper.

courses with pesticides and herbicides. The industry took a nasty knock in 1986 when radiation from the Chernobyl accident descended on the Scottish uplands, and found its way into the fat and muscle of the red deer.

Stalking these red deer is one of Scotland's prime attractions to wealthy foreigners. At the last count there were more than 290,000 red deer in Scotland, most of them wandering north of the "Highland line" (between Helensburgh and Stonehaven), with a few small herds in the higher hills of Dumfries and Galloway. With numbers now at an all-time high (there were only 150,000 in the 1950s), there are fears that there are just too many of the beasts. Sportsmen often

stag to get off a clean shot. And it has to be a clean shot; if the beast is just wounded, the shooter will be dragged endlessly across the hills until the beast is properly killed.

It's a bruising and usually expensive business. A week's stalking (six days) costs around £1,500 and only the trophy (the head) belongs to the hunter; the venison belongs to the estate.

Accommodation is extra and can cost anything from £100 a week for a self-catering chalet, to more than £100 a night at upmarket establishments like Mar Lodge in Deeside or Tulchan Lodge in Strathspey (both of which are owned by a Swiss businessman). Rifles can be hired, but most sportsmen bring their

claim they are doing the species a favour by "shooting out" the older stags and the weaklings. Around 40,000 red deer are shot in Scotland every year, 50 percent of which are hinds (females) culled by professional stalkers and foresters every winter to keep down the numbers.

Although the stalking season runs from 1 July to 20 October, very little shooting is done before the end of August. Thereafter shooters from all over Britain, Europe and North America descend on the Highlands to spend their days crawling on their bellies through heather and mud, often in sleet or snow, hopping to get near enough to jumpy

own. And a decent 0.270 or 7 mm stalking rifle with telescopic sight can cost anything from £300 to £3,000.

John Ormiston of Sport In Scotland, the biggest of the sporting-holiday agencies, reckons that the most enthusiastic deer hunters are the British and the Germans, followed by the Americans. "It's all a matter of tradition," he says. "The French and Italians prefer using shotguns." A more recent development is the shooting of roe deer bucks (males), usually in woodland, and often from "high seats" fixed in trees. "That's a bit less

Above, a catch from the River Don.

expensive," Ormiston says. "A red deer stag costs £250 to shoot. A roe deer buck costs around £180."

The "Glorious Twelfth" is the name given to 12 August, the day the season opens on red grouse, and the 500 moors of Scotland and northern England fill up with gents in expensive tweeds carrying even more expensive shotguns. Some estates can rake in as much as £250,000 in a season, but expenses are high. The past two decades have seen a gradual decline in the grouse population and, in recent years, the annual bag has been well under 500,000. This appears to be due to ticks, foxes, rabbits and winter moths.

Like deer stalking, grouse shooting doesn't come cheap. Driven grouse (grouse shot with the aid of beaters) can cost around £60 a brace. And even estate-reared pheasants can cost the shooter about £30 a brace. The cheapest shotgun will cost in the region of £250, while an over-and-under Purdy can cost the enthusiast more than £18,000.

Stalking the salmon: But the upmarket sport *par excellence* has to be salmon fishing in one of Scotland's great east-coast salmon rivers such as the Spey, the Dee, the Tay, the Tweed or the Conon. One recent survey estimated that it costs the affluent angler around $3,500 to land an Atlantic salmon from a Scottish river. Certainly, a week's fishing on a good "beat" at the height of the season (July to September) on one of the classier rivers is likely to set the fisherman back between £1,500 and £2,000. If, that is, he is lucky enough to find someone willing to take his money; the supply is strictly limited and the demand is always high.

So high, in fact, that a number of London-based firms have taken to operating salmon beats on a timeshare basis. It works like this: a company such as Salar Properties (owned by financier Jim Slater) buys a large stretch of a good salmon river such as the Tay in Perthshire or the Forss in Caithness, divides it into beats, and then sells a week's fishing on the beats "in perpetuity" for up to £25,000 a week, (depending when the slot occurs in the season and on the quality of the fishing). Despite the formidable sums involved, Slater has had no trouble peddling the weeks to wealthy *aficionados*.

With that kind of money at stake, the river proprietors are growing ever more anxious about the salmon stocks. They are right to be worried. In 1967 around 605,000 salmon were hauled out of Scottish rivers. Twenty years later, that figure had slumped to just over 270,000 and, of those, only 76,000 were caught by anglers. The rest were scooped up by nets-men using the traditional "net and coble" method of fishing, or stake nets which run out from the east coast beaches.

In an effort to make sure the dwindling numbers of salmon aren't intercepted before they can make their run up the rivers, some river proprietors set up in 1986 the Atlantic Salmon Conservation Trust. The idea was to raise several million pounds to buy out the coastal netting companies and increase the numbers of fish available to the anglers. The trust quickly acquired 53 netting stations near the approaches to the River Spey and the River Nairn; most were quickly closed and the remainder were shut down by 1990.

The Trust's efforts have been successful because, whereas in 1980 only 100 tonnes of farmed salmon were grown, by 1991 the figure had increased to 40,000 tonnes, and the value of netted salmon compared to that landed by rod was negligible.

However, problems still exist, says the trust: "An awful lot of salmon bound for Scottish rivers are being taken in drift nets off the coasts of Greenland, Iceland and Faroes." Also, a lot of poaching has traditionally gone on off the coast of Scotland with illegal fine-mesh nets.

Trout fishing: While salmon fishing may be the glamour end of the sport, many anglers feel that too much is made of it. They argue that the tourist authorities would do better to bang the drum about the brown trout fishing which is available on countless Scottish lochs, particularly on the west coast and its islands and in the far north where the salmon are not so abundant. Some remote lochs are seldom visited by fishing enthusiasts and 100 fish in a day on two rods is not just a dream.

"Our trout lochs are the most neglected resource we have," says Inverness fisherman, Allan Scott. "Brown trout weighing 3 or 4 lb (1.4 to 1.8 kg) aren't uncommon. And in the deep lochs around Fort William you get the occasional ferox trout. They're giant brown trout, some of them weighing up to 20 lb (9 kg). They're cannibals. Big-shouldered brutes that eat their own kind and prey on other fish. But a hell of an exciting fish to get on the end of your line."

At the end of the most sophisticated dinner parties in London, guests are invariably offered a choice of brandy or port but seldom a glass of Scotch. Familiarity, perhaps, has produced contempt for the native product – or, the Scots would argue, the English are showing their customary ignorance of all things Scottish.

The prejudice is an ill-founded one because good malt whiskies have a wider range of flavour and aroma than brandy, and – an extra bonus – they are less likely to make the over-indulger's head throb the morning after. Snobbery probably accounts for the attitude, too, for Scotland's unique drink has never quite managed to cultivate the exclusive image of cognac.

For one thing, there's a lot more of it on the international market. Scotch is one of Britain's top five export items: even the Vatican, on one recent annual reckoning, bought 18,000 bottles. More than 700 million bottles a year are exported; the major market is the United States, followed by France (which consumes more whisky than cognac), Japan and Spain.

Toddler's tipple: The lowly origins of Scotch may also be partly to blame for its fluctuating fortunes. In the 18th century, it was drunk as freely as the water from which it was made, by peasants and aristocrats alike. A spoonful was given to new-born babies in the Highlands and even respectable gentlewomen might start the day with "a wee dram". The poorest crofter could offer the visitor a drink, thanks to the ubiquity of home-made stills which made millions of gallons of "mountain dew" in the remote glens of the Highlands. Even in Edinburgh, no-one needed to go thirsty: excise officers estimated in 1777 that the city had eight licensed stills and 400 illegal ones.

Yet something as easy to make cannot be made authentically outside Scotland. Many have tried, and the Japanese in particular have thrown the most modern technology at the problem; but the combination of damp

climate and soft water flowing through the peat cannot be replicated elsewhere.

Indeed no-one – not even the most experienced professional taster – can agree on what elements create the best whiskies. Is the water better if it runs off granite through peat, or if it runs through peat onto granite? Does the secret lie in the peat used to dry the malt in a distillery's kiln? Or does it lie in the soft air that permeates the wooden casks of whisky as the liquid matures for anything from three to 18 years? The arguments con-

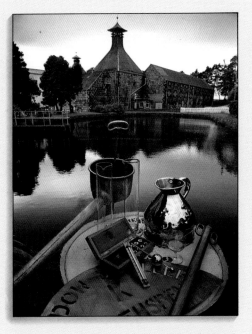

tinue – over a glass or two of the debated liquid, of course.

Some historians believe that the art of distilling was brought to Scotland by Christian missionary monks. But it is just as likely that Highland farmers discovered for themselves how to distil spirits from their surplus barley. The earliest known reference to whisky occurred in 1494, when Scottish Exchequer Rolls record that Friar John Cor purchased a quantity of malt "to make aquavitae".

These days there are two kinds of Scotch whisky: *malt*, made from malted barley only; and *grain*, made from malted barley together

Preceding pages: whisky maturing under the eye of the Customs officer. Left, whisky still. Right, tools of the distiller's trade.

with unmalted barley, maize or other cereals. Most popular brands are blends of both types of whisky – typically 60 percent grain to 40 percent malt.

A single malt, the product of one distillery, has become an increasingly popular drink, thanks largely to the aggressive marketing by William Grant & Sons of their Glenfiddich brand. But sales of single malts still account for only one bottle in 20 sold around the world, and most of the production of single malt distilleries is used to add flavour to a blended whisky.

So automated are Scotland's 100-plus distilleries that the visitor, sipping an end-of-tour glass of the product he has watched

heated by a peat fire. The dried malt is ground and mixed with hot water in a huge circular vat called a mash tun. A sugary liquid, "wort", is drawn off from the porridge-like result, leaving the remaining solids to be sold as cattle food. The wort is fed into massive vessels containing up to 45,000 litres of liquid, where living yeast is stirred into the mix in order to convert the sugar in the wort into crude alcohol.

After about 48 hours, the "wash" (a clear liquid containing weak alcohol) is transferred to the copper pot stills and heated to the point at which alcohol turns to vapour. This vapour rises up the still to be condensed by a cooling plant into distilled alcohol which

being manufactured, is left with an image of the beautifully proportioned onion-shaped copper stills and a lingering aroma of malted barely – but not with any clear idea of the process by which water from a Highland stream is transformed into *usquebaugh*, the water of life.

What happens is this. To make malt whisky, plump and dry barley (which, unlike the water, doesn't have to be local) sits in tanks of water for two or three days. It is then spread out on a concrete floor or placed in large cylindrical drums and allowed to germinate for between eight and 12 days. Next it is dried in a kiln, which ideally should be

is then passed through a second still. (One thing that distinguishes Scotch whisky from Irish whiskey, apart from the different spellings, is that Scotch is distilled twice and Irish three times.)

The trick is to know exactly when the whisky has distilled sufficiently. Modern measuring devices offer scientific precision, but the individual judgement of an experienced distiller is hard to beat. Some smaller distilleries, it was once said, were so afraid of disturbing any element in the delicate environment that they wouldn't allow the cob-

<u>Above</u>, rolling out the barrels on Islay.

webs to be swept off the vat-room rafters.

Once distilled, the liquid is poured into oak casks which, being porous, allow air to enter. Evaporation takes place, removing the harsher constituents of the new spirit and enabling it to mellow. Legally it can't be sold as whisky until it has spent three years in the cask and a good malt will stay casked for at least eight years.

It wasn't until the 1820s that distilling began to develop from small family-run concerns into large manufacturing businesses. What accelerated the change was the invention in 1830 by Aeneas Coffey of a patent still. This was faster and cheaper than traditional methods. More importantly, it did not need the perfect mix of peat and water, but could produce whisky from a mixture of malted and unmalted barley mashed with other cereals.

The real thing: But was the resulting grain whisky real Scotch? Some dismissed it as flavourless surgical spirits; others approved of it as "lighter-bodied". The argument rumbled on until 1905, when one of London's local authorities decided to test in the courts whether pubs could legally sell the patent-still (as opposed to the pot-still) product as "whisky". Even the courts couldn't agree. It was left to a Royal Commission to deliver the verdict that both drinks were equally wholesome and could call themselves whisky.

The Distillers Company, which was to swallow up more than 40 distillers until it too was taken over in 1986 by Guinness, lost no time in capitalising on the Royal Commission's decision. It advertised its patent-still grain whisky as "light, delicate, exquisite – not a headache in a gallon" and pitched its appeal particularly at city dwellers, claiming somewhat dubiously that pot still whisky was "too strongly flavoured for most people in sedentary occupations".

The industry's future, however, lay in a marriage between malt and grain whiskies. Blending tiny amounts of 30 or 40 malt whiskies with grain whisky, distillers found, could produce a palatable compromise between taste and strength. What's more, an almost infinite variety of combinations was possible, enabling each brand to claim its own unique taste.

The truth is that most people, in a blind tasting of blends, would be hard-pressed to say whether they were drinking Bell's, Teacher's, Dewar's, Johnnie Walker or J&B. Pure malt whiskies, on the other hand, are more readily identifiable. The experienced Scotch drinker can differentiate between Highland malts, Lowland malts, Campeltown malts and Islay malts, and there is certainly no mistaking the bouquet of a malt such as Laphroaig, which is usually described as tasting of iodine or seaweed.

So which is best?: Whole evenings can be whiled away in Scotland debating and researching the question, with no firm conclusions being reached. It all comes down to individual taste – after all, in the words of Robert Burns, who is not only the national poet of Scotland but also of Scotch: "Freedom and Whisky gang the gither."

However, the one point of agreement is that a good malt whisky should not be drunk with a mixer such as soda or lemonade which would destroy the subtle flavour. Yet, although it is said there are two things which a Highlander likes naked, connoisseurs may be permitted to add a little water to their single malt. After dinner, malts are best drunk neat, as a liqueur. Blended whisky, on the other hand, is refreshing in hot weather when mixed with soda.

In sales terms, Glenfiddich leads the market in single malts, exporting 6 million bottles a year to 185 countries. The Scots themselves tend to favour Glenmorangie, which is matured in old Bourbon casks, charred on the inside, for at least 10 years to produce a smooth spirit with hints of peat smoke and vanilla. The most popular malt in the United States is The Macallan, which is produced on Speyside and matured in 100 percent sherry casks seasoned for two years in Spain with dry oloroso sherry; connoisseurs argue that the 10-year-old is a better drink than the more impressive-sounding 18-year-old.

The brave should sample Glenfarclas, whose legendary 105 proof spirit made the *Guinness Book of Records* for its strength (over 60 percent alcohol). Those desiring a more diluted sample need only take one of the many distillery tours on the Scotch Whisky Trail. Because whisky "breathes" while maturing in its casks, as much as 4 million gallons (20 million litres) evaporate into the air each year. All you have to do is inhale.

Scotland, as the writer H. V. Morton once remarked, is the best place in the world to take an appetite; and although, on a permanent basis, the local diet has its hazards – many believe it to be the main cause of the country's internationally appalling level of heart attacks and strokes – the seafood at least can hardly fail to be good for the health. Certainly, lobsters, large langoustines and giant Orkney scallops do wonders for the most jaded of appetites.

No doubt Mr Morton's appetite was coaxed also by the Scottish air, which in the Highlands (and even the Lowlands) remains remarkably pure. Indeed, it has traditionally helped to determine the nature of the Scottish kitchen. It is vigorous and sometimes blustery air, calling for the inner warmth and energy produced by porridge (the Scottish equivalent of Italian *polenta*, though grey rather than yellow), by broth and haggis, by baps, butteries, barley bannocks, griddle scones, oatcakes and other examples of local baking; plus numerous nips of whisky and pot after pot of tea.

So at least the story goes – although the rise of Chinese and Indian restaurants and an increasingly international outlook on food have influenced Scottish taste in recent years almost as much as English. Scottish cookery still has its roots in the soil, however, especially in some of those isolated hotels and restaurants far from the main cities. There, real Scottish cuisine is something the proprietors are genuinely proud of serving. Elsewhere, Scotland has its own unedifying brand of fast food. "Scotch eggs", for example, are hard-boiled eggs wrapped in sausage meat and then fried; the result is as appetising as a greasy cannonball.

Fashionable restaurants may differ little from their English counterparts (though steak and game, if not vegetables, tend to be better north of the River Tweed) but historically the real Scots kitchen is no more like the English than the Portuguese is like the Spanish. That expert in the art of Scots gastronomy, F.

Marian McNeill, has rightly scolded that expert in the art of French gastronomy, André Simon, for mentioning Scottish dishes under the heading "English fare". Many good things come out of England, she admitted, but porridge isn't one of them.

If flour and meat still form the basis of English cookery, meat and fish form the basis of Scottish, along with bakery, which can sometimes be stodgy, heavy and mass-produced but is often really delectable. Not too long ago in Scotland there were fewer

restaurants than tea rooms. Here, people ate not only lunch and afternoon tea but also "high tea" which usually consisted of fish and chips and an array of scones and cakes.

Such establishments, sometimes with a piano trio providing gentle music, flourished in Edinburgh and Glasgow until after World War II, and their atmosphere can still be sampled in the elegantly renovated Willow Tea Room in Glasgow's Sauchiehall Street, originally designed by the great Charles Rennie Mackintosh. The tables and chairs may no longer be the real thing but they look good and the place still reeks of *art nouveau*, as also do a few Glasgow pubs (such as the

Left, fishmongers in Rothesay, on the Isle of Bute. **Right**, on offer: Scotland's most maligned native dish.

Griffin opposite the King's Theatre, in spite of modern attempts to interfere with its *Jugendstil* beauty).

It is also significant that biscuit-making remains an extensive and popular industry in both Edinburgh and Glasgow and as far north as Kirkwall in Orkney (where the oat-cakes are arguably the best in the land). Dundee is renowned for its eponymous cake and for orange marmalade, its gift to the world's breakfast and tea tables – though the theory that the name "marmalade" derives from the words *Marie est malade* (referring to the food given to Mary Queen of Scots when she was ill) must be considered rather far-fetched.

Flavourful fish: Kippers, too, are a treat. The best of them are from Loch Fyne or the Achiltibuie smokery in Ross and Cromarty, where their colour emerges properly golden, not dyed repellent red as they are in so many places. Finnan-haddies (*alias* haddock) are a tasty alternative, boiled in milk and butter. Salmon and trout, sadly, are just as likely to come from some west-coast or northern fish farm as fresh from the river, but the standard remains high. If you're buying from a fish-monger, ask for "wild" salmon, more fla-vourful than the farmed variety. On the other hand, farmed salmon is generally preferred, to help ensure uniformity, in the production of justifiably renowned smoked salmon.

The beef of the Aberdeen Angus remains the most famous in the world, though Clive Davidson of the Champany Inn near Linlith-gow – which serves, according to the *Good Food Guide*, the best steak in Britain – would challenge its supremacy, naming Scots Blue-Grey ("the ugliest beast you ever saw") as a more than worthy rival, and pope's eye as a better cut than the more fashionable but flabby fillet. Good Scottish meat, he claims, should be hung for at least four weeks or even for eight – unlike supermarket steak, which is not aged at all – and should never be sliced less than 1¼ inches (3 cm) thick.

Venison, pheasant, hare and grouse are also established features of the Scottish kitchen. Admittedly, the romance of eating grouse after it has been ritually shot on or around 12 August should be tempered (if you are honest with yourself) by this bird's quite depressing fibrous toughness, which makes grouse shooting seem, at least to a gourmet, an unutterable waste of time.

As for haggis – though it, too, is hardly a gourmet delight – it does offer a fascinating experience for brave visitors. Scotland's great mystery dish is really only a sheep's stomach stuffed with its minced heart, liver and lights, along with suet, onions and oatmeal. After being boiled, the stomach is sliced open, as spectacularly as possible, and the contents served piping hot.

Butchers today often use a plastic bag instead of a stomach; this has the advantage that it is less likely to burst during the boiling process, resulting in the meat being ruined. But no haggis devotee would contemplate such a substitute.

The tastiest haggis, by popular acclaim, comes from Macsween's of Edinburgh, who also make a vegetarian haggis. (That's progress, as the Orkney poet George Mackay Brown would cynically say.) Small portions of haggis are sometimes served as starter courses in fashionable Scottish restaurants, though the authentic way to eat it is as a main course with chappit tatties (potatoes), bashed neeps (mashed turnips) and a number of nips (Scotch whisky, preferably malt). This is especially so on Burns Night (25 January), when the haggis is ceremonially piped to table, and supper is accompanied by poetry reading, music and Burns's own *Address to the Haggis*; or on St Andrew's Night (30 November), when haggis is again attacked with gusto by loyal Scots the world over.

Many of Scotland's national dishes have names as rugged as Scottish speech. No adventurous eater should pass up the chance to sample fare with such names as feather fowlie (a chicken soup), cock-a-leekie (a soup made from chicken and leeks, but au-thentic only if it also contains prunes), cullen skink (soup made from smoked haddock and potatoes), hugga-muggie (Shetland fish hag-gis, using the fish's stomach), Arbroath smokies (smoked haddock stuffed with but-ter), crappit heids (haddock heads stuffed with lobster), partan bree (a soup made from giant crab claws, cooked with rice), stovies (potatoes cooked with onion), carageen mould (a Hebridean dessert), cranachan (a mixture of cream, oatmeal, sugar and rum), or hattit kit (an ancient Highland sweet made from buttermilk, milk, cream, sugar and nut-meg).

Though the Scots are said to like far more salt in their soup – and with their fish and vegetables – than the English, they also possess an exceptionally sweet tooth, as some of the above dishes confirm. This is also seen in their penchant for fizzy lemonade and the Glaswegian's favourite thirst-quencher, Irn-Bru, a sparkling concoction said to be "made from girders".

Real cheese, at last fighting back against the marketing boards' anonymous mass production, has been making progress in Scotland. Lanark Blue, hand-made from unpasteurised ewe's milk, has been one recent success, worth looking out for in go-ahead restaurants. Unpasteurised (hard) Teviotdale or (soft) Bonchester from the Border country make a welcome change

tion, for a long time almost defunct but now showing happy signs of revival. Hot savouries have always tended to have mysterious, sometimes misleading, names. Scotch woodcock, for instance, is no more a bird than Welsh rarebit is a rabbit; a woodcock, in this context, is a portion of anchovies coated with scrambled eggs and served (like most savouries) on small fresh slices of toast. At best, it rounds off a meal most piquantly, as also do Loch Fyne toasts, where kipper fillets replace the anchovies.

Many hotels and restaurants, encouraged by a "Taste of Scotland" scheme devised by the Scottish Tourist Board, offer their customers supposedly authentic menus, often

from tinted Scottish Cheddar. Crowdie, Scotland's original creamed cottage cheese, has evolved into Caboc from the Highlands; with its original oatmeal coating, it is almost as creamy as France's *crème fraîche*. Pentland and Lothian cheeses are Scotland's answer to camembert and brie.

Cheese before pudding, as a running order, reflects Scotland's Auld Alliance with France, as does the amount of fine claret to be found on the wine-lists of good restaurants and hotels and in many homes. But pudding before savoury is also an admirable tradi-

Above, preparing smoked haddock.

with flowery descriptions of dishes in self-consciously broad Scots. However good the intentions, these may be no more reliable than some of their English counterparts. Scottish cuisine at its best tends to have a French accent; it is a marriage between fine local ingredients and French flair. This is the hallmark of David Wilson's cooking at the Peat Inn in Fife – widely hailed as one of Scotland's best restaurants. The Auld Alliance is something which he and others like him believe in. Not only has it helped to give Scotland a culinary vocabulary – the Scottish "ashet" derives from the French *assiette* – but is still inspires chefs.

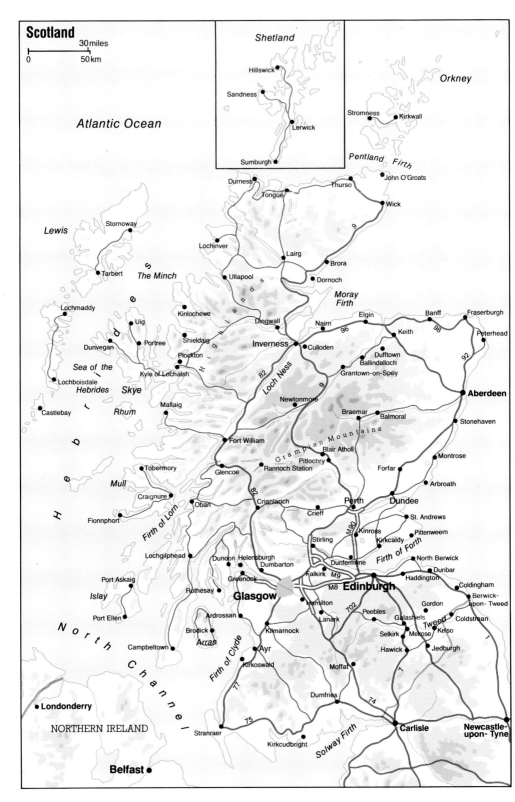

Scotland

30 miles
0   50 km

Atlantic Ocean

Shetland

Hillswick
Sandness
Lerwick
Sumburgh

Orkney

Stromness ● Kirkwall

Pentland Firth

Durness
Tongue
Thurso
John O'Groats
Wick

Lewis

Stornoway
Lochinver
Lairg
Brora
Tarbert
The Minch
Ullapool
Dornoch

Moray Firth

Lochmaddy
Kinlochewe
Dingwall
Nairn
Elgin
Banff
Fraserburgh
Peterhead
Keith
Uig
Portree
Shieldaig
Inverness
Culloden
Dunvegan
Plockton
Dufftown
Lochboisdale
Kyle of Lochalsh
Ballindalloch
Grantown-on-Spey
Hebrides
Sea of the
Skye
Castlebay
Rhum
Mallaig
Newtonmore
Aberdeen
Braemar
Balmoral
Stonehaven
Fort William
Grampian Mountains
Blair Atholl
Montrose
Tobermory
Glencoe
Pitlochry
Rannoch Station
Forfar
Mull
Craignure
Arbroath
Oban
Crianlarich
Perth
Dundee
Fionnphort
Crieff
St. Andrews
Firth of Lorn
Kinross
Pittenweem
Stirling
Kirkcaldy
Lochgilphead
Dunoon Helensburgh
Dunfermline
Firth of Forth
North Berwick
Dumbarton
Port Askaig
Rothesay
Greenock
Falkirk
Dunbar
Haddington
Islay
Glasgow
Edinburgh
Coldingham
Berwick-upon-Tweed
Hamilton
Gordon
Port Ellen
Ardrossan
Peebles
Galashiels
Coldstream
Brodick
Lanark
Tweed
Kelso
Arran
Kilmarnock
Selkirk
Melrose
Campbeltown
Ayr
Hawick
Jedburgh
Firth of Clyde
Kirkoswald
Moffat

North Channel

● **Londonderry**
NORTHERN IRELAND
Stranraer
Dumfries
Carlisle
Newcastle-upon-Tyne
Kirkcudbright
Solway Firth

Belfast ●

H e b r i d e a n   S e a

Loch Ness
H i g h l a n d s

82
96
9
92
98
82
A9
M90
M9
M8
702
77
75
74
A7
A1

Like Greece, Scotland is a hilly country with many small islands and a complicated history that attracts romantics. There, the similarity ends. The ethic bequeathed by Scottish Presbyterianism is a world away from Mediterranean attitudes and, at the height of summer, an umbrella is often needed as protection from the rain, not the sun. Few complain. The wildest Highland thunderstorm only enhances the magnificence of one of Europe's most captivating regions.

Edinburgh, a majestic capital city, enchants effortlessly, its castle towering over it on a rugged crag as a daily reminder of its turbulent history. These days, as a "court city" whose court long ago emigrated to London, Edinburgh cultivates culture and rejoices in its appellation of "the Athens of the North" (even though a character in a Tom Stoppard play suggested that a more appropriate title would be "the Reykjavik of the South").

Just 40 miles (64 km) away, Glasgow, by contrast, is Britain's great unknown city, still suffering from an outdated image of industrial grime and urban decay. Yet, having had its heart ripped out by motorways in the 1960s, it remodelled itself radically enough to take centre stage as European City of Culture in 1990, and its Burrell Collection museum has, to Edinburgh's chagrin, soared to the top of tourism's league table.

Outside the two great cities lies an astonishingly varied landscape. To the south-west are the moorlands, lochs and hills of Dumfries and Galloway, haunt of Scotland's national poet Robert Burns; to the south-east, the castles, forests and glens of the Borders, one of Europe's unspoilt areas; to the west, the rugged splendour of the West Highlands, a fragmented wilderness of mountain and moor, heather and stag, and the jumping-off point for Skye and the Western Isles; to the north-east, the farms and fishing villages of Fife and the swing along the North Sea coast through Dundee towards the granite city of Aberdeen, Scotland's oil capital; and, to the north, the elusive monster of Loch Ness, the awesomely empty tracts of the Highlands, and the islands of Orkney and Shetland that are more Norse than Scottish.

Scotland's greatest appeal is to people who appreciate the open air, whether scenery or outdoor pursuits. The attractions range from pleasant rambling across moors and treks along long-distance footpaths to arduous hill walking, hair-raising rock climbs, and pony trekking. You can ski down snow-capped mountains, canoe in fast-flowing white water, thrill to some of Europe's best surfing, fish for salmon in crystal-clear streams, or play golf in the country that invented the game.

"Scotland's For Me!" chorused a Scottish Tourist Board advertising campaign. Few visitors find any reason to disagree.

Preceding pages: Blackrock Cottage, Glencoe; the much photographed Eilean Donan Castle, Wester Ross; Edinburgh Castle from the air.

EDINBURGH

Not for nothing was that great parable of the divided self, *Dr Jekyll and Mr Hyde*, written by an Edinburgh man, Robert Louis Stevenson. He may have set the story in London but he conjured it out of the bizarre life of a respectable Edinburgh tradesman called William Brodie.

Brodie, a Deacon of Wrights and Masons of Edinburgh, was a pillar of 18th-century rectitude by day and a ruthless thief by night who ended his days dangling at the end of the Edinburgh hangman's rope. Stevenson, it seems, was fascinated by Brodie and other such Edinburgh double-dealers like Major Weir, who contrived to be both a pious Presbyterian elder and a necromancing wizard, and Dr Robert Knox, the respected Edinburgh University anatomist who bought about 15 freshly-murdered corpses from the Burke and Hare partnership. Burke himself was a "respectable man" apart from the fact that he was a murderer.

All of which has led more than one critic to see the Jekyll and Hyde story as a handy metaphor for the city of Edinburgh itself: something at once universal yet characteristically Scottish. Where else does a semi-ramshackle late medieval town glower down on such Georgian elegance? What other urban centre contains such huge chunks of sheer wilderness within its boundaries? Does any other city in Europe have so many solid Victorian suburbs surrounded by such bleak housing estates? Stevenson himself was inclined to agree. "Few places, if any" he wrote, "offer a more barbaric display of contrasts to the eye."

And not just to the eye. Edinburgh's renowned civic pride conceals some of the hardest-pressed police stations in Britain, and the worst hard drugs problem outside London. Edinburgh may have one of Europe's most venerable medical establishments, but it also has an appalling incidence of AIDS (needle sharing is more often to blame than sexual activity). And, while Edinburgh's financiers may juggle with billions every year, the local authorities never seem to have enough money to keep the streets clean. Behind the amiable and rational intelligence of Dr Henry Jekyll stands the cold glare of Mr Edward Hyde.

Raw weather: Just as Edward Hyde "gave an impression of deformity without any nameable malformation" so the meaner side of Edinburgh tends to lurk unnoticed in the beauty of its topography and the splendour of its architecture. Even the weather seems to play its part. "The weather is raw and boisterous in winter, shifty and ungenial in summer, and downright meteorological purgatory in spring," Stevenson wrote of his home town.

But the Jekyll and Hyde metaphor can be stretched too far. For all its sly duality and shifty ways, Edinburgh remains one of Europe's most beautiful and amenable cities, a stunning confection of late medieval tenements, neoclassical terraces, tidy suburbs, rivers and wooded gardens set among a series of volcanic hills and small lochs.

To the south the city is hemmed in by

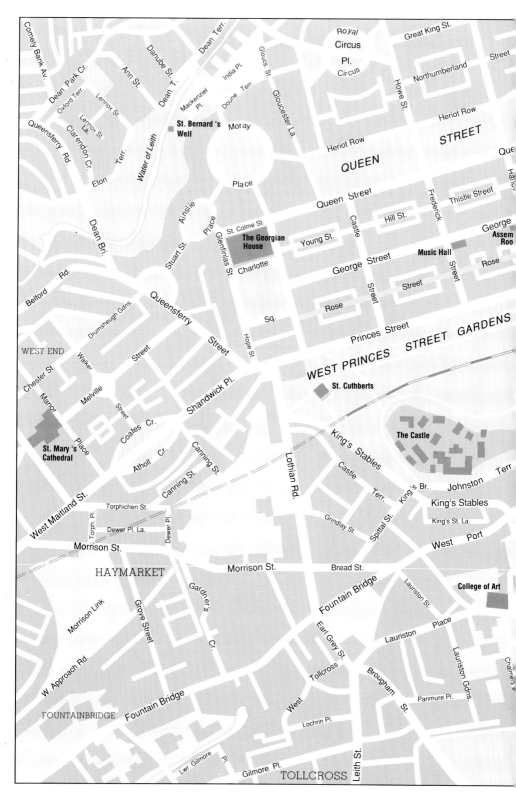

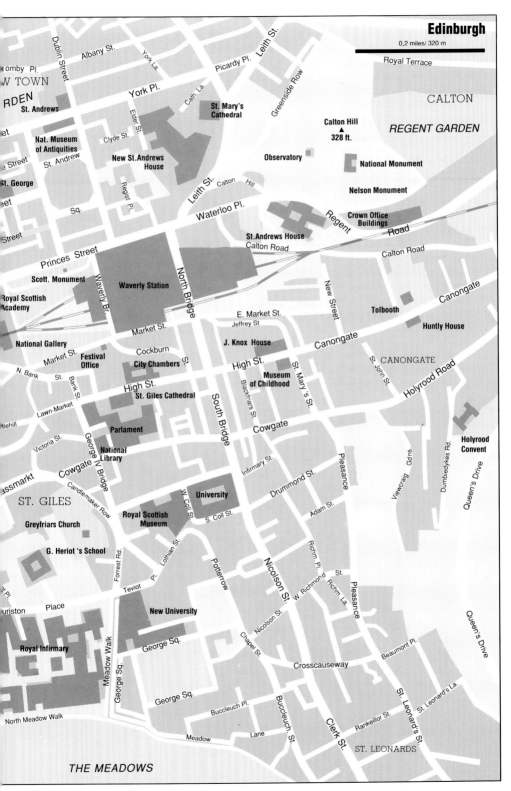

Edinburgh

0,2 miles/ 320 m

Royal Terrace

CALTON

REGENT GARDEN

Dublin Street
Albany St.
York La.
Picardy Pl.
Leith St.
Greenside Row

omby Pl.
W TOWN

RDEN
St. Andrews

York Pl.

St. Mary's Cathedral

Calton Hill
▲
328 ft.

Nat. Museum of Antiquities

Elder St.
Clyde St.

St. Andrew

Observatory

National Monument

e Street

New St.Andrews House

Leith St.
Calton Hill

Nelson Monument

St. George

Regist. Pl.

Sq.

Waterloo Pl.

Regent

Crown Office Buildings

Street

St.Andrews House
Calton Road

Road

Calton Road

Princes Street

Scott. Monument

Waverly Br.

North Bridge

Waverly Station

New Street

Canongate

Tolbooth

Royal Scottish Academy

E. Market St.
Jeffrey St

Huntly House

National Gallery

Market St.

Cockburn

J. Knox House

Canongate

St. John St.

CANONGATE

Holyrood Road

N. Bank St.
Bank St.

Festival Office

City Chambers

St.

High St.

Museum of Childhood

St. Mary's St.

Lawn-Market

High St.

St. Giles Cathedral

Blackfriars St.

Cowgate

Holyrood Convent

tlehill

Victoria St.

Parlament

South Bridge

George IV. Bridge

National Library

Infirmary St.

Pleasance

Viewcraig Gdns.

Dumbiedykes Rd.

Queen's Drive

assmarkt

Cowgate

Candlemaker Row

Drummond St.

Adam St.

ST. GILES

University

S. Coll St.

Greyfriars Church

W. coll St.

Royal Scottish Museum

S. Coll St.

Richm. Pl.

W. Richmond

Richm. La.

Pleasance

Queen's Drive

G. Heriot 's School

Forrest Rd.

Lothian St.

Potterrow

Nicolson St.

St.

l Pl.

uriston
Place

Teviot Pl.

New University

Nicolson St.

Chapel St.

Beaumont Pl.

Royal Infirmary

Meadow Walk

George Sq.

George Sq.

Crosscauseway

St. Leonard's La.

George Sq.

George Sq.

Buccleuch Pl.

Buccleuch St.

Clerk St.

Rankeillor St.

St. Leonard's St.

North Meadow Walk

Meadow

Lane

ST. LEONARDS

THE MEADOWS

the Pentland Hills – some of which are almost 2,000 ft (600 metres) high – and to the north by the island-studded waters of the Firth of Forth. In 1878 Stevenson declared himself baffled that "this profusion of eccentricities, this dream in masonry and living rock is not a drop-scene in a theatre, but a city in the world of everyday reality".

Which, of course, it is. At the last count, Edinburgh contained almost 440,000 people rattling around in 100 sq. miles (26,000 hectares) on the south bank of the Firth of Forth. While the city's traditional economy of "books, beer and biscuits" has been drastically whittled away by the ravages of recession and change, there is a powerful underpinning of banking, insurance, shipping, the professions (especially the law), the universities, a lot of hospitals, and of course government bureaucracies (local and central). By and large, the great North Sea oil boom passed Edinburgh by, although some of the city's financiers did well enough by shuffling investment funds around, and

for a while Leith Docks was used as an onshore supply base, to coat pipes, and to build steel deck modules.

And, like every other decent-sized city in the western hemisphere. Edinburgh is now a fairly rich cultural mix. The "base" population remains overwhelmingly Scots with a large Irish content, but there are big communities of Poles, Italians, Ukranians, Jews, Pakistanis, Sikhs, Bengalis, Chinese and, of course, English. Within that mix there are echoes of Ulster.

Although Edinburgh has been spared the kind of religious bigotry which bedevils Glasgow, it still has separate schools for Catholic and Protestant children. And every July the city stages one of the biggest "Orange Walks" outside of Northern Ireland.

To some extent Edinburgh is a city with a hole in its psyche where a Scottish legislature should have been, the mock capital of a country without sovereignty. The last attempt to claw back some power from London came to grief in 1979 when the British Government

A city by design: Edinburgh's West End.

refused to set up a Scottish Assembly because the Scots did not vote in favour of one by a big enough margin, although they did vote in favour. Plans to hold the Assembly in the converted **Royal High School** in Waterloo Place were abandoned and the building was sold in 1994.

For all that, Edinburgh wields more power and influence than any British city outside of London. It is the centre of the Scots legal system, home to the Court of Session (the civil court) and the High Court of Justiciary (criminal court) from which there is no appeal to the House of Lords: Edinburgh's decision is final. Edinburgh is also the base of the Church of Scotland (the established church) whose General Assembly every May floods Edinburgh with sober-suited Presbyterian ministers from all over Scotland.

And the British Government runs its policies in Scotland through the Edinburgh-based **Scottish Office**, whose boss, the Secretary of State for Scotland, is a member of the British cabinet. Anyone seeking to consult the records of Scotland (land titles, company registration, government archives, lists of bankrupts, births, marriages, deaths) must come to Edinburgh.

And *The Scotsman* newspaper, published in Edinburgh, is still arguably the most influential piece of media north of the border, a kind of notice-board of the Scottish establishment.

The early days: No-one is quite sure just how old Edinburgh is, only that people have been living in the area for more than 5,000 years. But it seems certain that the city grew from a tiny community perched on the "plug" of volcanic rock which now supports **Edinburgh Castle**. With its steep, easily-defended sides, natural springs of water, and excellent vantage points, the castle rock was squabbled over for hundreds of years by generations of Picts, Scots, British (Welsh) and Angles, with the Scots (from Ireland) finally coming out on top. But it was a Northumbrian (i.e. Angle) king, Edwin, who gave his name to the city.

It was not until the 11th century that

A City Halberdier, called after the halberd (pike) he carries.

Edinburgh settled down to be the capital city of Scotland, and a royal residence was built within the walls of Edinburgh Castle.

But Edinburgh proved to be a strategic liability in the medieval wars with the English. It was too close to England. And, time after time, powerful English armies came crashing across the border laying waste the plump farmlands of the southeast, and burning Edinburgh itself. It happened in 1174 (when the English held Edinburgh Castle for 12 years), in 1296, in 1313 (during the Wars of Independence), in 1357, in 1573, in 1650 and as late as 1689 when the Duke of Gordon tried, and failed, to hold Edinburgh Castle against the Protestant army of William of Orange.

The hammering of Edinburgh by the English military came to an end in 1707 when the Scottish Parliament, many of whose members had been bribed by English interests, voted to abandon the sovereignty of Scotland in favour of a union with England. "Now there's an end of an auld sang," the old Earl of

Seafield was heard to mutter as he signed the Act. But in fact, power and influence had been haemorrhaging out of Edinburgh ever since the Union of the Crowns in 1603 when the Scottish King James VI (son of Mary Queen of Scots) became the first monarch of Great Britain and Ireland.

Stripped of its Royal Family, courtiers, parliament and civil service, 18th-century Edinburgh should have lapsed into a sleepy provincialism. But that didn't happen. The Treaty of Union guaranteed the position of Scots law and the role of the Presbyterian Church of Scotland. With both these powerful institutions still firmly entrenched in Edinburgh, the city was still a place where men of power and influence met to make important decisions.

The Scottish Enlightenment: In fact, for reasons which are still not clear, 18th-century Scotland became one of Europe's intellectual powerhouses, producing scholars and philosophers like David Hume, Adam Smith and William Robertson, architect-builders like

Sir Walter Scott stares stonily at modern Edinburgh.

William Adam and his sons Robert and John, engineers like James Watt, Thomas Telford and John Rennie, surgeons like John and William Hunter, and painters like Henry Raeburn and Alan Ramsay. It was a concentration of talent that led the amiable Englishman John Amyat, the King's Chemist, to remark that he could stand at the **Mercat Cross** near St Giles and "in a few minutes, take 50 men of genius by the hand".

That explosion of talent became known as the Scottish Enlightenment, and one of its greatest creations was the **New Town** of Edinburgh. Between 1767 and 1840 a whole impeccable new city – bright, spacious, elegant and rational – was created on the land to the north of the **Old Town**. It was one of the wonders of the world, and was very quickly occupied by the aristocracy, gentry and "middling" classes of Edinburgh who left the Old Town to the poor and to the waves of Irish and Highland immigrants who flooded into Edinburgh from the 1840s on.

Like most British (and European) cities, Edinburgh's population burgeoned in the 19th century, from 90,786 in 1801 to just over 413,000 in 1901. There was no way that the Old Town and the New Town could house that kind of population, and Victorian Edinburgh became ringed by a huge development of handsome stone-built tenements and villas in suburbs such as **Bruntsfield**, **Marchmont**, **the Grange** and **Morningside**, which in turn became ringed about by 20th-century bungalows and speculative housing. And, beginning in the 1930s, the Edinburgh Corporation (and later the Edinburgh District Council) outflanked the lot by throwing up an outer ring of huge council-housing estates, some of which are now fraught with awful problems.

The Old Town: Although the Old Town has been allowed to deteriorate in a way that is nothing short of disgraceful, it is being revived. In the past 20 years or so, a serious effort had been made to breathe new life into its labyrinth of medieval street, wynds and closes.

A few developers have been restoring

Two's company in St Andrew Square.

17th-century tenements, and converting 19th-century breweries to cater for those who have discovered the heady delights of city-centre living. As a way of rescuing Edinburgh's many down-at-heel architectural treasures, the city fathers have been literally giving away some of the buildings (along with handsome grants) to private developers.

Even after two centuries of neglect, Edinburgh's Old Town packs more historic buildings into a square mile than just about anywhere in Britain. Stevenson, again, provides the reason. "It (the Old Town) grew, under the law that regulates the growth of walled cities in precarious situation, not in extent, but in height and density. Public buildings were forced, whenever there was room for them, into the midst of thoroughfares; thoroughfares were diminished into lanes; houses sprang up storey after storey, neighbour mounting upon neighbour's shoulder, as in some Black Hole in Calcutta, until the population slept 14 to 15 deep in a vertical direction."

In this late-medieval version of Man-hattan, the aristocracy, gentry, merchants and commoners of Edinburgh lived cheek by jowl. Often they shared the same "lands" (tenements), the "quality" at the bottom and hoi polloi at the top. They rubbed shoulders in dark stairways and closes, and knew one another in a way that was socially impossible in England. Any Lord of Session (high court judge) whose verdict was unpopular could expect to be harangued or even pelted with mud and stones as he made his way home.

Politicians, aristocracy and church leaders came under close scrutiny. When the Scottish parliament approved the treaty of Union with England in 1707, the Edinburgh mob went on the rampage trying to track down the "traitors" who, they felt, had sold Scotland out to the "Auld Enemy" (the English).

In fact, the Edinburgh mob was a formidable political force. For much of the 18th century it was led by a certain "General" Joe Smith, a bow-legged cobbler who believed passionately in the inferiority of women (his wife had to

Old Edinburgh up for sale.

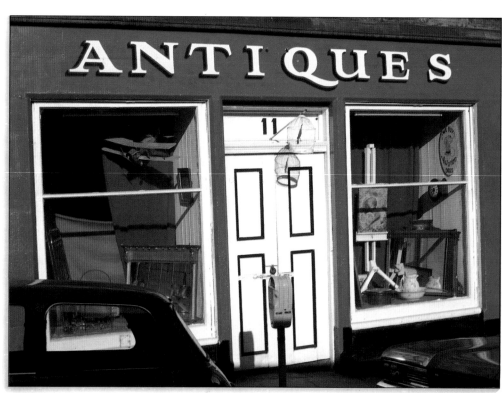

walk several paces behind him) and who could drum up a crowd of thousands within a few minutes. With the mob at his back, Joe Smith could lay down the law to the Magistrates of Edinburgh, and ran a kind of rough justice against thieving landlords and dishonest traders. His career came to an abrupt end in 1780 when, dead drunk, he fell to his death off the top of a stagecoach.

Not that life in the Old Town was entirely dominated by the mob rule of "General" Joe Smith. Far from it. Until the end of the 18th century the Old Town was the epicentre of fashionable society, a tight little metropolis of elegant drawing rooms, fashionable concert halls, dancing academies, and a bewildering variety of taverns, *howffs* (meeting places), coffee-houses and social clubs. "Nothing was so common in the morning as to meet men of high rank and official dignity reeling home from a close in the High Street where they had spent the night in drinking," wrote Robert Chambers, a lively chronicler.

The heady social life of the Old Town came to an end at the turn of the 19th century when it was progressively abandoned by the rich and the influential, whose houses were inherited by the poor and the feckless. "The Great Flitting" it was called, and crowds used to gather to watch all fine furniture, crockery and painting being loaded into carts for the journey down the newly-created "earthen mound" (now called **The Mound**) to the New Town.

The Royal Mile: The spine of the Old Town is the **Royal Mile**, a wide thoroughfare which runs down from the Castle to the **Palace of Holyrood House**, and comprises (from top to bottom) Castlehill, Lawnmarket, the High Street, and the Canongate. This street was described by the author of *Robinson Crusoe*, Daniel Defoe (who lived in Edinburgh at the beginning of the 18th century), as "perhaps the largest, longest, and finest Street for Buildings, and Number of Inhabitants, not in Britain only, but in the world."

The **Castle** itself is well worth a visit, if only for the views over the city. Many of the castle buildings are 18th- and 19th-century, although the tiny Norman chapel dedicated to the saintly Queen Margaret dates to the 12th century.

Also worth seeking out are the **Scottish National War Memorial**, **Great Hall** (which has a superb hammer-beam roof), and the **Crown Room** which houses the Regalia (crown jewels) of Scotland, which were lost between 1707 and 1818 when a commission set up by Sir Walter Scott traced them to a locked chest in a locked room in the castle.

Just below the castle esplanade, on **Castlehill**, an iron fountain marks the spot where, between 1479 and 1722, Edinburgh used to burn its witches; **Ramsay Gardens**, the tenements designed by the 19th-century planning genius Patrick Geddes; and a **Camera Obscura** built in the 1850s. Across the road is the **Scotch Whisky Heritage Centre**, where visitors can learn about the drink's origin from an audio-visual show and by travelling in a whisky barrel through 300 years of history. The shop sells a good selection of whiskies.

Beside the centre is the huge but now

The Royal Mile.

closed **Tolbooth Kirk**, where the city's Gaelic speakers used to worship.

On the north side of the Lawnmarket is **Gladstone's Land**, a completely restored six-storey 17th-century tenement now owned by the National Trust for Scotland (NTS) which gives some insight into 17th-century Edinburgh life (dirty, difficult and malodorous).

Next door is **Lady Stair's House**, now a museum dedicated to Burns, Scott and Stevenson, and **Deacon Brodie's Tavern**, named after William Brodie, the model for the Jekyll and Hyde story.

Further along, on what is now **High Street**, are **Parliament House** (now the law courts), the **High Kirk of St Giles** (often miscalled St Giles Cathedral), the **Mercat Cross** from which kings and queens are proclaimed, the **City Chambers** which was built as an "exchange" (i.e office block) and was one of the first buildings in the great drive to "improve" Edinburgh in the late 18th century. The lower part of the High Street contains the 15th-century **Moubray House** which is probably the oldest inhabited building in Edinburgh, **John Knox's House**, and the **Museum of Childhood** where, to see the displays, children have to fight their way through crowds of wistful adults.

Across the road in **Trinity Church** in **Chalmer's Court** enthusiasts can make rubbings of rare Scottish brasses and stone crosses in the **Scottish Stone and Brass Rubbing Centre**.

The **Canongate** is particularly rich in 16th- and 17th-century buildings. These include the **Tolbooth**, which houses *The People's Story*, an exhibition about ordinary Edinburgh folk from the late 18th century to the present; **Bakehouse Close, Huntly House**, the city's main museum of local history); **Moray House** (the most lavish of the aristocracy's town houses), the Dutch-style **Canongate Church**, **White Horse Close** (once a coaching inn), and the 17th-century **Acheson House**. Just beyond the Canongate Church is the "**mushroom garden**", a small walled garden laid out in the 17th-century manner, and almost completely unknown.

The Tolbooth, an ancient entry into Edinburgh.

The **Palace of Holyrood House** began as an Abbey in the 12th century, grew into a Royal Palace in the early 16th century, and much was added in the late 17th century by Sir William Bruce for Charles II, who never set foot in the building. Holyrood's history is long and often grisly. It was here that Mary Queen of Scots witnessed the butchery of her Italian favourite, David Rizzio, in 1558, and where the severed and scattered remains of the Marquis of Montrose were reassembled prior to being given a decent burial in 1661. Bonnie Prince Charlie held court here in 1745 during his short-lived triumph.

And Holyrood Palace was used by George IV during his hilarious state visit to Edinburgh in 1822. The portly Hanoverian stalked the palace wearing flesh-coloured tights under an exceedingly brief Royal Stewart tartan kilt. "As he is to be here so short a time," remarked one waggish Edinburgh lady, "the more we see of him the better."

But he set a precedent which the British royals have been following ever since. Queen Victoria and Prince Albert favoured Holyrood as a stop-over on their way to and from Balmoral. And every June, when the Queen is in residence the dress-hire business booms and polite Edinburgh goes into a flap over who has and who has not been invited to the Royal Garden Party in Holyrood's gardens. It usually rains.

South of the Royal Mile, on George IV Bridge, are the **National Library of Scotland** (one of the few copyright libraries in Britain) and the little bronze statue of **Greyfriars Bobby**, the devoted Skye terrier immortalised by Walt Disney. In Chambers Street the **Royal Museum of Scotland's** dazzling collection of 19th-century machinery and scientific instruments is well worth seeing, which is more than can be said for its collection of badly stuffed animals. And on the corner of Chambers Street and the South Bridge lies Robert Adam's **The Old College**, the finest of the university's collection of buildings.

Running roughly parallel with the Royal Mile to the south are the **Grass-**

Holyrood Palace.

market – the site of many a riot and public execution – a long and now rather dismal street called the **Cowgate**, which in the 19th century was crammed with Irish immigrants fleeing the Great Famine. James Connolly, one of the martyrs of the Easter Rising in Dublin in 1916, was born and reared in the Cowgate. He worked as a printer on the *Edinburgh Evening News*, and did a spell of military service with the Royal Scots, the oldest regiment in the British Army.

The Irish Catholic nature of the Cowgate is testified to by the huge but inelegant bulk of **St Patrick's Roman Catholic church**. A much more interesting Cowgate building is **St Cecilia's Hall**, which now belongs to Edinburgh University, but was built by the Edinburgh Musical Society as a fashionable concert hall in 1762 and modelled on the Opera House at Parma.

A landmark of Europe: "A sort of schizophrenia in stone" is how the novelist Eric Linklater once described **Princes Street**, going on to contrast the "natural grandeur solemnised by memories of human pain and heroism" of the castle rock with the tawdry commercialism of the north side of the street. This "municipal anarchy," he argued, had created a street "whose resemblance to an oriental bazaar is truly startling". In Linklater's view, the kind of tourist junk on sale in Princes Street "would look equally at home on the boat of a native vendor in Port Said". Linklater wrote that in 1960, and nothing much has changed since.

If Princes Street is still one of Europe's more elegant boulevards it is no thanks to the architects, developers and retailers of the 20th century. Just about every decent building has been gouged out of the north side of the street and replaced by some undistinguished piece of Marks & Spencer modern. What has saved Princes Street from tragedy is the fact that the south side remains the "broad and deep ravine planted with trees and shrubbery" that so impressed the American writer Nathaniel Willis in 1834. So unless the powers-that-be are plotting to fill **Princes Street Gardens** with car

Left, the circus comes to town. **Right**, Greyfriars Bobby's statue.

parks (it has been suggested) and level the Edinburgh Castle, Princes Street's role as one of the glorious landmarks of Europe should be secure.

Princes Street has always been the venue for Edinburgh promenaders, out to enjoy what the local historian Thomas Carlyle called "the finest city prospect in the World and the sight of one another". Generations of Edinburgh youths and girls have ambled up and down Princes Street, eyeing one another in the hope of striking up a conversation on the return journey. The poet Edwin Muir compared an evening stroll on Princes Street to waiting on a country railway platform for a train which is late. "There is the same intense and permitted scrutiny of one's fellow passengers, the same growing expectation…"

With the exception of the superb **Register House** by Robert Adam at the far northeast end of the street, and a few remaining 19th-century shops (such as Jenners and Debenhams) everything worthwhile is on the south side of the street. The most startling edifice, which may be ascended for splendid views, is the huge and intricate Gothic **monument to Sir Walter Scott** (the "Gothic Rocket"), erected in 1844 and designed by a self-taught architect called George Meikle Kemp. The unfortunate Kemp drowned in an Edinburgh canal shortly before the monument was completed, and was due to be buried in the vault under the memorial until some petty-minded member of Scott's entourage persuaded the Court of Session to divert the funeral. Another blow for Edward Hyde.

Much more typical of Edinburgh are the two neo-classical art galleries at the junction of Princes Street and The Mound. Now known as the **Royal Scottish Academy** and the **National Gallery of Scotland**, both buildings were designed by William Playfair between 1822 and 1845. The space around the galleries has long been Edinburgh's version of London's Hyde Park Corner, and is heavily used by preachers, polemicists and bagpipers. During the

A timely trim for the flower clock in Princes Street Gardens.

Edinburgh Festival it becomes the greatest free show on earth, with brass bands, string quartets, magicians, fire-eaters, comic turns and rock guitarists jostling for the attention (and silver) of the festival-going crowds.

Exhibitions at the Royal Scottish Academy come and go, but the National Gallery of Scotland houses the biggest permanent collection of Old Masters outside London. There are paintings by Raphael, Rubens, El Greco, Titian, Goya, Vermeer and a clutch of superb Rembrandts. Gaugin, Cézanne, Renoir, Degas, Monet, Van Gogh and Turner are well represented, and the gallery's Scottish collection is unrivalled. There are important paintings by Raeburn, Ramsay, Wilkie, and the astonishing (and underrated) James Drummond.

At the southwest end of Princes Street is a brace of fine churches: **St John's** (Episcopalian) and **St Cuthbert's** (Church of Scotland). St John's supports a lively congregation which is forever decking the building out with paintings in support of various Third World causes and animal rights. The church, a Gothic revival building designed by William Burn in 1816, has a fine ceiling which John Ruskin thought "simply beautiful". There is also a thriving café in the basement which specialises in Nicaraguan coffee and other politically-sound comestibles.

It is an extraordinary fact of Edinburgh life that there is not one pub the whole length of Princes Street. A few plushy clubs, certainly, but no pubs. But **Rose Street**, a narrow and once infamous thoroughfare that runs just behind it, has more than its share. The more diverting Rose Street hostelries are **the Kenilworth** (which has a lovely ceramic-clad interior), **Scotts**, **Paddy's**, **the Abbotsford** and a *howff* called **Milnes Bar**, once the haunt of 20th-century Edinburgh literati. In the 1950s and 1960s a favourite Edinburgh sport was to try to get from one end of Rose Street to the other, downing half a pint in every pub and remain standing. Few succeeded. (Incidentally, the *Good Pub Guide* lists Edinburgh, with more than 700 pubs for

Looking down on Princes Street.

fewer than 500,000 people, as the best place in Britain for boozers.)

The New Town: But what makes Edinburgh a truly world-class city, able to stand shoulder to shoulder with Prague, Amsterdam or Vienna, is the great neoclassical New Town, built in an explosion of creativity between 1767 and 1840. The New Town is the product of the Scottish Enlightenment. And noone has really been able to explain how, in the words of the historian Arthur Youngson, "a small, crowded, almost medieval town, the capital of a comparatively poor country, expanded in a short space of time, without foreign advice or foreign assistance, so as to become one of the enduringly beautiful cities of western Europe".

It all began in 1752 with an anonymous pamphlet entitled *Proposals for carrying on certain Public Works in the City of Edinburgh*. It was published anonymously, but was engineered by Edinburgh's all-powerful Lord Provost (Lord Mayor), George Drummond. Drummond was determined that Edin-

burgh should be a credit to the Hanoverian-ruled United Kingdom which he had helped create, and should rid itself of its (justifiable) reputation for overcrowding, squalor, turbulence and Jacobitism.

To some extent the New Town is a political statement in stone. It is Scotland's tribute to the Hanoverian ascendancy. Many of the street names reflect the fact: **Hanover Street**, **Cumberland Street**, **George Street**, **Queen Street**, **Frederick Street** etc.

But the speed with which the New Town was built is still astonishing, particularly given the sheer quality of the building. Built mainly in calciferous sandstone from Craigleith Quarry to a prize-winning layout by a 23-year-old architect/planner called James Craig, most of the more important New Town buildings were in place before the end of the century: **Register House** (1778), the North side of **Charlotte Square** (1791), the **Assembly Rooms and Music Hall** (1787), **St Andrew's Church** (1785), most of **George Street**,

THE MONEY MEN OF CHARLOTTE SQUARE

One of the more remarkable facts about Edinburgh is that it is the biggest financial centre in Europe apart from the City of London. Occasionally the bankers of Frankfurt, the Gnomes of Zurich or even the upstarts of Manchester dispute Edinburgh's claim, but their protests are never conceded. "Of course it's very difficult to measure these things," says Professor Jack Shaw of Scottish Financial Enterprises (the Edinburgh financiers' mouthpiece). "But Edinburgh handles more fund money than anyone outside of London. We calculate that it amounts to around £50 billion. And that's a lot of money."

Naturally, this huge community of bankers, investment-fund managers, stockbrokers, corporate lawyers, accountants, insurance executives and unit-trust operators has to be "serviced". Which means nice business for Edinburgh's glossier advertising agencies, public relations firms, design studios

and photographers – not to mention restaurants, wine bars and auction houses like Sotheby's, Philips and Christie's.

Just as "the City" is shorthand for London's vast financial community, so Edinburgh's is known as "Charlotte Square". But the financial district it inhabits extends far beyond the elegant boundaries of the square itself. It now takes in much of George Street, St Andrew Square, Queen Street, Melville Street and various other large chunks of the New Town.

Edinburgh's star role in the financial world can be traced back to the enthusiasm of the Scots for making and then keeping money. The Scots have always been among the modern world's best and canniest bankers. Which is why the Scottish clearing banks have a statutory right (dating from 1845) to print their own distinctive banknotes. This is a right the Scottish banks relish, particularly as the English banks were stripped of it following a string of bank failures in the 19th century, and the Scots are remarkably attached to their Edinburgh-based banks.

Probably the biggest fish in Edinburgh's financial pond are the giant Scottish insurance companies which handle funds in the region of £30 billion. The most important by far is the Standard Life Assurance Company which has offices all over Britain, Ireland and Canada and is now Europe's biggest "mutual fund". Like most of the Edinburgh insurance companies, the Standard Life is a vintage operation (1825). Some are even older, with names that have a satisfyingly old-fashioned ring, like the Scottish Widows Fund & Life Assurance Society or the Scottish Provident Institution for Mutual Life Assurance.

Although Charlotte Square took much stick for being slow to get in on the booming unit trust business (a complaint it fast put right) there's no shortage of old-fashioned "investment trusts". It was with money from these trusts that much of the American west was built. In the 19th century, Charlotte Square was heavily into cattle ranching, fruit farming and railways in the USA. Nowadays it prefers to sink its "bawbees" into the high-tech wizardry of Silicon Valley or east Texas oil wells. And while Edinburgh as a whole benefitted little from North Sea oil, parts of Charlotte Square did very nicely, thank you. ■ **Charlotte Square.**

Castle Street, **Frederick Street** and **Princes Street**.

The stinking Nor' Loch (north loch) under the castle rock was speedily drained to make way for the "pleasure gardens" of Princes Street. Two million cart-loads of soil from the New Town excavations were used to create an "earthen mound" (now known as **The Mound**) linking Princes Street with the Old Town.

By the 1790s the New Town was the height of fashion, and the gentry of Edinburgh were abandoning their roots in the Old Town for the Georgian elegance on the other side of the newly-built North Bridge. Some idea of how they lived can be glimpsed in the **Georgian House** at 7 Charlotte Square (on the block designed by Robert Adam). The house has been lovingly restored by the National Trust for Scotland to its original state. It is crammed with the furniture, crockery, glassware, silver and paintings of the period, and even the floorboards have been dryscrubbed in the original manner. The basement kitchen is a masterpiece of late 18th-century domestic technology.

Also in Charlotte Square is **West Register House** (part of the Scottish Record Office) which was built by Robert Reid in 1811 and began life as St George's Church. A few hundred metres along George Street are the **Assembly Rooms and Music Hall** (1787), once the focus of social life in the New Town, and still a top venue during the festival.

Across the road is the **Church of St Andrew and St George** (1785) whose oval-shaped interior witnessed the "Great Disruption" of 1843. The Church of Scotland was split down the middle when the "evangelicals", led by Thomas Chalmers, walked out in disgust at the complacency of the church "moderates" who were content to have their ministers foisted on them by the gentry (as was the custom in England). Chalmers and his colleagues went on to form the Free Church of Scotland, a sterner but more democratic form of Presbyterianism.

Parallel to George Street lies **Queen**

The Georgian House in Charlotte Square.

Street whose only public building of any interest is an eccentric Doge's Palace housing the **Scottish National Portrait Gallery** and the **Royal Museum of Scotland (Antiquities)**. The rather gloomy portrait gallery is well stocked with pictures of generations of Scots worthies, while the museum contains many an intriguing artefact. The Pictish and Gaelic cross stones and carvings are extraordinary. The children's favourite seems to be "the maiden", the guillotine that stood in the Old Town and was used to shorten malefactors.

Although **St Andrew Square** at the west end of George Street has been knocked about a bit, it is still recognisable, with the most noteworthy building in the square being the head office of the Royal Bank of Scotland. Originally built in 1774 as the Town House of Sir Laurence Dundas, it was remodelled in the 1850s when it acquired a quite astonishing domed ceiling with glazed star-shaped cofers. The 150-ft-high (45-metre) monument in the centre of St Andrew Square is to Henry Dundas, 1st Viscount Melville, who was branded "King Harry the Ninth" for his autocratic (and probably corrupt) way of running Scotland.

To the north of the Charlotte Square/ St Andrew Square axis lies a huge acreage of Georgian elegance which is probably unrivalled in Europe. Only the English city of Bath comes close. Most of it is private housing and offices. Particularly worth seeing are **Heriot Row**, **Northumberland Street**, **Royal Circus**, **Ainslie Place**, **Moray Place** and **Drummond Place**. **Ann Street** near the Water of Leith is beautiful but atypical, with its gardens and two- and three-storey buildings. The street is the creation of the painter Henry Raeburn who named it after his wife Ann.

But elegant appearances can deceive. Nearby **Danube Street** used to house Edinburgh's most notorious whorehouse, run by a flamboyant madame called Dora Noyes and much frequented by foreign seamen. Mrs Noyes is long since dead, the whores are scattered, and the house has reverted to middle-class decency.

The **Stockbridge** area on the northern edge of the New Town is an engaging bazaar of antique shops, curiosity dealers, picture framers, second-hand book stores, with a sprinkling of decent restaurants and noisy pubs. The **Royal Botanic Garden** (half a mile north of Stockbridge) is 70 acres (28 hectares) of woodland, green sward, exotic tees, heather garden, rockeries, rhododendron walks and exotic planthouses.

Also in this area, on Bedford Road, is the **Scottish National Gallery of Modern Art**, with a fine permanent collection of 20th-century art including works by Matisse and Picasso, Magritte and Hockney and frequent special shows.

Edward Hyde lurks in the New Town, too. The designers of the New Town provided it with a plethora of handsome "pleasure gardens" which range in size from small patches of grass and shrubbery to the three **Queen Street Gardens** which cover more than 11 acres (4.5 hectares). All three are closed to the public and accessible only to the "key-holders" who live nearby. One of the

A leg-up for the Festival Fringe.

drearier summer sights is to see puzzled tourists shaking the gates, at a loss of understand why they are barred from ambling round the greenery. The locked pleasure gardens of the New Town is middle-class Edinburgh at its most mean-spirited.

Between 1815 and 1840 another version of the New Town grew beyond the east end of Princes Street and Waterloo Place. **Regent Terrace**, **Royal Terrace**, **Blenheim Terrace** and **Leopold Place** were its main thoroughfares.

This eastward expansion also littered the slopes of **Calton Hill** with impressive public buildings which probably earned Edinburgh the title "Athens of the North" (although a comparison between the two cities had been made in 1762 by the antiquarian James Stuart). On the hill are monuments to Dugald Stewart, the 18th/19th-century philosopher, and Horatio Nelson, whose memorial in the shape of a telescope may be ascended for great views, and the old **City Observatory**, now home to *The Edinburgh Experience* show.

The oddest of the early 19th-century edifices on the Calton Hill is known as "Scotland's Disgrace" and was meant to be a war memorial to the Scots killed in the Napoleonic wars, and was to be modelled on the Parthenon in Athens. The foundation stone was laid with a great flourish during George IV's visit to Edinburgh in 1822, but the money ran out after 12 columns were erected.

Beyond Calton Hill, on Regent Road, are the former **Royal High School** (called "the noblest monument of the Scottish Greek Revival"), the **Robert Burns Monument**, modelled on the Choragic Monument of Lysicrates in Athens, and the **Old Calton Burial Ground**, with 18th and 19th-century memorials (including one honouring David Hume), in the lee of the empty, semi-derelict **Governor's House** of the Old Calton Jail.

Maritime Edinburgh: Although more ships now sail in and out of the Firth of Forth than use the Firth of Clyde, maritime Edinburgh has taken a terrible beating over the past 20 years. Edinburgh's

Street art defies Scotland's rainy climate.

port of **Leith** was, until recently, one of the hardest working harbours on the east coast of Britain, and the city's coastline on the Firth of Forth is studded with fishing villages: **Granton, Newhaven, Portobello, Fisherrow**, and further east, **Cockenzie**, **Port Seton** and **Prestonpans**. Ships from Leith exported coal, salt fish, paper, leather and good strong ale, and returned with (among much else) grain, timber, wine, foreign foods and Italian marble. The destinations were Hamburg, Bremen, Amsterdam, Antwerp, Copenhagen and occasionally North America and Australia.

Right up to the mid 1960s at least four fleets of deep-sea trawlers plied out of Leith and the nearby harbour of **Granton**, and the half-Scottish, half-Norwegian firm of Christian Salvesen was still catching thousands of whales every year into the 1950s (which is why there is a Leith Harbour in South Georgia). The 2-mile (3-km) stretch of shore between Leith and Granton used to be littered with shipyards, ship repair yards, a ship breaking yard, drydocks, marine engineering shops, a ropeworks and wireworks. The women of Leith and Granton would earn extra money by making fishing nets at home. The streets of Leith itself were full of shipping agents, marine insurance firms, grain merchants, ships' chandlers, plus a burgeoning "service sector" of dockside pubs, clubs, flophouses, bookies and whores.

But most of it is gone. The trade has shifted to the container ports on the east coast of England. The maritime heart has gone out of Leith, and therefore Edinburgh. A few cruise liners still make an occasional appearance, and every now and again an oil-industry supply boat or a visiting naval vessel comes through the harbour mouth.

There have been attempts to turn Leith round. Scottish Enterprise and the local authorities have been spending millions restoring the exteriors of some of Leith's handsome commercial buildings such as the old **Customs House**, the **Corn Exchange**, the **Assembly Building**, and **Trinity House** in the Kirkgate. At the same time private developers have been

Leith: was Scotland's major port.

More interesting is **Duddingston**, tucked under the eastern flank of Arthur's Seat, beside a small loch which is also a bird sanctuary. Duddingston claims that its main pub, *The Sheep's Heid*, is the oldest licensed premises in Scotland. It also has a fine Norman-style church, and a 17th-century house which was used by Bonnie Prince Charlie in 1745.

And on the northern slopes of the Pentland Hills lies **Swanston**, a small huddle of white-painted thatched cottages, near where the Stevenson family used to rent Swanston Cottage as a summer residence for the sickly RLS. For some odd reason, the gardens of Swanston are decorated with statuary and ornamental stonework taken from the High Kirk of St Giles when it was being "improved" in the 19th century.

The hills of Edinburgh: If there is such a creature as the Urban Mountaineer, then Edinburgh must be his or her paradise. Like Rome, the city is built on and around seven hills, none of them very high but all of them offering good stiff walks and spectacular views of the city. They are, in order of altitude, **Arthur's Seat** (823 ft/247 metres), **Braid Hill** (675 ft/203 metres), **West Craiglockhart Hill** (575 ft/173 metres), **Blackford Hill** (539 ft/162 metres), **Corstorphine Hill** (531 ft/159 metres), **Castle Hill** (435 ft/131 metres) and **Calton Hill** (328 ft/98 metres).

In addition, Edinburgh is bounded to the south by the Pentland Hills, a range of amiable mini-mountains which almost (but not quite) climb to 2,000 ft (600 metres), and which are well used by Edinburgh hill walkers, fell runners, mountain bicyclists, rock scramblers and the British Army.

Here, too, is the **Hillend Ski Centre**, which has the largest dry ski slope in Europe. Non-skiers can take the lift to the top station for magnificent panoramic views of Edinburgh and beyond to Loch Lomond.

Of the "city-centre" hills, Calton Hill at the east end of Princes Street probably offers the best view of Edinburgh. But it is **Arthur's Seat**, that crag-girt

The glory that was Edinburgh: the view from Calton Hill.

old volcano in the Queen's Park, which must count as the most startling piece of urban mountainscape. It is one of the many places in Britain named after the shadowy (and possibly apocryphal) King Arthur. But, surprisingly enough, Edinburgh has a better claim to Arthur than most other regions. The area around Edinburgh was one of the British (Welsh) kingdoms before it was overrun by the Angles and the Scots.

On the flanks of Arthur's Seat, the feeling of *rus in urbe* can be downright eerie. Dorothy Wordsworth pointed this out in 1803 when she described the old hill as being "as wild and solitary as any in the heart of the Highland mountains". And its 853 ft (260 metres) high bulk provides some steep climbing, rough scrambling and dangerous (and now illegal) rock climbing on **Salisbury Crags**. But one of the choicest experiences Edinburgh has to offer is to watch the sun go down over the mountains of the west from the top of Arthur's Seat and then descend to the darkened hillside into a sea of lights.

The outer darkness: Although Edinburgh may not have an "inner city" problem, it certainly has its "outer city" difficulties. It is ringed to the east, south and west with some of the most dreadfully depressing, crime-ridden council-housing estates in Britain, places like **Craigmillar** and **Niddrie**, **Oxgangs** and **Gilmerton**, **Pilton**, **Muirhouse** and **Wester Hailes**. Most of the people who live in these sprawling schemes were "decanted" there from the High Street, the Cowgate and Leith, and many would go back at the drop of a hat if only they could find a tolerable house they could afford to live in.

Foreign visitors are often shocked that a city with the style (and affluence) of Edinburgh tolerates such conditions. But respectable Edinburgh has long since learned to contemplate the other Edinburgh with the equanimity of Henry Jekyll seeing the face of Edward Hyde in the mirror for the first time. "I was conscious of no repugnance," Dr Jekyll says, "rather of a leap of welcome. This, too, was myself."

Colourscape created for the Edinburgh Festival.

THE WORLD'S BIGGEST ARTS FESTIVAL

When the Edinburgh International Festival explodes into life every August, the city, as the *Washington Post* once pointed out, becomes "simply the best place on Earth". Certainly the display of cultural pyrotechnics is awesome. Every concert-hall, basement-theatre and church hall in the centre of Edinburgh overflows with dance groups, theatre companies, string quartets, puppeteers, opera companies and orchestras. And for three weeks the streets of Edinburgh are awash with fire eaters, jugglers, bagpipers, clowns, warblers, satirists and theatrical hopefuls of every shape, size and colour.

All of which is a distant cry from the dead and dreary days after World War II when the idea of the festival was hatched by Sir John Falconer, then Lord Provost of Edinburgh, Harry Harvey Wood of the British Council, and Rudolf Bing, the festival's first artistic director. The notion was, said the novelist Eric Linklater, "the triumph of elegance over drab submission to the penalties of emerging victorious from a modern war".

Today 180,000 people buy tickets for the main events, a figure which doesn't include the 80,000 or so who troop into the (free) art shows or the thousands who pack the "esplanade" of Edinburgh Castle every night to relish the stunning (if occasionally somewhat sinister) glamour of the Edinburgh Military Tattoo. Not that it has been all plain sailing: there has been much wrangling with the Scottish Arts Council over money, and bickering with the Edinburgh District Council over the "elitism" of the Edinburgh Festival Society, the festival's ruling body.

During the 1980s artistic director Frank Dunlop sounded off regularly about upstart arts festivals trying to "poach" Edinburgh's hard-won commercial sponsors. In fact, in spite of relatively small loans, the Edinburgh Festival is now doing very nicely out of big business, and box office takings are running at over £1 million. This sounds a lot; but, as Dunlop said, "no major festival in the world has to make do with as little money as Edinburgh does. Salzburg gets 10 times as much public money."

Dunlop felt that he broke down the élitism that often cocoons culture. His successor, Brian McMaster, says: "Elitist I'm certainly not. Having worked in opera, which suffers from that label, I've always had to break that down. And populist? If it means patronising, then No."

Edinburgh's "other" festival, the Festival Fringe (which also began in 1947) has become a behemoth – so big, in fact, that it is in real danger of outgrowing the city. In 1992 the 539 companies on the Festival Fringe staged more than 10,650 performances of 1,129 shows in 149 venues all over the city. Over the years it's been a nursery for new talent: Maggie Smith, Tom Stoppard, Rowan Atkinson, Billy Connolly and Emma Thompson all made their entrance into the business on the Festival Fringe.

Nor is that all. On the fringe of the Fringe (as it were) there is also a Television Festival (full of heavyweight discussions about the Role Of The Media), a Film Festival (which gets many a good movie long before London), a Book Festival (staged every two years), and a Jazz Festival (staged in just about every pub in the city centre). ∎

Face at the Festival Fringe.

THE BORDERS

"When you pass the *Welcome to Scotland* sign, just press on." That, at least, is how received wisdom goes, the accompanying assumption being that, compared with all those northerly lochs and glens, rushing rivers and barren moors, the Borders have only borderline appeal.

In reality the region is much more magnificent than the name suggests. The Borders (administratively, it includes the four "shires" of Peebles and Berwick in the north and Selkirk and Roxburgh in the south) comprises one of Europe's last unspoilt areas.

There are castles here, barren moorland, ruined abbeys, baronial mansions, historic houses and evidence of past turbulent struggles against the English that give the region a romance all of its own. It even has a loch. And, when it comes to rushing rivers, you can't do better than the Tweed, which has inspired romantic Borders ballads for hundreds of years and was held by the novelist Sir Walter Scott to be the most precious river in the world. The Tweed, also noted for its salmon, has its source in the Borders and cuts right through three of the most important Border towns: Peebles, Melrose and Kelso.

Quiet beginnings: Directly south of Edinburgh, **Peebles** owes much of its charm to its Tweedside location. Here the river already runs wide and fast. Peebles' central throughfare is equally wide but much more sedate. The town was never renowned for its hustle and bustle: an 18th-century aristocrat coined an ungenerous simile: "As quiet as the grave – or Peebles". While each June things liven up considerably with the week-long Beltane festival, during the rest of the year Peebles is still a quiet introduction to the Borders and offers a wide variety of good accommodation: attractions usually recommended to visitors owe their origins to either religion or dictionaries.

The **Cross Kirk**, was erected in 1261 after the discovery of a large cross on

this site. The remains include a large 15th-century tower and foundations of cloister and monastic buildings. St Andrew's Collegiate Church, the fore-runner to the Cross Kirk, sits in a cemetery on the Glasgow road. Here, too, only a tower remains; the remainder was burnt by the English at the time of the sacking of the four great Border abbeys. At the bottom of Peebles High Street, the Gothic outline of Peebles Parish Church adds to the town's air of sobriety.

The **Chambers Institute**, Peebles's civic centre and museum, was a gift to the place from William Chambers, a native of the place and the founding publisher of Chambers Encyclopedia.

Following the Tweed: Just a few minutes out of Peebles (west on the A72), perched high on a rocky bluff overlooking the Tweed, **Neidpath Castle**, a well preserved example of the many medieval Tower Houses in the region, offers more excitement. Wordsworth visited in 1803 and wrote a famous poem lamenting the desolation caused in 1795 when the absentee landowner, the 4th

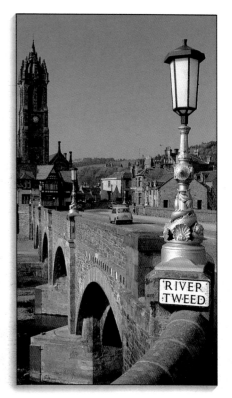

Duke of Queensberry, cut down all the trees for money to support his extravagant London lifestyle.

Wordsworth would have been happier had he journeyed 8 miles (13 km) southwest of Peebles on the B712 to **Dawyck Botanic Gardens**, an outstation of Edinburgh's Royal Botanic Garden which contains a fine collection of mature specimen trees, many over 100 years old. In fact, the earliest record of tree planting here dates back to 1680.

Continue on the B712 to **Broughton**, the site of Broughton Place, an imposing castillian house that looks as if it was built centuries ago: it was in fact designed this century. Inside, Broughton Gallery has a fine collection of work by British artists and craftsmen for sale. John Buchan, author of the best-selling *The Thirty Nine Steps*, grew up in this village. In later life he wrote that he "liked Broughton better than any place in the world". Just south of the village, the **John Buchan Centre** is a small museum that paints a detailed picture of a man who led a varied and distinguished life which eventually saw him become Governor General of Canada.

Buchan also liked the **Crook Inn**, just outside **Tweedsmuir**, a few miles south of Broughton. One of the oldest Border inns, it has strong literary associations. Robert Burns was inspired to write his poem "*Willie Wastle's Wife*" in the kitchen (now the bar). Sir Walter Scott used to visit here, as did his lesser known contemporary James Hogg, the poet known locally as "The Ettrick Shepherd". Buchan was born nearby and took his title of Baron of Tweedsmuir from this parish.

The source of the Tweed is just a few miles south of the village of Tweedsmuir. The two highest points in the Borders, Broad Law and Dollar Law rise to more than 2,750 ft (840 metres) and 2,680 ft (820 metres) respectively. If it's rugged moorland and craggy terrain you're after, you won't find much better outside the Scottish Highlands. Draw a line between Hawick and Broughton and then stay south of it and you'll see the best the Borders has to offer. A popular route is the side-road

out of Tweedsmuir up to the **Talla** and **Megget Reservoirs**. Steep slopes and rock-strewn hillsides provide a stunning panorama as you twist and turn your way down to the A708, where, to the south, you reach another favourite spot: **St Mary's Loch**, the only loch in the Borders region.

Step southwards outside the Borders towards Eskdalemuir, and you'll be greeted by a real surprise: the **Kagyu Samye Ling Tibetan Monastery**. This Tibetan Buddhist centre was founded in 1967 for study, retreat and meditation and incorporates Samye Temple, an authentic Tibetan Buddhist monastery in the centre's grounds. Samye Ling, which long ago threw off its "hippy" image, has received written support from David Steel, the former Liberal Party leader who lives just a few miles north. Visitors, regardless of faith, can join free tours around the centre's facilities.

Traquair House is still owned by the family that acted as hosts when Mary Queen of Scots stayed there with her husband Darnley in 1566. Its history

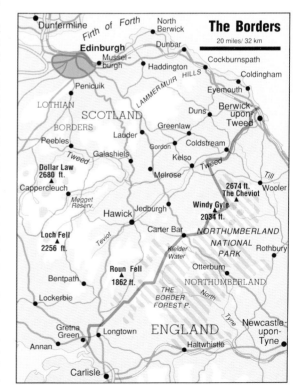

166

goes much further back; parts of it date from the 12th century. The wide avenue leading away from the house to the large gates by the main road has been disused for more than two centuries. After Bonnie Prince Charlie visited in 1745, the 5th Earl of Traquair closed the Bear Gates after him and swore they would not open until a Stuart king had been restored to the throne. Traditional ale, which may be purchased, is regularly brewed in the 18th-century alehouse.

On the road west back towards Peebles, **Kailzie Gardens** adds to the beauty of the Tweed Valley with its formal walled garden, greenhouses and woodland walks.

Heart of the Borders: Though it has little to tempt today's visitor, **Galashiels** has played a pivotal role in the Borders economy as a weaving town for more than 700 years. The world-famous Scottish College of Textiles, founded in 1909, has helped to cement the reputation of the tartans, tweeds, woollens and other knitted materials sold in the mills here. Most people understandably as-sume, therefore, that the word "tweed" was adopted by the woollen industry because of the river; in fact, it was originally a misprint – by an English publisher, naturally – for *tweels*, the Border name for woollen fabrics. Al-though the industry across the region has gone into decline, there are numer-ous working mills open to the public: **Peter Anderson of Scotland** in Hud-dersfield Street, which holds conducted tours and features a textiles museum, is one of the most popular.

It's not only Galashiels that lets you sample the Borders' textiles. Tourism has fashioned the **Borders Woollen Trail**, which includes eight other towns involved in this industry. One of them, **Selkirk**, became a textile centre in the 19th century only when the growing demand for tweed could no longer be met by the mills of Galashiels. Like Galashiels, Selkirk's manufacturing background leaves little for you to en-joy other than shopping for tweeds and woollens. The one exception is 18th-century **Haliwell's House**, an old iron-

Left, parade at Traquair House. **Right**, peace at Samye Ling Monastery.

mongers that is now a small museum telling the story of Selkirk in entertaining detail.

Don't leave the locality without visiting **Bowhill House**. Dating from 1812, Bowhill has for eight generations been the home of the Scotts of Buccleuch and Queensberry, once one of the largest landowners of all the Border clans. More than 300 years of discerning art collecting has resulted in a collection that includes works by Canaletto, Guardi, Leonardo, Reynolds and Gainsborough.

If the Borders have a sort of visitors' Mecca, then **Abbotsford House**, home of Sir Walter Scott from 1811 to 1832, undoubtedly lays claim to that title, and nobody can really claim to have "done" this part of Scotland unless they pay homage to the man and his home. Scott spent £50,000 and the rest of his life turning a small farm into an estate that could do justice to his position as a Border laird. Yet Abbotsford is not visited for its architecture; Ruskin said the house was "the most incongruous pile that gentlemanly modernism ever de-signed". People come instead to enjoy its baronial, literary and magnificently preserved interior. All of the Waverley novels were written here, though Scott didn't admit to being the author until 1827, feeling that it wasn't "decorous" of a Clerk of Session at Selkirk to be seen writing novels. This is just one detail in the long and fascinating account of Scott's rise to fame and celebrity status, his financial ruin and his final days at Abbotsford, all colourful chapters that make for a highly romantic story in themselves.

Scott was buried at **Dryburgh**, one of the four great 12th-century abbeys in the Borders. While the ruins at Jedburgh, Kelso and Melrose lie near the edge of their respective towns, Dryburgh, founded by Hugh de Morville for monks from Alnwick in Northumberland, is tucked away in an idyllic location among trees by the edge of the Tweed. Until 1544, Dryburgh referred to an important town as well as the Abbey. Both suffered a violent and fiery end (as did the three other Border abbeys) on the orders of

Dryburgh Abbey: a brooding reminder of a bloody history.

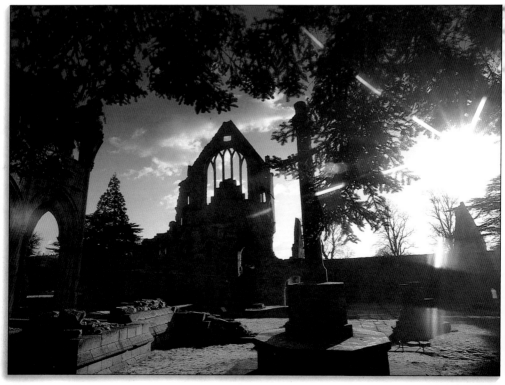

Henry VIII, who was intent on orchestrating a marriage between the infant Queen Mary and his own son Edward.

Dryburgh's setting is no match for **Scott's View**, which offers a sweeping view of the unmistakeable triple peaks of the **Eildon Hills** (reputed to be the legendary sleeping place of King Arthur and his knights) and a wide stretch of the Tweed Valley. Scott came here many times to enjoy the panorama. When his mile-long funeral cortege was on its way from Abbotsford to Dryburgh, it is said the horses stopped at this point of their own accord.

The town of **Melrose** escaped much of the industralisation that affected Selkirk, Hawick and Galashiels and is more attractive because of it. **Melrose Abbey** seals the town's pedigree. It even accounts for the beginning of Sir Walter Scott's rise to fame, for it was eloquently described in *The Lay of the Last Minstrel*, the great narrative poem of 1805 that made him famous. The Abbey was founded in 1136 by King David I, who founded all four of the great Border abbeys, and was the first Cistercian monastery in Scotland. Tragically it lay in the path of repeated English invasions long before Henry VIII made his presence felt in the 16th century. An attack in 1322 by Edward II prompted Robert Bruce to fund its restoration. Bruce's heart, it is said, was buried near the high altar, though subsequent excavation has failed to locate any trace of it.

North of Melrose, on the outskirts of **Lauder**, is **Thirlestaine Castle**, once the seat of the Earls of Lauderdale. One of Scotland's oldest and finest castles, it was built on a 12th-century foundation and today houses an impressive collection of furniture and paintings as well as some renowned 17th-century plaster ceilings. Local enthusiasts were responsible for the castle's **Border Country Life Museum**, an exhibition on the history of Borders agriculture.

Roman reminders: Historically, **Jedburgh** is the most important of the Border towns. It was also strategically important; as the first community across

the border it frequently received the full brunt of invading English armies. Earlier invaders came from even more distant lands than the English. Two miles north of Jedburgh it is possible to follow the course of Dere Street, the road the Romans built in southern Scotland more than 1,900 years ago.

The most ancient surviving building, **Jedburgh Abbey**, was founded in 1138 by Augustinian canons from northern France. Stonework in the abbey's museum dates from the first millennium AD and proves that the site had much older religious significance. Malcolm IV was crowned here and Alexander III married his second wife in the abbey in 1285. Legend tells of a ghostly figure appearing at the wedding feast in nearby Jedburgh Castle prophesying the death of the King and disaster for Scotland. Alexander died the following year and Scotland from then on suffered the centuries of strife that accompanied the struggle to find a new Scottish king.

The castle at which Alexander confronted the prophetic spectre occupied a site in Castlegate. It was demolished in 1409 to keep it out of English hands. In 1823 the **Castle Gaol** was built on the old castle's foundations; its museum of social history is well worth a visit.

Near the High Street, display panels and artefacts in **Mary Queen of Scots' House** tell a short but crucial chapter in Scotland's history. It was in this house in late 1566 that Queen Mary spent several weeks recovering from serious illness (at one point she was left for dead) after her renowned dash on horseback to Hermitage Castle to see her injured lover James Hepburn, Earl of Bothwell. Her ride resulted in scandal that was made all the worse by the murder of her husband Darnley in the following February. From there on, her downfall was steady. Years later, during her 19 years of imprisonment, Mary Queen of Scots regretted that her life hadn't ended in the Borders before her many misfortunes: "Would that I had died at Jedburgh."

If you decide to retrace Mary's footsteps to Hermitage Castle, you're more

Old money: the Duke of Roxburgh at home in Floors Castle.

than likely to pass through **Hawick** (pronounced *Hoik*). The Borders' textile industry is all around you here. World-famous knitwear and clothing brand names are emblazoned boldly above factory gates, while at the **Hawick Museum** in **Wilton Lodge Park** a fascinating collection of exhibits picks up older sartorial threads.

Kelso and castles: Still retaining its central cobbled streets leading into a spacious square, **Kelso** is one of the most picturesque of the Border towns. Sir Walter Scott, who was a pupil at the Grammar School in the nave of the ruined abbey, wrote and spoke fondly of it. Just 100 metres from the town's centre, **Kelso Abbey**, once the largest and richest of the Borders abbeys, suffered the same fate as its counterparts at Melrose, Jedburgh and Dryburgh and is today the least complete of all of them.

It's ironic that, while the English destroyed Kelso's abbey, the Scottish were responsible for the much greater devastation of the town of **Roxburgh** and its castle. Roxburgh had grown up on the south bank of the Tweed (Kelso occupies the north bank) around the mighty fortress of Marchmount. An important link in the chain of border fortifications, Marchmount controlled the gateway to the north.

In the 14th century the English took Roxburgh and its castle and used it as a base for further incursions into Scottish territory. The fortress built for protection had begun to serve precisely the opposite purpose. In 1460 James II of Scotland attacked Marchmount but was killed by a bursting cannon. His widow urged the Scottish troops forward.

On achieving victory they destroyed Roxburgh's castle (to make sure it stayed out of enemy hands for good) with a thoroughness that the English would have found hard to match. The town itself quickly fell into decay. Today, on a mound between the Teviot and the Tweed about a mile to the west of Kelso (the plain village of Roxburgh a few miles on is no direct relation of the ancient town), only fragments of Marchmount's walls survive.

On the north bank of the Tweed, Kelso thrived, however. So far as castles go, Kelso picked itself up, brushed itself off and went one better with **Floors Castle**. The original house was designed by Robert Adam and built between 1721 and 1726. It owes its present flamboyant appearance to William Playfair who re-modelled and extended it between 1837 and 1845. An outstanding collection of German, Italian and French furniture, Chinese and Dresden porcelain, paintings by Picasso, Matisse and Augustus John, and a prized 15th-century Brussels tapestry are some of the many glittering prizes that give Floors an air of palatial elegance. Tradition has it that a holly tree in the large grounds marks the spot where James II was killed by the cannon.

Smailholm Tower stands gaunt and foreboding 6 miles (10 km) northwest of Kelso (B6404). Walter Scott made a deal with the owner of this superb 16th-century peel tower: in exchange for saving it, Scott would write a ballad – *The Eve of St John* – about it. Today, the stern-faced fortress is a museum of costume figures and tapestries relating to Scott's *Minstrelsy of the Borders*.

Outsiders could be forgiven for thinking the Borders region is too generously endowed with aristocratic art and architecture. They only have to drive 8 miles (13 km) northwest from Kelso on the A8069 to make their point. **Mellerstain House** is one of Scotland's finest Georgian mansions, the 18th-century product of the combined genius of William Adam and his son Robert. Externally it has the dignity, symmetry and well-matched proportions characteristic of this period. Inside there's furniture by Chippendale, Sheraton and Hepplewhite as well as paintings by Gainsborough, Constable, Veronese and Van Dyck, and some exquisite examples of moulded plaster ceilings, doorheads, mantelpieces and light-fittings.

As if all this weren't enough to impress, formal Italian gardens were laid out in 1909 to create a series of gently sloping terraces and the house became a popular venue for fashionable dances. If all else in the Border Country fails to whet your appetite, Mellerstain, and its neighbour Floors, are reason enough for visiting.

Border crossings: East of Kelso the Tweed marks the natural boundary between England and Scotland. **Coldstream**, one of the last towns on this river before Berwick, has little to offer the visitor other than history. The town's name was taken by the famous regiment of Coldstream Guards that was formed by General Monck in 1659 before he marched south to support the restoration of the Stuart monarchy. The regiment today loans material to the **Coldstream Museum**, set up in a house that served as Monck's headquarters.

Nearly 150 years earlier, in 1513, James IV of Scotland crossed the Tweed at Coldstream to attack the English with a much larger force. Though Henry VIII was at that time fighting in France (James IV's invasion was a diversion intended to aid the French) an English army was sent north to meet the threat. The encounter, which took place near the English village of Branxton but was known as the Battle of Flodden, was a

military disaster for Scotland: the king, his son, and as many as 46 nobles and 9,000 men were slain.

Happier endings are to be had at **Kirk Yetholm**, just yards from the English border. Overlooking the village green, the part-thatched Border Hotel bills itself as the "End of the Pennine Way". A few miles away **Lonton Kirk**, said to be the oldest building in continuous use for Christian worship in the area, sits proudly on a hummock of sand in a picturesque valley. Here the slopes rise steeply to join the Cheviots – a ridge of hills that forms another natural ingredient in the border between Scotland and England.

When it comes to identifying precise borderlines, **Berwick-upon-Tweed** can be forgiven for feeling a little confused. Boundaries around here lack a sense of fair play: Berwick is not part of Berwickshire. But there's worse to come. For, although the town takes its name from a river that has its source in the Scottish Borders, runs through their heart and even forms part of the Scottish/English border, Berwick-upon-Tweed

Mellerstain, one of Scotland's most glorious Georgian houses.

is not part of Scotland. It's in Northumberland, England.

It wasn't always like that. Berwick made its way into Scotland many times previously. For well over 300 years it was nothing less than a strategic shuttlecock. The town changed hands no fewer than 13 times between 1147 (when it was surrendered by William the Lion after his capture at the Battle of Alnwick) and 1482 (when it was finally taken for England by Richard, Duke of Gloucester – later Richard III).

Historically Berwick is very much a part of the Borders. The town's castle, built in the late 12th century by Henry II, once towered high above the Tweed. Much of it was demolished in 1847 to make space for the station, which bears an appropriate inscription by Robert Stephenson: "The Final Act Of Union". Berwick's Town Wall, built on the orders of Edward I, has fared better and is one of the most complete of its kind in Britain. Berwick still retains its medieval street plan and there are several steep, cobbled streets that are worth exploring.

Situated in Scotland, along the coast just north of Berwick, **Eyemouth** is a small, working fishing town whose museum vividly outlines Eyemouth's long tradition as a fishing port. The museum's centrepiece is the Eyemouth Tapestry, made by local people in 1981 to commemorate the Great Disaster of 1881 when 189 local fishermen were drowned, all within sight of land, during a storm.

A few miles north, **Coldingham's Medieval Priory and St Abbs' Nature Reserve** are two further justifications for making this detour off the A1 to Edinburgh. You could head inland and take another route to Edinburgh: the A68. If you do, make a point of stopping at **Manderston House**, just outside Duns, to enjoy what has been dubbed "the finest Edwardian country house in Scotland". Each of the 36 bells in the servants' quarters has a different tone, and the cacophony must have been deafening when the servants were summoned to clean the silver staircase, the only one in the world.

Hallowe'en trick-or-treat for children in Berwickshire.

THE SOUTH-WEST

It's often said that the substantial island of **Arran**, in the Firth of Clyde, represents a topographical microcosm of Scotland: "Scotland in miniature," say its publicists. It has highlands, lowlands, coast (of course), its own offshore island and a handsome castle. But Arran's character is exclusively rural, with an economy rooted in agriculture, forestry and tourism. A more appropriate scaled-down version of modern Scotland can be found on the nearby mainland, between the great estuaries of Clyde and Solway.

In the landscape and seascapes of South-west Scotland, in the pretty villages of Dumfries and Galloway and the hill farms of south Lanarkshire, in the industrial townships of Ayrshire and the ports and holiday resorts of the Clyde coast you will find something of the rest of Scotland. All that is missing, perhaps, is the intimidating grandeur of the West

Preceding pages, interior of **Culzean Castle.** **Left**, the castle's exterior.

Highlands. The **Galloway Hills** are lonely, lovely places in their own right, but none rises to more than 2,800 ft (850 metres). The South-west is altogether a kindlier country, yet with a Covenanting history whose sometimes brutal nature belies the comeliness of the land, and with a dense concentration of literary associations.

Travellers from England often bypass the rewarding littoral of the Solway with its pastoral hinterland in their scamper up the grim A74 to points north and the Highlands, hesitating only at a name which is legendary for rather trivial reasons. **Gretna Green**, just over the Border (until the boundary between England and Scotland was agreed in 1552, this area was known simply as the Debatable Land) became celebrated for celebrating marriages. It was the first available community where eloping couples from England could take advantage of Scotland's different marriage laws. Many a makeshift ceremony was performed at the **Old Smithy**, which is now a museum, and, although seldom pursued by horse-whipping fathers, many a romantic bride still chooses to be married at Gretna Green today.

The Burns legend: A few miles farther north is the village of **Ecclefechan**, where the pretty white **Arched House** in which Thomas Carlyle was born in 1795 is now a modest literary shrine. (The man of letters, who was soon to make a dazzling reputation for himself in London, returned to South-west Scotland for a brief, bleak period of farming at Craigenputtock, on the moors above Moniaive). But the South-west is more inescapably identified with the poet Robert Burns, whose life and legend remains one of the main props of Scottish tourism.

The urban epicentres of the Burns industry are Dumfries and Ayr. **Dumfries** is also "the Queen of the South", an ancient and important Border town whose remaining character survives the unsightly housing estates and factories on its periphery, and which is within easy striking distance of the haunting, history-rich Solway coast. Burns, the farmer-poet, took over Ellisland Farm

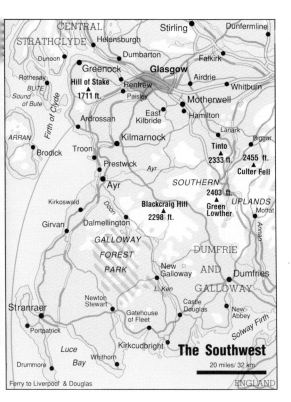

The Southwest

20 miles/ 32 km

some 6 miles (10 km) outside the town in 1788, built the farmhouse and tried to introduce new farming methods. His venture collapsed and he moved to Dumfries to become an exciseman, but the farm where he wrote *Tam o' Shanter* and *Auld Lang Syne* is now a museum – as is the house in Mill Vennel (now Burns Street), Dumfries, where he died in 1796. His first home in the town was a three-room flat in the Wee Vennel (now Bank Street), which Burns rechristened Stinking Vennel, but it isn't open to the public.

To bring it all together, visit the stone mill on the River Nith. This is home to the **Robert Burns Centre**, the major feature of the Scottish Tourist Board's Burns Heritage Trail. Then adjourn for a drink at the **Globe Inn**, where you can sit in the poet's favourite chair.

The handsome waterfront of the **River Nith**, with its 15th-century bridge, and the red sandstone dignity of nearby **St Michael's Church**, in whose churchyard Burns is buried, give Dumfries its distinctive character. Its environs have just as much to offer. On opposing banks of the Nith estuary, where it debouches into the Solway, are **Caerlaverock Castle and National Nature Reserve** (winter haunt of wildfowl) and **Sweetheart Abbey**.

The castle, strikingly well-preserved, dates back to the 13th century and was the seat of the Maxwell family, later Earls of Nithsdale – one of the most powerful local dynasties. It was besieged by Edward I during the Wars of Independence and in 1640 fell to a 13-week siege mounted by the Covenanters.

The graceful ruin of **Sweetheart Abbey**, in the pretty village of New Abbey, is a monument to the marital devotion of the noble Devorguilla Balliol, who not only founded this Cistercian abbey in 1273 but founded Balliol College, Oxford, in memory of her husband. She also carried his heart around her until her own death in 1290, when she and the heart were buried together in front of the high altar.

Good beaches: The shallow estuary of the Solway has some notoriety for the

Sculptures by Rodin (**left**) and Henry Moore gaze from Shawhead towards nearby Dumfries.

speed of its tidal race and the treachery of its sands, but the hazardous areas are well signposted and if you follow the coastal roads from River Nith to **Loch Ryan** you will find an amiable, undemanding succession of villages, yachting harbours, attractive small towns and good beaches marred only by the ubiquitous caravan parks; not to mention many secret coves and snug, deserted little bays available to those who can use their feet.

This is the ancient territory of Galloway, whose people once fraternised with the Norse raiders who settled on the coast and whose lords preserved a degree of independence from the Scottish crown until the 13th century. Many of Scotland's great names and great causes have seen action among the hills and bays of Galloway. At **Dundrennan Abbey**, 7 miles (11 km) southeast of Kirkcudbright on the A711, Mary Queen of Scots is believed to have spent her last night in Scotland, on 15 May 1568, sheltering in this 12th-century Cistercian house on her final, fatal flight from the Battle of Langside to her long imprisonment in England.

Kirkcudbright (pronounced *Kir-koo-bree*), at the mouth of the River Dee, has the reputation of being the most attractive of the Solway towns, with a colourful waterfront (much appreciated and colonised by artists) and an elegant Georgian town centre. Little remains of the Kirkcudbright which took its name from the vanished Kirk of Cuthbert (which once played host to the saint's bones) but it has a **Market Cross** of 1610 and a **Tolbooth** from the same period which entertained John Paul Jones. He was imprisoned for the manslaughter of his ship's carpenter, who had died after a flogging but he went on to take the credit for laying the foundations of the American navy.

Ten miles (16 km) northeast from Kirkcudbright is another neat and dignified little town, **Castle Douglas**, which stands on the small loch of Carlingwark, where you will find one of the most formidable tower strongholds in Scotland. **Threave Castle** was built towards

Keeping the telephones in working order in the rural south-west.

the end of the 14th century by the wonderfully named Archibald the Grim, third Earl of Douglas, and was the last Douglas castle to surrender to James II during the conflict between the king and the maverick Border family. It also has associations with the Covenanters, who seized it in 1640 and vandalised the interior. (Like all men of God, they had their violent moments.)

Gourmet's Galloway: It's worth mentioning, for the benefit of self-caterers, that Castle Douglas has some of the best food shops in Scotland, particularly butchers' shops, as it serves as market centre to a large tract of Galloway's rural hinterland. Here you will find villages unusually pretty for a country which isn't famous for the aesthetics of its small communities. Their characteristic feature is whitewashed walls with black-bordered doors and windows – as if they have taken their colour scheme from the black and white Belted Galloway cattle.

Many of the most pleasant villages – **New Galloway**, **Balmaclellan**, **Crossmichael** – are in the region of long, skinny **Loch Ken**, which feeds the River Dee; while to the west, shrouding the hills to the very shoulders of the isolated **Rhinns of Kells**, a tableland of hills around 2,600 ft (800 metres), is the massive Galloway Forest Park, 150,000 acres (60,000 hectares) criss-crossed by dull Forestry Commission trails.

Despite the conifers, you *can* sometimes see something interesting for the trees: **Clatteringshaws Loch**, 12 miles (19 km) north of Newton Stewart (a "planned town" built in the late 17th century by a son of the Earl of Galloway) on the A712 is the site of the **Galloway Deer Museum**. It will not only improve your knowledge of the habits of the Red Deer but will alert you to the range of the area's natural history.

Nearby, **Bruce's Stone** represents the site of the Battle of Rapploch Moss, a minor affair of 1307 but one in which the energetic Robert the Bruce routed the English. There are, in fact, two Bruce's stones in **Galloway Forest Park**, which creeps within reach of the coast at Turnberry, where he may have been born. The second stone – reached only if one backtracks from Newton Stewart and then travels northwest for 10 miles (16 km) on the A714 before taking an unmarked road to the west – is poised on a bluff above Loch Trool, at the heart of the park, and recalls those hefted down the hill by the hero in another successful wrangle with the English. Below is a sombre landmark: the **Memorial Tomb** of six Covenanters murdered at prayer. It is a simple stone which records their names and the names of their killers.

Back on the coast, the A75 between benign **Gatehouse of Fleet** and **Creetown**, which hugs the sea below the comely outriders of the distinctive hill **Cairnsmore of Fleet**, was said by Thomas Carlyle to be the most beautiful road in Scotland. This was very much a subjective judgement, and considered something of a Scottish slight to Queen Victoria, who posed the question hoping for a reference to her favoured Deeside. But it's certainly an agreeable road, with views across **Wigtown Bay** to the flat green shelf which was the cradle of Scottish Christianity.

Saints and stones: On the other side of the bay is the pleasant town of Wigtown, whose **Martyrs' Monument** is one of the most eloquent and moving testaments to the Covenanters, who were heroically supported in the Southwest; the site of the stake where in 1685 two women, one elderly and one young, were left to drown on the estuary flats.

On the promontory south of Wigtown, the coast becomes harsher and the villages bleaker, as if it indeed required the gentling influence of Christianity. **Whithorn** is the birthplace of Christianity in Scotland, and at the **Whithorn Dig** in the centre of the town the first known Christian church in Britain, built by St Ninian around the year 400, was recently uncovered. Next to the Dig is the **Priory** where Mary Queen of Scots once stayed. Here you will find the Latinus Stone of 450, the earliest Christian memorial in Scotland, as well as a significant collection of early Christian crosses and stones.

Four miles (6 km) away is the misnamed **Isle of Whithorn**, a delightful town built around a busy yachting harbour and with more St Ninian connections: there is the ruined **St Ninian's Chapel**, which dates from 1300 and may have been used by overseas pilgrims; and along the coast is **St Ninian's Cave**, said to have been used by the saint as an oratory.

A little inland from the undistinguished shoreline of Luce Bay, playground of the Ministry of Defence, are some relics of the Iron Age and Bronze Age, including **Torhouse Stone Circle**, a ring of 19 boulders standing on a low mound. The most impressive sight in this corner, however, is **Glenluce Abbey**, a handsome vaulted ruin of the 12th century where, says legend, Michael Scott the Wizard lived in the 13th century and where he lured the plague, which was then raging, to trap it in a vault.

Resort towns: From Glenuce the traveller crosses the "handle" of that hammer of land called the **Rhinns of Galloway**, the south-west extremity of Scotland terminating in the 200-ft (60-metre) high cliffs of the Mull of Galloway, from which Ireland seems within touching distance. At the head of the deep cleft of **Loch Ryan** is the port of **Stranraer**, market centre for the rich agricultural area, modest holiday resort and Scotland's main seaway to Northern Ireland. The Rhinns' other main resort is **Portpatrick**, and among the somewhat limited attractions of this remote peninsula are two horticultural ones; the sub-tropical plants of **Logan Botanic Garden** and the great monkey puzzle trees of **Castle Kennedy Gardens**, near Stranraer.

Stranraer's trunk roads are the A75, infamous for the volume of heavy traffic disembarking from the ferries from Ireland, which strikes west to Dumfries and points south and blights Thomas Carlyle's "loveliest stretch" between Creetown and Gatehouse of Fleet; and the A77, which conducts you north past the cliffs of **Ballantrae** (*not* the Ballantrae of R.L. Stevenson's novel) to the mixed pleasures of Ayrshire and,

Cattle auction at Newton Stewart, a busy market town in Wigtownshire.

THE PLOUGHMAN POET

Few poets could hope to have their birthday celebrated in the most unexpected parts of the world 200 years after their death. Yet the observance of Burns Night, on 25 January, goes from strength to strength. It marks the birth in 1759 of Scotland's national poet, Robert Burns, one of seven children born to a poor Ayrshire farmer. It was an unpromising beginning, yet today Burns's verses are familiar in every English-speaking country (with the exception of England) and are especially popular in Russia, where Burns Nights is toasted in vodka. He has even appeared on a postage stamp in Romania.

Millions who have never heard of Burns have, at some celebration or another, joined hands and sung his words to the tune of that international anthem of good intentions, *Auld Lang Syne* (dialect for "old long ago"):

> *Should auld acquaintance be forgot,*
> *And never brought to mind?*
> *Should auld acquaintance be forgot,*
> *And days o' auld lang syne?*

This was one of many traditional Scottish songs which he collected and rewrote, in addition to his original poetry. He could and did write easily in 18th-century English as well as in traditional Scots dialect (which, even in those days, had to be accompanied by a glossary). His subjects ranged from love songs (*Oh, my luve's like a red, red rose*) and sympathy for a startled fieldmouse (*Wee, sleekit, cowrin', tim'rous beastie*) to a stirring sense of Scottishness (*Scots, wha hae wi' Wallace bled*) and a simple celebration of the common people (*A man's a man for a' that*).

The key to Burns's high standing in Scotland is that, like Sir Walter Scott, he promoted the idea of Scottish nationhood at a time when it was in danger of being obliterated by the English. His acceptance abroad, especially in Russia, stems from his championing of the rights of ordinary men and women and his satirical attack on double standards in both church and state.

An attractive and gregarious youth, Burns had a long series of amorous entanglements and, once famous, took full advantage of his acceptance into Edinburgh's high society. Living life to excess did little for his health but seems to have been a source of poetic inspiration. Finally, he married Jean Armour, from his own village, and settled on a poor farm at Ellisland, near Dumfries.

No more able than his father to make a decent living from farming, he moved to Dumfries in 1791 to work as an Excise Officer. It was a secure job, and riding 200 miles (320 km) a week on horseback around the countryside on his duties gave him time and inspiration to compose prolifically. His affairs continued: the niece of a Dumfries innkeeper became pregnant, but died during childbirth. Four years later, Burns too was dead, of rheumatic heart disease. He was 37.

The 612 copies of his first edition of 34 poems sold in Kilmarnock in 1786 for three shillings (15p); today each will fetch £10,000. Almost 100,000 people in more than 20 countries belong to Burns clubs and the poet's enduring popularity embraces the unlikeliest of locations. The story is told, for example, of a black gentleman who rose to propose a toast at a Burns Night supper in Fiji. "You may be surprised to learn that Scottish blood flows in my veins," he declared. "But it is true. One of my ancestors ate a Presbyterian missionary." ■

Burns, pictured at Alloway.

ultimately, the edge of the Glasgow conurbation. It, too, is a busy road, giving early intimations of a return to urban life, and it takes you to the heart of Burns country.

En route, you will encounter the pleasant resort of **Girvan**, first of a series of resorts interspersed with ports and industrial towns which stretches to the mouth of the Clyde. Ten miles offshore is a chunky granite monolith over 1,000 ft (300 metres) high – the uninhabited island of **Ailsa Craig**, sometimes called Paddy's Milestone for its central position between Belfast and Glasgow.

Here, too, you begin to see more clearly the mountains of Arran and the lower line of the Kintyre peninsula, while at **Turnberry**, a mecca for golfers and site of some fragments of castle which promotes itself as the birthplace of Robert the Bruce, there is a choice of roads to Ayr.

The coast road (A719) invites you to one of the non-Burnsian showpieces of Ayrshire – **Culzean Castle**, magnificently designed by Robert Adam, built between 1772 and 1792 for the Kennedy family, now owned by the National Trust for Scotland and, with its country park of 560 acres (226 hectares) – the first in Scotland – open to the public. Transatlantic visitors are entertained by the **Eisenhower Presentation**, which recalls the flat presented to the General for his private use for life. A few miles beyond Culzean the road entertains drivers at the **Electric Brae**, where an optical illusion suggests you are going downhill when in fact you are going up.

The inland road (A77) takes you through the village of **Kirkoswald**, where Burns went to school, and the first of the cluster of Burns shrines and museums: **Soutar Johnnie's Cottage**, once the home of the cobbler who was the original of Soutar Johnnie in *Tam o' Shanter*. The B7024 then conducts you to the Mecca of Burns pilgrims, the village of **Alloway**, where he was born. Here, amid the usual visitor and "interpretation" centres, you can pick up the **Burns Heritage Trail** and visit in quick succession: Burns Cottage, Alloway

Burns characters converse eternally at Soutar Johnnie's Cottage.

Kirk (where his father is buried and which features critically in *Tam o' Shanter*), the pretentious Burns Monument (a neo-Classical temple) and the 13th-century **Brig o' Doon**, whose single span permitted Tam o' Shanter to escape from the witches.

You are now on the doorstep of **Ayr** – unsurpassed, according to Burns, "for honest men and bonnie lasses" – which is the principal resort of the Clyde coast and a busy, bustling centre at any time of the year. It has associations, too, with the warrior-partriot William Wallace, who was born not that far away at **Elderslie**, near Paisley, and who was once imprisoned in Ayr. (**Paisley**, incidentally, is worth a visit for its abbey and art galleries, which house a celebrated collection of Paisley shawls.)

Inland from Ayr, to the west and north, is another clutch of Burns associations: the village of **Mauchline**, where he married Jean Armour and where their cottage is now yet another museum; and **Poosie Nansie's Tavern**, the ale-house (still a pub) which in-

spired part of his cantata *The Jolly Beggars*. Nearby at **Failford** is Highland Mary's Monument, which allegedly marks the spot where Burns said farewell to the doomed Mary Campbell, who died before they could marry; while the sprawling, cheerless industrial town of **Kilmarnock** also claims intimacy with Burns, who published the first edition of his poems there in 1786. A hundred years later the town built him a monument, which contains – no prizes for guessing – yet more Burns material.

The A77 from Kilmarnock – that road which began life in Stranraer – takes you straight to the heart of Glasgow. But, if you are island or Highland bound, you should return to the coast. Between the industrial port and new town of **Irvine** – which is the home of the **Scottish Maritime Museum** and whose **Magnum Centre** claims to be Scotland's largest leisure centre – and the increasingly desolate shipbuilding town of **Greenock** are various ferry points for the Clyde islands and the Cowal peninsula. South of Irvine are two golfing resorts, **Troon** and **Prestwick**.

Ardrossan serves the island of **Arran**, the ferries disembarking passengers and cars at **Brodick**, the capital. Arran is popular with walkers and climbers (the sharp profile of the Arran ridge, which reaches 2,866 ft/860 metres at the elegant summit of Goatfell, provides some challenging scrambles) and even unenthusiastic pedestrians will find the 2 miles (3 km) from Brodick's attractive harbour to **Brodick Castle** congenial and effortless. The castle, parts of which date from the 14th century, is the ancient seat of the dukes of Hamilton and, with its country park, is open to the public. It contains various paintings and *objets d'art* from the collections of the dukes, and its woodland garden justly claims to be one of the finest rhododendron gardens in Britain.

Arran's other main villages are **Lochranza**, **Blackwaterfoot**, **Whiting Bay** and **Lamlash**, where a precipitous offshore island spans the mouth of Lamlash Bay. **Holy Island** owes its name to St Molaise, who lived and meditated in a cave on its west coast.

Brodick Castle on Arran: art inside, flowers outside.

The other Clyde islands regularly served by ferry are **Bute**, with its attractive, ancient capital **Rothesay**, and **Great Cumbrae**, with the family resort of **Millport**. The amiable little island of Great Cumbrae is reached from **Largs**, the most handsome of the Clyde resorts and the scene, in 1263, of a battle which conclusively repelled persistent Viking attempts to invade Scotland when the forces of Alexander III defeated those of Haakon, King of Norway.

Rothesay was once the premier destination for day trippers on the Clyde paddle steamers which took Glaswegians "doon the water" from the heart of their city, and is still a popular resort despite the mass exodus to the Mediterranean every Glasgow Fair holiday. It's a Royal burgh which gives the title of Duke to the Prince of Wales, and the ruin of its unusual castle with four round towers dates back to the early 13th century, when it was stormed by the Norsemen soon to be routed at Largs.

Bute is a comely, undemanding island with no great heights to scale, but provides its own spectacle at the narrow **Kyles of Bute**, where the northern end of the island almost closes the gap with the Cowal peninsula. But the ferry crossing is from **Wemyss Bay**, between Largs and Gourock – from where you can also board a ferry for Dunoon and the Cowal peninsula.

For many people in west central Scotland, the **Cowal peninsula** represents Highland escapism. It has a new population of second home-owners from the Glasgow conurbation, which makes it busy during weekends and holidays, despite the time it takes to negotiate its long fissures of sea-lochs (**Loch Fyne** to the west and **Loch Long** to the east, with several others in between). **Dunoon** is its capital, another ancient township turned holiday resort with another 13th-century castle, of which only remnants remain on **Castle Hill**, where you will again meet Highland Mary. Close by is the **Holy Loch**, which achieved fame as host to an American naval base.

First resort: West of Gare Loch (not to be confused with Gairloch in the north-

Lochranza, one of Arran's villages.

west), the Clyde begins to be compressed between the once-great shipbuilding banks of **Clydeside**, with the first of its resort towns on the north bank at **Helensburgh**, now more a stately dormitory for Glasgow. Those smitten with "Mackintoshismus" will wish to visit here the **Hill House**, Charles Rennie Mackintosh's finest domestic commission.

Industrial **Dumbarton** is even closer to the city and its name confirms it has been there since the days of the Britons. Its spectacular lump of rock was their fort, and supports a 13th-century castle which has close connections with – inevitably – Mary Queen of Scots.

The eastern edge of South-west Scotland is dominated – some might say intimidated – by the A74, the frenzied dual-carriageway which is Glasgow's access to the Border and England. Yet this unpleasant road is carved through some of the shapeliest hills in Scotland, with some lovely, lonely places and unexpected treasures tucked away in their folds.

The briefest of detours will bring you

to **Moffat**, an elegant little town which was once a minor spa and has the broadest main street in Scotland. On to the **Devil's Beef Tub**, a vast, steep, natural vat in the hills where Border raiders used to hide stolen cattle.

Nearby is the **Grey Mare's Tail**, a waterfall which drops 200 ft (60 metres) from a hanging valley. Here, too, is **Tibbie Sheil's Inn**, the meeting place of the renowned writer James Hogg (the "Ettrick Shepherd") and friends.

On either side of the A74, a few miles driving on suddenly silent roads will take you to the highest villages in Scotland (**Leadhills** and **Wanlockhead**, once centres of lead, gold and silver mining), glorious Drumlanrig Castle, a home of the Dukes of Buccleuch and Queensberry, the historic market town of Lanark and the social experiments of Robert Owen at New Lanark, and the lush orchards and dramatic falls of the River Clyde.

Drumlanrig Castle and Country Park is reached by descending the gloomy, precipitous **Dalveen Pass**, a natural stairway between the uplands of South Lanarkshire and the rolling pastures and exquisite broadleaf woodland of Dumfriesshire. It is a palace of pink sandstone fashioned in late 17th-century Renaissance style on the site of an earlier Douglas stronghold and near a Roman fort. The first Duke of Queensberry, for whom it was built, was so horrified by its cost that he spent only one night in it. Its rich collection of French furniture and Dutch paintings (Holbein and Rembrandt are represented) includes interesting relics of Prince Charles Edward Stuart, and its benign parkland offers an exciting adventure playground for children.

Bigger and Biggar: The A74's tributary to **Lanark** skirts the perfect breast of **Tinto Hill**, the highest in Lanarkshire, much-climbed and much-loved by Lanarkshire schoolchildren who traditionally carry stones to add to the enormous cairn which now forms the hill's nipple.

Biggar is a lively and rewarding little town, with an active museum life focusing on local history as if in defiance of the greater celebrity of its big neigh-

Largs: the Clyde resorts are magnets for Glasgow holidaymakers.

bour, **Lanark**. The high, handsome old Royal burgh was already important in the 10th century, when a parliament was held there, but is more closely identified with the origins of William Wallace's rebellion against the English. Wallace is said to have lived in the Castlegate and hidden in a cave in the Cartland Craigs, just below the town, after killing an English soldier in a brawl. When he heard that his wife had been murdered he attacked the English garrison with a band of friends, who became his first army of resistance against the invaders.

Lanark was also a Convenanting centre and is still a place of great character, much of it due to its weekly livestock market and the steep fall of the Clyde below the town at **New Lanark**, Scotland's most impressive memorial to the Industrial Revolution which has been honoured as a World Heritage Site. Here, between 1821 and 1824, a cotton spinning village became the scene of the pioneering social and educational experiment of Robert Owen. The old, handsome buildings have been brought back to life and feature an imaginative Visitor Centre and working models.

The cataracts of the **Falls of Clyde Nature Reserve**, lauded by the Romantic poets and painted by Turner, are the preface to one of the river's prettiest passages, its last Arcadian fling among the orchards and market gardens of Kirkfieldbank and Hazlebank and Rosebank before it reaches the industrial heartland of North Lanarkshire. Near one of those pastoral villages, **Crossford**, you will find one of Scotland's best-preserved and most impressive medieval castles. **Craignethan Castle**, was built between the 15th and 16th centuries on a splendid site above a wooded pass two miles from the Clyde, and was a stronghold of the Hamiltons, fierce friends of Mary Queen of Scots.

Its claim to be the original Tillietudlem in Sir Walter Scott's *Old Mortality* is pretty well authenticated. It represents a stirring farewell to the romance (and brutality) of the Middle Ages before the Reformation reached Scotland, together with a harsh new realism.

New Lanark: memories of old industries.

GLASGOW

Glasgow is a city for connoisseurs. It always has been, from the days when one of its earliest tourists, the 18th-century writer Daniel Defoe, described it as "the cleanest and beautifullest and best built city in Britain", to its recent, silver-tongued, brass-necked promotion of itself as the city "that's miles better". Yet there are few places in Europe which have been more publicly misunderstood and misrepresented than this monstrous, magnificent citadel to the worst and the best of commerce and capitalism, to the price and the prizes of Empire and the Industrial Revolution. And few cities can have inspired more furious conflicts of opinion of its worth, or ignited so many conflagrations of controversy.

Invincible spirit: Glasgow accommodates no neutrality. It is either loved or loathed by native Scots (exempting Glaswegians, whose chauvinism has been called "a formidable if ill-founded kind of sub-nationalism") and it is either admired or avoided by visitors who know only its two reputations: its friendly one or its fearsome one.

Yet even in the darkest days of its reputation, when Glasgow slums and Glasgow violence were the touchstone for every sociologist's worst urban nightmares, it was still a city for connoisseurs. It appealed to those who were not insensitive to the desperate consequences of its 19th-century population explosion, when the combination of cotton, coal, steel and the River Clyde transformed Glasgow from elegant little merchant city to industrial behemoth; and who were not blind to the dire effect of 20th-century economics which, from World War I onwards, have presided over the decline of its shipbuilding and heavy industries; but who were nevertheless able to uncover, behind its grime and grisliness, a city of noble character, handsome buildings and invincible spirit. Glasgow, in other words, has always appealed to the kind of tourist who responds to the very nature of cities – their sublime expression of human achievement at its most aspirational and its most problematic.

Its enthusiasts have always recognised Glasgow's qualities, and even at the height of its notoriety they have been able to give Glasgow its place in the pantheon of great Western cities. Today, it has become fashionable to describe it as European in character, for the remarkable diversity of its architecture and a certain levity of heart, or even to compare it with North America for its grid-iron street system and wisecracking street wisdom.

But these resonances have long been appreciated by experienced travellers. In 1929, at a time when social conditions were at their worst, the romantic but perceptive travel writer H.V. Morton found "a transatlantic alertness about Glasgow which no city in England possesses" and – the converse of orthodox opinion – was able to see that "Edinburgh is Scottish and Glasgow is cosmopolitan". And in 1960, as the demoralised city was poised to lose many of its finest buildings to the brutal sur-

Preceding pages: re-generated Glasgow. **Left**, old-style Glasgow pub. **Right**, new-style Glasgow coffee lounge.

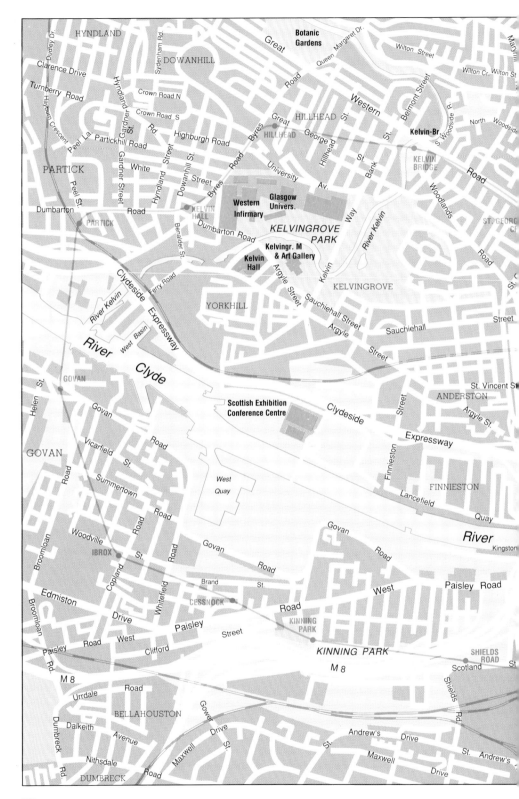

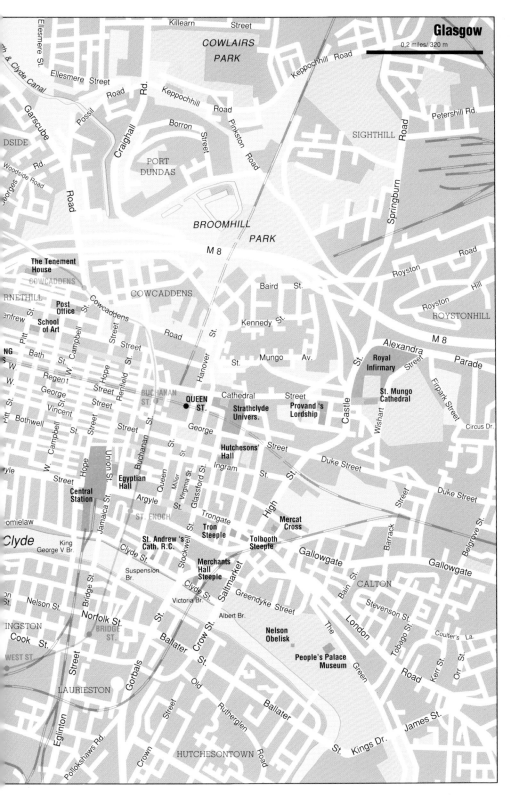

0,2 miles/ 320 m

Killearn Street

COWLAIRS PARK

Keppochhill Road

Ellesmere St.

h & Clyde Canal

Ellesmere Street

Garscube

Road

Rd.

Road

Keppochhill

Road

Petershill Rd.

Woodside Road

DSIDE

Craighall Rd.

Possil Rd.

Borron Street

Pinkston Road

Keppochhill Road

SIGHTHILL

Springburn Road

George...

Road

PORT
DUNDAS

BROOMHILL PARK

M 8

Royston

Road

Royston Road

Hill

ROYSTONHILL

The Tenement
House

COWCADDENS

Baird St.

M 8

RNETHILL

Post
Office

COWCADDENS

Cowcaddens

Kennedy St.

Royston Road

enfrew

Pitt St.

School
of Art

Campbell St.

Street

Street

Road

St.

Mungo Av.

Alexandra Parade

Royal
Infirmary

St.

Firpark Street

NG
S

Bath St.

Hope Street

Renfield St.

Hanover St.

St. Mungo
Cathedral

W.

Regent Street

Cathedral Street

Circus Dr.

W.

George St.

BUCHANAN
ST.

QUEEN
ST.

Castle St.

Wishart Street

tt St.

Vincent

Strathclyde
Univers.

Provand 's
Lordship

Bothwell St.

Buchanan St.

Street

George

Street

Duke Street

Duke Street

W. Campbell St.

Hope St.

Union St.

Queen St.

Miller St.

Glassford St.

Virginia St.

Hutchesons'
Hall

Ingram St.

St.

yle

Street

Egyptian
Hall

Argyle

Street

High St.

Street

Barrack Street

Central
Station

Jamaica St.

ST. ENOCH

Trongate

Mercat
Cross

Belgrove St.

omielaw

Tron
Steeple

Clyde

King
George V Br.

Clyde St.

Stockwell St.

Tolbooth
Steeple

Gallowgate

Gallowgate

Bridge St.

St. Andrew 's
Cath. R.C.

Saltmarket

Bain St.

CALTON

Stevenson St.

on
St.

Nelson St.

Suspension
Br.

Merchants
Hall
Steeple

Clyde St.

Greendyke Street

London

Tobago St.

Coulter's La.

INGSTON

Cook St.

BRIDGE
ST.

Victoria Br.

Albert Br.

Nelson
Obelisk

The Green

Road

Kerr St.

Orr St.

WEST ST

Ballater St.

Crow St.

People's Palace
Museum

LAURIESTON

Street

Gorbals Street

Old

Ballater

James St.

Eglinton Street

Pollokshaws Rd.

Crown St.

Rutherglen

St.

Kings Dr.

HUTCHESONTOWN Road

gery of redevelopment, the "British place-taster" Ian Nairn discovered with a sense of shock that "Glasgow was without doubt the friendliest of Britain's big cities, and probably the most dignified and coherent as well."

Nairn was immediately struck by what you might call the multinational look of the place, aware that "there is far more Continental influence in Scottish architecture (first French, then Dutch) than there ever is in English", and detecting, too, that influence which Glasgow's Victorian architects and planners shared with and sometimes exported to America: "In looks it is much more like the best parts of some American cities – Boston or Philadelphia – than anywhere in England." But above all he identified that celebrated quality (celebrated into myth, in many ways) which makes Glasgow an experience for those who care nothing for fine buildings: "Any Glasgow walk is inflected by a multitude of human contacts – in shops, under umbrellas (there *is* a good deal of rain in Glasgow), even from policemen – and

each of them seems to be a person-to-person recognition, not the mutual hate of cogs in a machine who know their plight but cannot escape it."

Iron fists: Yet Glaswegians themselves will admit that their positive qualities have a negative side. Even today, matiness can turn to menace in certain dismal pubs where too much whisky is chased by too much beer. (The working man's tipple here has traditionally been "a wee hauf and hauf" – a measure of whisky pursued by a half pint of beer – although the disaffected young have turned more to the lethal mixture of vodka and cheap wine). Religious bigotry, the obverse of honest faith, still exists, finding its most aggressive focus in the sub-culture of football.

And Glasgow's legendary humour, made intelligible even to the English through the success of comedians like Billy Connolly but available free on every street corner, is the humour of the ghetto. It has been nurtured on hard times. It is dry, sceptical, irreverent and often black. It's the humour of self-

Close scrutiny in the city's art gallery for Sir James Guthrie's *Old Willie, a Village Worthy.*

defence, the wit of people who know if they don't laugh they will cry. The Glasgow writer Cliff Hanley compares it to American-Jewish humour in its fast pace but places it in "the hard, subversive, proletarian tradition of the city".

Glasgow today is visibly, spectacularly, a city in transformation. Unlike the English port of Liverpool, which has suffered similar problems of economic decline and urban devastation, it hasn't allowed its "hard, subversive, proletarian tradition" to lead it into brick walls of confrontation with central government. The result? A city which has massively re-arranged its own environment; which sees its future in the service industries, in business conferences, exhibitions and indeed in tourism; which has already achieved some startling coups on its self-engineered road to becoming "Europe's first post-industrial city"; and which has probably never been more exciting to visit since, at the apogee of its Victorian vigour, it held the International Exhibition of Science and Art more than 100 years ago.

Glaswegians allow themselves a sly smile over their elevation to the first rank of Europe's cultural centres, and have taken to calling their home town "Culture City". But the smile becomes a little bitter for those who live in those dismal areas of the city as yet untouched by the magic of stone-cleaning, flood-lighting or even modest rehabilitation. Defenders of the new Glasgow argue that their turn will come; that you can't attract investment and employment to a city, with better conditions for everyone, unless first you shine up its confidence on the inside and polish up its image on the outside.

"Instant city": Like all four Scottish cities, Glasgow is defined by hill and water. Its suburbs advance up the slopes of the vast bowl which contains it, and the pinnacles, towers and spires of its universities, colleges and cathedral occupy their own summits within the bowl. It is, therefore, a place of sudden, sweeping vistas, with always a hint of ocean or mountain just around the corner. Look north from the heights of **Queen's Park**

Glasgow traders: fast-talking and hard-bargaining.

and you will see the cloudy humps of the Trossachs and the precipitous banks of Loch Lomond. Look west from **Gilmorehill** to the great spangled mouth of the Clyde and you will sense the sea fretting at its fragmented littoral and the islands and resorts which used to bring thousands of Glaswegians "doon the watter" for their annual Fair Fortnight.

The antiquity of this July holiday – Glasgow Fair became a fixture in the local calendar in 1190 – gives some idea of the long-term stability of the town on the Clyde. But for centuries Glasgow had little prominence or significance in the history of Scotland. Although by the 12th century it was both market town and cathedral city (with a patron saint, St Mungo) and flourished quietly throughout the Middle Ages, it was largely by-passed by the bitter internecine conflicts of pre-Reformation Scotland and the running battles with England. Most of Scotland's trade, too, was conducted with the Low Countries from the East Coast ports. But it had a university, now five centuries old and a distinguished centre of medical and engineering studies, and it had the Clyde. When trade opened up with the Americas, Glasgow's fortune was made.

Today, the names of the streets of 18th-century Glasgow – Virginia Street, Jamaica Street and the vanished Havannah Street – tell something of the story which turned a small town into the handsome fief of tobacco barons. The tobacco trade with Virginia and Maryland brought the city new prosperity and prestige and prompted it to expand westwards from the medieval centre of the High Street. (Little of medieval Glasgow remains.) In the late 18th century the urbanisation of the city accelerated with an influx of immigrants, mainly from the West Highlands, to work in the cotton mills with their new machines introduced by merchants who were forced to desert the tobacco trade. The Industrial Revolution had begun, and from then on Glasgow's destiny – grim and glorious – was fixed.

The deepening of the Clyde up to the Broomielaw, near the heart of the city,

Motorway city: old-timers wouldn't recognise the place.

in the 1780s and the coming of the steam engine in the 19th century consolidated a process of such rapid expansion that Glasgow has been called an "instant city". In the 50 years between 1781 and 1831 the population of the city quintupled, and was soon to be further swelled by thousands of Irish immigrants crossing the Irish Sea to escape famine and seek work. The Victorians completed Glasgow's industrial history and built most of its most self-important buildings as well as the congested domestic fortifications which were soon to become infamous as slum tenements. Since World War II, its population has fallen below the million mark to fewer than 700,000, the result of policies designed to decant citizens into "new towns". New policies are now encouraging the repopulation of the inner city.

The dear green place: There's some dispute about the origins of the name Glasgow. Scholars say it derives from the language of the British Celts, but variously interpret the genesis of its two syllables to mean anything from "dear

stream" to "greyhound" (which some say was a nickname of St Mungo). But there's no dispute about the version which has been adopted by the city, which was the title of a novel about Glasgow and which has now worked its way assiduously into its tourist literature and marketing lore: Glasgow means "dear green place". What else? It has, after all, over 70 parks – "more green space per head of population than any other city in Europe," as the tour bus drivers tell you.

The most unexpected, idiosyncratic and oldest of its parks – in fact, the oldest public park in Britain – is **Glasgow Green**, once the common grazing ground of the medieval town and acquired by the burgh in 1662. To this day Glasgow women have the right to dry their washing on Glasgow Green, and its Arcadian sward is still spiked with clothes poles for their use, although there are few takers. Municipal Clydesdale horses, used for carting duties in the park, still avail themselves of the grazing, and the general eccentricity of

Glasgow University: some traditions haven't changed.

CULTURE COMES IN FROM THE COLD

Glasgow's elevation to the position of European City of Culture 1990 (a title bestowed by the Ministers of Culture of the 12 member states of the European Community) was received with a mixture of astonishment and amusement in Edinburgh, which had long perceived itself as guardian of Scotland's most civilised values.

But, ever so quietly, Glasgow had been stealing the initiative. Edinburgh had been trying to make up its mind for nearly 30 years about building an opera house, but Glasgow went ahead and converted one of its general-purpose theatres, the **Theatre Royal**, into a home for the Scottish Opera. The city is also the home of four major orchestras, the acclaimed Scottish Ballet and the Royal Scottish Academy of Music and Drama.

Besides its traditional theatres – the **King's** and the **Pavilion** – the city boasts the cavernous **Tramway Theatre**, the former home of the City's tramcars in which Peter

Brook staged his ambitious *Mahabharata*. There are several interesting studio theatres. The **Tron** was founded in 1979; the **Mitchell Theatre** is housed in an extension of Glasgow's distinguished Mitchell Library; and the dynamic **Centre for Contemporary Arts** has two small theatres in its multi-media arts complex on Sauchiehall Street. However, Glasgow's most distinctive stage is the innovative **Citizens' Theatre**.

Each year, or so it seems, Glasgow adds a new festival to its calendar. Mayfest, a general celebration of the arts, has been followed by international jazz, folk music and Early music festivals, each held during successive months of the summer to keep the visitors coming. But the turning point in Glasgow's progress towards cultural respectability in the wider world came with the opening, in 1983, of the new building in Pollok Country Park which houses the Burrell Collection. The cliché about the **Burrell Museum** is that the building outshines the collection. Certainly, its inventive design attracts people with only a slight interest in the eclectic taste of Sir William Burrell, the Glasgow shipowner who bequeathed his collections to the city in 1944.

It claims to be Scotland's most popular tourist attraction, and its popularity has tended to overshadow Glasgow's other distinguished art galleries and museums: **Kelvingrove**, at the Western end of Argyle Street, which has a strong representation of 17th-century Dutch paintings and 19th-century French paintings as well as many fine examples of the work of the late 19th-century Glasgow Boys; the university's **Hunterian Museum and Art Gallery**, and the **St Mungo Museum of Religious Life and Art**. In addition, the restored **McLellan Galleries** mount half a dozen major exhibitions a year in the largest temporary exhibition space outside London.

Other museums of special interest are the **Museum of Transport**, which contains the UK's largest range of vehicles and an unsurpassed collection of model ships; **Haggs Castle**, a period museum with a focus on children's educational activities, on the South Side; and the charming, miniature repository of social history, the **Tenement House**, a two-room-and-kitchen flat in a 1892 tenement in Garnethill, wonderfully preserved in its original state. ■

A night at the opera.

the place is compounded by the bizarre proximity of Templeton's Carpet Factory, designed in 1889 by William Leiper who aspired to replicate the Doge's Palace in Venice. (The factory is now a business centre.)

Here, too, you will find the **People's Palace**, built at the turn of the century as a cultural centre for the East End community, for whom its red sandstone munificence was indeed palatial. It's now a museum dedicated to the social and industrial life of the 19th-century city, and the adjacent Winter Gardens has been turned into the cosiest and most verdant cafeteria in town.

The most distinguished of the remaining 69-odd parks include the **Botanic Gardens**, in the heart of Glasgow's stately West End, with another palace – the **Kibble Palace** – the most enchanting of its two large hot-houses. It was built as a conservatory for the Clyde Coast home of a Glasgow businessman, John Kibble, and shipped to its present site in 1873. The architect has never been identified, although legend promotes Sir Joseph Paxton, who designed the Crystal Palace in London.

Kelvingrove Park, in the city's west end, was laid out in the 1850s and was the venue of Glasgow's principal Victorian and Edwardian international exhibitions, although that function is now performed by the new Scottish Exhibition and Conference Centre. It is a spectacular park, however, traversed by the River Kelvin and dominated on one side by the Gothic pile of **Glasgow University** (this seat of learning was unseated from its original college in the High Street and rehoused on Gilmorehill in 1870) and by the elegant Victorian precipice of **Park Circus** on the other side.

Pollok Country Park, on the city's South Side (those who live south of the Clyde consider themselves and are considered to be a separate race of Glaswegian) has now got a well-worn path beaten to the door of the new **Burrell Museum** but is also the home of the 18th-century **Pollok House**. It, too, is an art gallery with works by El Greco, Murillo, Goya and William Blake. From the windows of Pollok House visitors

see a prize-winning herd of Highland cattle and Pollok Golf Course, one of 30 courses in and around the city.

Yet more greenery can be found among the sylvan glades of **Queen's Park**, also on the South Side, and in **Victoria Park**, near the north mouth of the Clyde Tunnel, which has a glasshouse containing several large fossil trees of some 350 million years' antiquity. Back across the river is **Bellahouston Park**, a magnet for the city's active sports people.

Dark welcome: In his book *In Search of Scotland*, H.V. Morton describes the launching of a ship on the Clyde in a passage which brings tears to the eyes: "Men may love her as men love ships…. She will become wise with the experience of the sea. But no shareholder will ever share her intimacy as we who saw her so marvellously naked and so young slip smoothly from the hands that made her into the dark welcome of the Clyde."

That was written in 1929 – at a time when that Clyde's shipbuilding industry was on the precipice of the great

The Burrell Collection.

depression from which it never recovered. Soon another writer, the novelist George Blake, was calling the empty yards and silent cranes "the high, tragic pageant of the Clyde", and today that pageant is nothing more than a sideshow. At Stobcross Quay, site of the **Scottish Exhibition and Conference Centre** on the north bank, you can marvel at the industrial colossus of the **Finnieston Cran** (crane), preserved to remind us of the heavy locomotives once hefted on board ships which carried them all over the world.

Stobcross Quay is also a terminus of the **Clyde Walkway**, Glasgow's first attempt to direct its great river towards the new industries of leisure and tourism. You can walk from the quay through the centre of the city past Glasgow Green to the suburb of **Cambuslang**, but somehow the journey isn't as cheerful as it should be, still lacking the kind of vigorous commercial, social and domestic life which has turned other derelict waterfronts into major attractions.

The central section is the most interesting, taking in the city's more distinguished bridges and many of the buildings associated with its maritime life. (The architectural historians Gomme and Walker identify only two bridges, the pedestrian Suspension Bridge and the Victoria Bridge, as worthy of notice, dismissing the others as "a sorry lot".) The Victoria Bridge was built in 1854 to replace the 14th-century Old Glasgow Bridge, and the graceful Suspension Bridge was completed in 1871 and designed by Alexander Kirkland, who later became Commissioner of Public Buildings in Chicago.

Custom House Quay, which looks across to the delicate, newly restored Georgian facades of Carlton Place on the south bank, has opulent sandstone landscaping, a bandstand and a pub.

There's much still to be done for the **Broomielaw**, which is rich in sailing history. To the west of George IV Bridge and Central Station's railway bridge, it was once the departure point for regular services to Ireland, North America and the west coast towns of Scotland. From here, up to 50 passenger steamers a day would depart for Port Glasgow, Greenock, Gourock, Helensburgh and the islands in the Firth; these were the forerunners of today's suburban trains. When moorings were not available, steamers would tie up across the river at Bridge Quay, now called **Clyde Place Quay**. The result was often "a regatta of demented chimney-pots".

There is new life stirring, however, on the vast deserted wharfs of the Clyde. On the south bank, near Govan, upmarket apartments have been built at the old **Princes Dock**, and the massive Rotunda at the north of the old Clyde Tunnel, designed for pedestrians and horses and carts (a new road tunnel was built in the early 1960s) has been restored as a restaurant complex.

Central points: "Rough, careless, vulnerable and sentimental". That's how the writer Edwin Morgan described Glaswegians, and they are certainly qualities which Glaswegians have brought to their environment. The city has been both brutal and nostalgic about its own fabric, destroying and lament-

Teeing off by the River Clyde.

ing with equal vigour. When the city fathers built an urban motorway in the 1960s they liberated Glasgow for the motorist but cut great swathes through its domestic and commercial heart, and were only just prevented from extending the Inner Ring Road which would have demolished in the process much of the Merchant City.

But the disappearance of the last tramcars in the 1960s has been regretted ever since and today there is nostalgic talk of retrieving them; while Glaswegians have taken a long time to accept their updated underground transport system and to grow to love the "Clockwork Orange" – the violently coloured new rolling stock which replaced the original carriages in the 1970s. (**Glasgow District Subway**, opened in 1896, was one of the earliest in Britain and the only one in the country which is called, American-style, "the Subway".)

But to Morgan's list of adjectives might have been added "pretentious" and "aspirational", two sides of the architectural coin which represents Glas-

gow's legacy of magnificent Victorian buildings. They aren't hard to find: the dense grid-iron of streets around George Square and westwards invites the neck to crane at any number of soaring facades, many bearing the art of the sculptor and all signifying some chapter of the 19th-century history.

George Square is the heart of modern Glasgow. Like most Scottish squares, it contains a motley collection of statues, commemorating 11 people who seem to have been chosen by lottery. The 80-ft (24-metre) column in its centre is mounted by the novelist Sir Walter Scott, gazing southwards, so they say, to the land where he made all his money. But the square is more effectively dominated by the grandiose **City Chambers**, designed by William Young and opened in 1888. The marble-clad interior, which you can visit on guided tours, is even more opulent and self-important than the exterior. The *pièce de résistance* is the huge banqueting hall, 110 ft (33 metres) long, 48 ft (14 metres) wide and 52 ft (16 metres) high; it has a glorious

arched ceiling, leaded glass windows and paintings depicting scenes from the city's history. The south wall is covered by three large murals, works of the Glasgow Boys (*see pages 90–91*).

George Square's other monuments to Victorian prosperity are the **Head Post Office** on the south side and the noble **Merchants' House** on the northwest corner (now the home of Glasgow Chamber of Commerce). Its crowning glory is the gold ship on its dome, drawing the eye ever upwards – a replica of the ship on the original Merchants' House.

Just off Buchanan Street is **Nelson Mandela Place** (its name having been changed from St George's Place in tribute to the South African political leader). Here you will find **Glasgow Stock Exchange**, designed in the 1870s by John Burnet, whose reputation was to be eclipsed by his more celebrated son J.J. Burnet; and the **Royal Faculty of Procurators** (1854), which is rich in decorative stonework and influenced by Italian Renaissance style.

In nearby streets are examples of the work of another distinguished Glasgow architect, the younger James Salmon, who designed the Mercantile Buildings in **Bothwell Street** (1897–98) and the curious "Hat-rack" in **St Vincent Street**, named for the extreme narrowness and the projecting cornices of its tall facade.

Further west, J. J. Burnet's extraordinary **Charing Cross Mansions** (1891), with its grandiloquent intimations of French Renaissance style, was spared the surgery of motorway development which destroyed many 19th-century buildings around Charing Cross.

On the other side of one of these motorways are the first buildings of the **Park Conservation Area**. These buildings have resulted in the statement that Glasgow is the "finest piece of architectural planning of the mid-19th century" and led John Betjeman, an architectural enthusiast as well as the Poet Laureate, to describe Glasgow as the "greatest Victorian city in Europe". Stroll upwards through this area to a belvedere above **Kelvingrove Park** and marvel at the glorious vistas. The belvedere is

Charing Cross: full of 19th-century confidence.

backed by **Park Quadrant** and **Park Terrace**, which are probably the most magnificent of all the terraces in the Park Conservation Area.

Still in the west end, in Great Western Road, you will find **Great Western Terrace**, one of the best examples of the work of Glasgow's most famous Victorian architect, Alexander "Greek" Thomson, called "Greek" for the passion of his classicism.

Back towards the city centre in St Vincent Street is Thomson's prominent **St Vincent Street Church**. It is fronted by an Ionic portico, with sides more Egyptian than Greek and a tower that wouldn't have been out of place in India during the Raj. Here the streets rise towards **Blythswood Square**, once a haunt of prostitutes but now, with its surroundings, providing a graceful mixture of late Georgian and early Victorian domestic architecture. No. 7 was the home of one Madeleine Smith, who poisoned her French lover there in 1858. (It must be said that this "respectable" young woman was discharged by the Edinburgh jury with the verdict of "not proven" – which generally means "We know you did it but we can't prove it, so go away and don't do it again." She took the implicit advice to heart, moved to London, entertained George Bernard Shaw and married a pupil of the designer William Morris.)

Across Buchanan Street in **St Vincent Place** are the offices of Greater Glasgow Tourist Board. When you drop in to pick their brains and pick up their brochures you'll find yourself mounting the steps of another imposing mid-Victorian building, although the interiors have been reconstructed. Behind St Vincent Place is **Royal Exchange Square**, which is pretty well consumed by the city's new **Gallery of Modern Art** (opens 1996). The glorious building in which it is housed began life as the 18th-century mansion of a tobacco lord, has since been a bank and the Royal Exchange and in 1832, to the design of David Hamilton, it was extended to include the portico and the cupola.

Among the city centre's most distin-

Two local entertainers: Lulu at the Pavilion, and a street musician.

guished Georgian buildings are, in Ingram Street, **Hutcheson's Hall**, also designed by David Hamilton and now the Glasgow home of the National Trust for Scotland with a National Trust visitor centre and shop; and, in nearby Glassford Street, **Trades House** which, despite alterations, has retained the facade designed by the great Robert Adam.

But any excursion around Glasgow's architectural treasures must be highlighted by the work of the city's most innovative genius, Charles Rennie Mackintosh, who overturned the Victorians in a series of brilliant designs between 1893 and 1911. Mackintosh's influence on 20th-century architecture, along with his leading contribution to *art nouveau* in interiors, furniture and textile design, has long been acknowledged and celebrated throughout Europe, although all his finest work was done in and around Glasgow.

His sometimes austere, sometimes sensuous style, much influenced by natural forms and an inspired use of space and light, can be seen in several important buildings: his greatest achievement, the **Glasgow School of Art** (designed in 1896) in Renfrew Street; **Scotland Street School**, on the South Side, opened in 1904 and now a Museum of Education; and the **Martyrs' Public School**, perched above a sliproad to the M8 motorway near Glasgow Cathedral.

In Sauchiehall Street the facade of his **Willow Tea-Room** (1903) remains, and a room on the first floor has been turned over to tea-time again, with reproduction Mackintosh furniture. But more stunning examples of his interior designs can be seen at the **Mackintosh House** at the University of Glasgow's Hunterian Art Gallery on Gilmorehill. There, rooms from the architect's own house have been reconstructed and exquisitely furnished with original pieces of his furniture, water-colours and designs.

There's not much left in Glasgow which is old by British standards. The oldest building is **Glasgow Cathedral**, most of which was completed in the 13th century, but the only pre-Reformation dwelling house is **Provand's Lordship**, built in 1471 as part of a refuge for poor people and extended in 1670. It's now a museum of medieval material and, less logically, hosts an early 20th-century sweet shop.

Both old buildings stand on **Cathedral Street**, at the top of the High Street – the cathedral on a site which has been a place of Christian worship since it was blessed for burial in AD 397 by St Ninian, the earliest missionary recorded in Scottish history. A severe but satisfying example of early Gothic, it contains the tomb of St Mungo. Behind the cathedral, overseeing the city from the advantage of height, are more tombs – the intimidating Victorian sepulchres of the **Western Necropolis**. This cemetery is supervised by a statute of John Knox, the 16th-century reformer, and among the ranks of Glaswegian notables buried there is one William Miller, "the laureate of the nursery". He wrote the popular bedtime jingle, "Wee Willie Winkie".

A brand-new cream-coloured Scottish baronial building in front of the cathedral is home to the **St Mungo Museum of Religious Life and Art**,

Behind the Necropolis are the Cathedral and the Royal Infirmary.

with its Japanese Zen garden. Don't miss the comments on the visitors' board.

Glasgow's two oldest churches, other than the cathedral, are **St Andrew's Parish Church**, which contains some spectacular plaster-work, and the episcopal **St-Andrew's-by-the-Green**, once known as the Whistlin' Kirk because of its early organ. Both were built in the mid-18th century and both can be found to the northwest of Glasgow Green, in the Merchant City.

There you will also find two remnants of the 17th century, the **Tolbooth Steeple** and the **Tron Steeple**. The Tolbooth Steeple, at Glasgow Cross (where the Mercat Cross is a 20th-century replica of a vanished one) is a pretty substantial remnant of the old jail and courthouses, being seven storeys high with a crown tower. The Tron Steeple was once attached to the Tron Church, at the Trongate, and dates back to the late 16th and early 17th centuries. (Glasgow does have a habit of losing bits of its buildings.) The original church was burnt down in the 18th century and the re-

placement now accommodates the lively Tron Theatre.

Those truly dedicated to the pursuit of antiquity, however, could always proceed to the refined northwest suburb of **Bearsden**, where once rough Romans roamed. Bearsden lies on the line of the Antonine Wall, built during the 2nd century, and chunks of the Roman occupation remain to be seen.

Market forces: Heavy industry has come and gone, but Glasgow still flourishes as a city of independent enterprise – of hawkers, stallholders, street traders and marketeers. Even the dignified buildings of its old, more respectable markets – fish, fruit and cheese – have survived in a city which has often been careless with its past, and have now become part of the rediscovery of the Merchant City area, which stretches from the **High Street** and the **Saltmarket** in the east to **Union Street** and **Jamaica Street** in the west, and which contains most of the city's remaining pre-Victorian buildings.

The old **Fishmarket** in Clyde Street

Left, a Mackintosh room in the Hunterian Art Gallery. Right, Glasgow's School of Art.

is in fact Victorian, but it accommodates a perpendicular remnant of the 17th-century Merchants' House, demolished in 1817. This slender steeple was built in the Dutch style in 1659.

In **Candleriggs**, slightly to the north, the old Fruitmarket now houses a more traditional style of weekend market selling fresh produce and inexpensive clothes, but Glasgow's market celebrity still belongs to the **Barrows**, in the Gallowgate to the east, where both repartee and bargains were once reputed to rival those of Paris's Flea Market and London's Petticoat Lane. Founding queen of "the Barras" was a certain Mrs McIver, who started her career with one barrow, bought several more to hire out on the piece of ground she rented in the Gallowgate and was claimed to have retired a millionaire.

More local colour and open-air tat, useful or useless, can be found in **Paddy's Market**, in the lanes between Clyde Street and the Bridgegate, many of the stalls occupying the arches of an old railways bridge. This market has its genesis in Ireland's "Hungry Forties", when the great potato famines of the 1840s sent thousands of destitute Irish people to Glasgow (and elsewhere) to find a toehold or to starve.

The West Highlands of Scotland were almost as badly affected by the potato famines and they, too, looked to Glasgow for salvation. Comic tradition has it that they also looked to **Argyle Street** for shelter. This famous shopping street is traversed by the railway bridge to Central Station. The bridge has always been called the Heilanman's Umbrella. The slander is that Highlanders stood under it when it rained rather than buy umbrellas; but the truth is that it has long been a favourite rendezvous of Glasgow's Highland community.

Argyle Street, **Sauchiehall Street** and the more upmarket **Buchanan Street** are Glasgow's great shopping thoroughfares, although an area round **Byres Road**, in the West End, has recently become a centre for interesting bric-a-brac and boutiques. **West Regent Street** has a Victorian Village (a collection of small antique shops in old business premises) and the old Tobacco Market in **Virginia Street**, where once the American shipments were auctioned, now houses the Virginia Antique and Crafts Galleries.

Glaswegians have always spent freely, even flashily, belying the slur on the open-handedness of Scots, and the city's commercial interests still seem to believe that the appetite for shopping is insatiable. An open loading area just off Buchanan Street has been converted with great imagination into the **Princes Square** shopping mall, which is worth visiting even for those who don't wish to shop, eat or cease being fully paid-up misanthropes.

The site of the demolished St Enoch Railway Station and hotel (one of Glasgow's major acts of vandalism) is now occupied by **St Enoch Centre**, a spectacular £62 million glass-covered complex of 50 shop units, a fast-food "court", ice rink and multi-storey car park. "Edinburgh is the capital," as an old joke goes, "but Glasgow *has* the capital." And, as always, it flaunts it.

Left, pawnbroker's sign, traditionally a familiar sight in the Gorbals. **Right**, St Enoch Centre.

FORTH AND CLYDE

The royal burgh of **Stirling**, whose name resounds down the more turbulent corridors of Scottish history, stands at the apex of a triangle rich in character but poor in obvious tourist appeal. Stirling is the ornamental brooch on the plain, workmanlike belt which clasps the waist of central Scotland. The lower reaches of the rivers Forth and Clyde have been the waterways of that belt since the opening of the Forth and Clyde Canal in 1790 linked the industrial towns of west central Scotland with the east coast at Grangemouth – now the epicentre of a vast petrochemical plant. The canal, closed to working navigation in 1963, offers modest recreational activities.

Preceding pages, men at work in Lanark. **Left**, the Forth Railway Bridge.

Natural fortress: Stirling's title of "gateway to the Highlands" is no invention of its tourist officers. Its Old Bridge was of great strategic importance, giving access to the north across the lowest bridging point of the River Forth, while the 250-ft (75-metre) volcanic plug which supports its castle – every bit as impressive as Edinburgh Castle – was the natural fortress which made Stirling significant from the 12th century onwards.

The **castle** had its most active moments during Scotland's Wars of Independence. Surrendered to the English in 1296, it was recaptured by the warrior-patriot William Wallace after the Battle of Stirling Bridge (not today's stone bridge, built around 1400, but a wooden structure). It became the last stronghold in Scotland to hold out against Edward I, the "Hammer of the Scots". Eventually, it went back to the English for 10 years, until Robert the Bruce re-took it in 1314 after the Battle of Bannockburn, which decisively secured Scotland's independence. There's much to see at the castle; the Stewarts favoured it as a Royal residence, James II was born in it, Mary Queen of Scots was crowned there at the age of nine months, and its splendid collection of buildings reflects its history as palace and fortress.

The achievements of both Wallace and Bruce are conspicuously recalled in the environs of Stirling. On the rock of **Abbey Craig**, above the site where Wallace camped, is the ostentatious, overbearing **Wallace Monument**, built by the Victorians in one of their more vulgar moods and home of the hero's two-handed sword. From its elevation, however, you feel you can almost touch the leaping ramparts of the **Ochil Hills**, while to the south-east the Forth spreads across its flat plain to the spectacular flare-stacks of **Grangemouth**.

The site of the Battle of Bannockburn, a few miles south of Stirling, has been more or less consumed by a housing estate. No one is precisely sure where the battle was fought, but the rotunda beside the heroic bronze equestrian statue of Bruce is said to mark his command post. The **Bannockburn Heritage Centre** gives an audio-visual account of the matter – but, as Scotland's battlefields go, this most famous one could hardly be called atmospheric.

Stirling is almost equidistant from Edinburgh and Glasgow. If you take the uncongested M9 motorway to Edin-

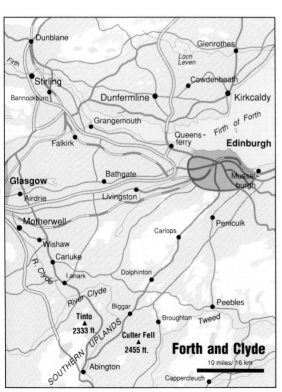

Forth and Clyde

10 miles/ 16 km

burgh, you will find yourself keeping roughly parallel to the broadening course of the Forth. There are rewarding diversions to be made on this route. Near the industrial town of Falkirk are four good sections of the Roman **Antonine Wall**, a turf rampart on a stone base which the Emperor Antoninus Pius caused to be built between the firths of Clyde and Forth around AD 140; while the motorway itself has opened up a distracting view of the loch and **palace of Linlithgow**, the well-preserved ruins of Scotland's most magnificent palace.

The birthplace of Mary Queen of Scots, Linlithgow's chapel and great hall are late 15th-century, while its handsome courtyard has an elaborate 16th-century fountain. Adjacent and worth visiting is the **Church of St Michael**, Scotland's largest pre-Reformation parish church; note the abstract golden crown mounted on its tower in 1964.

From the M9, you can also visit the village of **South Queensferry** on the southern bank of one of the Forth's oldest crossings, where river becomes estuary. Until the Forth Road Bridge was built, ferries had plied between South and North Queensferry for 900 years. Today, South Queensferry huddles between and beneath the giant bridges which provide such a spectacular contrast in engineering design – the massive humped girders of the 1890 rail bridge and the delicate, graceful span of the suspension bridge, opened in 1964. Pedestrians, incidentally, have their own footpath on the road bridge and can tramp for over a mile through the boisterous air between river and sky.

At South Queensferry, you can take a boat excursion to the island of **Incholm** in the Firth and visit the 12th-century ruined abbey, well-preserved monastic buildings and gardens. Before leaving this part of the world, cross the Forth Road Bridge or take the train to North Queensferry and the new **Deep Sea World** for a diver's eye-view of myriad fish in the "Underwater Safari", Europe's largest aquarium.

Near South Queensferry are two of Scotland's stately homes, both open to the public: **Hopetoun House**, home of the Earls of Hopetoun, magnificently situated in parkland beside the Forth and splendidly extended and rebuilt by William Adam and his son John between 1721 and 1754; and **Dalmeny House**, home of the Earls of Rosebery and a fine collection of paintings.

You can walk delightfully beside the Forth through the wooded Rosebery estate to the **River Almond**, where a little rowing-boat ferry transports you across this minor tributary to the red pantiles and white crowstep gables of **Cramond**. Now a suburb of Edinburgh, Cramond is still very much its own 18th-century village, with a harbour which was used by the Romans. Its **Roman Fort**, whose foundations have been exposed, was built around AD 142, and may have been used by Septimius Severus.

Scotland's pre-eminent river, the **Clyde**, undergoes more personality changes than any other in its progress to the western seaboard. The limpid little stream which has its source in the hills of Tweedale, 80 miles (130 km) south-

Stirling Castle: it changed hands often between Scots and English.

212

east of Glasgow, moves prettily through the orchards and market gardens of Clydesdale before watering the industries of North Lanarkshire and welcoming the ships and shipyards of Glasgow. The lower reaches of its valley have been colonised by the city's satellites, and by a clutter of hill towns which more or less run into each other: Wishah, Motherwell and Hamilton.

Once drab coal and steel towns, they are attempting to recover their dignity and vitality through (among other things) the creation of **Strathclyde Country Park**, a huge recreational area which includes a 200-acre (80-hectare) loch, formed by diverting the Clyde, and part of the old estate of the Dukes of Hamilton. Of the three towns, **Hamilton** has the longest history, with associations with Mary Queen of Scots, Cromwell and the Covenanters, who were defeated by Monmouth at nearby Bothwell Bridge in 1679. Many of the escaping Covenanters sheltered in the woods of the sympathetic Duchess of Hamilton, who urged the victor not to disturb her game.

Immediately south of Hamilton is the recently restored **Chatelherault**, a glorious hunting lodge and kennels built in 1732 for the Duke of Hamilton by William Adam. More Hamilton grandeur is seen in the nearby 18th-century **Mausoleum**, whose acoustics endow it with the longest echo in Europe.

Bothwell Castle, a red ruin above the Clyde which is often called the finest 13th-century castle in Scotland, was repeatedly fought over by the Scots and the English. Memories of more recent adventures can be found in the adjacent community of **Blantyre**, birthplace of the explorer and missionary David Livingstone. The **Livingstone National Memorial and Museum** imaginatively incorporates the mill tenement where he was born, and exhibits recall his harsh early life and his great mission in Africa against the slave trade. Livingstone was buried in London's Westminster Abbey, but only after his bearers had transported his body 1,500 miles (2,400 km) from the interior to the coast – an episode described in sculptured wood.

Bothwell Castle: the country's finest 13th-century stronghold.

215

THE WEST COAST

From the long finger of Kintyre to the deep fissure of Loch Broom, the west coast is that part of Scotland which most perfectly conforms to its romantic image. Mountain and moor, heather and stag, castle and loch – and the magical seaboard of isolated villages and small ports where, on a whim, you can jump a ferry to the Western Isles – are all to be found on this gloriously intricate and spectacular littoral. Nowhere else in Scotland (outside Caithness and Sutherland) is a physical sense of travelling more thrillingly experienced; and few other areas provide such opportunities for solitude and repose, as well as the slightly scary impression that this dramatic landscape of sometimes savage desolation is not to be trifled with.

It all begins gently enough at the Clyde estuary where the deep penetration of the sea at **Loch Fyne** has created Scotland's longest peninsula, which is 54 miles (87 km) from Crinan to the Mull of Kintyre and never wider than 10 miles (16 km). This mighty arm is nearly bisected by West Loch Tarbert into the two regions of Knapdale and Kintyre, and its isolated character makes it almost as remote as any of the islands.

Here there are rolling hills rather than mountains, rough moors and forests in Knapdale, grassy tops in Kintyre, and a coast which is most interesting on its west side, with its close view of the island of Jura from **Kilberry Head** (where you can also view a fine collection of late medieval sculptured stones). Farther south are **Tayinloan**, from which you can take the 20-minute car-ferry ride across to the tiny island of Gigha, and the vast beach of **Machrihanish**.

Tarbert is an agreeable little port very popular with yachties; car ferries leave from it for Islay and Jura. But of the Kintyre metropolis of **Campbeltown** the writer W.H. Murray has this to say: "It would be unjust to call it ugly but certainly it is not fair. Campbeltown is no more hideous to the eye than the grunt of a pig to the ear." However, you

are within easy reach of the tip of the peninsula, the **Mull of Kintyre** itself.

The north coast of Ireland is only 12 miles (19 km) away, and legend has it that St Columba first set foot in Scotland at **Keil**, near the holiday village of Southend. You can see his "footprints" imprinted on a flat rock near a ruined chapel. (There is also a St Columba's cave on the shores of **Loch Caolisport**, in Knapdale, a recess which was certainly used as a Christian chapel around the 6th century, but which archaeology has pronounced was occupied as far back as the Middle Stone Age.)

Scenic drama: From the great lighthouse of Mull, built in 1788 and remodelled by Robert Stevenson, the grandfather of Robert Louis Stevenson, there is nowhere else to go. You can retreat back up the secondary road (B842) of Kintyre's east coast, which has its own scenic drama in the sandy sweep of **Carradale Bay** and the view across the water to the mountainous Clyde island of Arran. On your way north you can take in the ruined walls

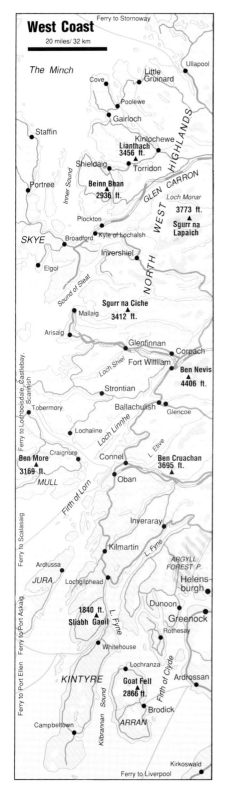

Ferry to Stornoway

The Minch

Ullapool

Little Gruinard

Cove

Poolewe

Gairloch

Staffin

Kinlochewe

Lianthach
3456 ft.

Shieldaig

Torridon

Portree

Beinn Bhan
2936 ft.

Loch Monar

3773 ft.
Sgurr na
Lapaich

Plockton

Broadford

Kyle of Lochalsh

SKYE

Invershiel

Elgol

Sound of Sleat

Sgurr na Ciche
3412 ft.

Mallaig

Arisaig

Glenfinnan

Corpach

Loch Shiel

Fort William

Ben Nevis
4406 ft.

Strontian

Ballachulish

Glencoe

Loch Linnhe

Tobermory

Lochaline

L. Etive

Craignure

Connel

Ben Cruachan
3695 ft.

Ben More
3169 ft.

Oban

MULL

Firth of Lorn

Inveraray

Kilmartin

L. Fyne

ARGYLL
FOREST P.

Ardlussa

Helens-
burgh

JURA

Lochgilphead

Dunoon

1840 ft.
Sliabh Gaoil

Greenock

Rothesay

Whitehouse

Lochranza

Loch of Clyde

KINTYRE

Goat Fell
2866 ft.

Ardrossan

Campbeltown

Brodick

ARRAN

Kilbrannan Sound

Kirkoswald

Ferry to Liverpool

and sculptured tombstones of **Saddell Abbey**, a 12th-century Cistercian house, and the rhododendron-filled gardens of **Carradale House**. The hump behind them is **Beinn an Tuirc**, Kintyre's highest peak (1,490 ft/447 metres). The name means Mountain of the Boar, from one fearsome specimen said to have been killed by an ancestor of the Campbells.

From **Lochgilphead**, where the Crinan Canal crosses the neck of the peninsula and connects Loch Fyne to the Atlantic Ocean, you have a choice of two main routes to the handsome port and resort of Oban (the tourist capital of the West Highlands). The longer route, up Loch Fyne by Inverary to Loch Awe (A83 and then A819), is probably the more dramatic, although the shorter route (A816) takes you close to the coast and its vistas of those low-lying islands which are the floating outriders of the mountains of Jura and Mull.

Both routes are punctuated with places of interest. The most celebrated castle in this part of Scotland is **Inverary**, which has been the seat of the chiefs of the

Music maker: craftsmen are much in demand.

Clan Campbell, the Dukes of Argyll, for centuries. The present building – Gothic-revival, famous for its magnificent interiors and art collection and open to the public – was started in 1743, when the third Duke also decided to re-build the village of Inverary. The result is a dignified community with much of the orderly elegance of the 18th century; even if its snowy buildings on the shores of Loch Fyne can look like a promotion for whitewash.

By means of wax figures and imaginative exhibitions, the **Inverary Jail** brings to life an 1820 courtroom trial and life in the cells in the 19th century.

Two very different museums are in the neighbourhood. One, attached to the castle, is the **Combined Operations Museum**, which recalls the passing of a quarter of a million Allied troops through this little Highland village during World War II, when Inverary was the British Combined Operations base. The other, some 5 miles (8 km) south of the village, is **Auchindrain Museum of Country Life**, whose dwellings and barns of the

18th and 19th centuries were once a communal-tenancy Highland farm, paying rent to the Dukes of Argyll.

Loch Awe, where the road takes you past the fallen house of the Breadalbane family – the romantic ruins of **Kilchurn Castle**, on a promontory on the water – is the longest freshwater loch in Scotland. At its north-west extremity, where it squeezes past the mighty mountain of Ben Cruachan and drains into Loch Etive through the grim slit of Brander, it's as awesome as its name promises.

The **Pass of Brander** is so steep and narrow that legend claims it was once held against an army by an old woman wielding a scythe. Almost a mile inside the mountain is the Cruachan pumped storage generating station, an artificial cavern which can be visited daily in the summer.

Ancient echoes: If you take the A816 to Oban by the coast on the A816, you will pass one of the ancient capitals of Dalriada, the kingdom of the early Celts. The striking eminence of **Dunadd Fort** (*circa* 500 to 800) sets the mood for a

Glen Tarbert: almost as remote as one of the Western Isles.

spectacular range of wondrous prehistoric sites near the village of **Kilmartin**: standing stones, burial cairns and cists, all accessible. As you drive north, the coast becomes more riven, while the natural harbours of the sea lochs and the protective islands of **Shuna** and **Luing** and **Seil** attract the yacht fraternity.

Seil and its neighbours were supported by a vigorous slate industry in the 19th century, until a great storm in 1881 flooded the quarries deep below sea level and efforts to pump them out failed. You can see vivid evidence of those days in **Easdale Island Folk Museum**, a short ferry crossing from Seil. The island of Seil itself comes so close to the mainland that it's reached by the single stone arch of the Clachan Bridge, "the bridge over the Atlantic". Built in 1791, this hump is also a site of the rare "fairy foxglove", and on its island side is the Tigh na Truish Inn, whose name – House of the Trousers – recalls the vindictive law which prohibited the wearing of the kilt after the 1745 Rising.

Oban, ringed by wooded hills and clasped within the sheltered bay which gives it the finest harbour on the Highland seaboard. Hotels and boarding houses abound – a far cry from 1773 when Dr Johnson had to content himself with a "tolerable inn". However, modern tourism hasn't been so kind to the dignity of its high street; it lost the delightful Victorian buildings of its railway station in an act of institutionalised vandalism. But the town still has atmosphere – mostly centred on the busy harbour which is the seaway to the Hebrides, and where even a landlocked traveller feels the pull of the islands.

All the usual (sometimes oppressive) infrastructure of tourism can be found in Oban, whose only beach, **Ganavan Sands**, is 2 miles (3 km) outside the town. There is local island-hopping to be done (the long island which lies across the bay is **Kerrera**) and there are castles to be visited: the scant fragment of **Dunollie** on its precipitous rock and the well-preserved 13th-century fortress of **Dunstaffnage**.

There are hills to be climbed – **Pulpit**

Oban, dominated by the folly of McCaig's Tower.

Hill is the town's best viewpoint – and there is the extraordinary folly of **McCaig's Tower** to be admired or despised. ("Its effect is damnable, if one feels in damning mood," says W.H. Murray). John Stuart McCaig was an Oban banker who financed this strange enterprise on a hill above the town centre to give work to the unemployed and provide himself with a memorial. The tower was raised between 1890 and 1900 but McCaig's grand plan was never completed. What remains looks like an austere Scottish Colosseum.

Three miles (5 km) north is the **Rare Breeds Animal Park**, where all sorts of exotic animals and birds are sheer joy, and the delightfully situated **Sea Life Centre** (10 miles/16 km) with its walk-through aquarium, touch tanks and fish farming exhibit.

Oban is also the gateway to the lovely lands of Benderloch and Appin (A828). Beyond, still on the A828, travel to **Corran** for the five-minute ferry voyage across **Loch Linnhe** to **Ardgour** and the tortuous car journey to isolated

Glencoe: even the unimaginative feel their spine tingle.

Ardnamurchan Point, the most westerly point of the Scottish mainland.

Appin is a name which evokes romantic tragedy: there, in a historical incident made famous by Robert Louis Stevenson in *Kidnapped*, James Stewart of the Glens was wrongly hanged for the murder of Colin Campbell, "the Red Fox" and government land agent, in yet another of the internecine feuds which followed the Jacobite Rising of 1745.

Bloody massacre: To the north and west of the Ballachulish Narrows the greatest grandeur of the West Highlands now lies before you. To the east is the forbidding dark gash which is probably the most famous glen in Scotland: **Glencoe**, where, in a savage winter dawn in 1692, 40 members of the Clan MacDonald were slaughtered by the government soldiers of the Argyll regiment (*see page 37*).

Today, Glencoe seems to have trapped the gloom and grisliness of that awful event. Even the unimaginative must feel a shiver of the spine as they descend the main road between its black buttresses

of mountain, which even ski development and a visitor centre have not been able to cosmeticise. These mountains – **Buachaille Etive Mor**, **Bidean nam Bian** and the **Aonach Eagach** – are notorious: they are one of Britain's supreme mountaineering challenges, and nearly every winter they claim lives.

Big Ben: Some 15 miles (24 km) to the north of Ballachulish on the A82 is **Fort William**. The Fort itself was demolished, not by the Jacobites but by the railway. The secret portrait of Bonnie Prince Charlie, and his bed, are among the Jacobite relics in the **West Highland Museum**. Despite its fine position below the Mammore Mountains on Loch Linnhe, this straggling, congested town has little to recommend it beyond its proximity to **Ben Nevis** and glorious Glen Nevis. Britain's highest mountain – a mere 4,406 ft (1,340 metres) – looks a deceptively inoffensive lump from below, where you can't see its savage north face, and it can be easily enough climbed. But there are risks. The volatile nature of the Scottish climate should never be underestimated when setting out on any hill or mountain expedition.

From Fort William, turn west along **Loch Eil** (A830), take the "Road to the Isles" and to **Mallaig**, another seaway to the Hebrides (particularly the "small isles" of Eigg, Rum, Canna and Muck). The road has a dense concentration of associations with Charles Edward Stuart, running between the clan territories of Moidart and Morar, whose chief, MacDonald of Clanranald, raised the clans in support of the prince along with Cameron of Lochiel.

At **Glenfinnan**, Charles raised the white-and-crimson Stuart banner to the mighty cheers of 5,000 men who rallied behind the charismatic young prince's impetuous adventure, which was to cost the Highlands dear. A monument was erected on the spot in 1815 – a grey column in baroque style with a bearded clansman on top which, says W.H. Murray, "impairs the splendid scene down the loch". The prince landed from his French brig at **Loch nan Uamh**, a bay on the Arisaig coast a few miles

The Glenfinnan Viaduct, still carrying trains from Glasgow to Mallaig.

west. Just over a year later, after the disaster of Culloden, he left from the same place, having wandered around the Highlands with a price of £30,000 on his head. It says something for the character of Highlanders – who were left to pay the prince's debts in death, persecution and attempted cultural genocide – that he was never betrayed, only helped to escape. A memorial cairn on the shore of Loch nan Uamh marks his final exit from Scotland.

From **Arisaig** the road passes between the silver sands of Morar and the very deep **Loch Morar** itself (reputedly the home of Scotland's other water monster) and comes to an end at **Mallaig**, the west coast's principal fishing port and the most important herring and shellfish port in Britain. Here you can catch a car ferry across the Sound of Sleat to **Armadale on Skye** or enjoy a hflf-day cruise which hugs the great, roadless mountain wilderness of Knoydart with its two long sea lochs, **Nevis** and **Hourn** – the lochs of Heaven and Hell.

The sail also takes you past **Glenelg**, which can also be reached by leaving Fort William on the A82 and, at **Invergarry**, turning west on to the A87. At **Shiel Bridge**, at the head of **Loch Duich**, brave the giddy mountain trip to Glenelg which is worth a visit not only for its beauty but for its two Iron Age brochs – circular towers with walls which still stand over 30 ft (9 metres) high. There, too, are the remains of **Bernera Barracks**, quartered by Hanoverian troops during the 18th century, and nearby you can cross the 500 metres of water to Kylerhea in Skye, as Dr Johnson and Boswell did, although the little car ferry runs only in summer.

The graceful **Five Sisters of Kintail** must be among Scotland's most photographed mountains, while the Mackenzies' restored **Eilean Donan Castle**, on its islet over a causeway in Loch Duich, is certainly the most photographed castle.

A more conventional route to Skye is the A87 until **Kyle of Lochalsh** and its bridge to **Kyleakin** in Skye.

Sublime scenery: From **Kyle of Lochalsh**, mainland travellers continue north by lovely **Loch Carron**, leaving Inverness-shire for the tremendous mountain massifs of **Wester Ross**. Here, on the isolated Applecross peninsula, among the famous peaks of **Torridon** with their views to the Cuillins of Skye and the distant, drifting shapes of the Outer Hebrides, is some of Europe's most spectacular scenery – with exhilarating driving yielding to richer rewards for those who are prepared to use their feet.

More gentle pursuits – amid equally wild and empty scenery – can be found at the village of **Poolewe**, where the road through the fishing port of Gairloch passes between Loch Ewe and **Loch Maree**, possibly the most sublime inland loch in Scotland, outranking Loch Lomond with no effort. (Loch Maree's particular features are the old Scots pines which line its shores and the impressive presence of Mount Slioch above it.)

Inverewe Gardens provides a sumptuous international collection of subtropical plants, growing – thanks to the mild climate created by the North Atlantic Drift – on the same latitude as Siberia. The gardens were created in the 19th century by Osgood Mackenzie, a son of the 12th chief of the Gairloch Mackenzies.

A few miles farther north is the glittering 4-mile (6-km) scoop of **Gruinard Bay**, with its coves of pink sand from the red Torridon sandstone, nearly 800 million years old. The road then takes you round **Little Loch Broom**, below the powerful shoulders of An Teallach (3,483 ft; 1,046 metres) highest of those Torridon peaks which, says W.H. Murray, make "most Munros of the south and central Highlands seem tame by comparison". (A Munro is a Scottish mountain of over 3,000 ft/900 metres, named for the man who collated them). And you are now within easy striking distance of **Loch Broom** itself, a seasonal home to fish factory ships from Russia and Eastern Europe, and the substantial northern fishing port of **Ullapool** (*see page 287*).

Ten miles (16 km) before Ullapool, stop at the **Measach Falls** which tumble down 120 ft (35 metres) into the spectacular **Corrieshalloch Gorge**.

SKYE

A giant "crab" slumbers off the north-western coast of Scotland. The crab is the romantic island of Skye – arguably the most magnificent of the dozens of Scottish islands – and justly described thus because of the many sea lochs that bite deep into its land mass and form several peninsulas, each of which can be compared to a crab's claws. So deep are these incisions that, although the island is about 50 miles (80 km) long and 30 miles (50 km) wide, no part is more than 5 miles (8 km) from the sea. The population, unlike that of most Scottish islands, is on the increase – mainly due to immigrants, many of whom are from south of the border.

Gaelic may soon, once again, become the first language of Skye. Road signs are already bilingual and in Portree the parents of more than half the children in early primary school have elected to have them taught in Gaelic. One hotel owner employs only those who speak the tongue. He also runs **Sabhal Mor Ostaig**, a centre of Gaelic learning.

Dominating the "Misty Island" are the jagged **Cuillins** whose snow-clad peaks, glistening remotely in the heaven, provide on a sharp winter's day as thrilling a landscape as any in Nepal or New Zealand. Soon, however, they shyly hide behind the gathering clouds of an approaching storm.

Strange that the Cuillins, the greatest concentration of tall peaks in Britain, are referred to as "hills" rather than mountains; although they attain a height of not much more than 3,000 ft (900 metres), they spring dramatically from sea level. They offer superb climbing, and most British mountaineering teams who have challenged Everest and other great 26,000-ft (8,000-metre) peaks of the world cut their teeth and did much of their serious training here.

Most visitors reach Skye by driving up and – except during August when there can be delays – driving on to a ferry for a 10-minute crossing between Kyle of Lochalsh and **Kyleakin**. Alternative car-ferry routes are from Glenelg to Kylerhea and from Mallaig to Armadale. The former, a ferry accommodating a mere handful of cars, runs only during the summer – never on a Sunday – while the latter becomes a passenger ferry only in the winter. The construction of a bridge between Kyle of Lochalsh and Kyleakin is under way but is meeting with much spirited opposition partially because, even although the ferry runs on Sundays, locals are against further desecration of the sabbath.

Overlooking Kyleakin harbour are the scanty ruins of **Castle Moil**, once a stronghold of the Mackinnons and a lookout post and fortress against raids by Norsemen. Six miles (10 km) out of Kyleakin, turn south on the A851 and, after 17 miles (27 km), arrive at **Armadale** and its ruined castle. This was formerly the home of the the MacDonalds who were once one of Scotland's most powerful clans and Lord of the Isles. The **Clan Donald Trust**, formed in the 1970s, which has members throughout the world, has turned

Preceding pages: looking towards the Hebrides. Left, Skyescape. Below, over the sea to Skye.

one wing of the ruined castle into a museum with audio-visual presentations. The old stables house an excellent restaurant, a good bookshop, and a giftshop and have luxurious self-catering accommodation. There's a ranger service and guided walks through the well-tended grounds with their mature trees and rhododendrons. Further exploration of this "claw" called **Sleat** (pronounced *Slate*) reveals why it bears the sobriquet "Garden of Skye".

Return to the A850 and immediately reach **Broadford** from where a diversion southwest on the A881 leads, after 14 miles (22 km), to the scattered village of **Elgol**. It was from here on 4 July 1746 that the Young Pretender, after being given a banquet by the Mackinnons in what is now called **Prince Charles's Cave**, finally bade farewell to the Hebrides. However, one visits Elgol not for history but for the view of the **Black Cuillins** which many claim is the most splendid view in all Britain.

In summer, motor-boats sail from Elgol across wide **Loch Scavaig**, past schools of seals, to land passengers on the rocks from where they can scramble upwards for half a mile to mile-long **Loch Coruisk** in the very heart of the Cuillins. Familiar? The scene was much painted by Turner and other romantics and written about by Sir Walter Scott.

Backtrack once more to the A850 and, after 7 miles (11 km) with the Red Cuillins to the left – they are much more rounded, much less dramatic than the Black Cuillins – you arrive at **Luib** and the **Old Skye Crofter's House**, the first of the Skye folk museums. Of particular interest is the collection of fading newspaper cuttings from the end of the 19th century which deal with crofters' grievances. Skye was the scene of some of the most intense fight-backs by crofters threatened with eviction during the Clearances and the Battle of the Braes (1882), when police were confronted by stone-throwing crofters, was the last battle fought in Britain.

The road continues through **Sligachan**, a base for serious climbers of the Black Cuillins and then descends into **Portree**, the island's capital, an attractive town built round a natural harbour and with neat and brightly painted houses rising steeply from the water. In 1773, when they visited Portree, Dr Johnson and James Boswell dined in the the Royal Hotel, then called MacNab's hostelry, believing it was "the only inn on the island". A quarter of a century before that, Prince Charlie bade farewell to Flora MacDonald at MacNab's. He repaid her half-a-crown she had lent him, gave her a miniature of himself and said: "For all that has happened I hope, Madam, we shall meet in St James yet." (St James was then the royal palace in London.) This was not to be and Flora never heard from the prince again. She did reach London, where she was imprisoned in the Tower for her part in the escapade. Later, she was released and returned to Skye where she married and had seven children.

Magnificent rock scenery and breathtaking views can be enjoyed by driving north from Portree on the **Trotternish Peninsula**. Seven miles (11 km) out along the A855 is **The Storr**, a 2,360-ft (708-metre) height which is shaped like a crown and offers a stiff two-hour climb; to its east is the **Old Man of Storr**, an isolated,150-ft (45-metre) pinnacle of rock. Further north is **Kilt Rock**, a sea cliff which owes its name to columnar basalt strata overlying horizontal ones beneath, the result bearing only the most fanciful relationship to a kilt.

A further 2 miles (4 km) leads to **Staffin**, immediately beyond which is **The Quiraing**, so broken up with massive rock faces that it looks like a range in miniature rather than a single mountain. The various rock features of the Quiraing – the castellated crags of **The Prison**, the slender unclimbed 100-ft (30-metre) **Needle** and **The Table**, a meadow as large as a football field – can be appreciated only on foot and can be reached readily by a path from a glorious minor road which cuts across the peninsula from Staffin to Uig.

However, to take this road rather than to loop around the tip of the Trotternish Peninsula is to forego some encounters with history. The annexe of the **Flodigarry Hotel** was Flora MacDonald's first home after her marriage in 1750 to Captain Allan MacDonald.

Adjacent to the museum is **Kilmuir churchyard**, where Flora lies buried, wrapped in a sheet from the bed in which the fugitive prince had slept. (Johnson would later sleep in this bed but "had no ambitious thoughts about it.") Her original gravestone is no more and a large Celtic cross now marks the spot. Inscribed on the base are Johnson's words: "A name that will be mentioned in history, and, if courage and fidelity be virtues, mentioned with honour." Look west from here: on a clear day there are fine views of the Outer Hebrides, from where Charlie and Flora fled to Skye.

Then, at the northwest tip of the peninsula, is the ruined **Duntulm Castle**, an ancient MacDonald stronghold commanding the sea route to the Outer Hebrides. It was abandoned after a nursemaid dropped the laird's infant son out of a window into the sea.

South of the castle is the **Skye Museum of Island Life** whose seven thatched cottages show how the crofters

lived. The cottages are built solidly of irregularly undressed stones painted white and topped by a rough thatch held by ropes weighted with heavy stones. A typical house had three rooms: a kitchen at one end, a room housing farm animals at the other and between a smaller room just large enough to accommodate a box bed. A peat fire would burn in a hearth in the centre of the kitchen and its smoke would escape through a hole in the roof. Much of the smoke would lodge in the thatch where it would congeal into a sticky liquid which, in damp weather, would drip on everyone below.

And so, after a few miles, to **Uig** from where ferries depart for Lochmaddy on North Uist and Tarbert on Harris. The road south from Uig returns to Portree but rather than turning left at the junction with the A850 turn right and travel westwards, across the base of the Trotternish peninsula, to arrive after 19 miles (30 km) at Dunvegan.

Just before Dunvegan, look south to **Macleod's Tables** which dominate the **Durinish Peninsula**. Their flatness is

The way we were: the Skye Museum of Island Life.

Skye 229

attributed to the inhospitality shown Columba when he preached to the local chief: in shame the mountains then shed their caps so that the saint might have a flat bed on which to lie.

No other castle in Scotland boasts so long a record of continuous occupation by one family as **Dunvegan** which has been home to the MacLeods for the past 700 years. Set on a rocky platform overlooking Loch Dunvegan, its stuccoed exterior lacks the splendour of at least a dozen other Scottish castle. Its interior, however, is another matter, with a wealth of paintings and memorabilia including a painting of Dr Johnson by Sir Joshua Reynolds and a lock of Bonnie Prince Charlie's hair.

Best known, though, is the "Faiery Flag", a torn and faded fragment of yellow silk spotted with red. Some say a fairy mother laid it over her half-mortal child when she had to return to her own people: others, more prosaic, that it was woven on the island of Rhodes in the 7th century and that a MacLeod captured it from a Saracen chief during the Crusades. Whatever its origins, the Faiery Flag is said to have three magic properties: when raised in battle it ensures a MacLeod victory; when spread over the MacLeod marriage bed it guarantees a child; and when unfurled at Dunvegan it charms the herring in the loch. The flag should be flown sparingly: its powerful properties will be exhausted when used three times. (So far, it has twice been invoked.)

Then there is the horn of "Rory Mor", the 15th chief. Tradition has it that at his inauguration the new chief must drink a claret-filled 4-pint (2-litre) horn (1½ bottles) to the dregs "without falling down or setting down".

Three miles (5 km) before Dunvegan, take the secondary B866 and travel northwards for 8 miles (13 km) to **Trumpan** where, in 1597 the "Faiery Flag" was unfurled. A raiding party of MacDonalds from the island of Uist landed and set fire to a church packed with worshipping MacLeods. The alarm was raised: the MacDonalds were unable to escape as a falling tide had left **Dunvegan Castle.**

their longboats high and dry: they were decimated. The bodies of friend and foe alike were laid out on the sands below the sea wall, which was then toppled to cover the corpses.

Primitive justice once practised on Skye is seen in the **Trumpan churchyard** in the shape a standing stone pierced by a circular hole. The accused would be blindfolded and, if he could put his finger unerringly through the Trial Stone, was deemed innocent.

A few miles west of Dunvegan are Colbost, then Glendale and Boreraig. The **Colbost Folk Museum** is very atmospheric, with a peat fire of the floor of the "black house" waiting to cook a stew and a boxbed uncomfortable enough to be genuine. Behind the house an illicit whisky still is sadly no longer in use but the fully restored 200-year-old watermill at **Glendale** is fully operational. **Boreraig** is as much a shrine to lovers of bagpipe music as Salzburg is to lovers of Mozart.

A cairn here marks the site of the piping school of the MacCrimmons, for 300 years the hereditary pipers to the MacLeods. According to legend, a fairy granted a young MacCrimmon great piping skills on condition that he obeyed when she summoned him. One day the fairy called the boy: he abandoned his pupils, walked to the shore, playing his silver chanter and disappeared forever into what is has become known as **MacCrimmon's Cave**. The school is now in ruins but opposite is a piping centre which records the feats of the MacCrimmon family, exhibits innumerable bagpipes and gives piping classes.

Heading south from Dunvegan, the A863 follows the shores of **Loch Bracadale**, one of the most magnificent fjords of the west coast, with the black basalt wall of **Talisker Head** away to the south. At **Dun Beag**, near Bracadale, is a well-preserved broch. A right turn onto the B885 before reaching Talisker leads back to Portree. Alternatively, remain on the B863 and either continue to Portree via Sligachan or, on reaching the head of **Loch Harport**, go right on B8009, and immediately cut back left into wooded **Glen Brittle** and more glorious views of the Black Cuillins. Remaining on the B8009 would have lead to **Carbost** and the renowned whisky distillery of Talisker.

The claim has been made that the sole purpose of Skye is to protect the small lush island of **Raasay**, just east of Skye. The Sabbath is strictly observed here and the ferry doesn't run on Sundays, when most of the population of 150, almost half of whom are over 60, are in church. There are two churches, one for the "Wee Frees", the other for a group of even stricter dissenters. In the 18th century the English burned all Raasay's houses and boats because the laird had sheltered Bonnie Prince Charlie after Culloden. **Dun Caan**, an extinct volcano, dominates the centre of the island.

Visitors can see the ruined **Brochel Castle**, home of the MacLeods of Skye and the grounds of Raasay House. When the exuberant Boswell stayed with Dr Johnson at Raasay House, now an outdoor pursuits centre, he danced a jig on top of the 1,500-ft (450-metre) high **Dun Caan** ridge.

THE INNER HEBRIDES

In the competition for visitors between Mull and Skye, the easiest Hebridean islands to reach, Skye wins hands down. "If Bonnie Prince Charlie had escaped over the sea to Mull, we'd been enjoying the benefits of mass tourism here," says one envious Mull hotelier.

Some scorn **Mull**'s green prettiness, dismissing it as Surrey with a tartan fringe. They might think again if they strolled on a wet day past Loch Scridain through the boggy desolation of the **Ross of Mull** or walked to the top of Mull's only mountain, **Ben More**, a respectable 3,169 ft (950 metres).

The island is shaped like a gigantic teddy bear, but don't be deceived by its size, only 25 by 26 miles (40 by 41 km). A drive on the mainly single-track roads, running mostly round the perimeter, is made even slower by Scotland's most feckless and fearless sheep, which regard roads simply as grassless fields.

Preceding pages: Tobermory, on Mull. Left, Iona Abbey.

Mull's trump card is **Tobermory**, the prettiest port in Western Scotland, captivating and cheerful. Skye has nothing to touch it; even the impeccably renovated stable block at Skye's Clan Donald Centre can't compete with the natural charm of Tobermory, tucked in a wooded protected bay whose waters are almost invariably unruffled. Yet, in 1588, an explosion reverberated across the bay and the waters gurgled as the Spanish galleon *Florida* sank to the bottom. The exact spot, just 100 metres straight out from the pier, is well defined. And here, it is believed, a vast treasure of gold awaits salvage. Not that innumerable attempts have not been made, unsuccessfully, to retrieve it.

The tall, brightly painted houses curving round the harbour go back to the late 18th century when the British Fisheries Society planned a herring port. But the fish were fickle and today Tobermory's sparkling harbour bobs with pretty pleasure yachts. The other towns, **Craignure** on the east where the Oban ferry docks, **Salen**, in the narrow neck of the island, and **Dervaig** in the northwest, are neat serviceable little places. Visitors come to the volcanic island of Mull for the contrasting scenery, wooded and soft to bleak and bare; for fishing in the lochs; and for walking. Drive through Glen More, the ancient royal funeral route to Iona which bisects Mull from east to west, for some of the best scenery on the island. Also in Dervaig is the most enjoyable **Mull Little Theatre** which, with 43 seats, is the smallest professional theatre in Britain.

Then, on the west of the island, there's **Calgary**, the silver-sand beach where, after the Clearances, despairing emigrant ships set sail for the New World. The beach held happy memories for one émigré: Colonel McLeod of the North West Mounted Police named a new fort in Alberta after it.

Further proof, if it be needed, that Scotland's two main exports are whisky and brains can be found just south of Calgary at **Loch Ba** near Salen. The MacQuarie Mausoleum houses the remains of Major-General Lachlan MacQuarie, the first Governor-General of

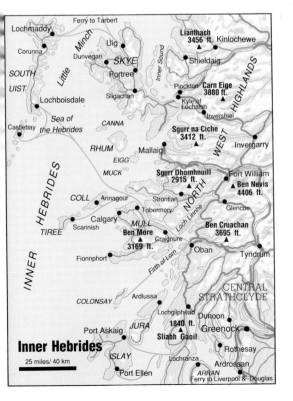

Inner Hebrides

25 miles/ 40 km

New South Wales who is sometimes called the "Father of Australia".

To understand what the 19th-century Clearances meant to all Hebrideans and to grasp the harshness of a crofting life, see the tableaux, with sound commentary, at the **Old Byre Heritage Centre** at Dervaig. They help explain the islanders' fatalistic attitude to life. Some charitable outsiders think this attitude stems from the trauma of the Clearances which still trouble the collective consciousness. But cynical mainlanders say the islanders are simply idle, and get lazier. Islanders – when you can find them, for many service jobs, particularly those connected with tourism, seem to be run by incomers – say they work as hard as anyone. Crofting and fishing, they argue, just aren't understood by urbanised outsiders.

Two castles are open to the public, both on the east. **Torosay**, with 19th-century Scottish baronial turrets and crenellations, is near Craignure and is reached from there on a 1½-mile (2-km) steam miniature railway. The castle is still lived in by the Guthrie-James family. It's full of family memorabilia and is a friendly, non-imposing house. On wet days (frequent), you can leaf through old books in the drawing room. There's shapely Italian statuary in the 11 acres (4½ hectares) of terraced grounds, fine clematis climbing on old brick walls, and a sweet-smelling rock garden.

The 13th-century **Duart Castle** on a dramatic headland overlooking the Sound of Mull was the MacLeans' stronghold. Mull belonged to the clan until it was forfeited when the MacLeans supported young Prince Charles Edward, who was defeated at Culloden in 1746. The castle was deserted for almost 200 years, then restored by Sir Fitzroy MacLean early this century. As a young Hussar, MacLean charged with the Light Brigade in the Crimea in 1854, and some of his mementoes are displayed in the Grand Banqueting Room.

Ferry tales: Mull is the jumping-off point for several islands: Iona, Staffa, the Treshnish Isles, Coll and Tiree.

You feel a bit like a pilgrim as you **Mull mails.**

board the serviceable little 10-minute shuttle to **Iona**. Cars and big coaches on day trips from the mainland line the ferry road at **Fionnphort** on Mull's southwest tip, for visitors must cross to the Holy Island on foot. Curiosity and a search for some intangible spiritual comfort draw well over half a million people from all over the world each year to this tiny 3-mile (5-km) island where Saint Columba and 12 companions landed from Ireland in the 6th century to set up the mission that turned Iona into the Christian centre of Europe.

In 1773 Dr Samuel Johnson was impressed with the piety of Iona. The abbey, which had been suppressed at the Reformation, was still in ruins and there were not many visitors then. In the 1930s the low, sturdy building, about half a mile from the ferry, was restored by the Iona Community; visitors have increased ever since. Accept the crowds and go round at your own pace. Some of the best restoration is the tiny cloister, especially the birds and plants on the slender replacement sandstone columns. They were meticulously copied from the one remaining medieval original. There's an unusual attention-grabbing modern bronze by Jacob Lipschitz in the green centre of the cloister.

The general store near the ferry has added bicycle hire to its varied services, so there's time in theory to see **Coracle Cove** where Columba landed in AD 563. From the abbey it is just 100 metres to the cemetery of **Relig Oran** where, it is alleged, lie the remains of 48 kings of Scotland, seven Norwegian and four Irish kings. The last king to be buried here was Duncan who, according to Shakespeare, was murdered by Macbeth: he too is supposedly buried in Relig Oran. Dr Johnson was sceptical: "the graves are very numerous and some of them undoubtedly contain the remains of men who did not expect to be soon forgotten".

Fingal's Cave on **Staffa** is a big attraction; supposedly it inspired Mendelssohn to compose his overture. The experience of going into the cave, if the weather is good enough for landing, is

Fascinating rock formations on Staffa.

well worth the 90-minute boat journey – tedious when the weather is bad. The primeval crashing of the sea, the towering height of the cave and the complete lack of colour in the sombre rocks make a powerful impression. Even if the little 47-ft (14-metre) partially covered passenger launch can't land, it's worth making the journey just to see the curious hexagonal basalt rocks with the gaping black hole of the cave. Birdwatchers, too, have plenty to enjoy.

Beyond Staffa are the uninhabited **Treshnish Islands** – uninhabited, that is, unless you count sheep, bewitching puffins, kittiwakes, razorbills, shags, fulmars, gannets and guillemots.

The ferry from Oban for Coll and Tiree calls at Tobermory for additional passengers. There's the usual rivalry between these sister islands, most distant of the Inner Hebrides. People from Tiree can't understand why anyone wants to get off the ferry at Coll. The people of Coll maintain that the inhabitants of Tiree are permanently bent by the island's ceaseless wind.

Purists, or those against progress, feel **Coll** is too civilised. A young cyclist, camping near the glorious west coast beaches, complained that the island's only hotel had gone suburban when it installed a sauna; while a 75-year-old resident of **Arinagour**, the island's only village, where most of the population of 150 live, spoke with astonishment of the local café's advanced ideas – recently revitalised and repainted, it had emerged as a bistro.

Young families go to Coll for the simple holiday, pottering on uncrowded beaches. Much of the coast can be reached only on foot – although bicycles can be hired. This isn't an island for antiquities, and the restored medieval castle of **Breacachadh** is only sometimes open to the public.

A later, 18th-century castle in much worse shape is where Samuel Johnson and James Boswell spent most of their time when stranded on Coll for 10 days during their Highland Tour. Johnson commented on the island's garden flowers but neither he nor Boswell attempted

Tiree farming: the wind never seems to drop.

to climb – neither was energetic – the giant dunes (100 ft/30 metres) separating the nearby long sandy beaches of Feall Bay and Crossapool Bay.

Tiree's Gaelic name, *Tir fo Thuinn*, means "land below the waves". It's a good description of this flat, sunny island whose two hills are only 400 ft high (120 metres). One of the islands' most eccentric visitors was Ada Goodrich Freer, who claimed telepathic gifts and an ability to receive messages through sea shells. She spent three weeks on Tiree in 1894 investigating Highland second sight. She spoke no Gaelic, but was finally defeated, not by the language but by the monotonous diet of tea, eggs, bread and jam provided by the Temperance hotel.

Nowadays international windsurfers, who call Tiree the Hawaii of the North, are attracted to the island by the great Atlantic rollers that break on the long, curving silver beaches.

Some people find **Colonsay** too bland. On the other hand, a woman from Oban claims it to be her favourite island sim-ply because it has no distinguishing features. She finds Mull too pretty and doesn't care for the lowering Cuillins of Skye. Colonsay, 40 miles (64 km) south-west of Oban, is just right. It has its antiquities, seven standing stones and six forts, and excellent wildlife – birds, otters and seals. It has good white beaches and isn't over-mountainous. Visitors are few as there are no organised day-trips and, because the ferry calls only three times a week, accommodation has to be found either at the one hotel or with families providing bed and breakfast.

The island, 8 miles (12 km) long and 3 miles (4 km) wide, has a population of 120 and is one of the largest British islands still in private hands. It is warmed by the North Atlantic Drift, and the gardens of **Colonsay House**, open to the public, have a variety of exotic plants. It's said that the island's wild goats are descended from survivors of the Spanish Armada ships wrecked in 1588.

At low tide it's possible to walk across muddy sands to tiny **Oronsay**, off the

Tiree fishing: calm now, but the Atlantic can be fearsome.

southern tip of Colonsay; alternatively there are boat trips. Oronsay is about 2 miles (3 km) square and has a population of six. Its fine 14th-century priory is the biggest medieval monastic ruin in the islands, after Iona.

Island-hopping: The small islands of Eigg, Muck, Rum and Canna can be reached from Mallaig on the Sleat peninsula, the end of the "Road to the Isles". There's not a great deal to do on the islands. Mostly people go for the wildlife, for a bit of esoteric island-hopping or to stay at Britain's most inaccessible luxury hotel on Rum.

The islands are all different and, if you just want to see them without landing, take the little boat that makes the five to seven-hour round-trip six times a week in the summer, less often in winter. It's a service for islanders rather than a pleasure boat for visitors, and carries provisions, mail, newspapers and other essentials. Only those planning to stay are allowed to disembark. However, in summer, boarding the *MV Shearwater* at Arisaig, 8 miles (13 km) before Mallaig, allows you to stop for several hours at either Eigg or Rum.

Eigg is famous for its laird, Yorkshire businessman Keith Schellenberg and his Games. These last for three days and involve all 70 permanent inhabitants and any visitors lucky (or rash) enough to visit the island in July. Schellenberg's friends and relatives fly in from all over the world for water sports and more Scottish pursuits. The grand finale is a reenactment of the struggle between the Jacobites and the Hanoverians. The silver trophies awarded at the end are of course Eigg Cups.

Muck gets its unfortunate name (Gaelic for pig) from the porpoises or sea-pigs that swim round its shores. It's the smallest of the four islands, only 2 miles (3 km) long, and has neither transport nor shops. Visitors must bring provisions and be landed by tender. Eighty breeds of birds nest on Muck.

There's an incongruous Greek temple on the rugged island of **Rum**: the mausoleum of Sir George Bullough, the island's rich Edwardian proprietor. His

Islay whisky is known for its peaty taste.

castellated **Kinloch Castle**, used as a convalescent home during the Boer War just after it was built, is an opulent hotel. Both hotel and island are owned by the Scottish Natural Heritage. There is fine bird watching and hill walking.

Graffiti adorn the rocks near the landing stage at **Canna**; they are at least 100 years old and record the names of visiting boats. The harbour's safe haven is one of the few deepwater harbours in the Hebrides. This sheltered island, most westerly of the four, is owned by the National Trust for Scotland and is particularly interesting to botanists. No holiday accommodation exists.

Islay's the place if you enjoy malt whisky. There are over half a dozen distilleries on this attractive little island, some with tours. Islay, where Clan Donald started, was once the home of the Lord of the Isles. It has some good beaches on the indented north coast. Also on this side of the island is one of the best Celtic crosses in Scotland: the 9th-century **Kildalton Cross** stands in the churchyard of a ruined, atmospheric

little chapel. **Port Askaig**, where the ferry from the Kintyre peninsula docks, is a pretty little place with a hotel, once a 16th-century inn on the old drovers' road a few steps away from the ferry.

Jura, Islay's next-door neighbour, is so close you can nip over for a quick inspection after dinner. Three shapely mountains, the Paps of Jura, 2,500 ft (750 metres) high, provide a striking skyline. Although palms and rhododendrons grow on the sheltered east side, it's a wild island inhabited by sheep and red deer and is much favoured by sportsmen, birdwatchers and climbers.

Gigha has one of the nicest hotels in the islands – bright, Scandinavian and beautifully neat and simple. No need to take a car on the 3-mile (5-km) crossing from **Tayinloan** to this small green island popular with yachting people: no walk is more than 3 miles from the attractive ferry terminal at **Ardminish** with its sparkling white cottages. The formal attraction is **Achamore Gardens**. Seals, barking amiably, cruise in the waters off the little used north pier.

Does a scarecrow also scare seagulls?

THE OUTER HEBRIDES

The Outer Hebrides, 40 miles (64 km) west of the mainland, are known locally as the Long Islands. They stretch in a narrow 130-mile (208-km) arc from the Butt of Lewis in the north to Barra Head in the south. Their eroded and often dramatic west coasts are relentlessly pounded by the cold Atlantic. Some visitors are thrilled by their wild bleakness, others find it disconcerting. Each island regards itself as the fairest in the chain. The people live mainly by crofting and fishing with commercial fish farming – crabs and mussels as well as the usual salmon and trout – growing fast.

There are enormous flat peat bogs on Lewis and North Uist and the islanders cut turf to burn rather than to export to the garden centres of England. The men cut it during the summer and stack it *in situ*; when it has dried the women and children cart it home and stack it against the house for winter fires. A traditional

Preceding pages: **Hercules Irvine,** **crofter. Left,** **Farne, a** **remote corner** **of the Outer** **Hebrides.**

blessing on Lewis is: "Long may you live, with smoke from your house."

Fierce loyalty: These climatically hostile Western Isles of few trees and stark scenery are the Gaidhealechd, the land of the Gael. When their Gaelic-speaking inhabitants change to English, as they politely do when visitors are present, they have virtually no accent and are among the easiest Scots for visitors to understand. They were fiercely loyal to Bonnie Prince Charlie. When, after the Battle of Culloden in 1746, the young man, with a £30,000 price on his head, dodged round the Outer Hebrides pursued by "Butcher" Cumberland, no-one betrayed him.

Harris and the larger **Lewis** are really one island. Lewis is mostly flat. Harris rises into high, rocky mountains culminating in North Harris in the peak of The Clisham (2,622 ft/690 metres).

Turn north from the ferry terminal at **Tarbert** for Lewis; south for Harris. (Beware of Tarberts in the Highlands, though: there are many, and it's all too easy to end up at the wrong one. The name means a narrow spit of land over which a boat can be pulled from one stretch of water to another.) The tiny Tarbert on the narrow isthmus joining Harris and Lewis is technically in Harris, a land of bare hills and fierce peaks. Ferries from Lochmaddy on North Uist and Uig on Skye dock in this sheltered port tucked into the hillside. There are a few shops, the Harris Hotel, a tourist office and sheds selling Harris tweed.

A drive around South Harris (40 miles/ 64 km) is rewarding. As you head south on the A859 down the west coast, you pass many glorious beaches – **Luskentyre, Scarista** – before reaching **Leverburgh**, with the remains of the buildings erected by the industrialist Lord Leverhulme (of Sunlight soap fame) for a projected fishing port. The road ends at **Rodel** with the 16th-century **St Clement's Church**, one of the best examples of ecclesiastical architecture in the Hebrides.

The single track road up the east coast offers superb seascapes and views across the Minch to Skye and tiny crofts from where you hear – as you do throughout

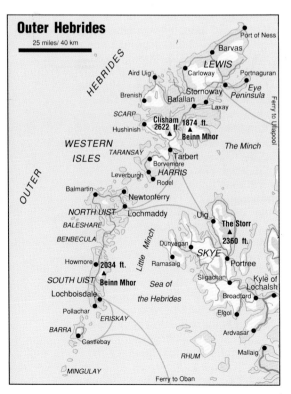

Outer Hebrides

25 miles/ 40 km

HEBRIDES

Port of Ness
Barvas
LEWIS
Aird Uig
Carloway
Portnaguran
Brenish
Stornoway
Eye Peninsula
Balallan
Laxay
SCARP
Clisham 2622 ft. 1874 ft.
Hushinish
Beinn Mhor
The Minch
WESTERN
TARANSAY
ISLES
Tarbert
Borvemore
Leverburgh
HARRIS
Rodel
Balmartin
Newtonferry
NORTH UIST Lochmaddy
Uig
BALESHARE
The Storr
BENBECULA
Dunvegan
2360 ft.
SKYE
Howmore 2034 ft.
Ramasaig
Portree
SOUTH UIST **Beinn Mhor** *Sea of*
Sligachan
Kyle of Lochalsh
Lochboisdale
the Hebrides
Broadford
Pollachar
Elgol
ERISKAY
BARRA
Ardvasar
Castlebay
RHUM
Mallaig
MINGULAY
Ferry to Oban

OUTER
Little Minch
Ferry to Ullapool

the Long Islands – the click-clack of crofters' looms producing tweed.

Back at Tarbert, a woman advised against Stornoway. "Nothing to see there," she said. "You're better off driving to **Hushinish Point**, especially in the evening when the salmon are rising." Visitors should try both.

Leave Tarbert for the north on the A859 and after 4 miles (6 km) turn onto the B887 which clings to the shore of **West Loch Tarbert**. The 16-mile (26-km) drive from Tarbert to golden **Hushinish Point** is dramatic, particularly in the evening if you see the setting sun silvering West Loch Tarbert and catching the peaks of Beinn Dhubh on Harris just across the water.

The road goes straight through the well maintained grounds of **Amhuinn-suidhe Castle** (pronounced *Avin-suey*), so close to the house you can almost see inside. This pale turretted castle, now a fishing lodge, was built in 1868 and James Barrie began his novel *Mary Rose* here. A stone's throw from the lodge, a salmon river runs into the sea. In late June and early July, salmon and sea trout leap the falls and swim from pool to pool on their way up river.

From Hushinish, ferries cross to the small island of **Scarp**. In the 1930s a new postal service was announced here. A special stamp was issued; the first rocket was fired, but unfortunately it exploded, destroying mail and project.

Back-track to the A859 which twists and turns past lochs and through mountains to arrive after 35 miles (56 km) at **Stornoway**, the capital of Lewis and the only large town in the Western Isles. Most activity in this solid town of 6,000 inhabitants is at the harbour where seals can nearly always be seen. They give Stornoway its nickname of Portrona (Port of Seals). Here too thousands of silver fish, which will be turned into fertiliser, can be seen being sucked by a giant vacuum hoses from boats' decks into waiting lorries. Here, the ferry from Ullapool, on the mainland, docks.

The best view of the **Lews Castle** is from the harbour. Lord Leverhulme bought the castle in 1918. In 1920 he purchased Harris, becoming Britain's largest landowner. His goals were admirable: to turn the islanders into a viable community not dependent on crofting but making its living from the sea. The "wee soap mannie's " visions were admirable. That he failed was only because of timing: today, fishing dominates the island's economy.

To explore Lewis's many antiquities, leave Stornoway on the A859 and, after a couple of miles, bear right onto the A858. **Callanish** and its magnificent standing stones is 16 miles (26 km) from Stornoway. The 13 ritual stones, some 12 ft (3 metres) high, are set in a circle like Stonehenge. Nobody is quite sure why they're there. Once, they were known as *Nu Fir Breige* – the false men. They have been claimed as a Viking parliament, a landing base for UFOs and a site for predicting eclipses. The standing stones, duns and burial cairns on or just off the west coast road that bends round East Loch Roag and Little Loch Roag hint at how important the Western Isles were in prehistoric times.

Keeping to the A858, you soon reach the upstanding remains of the 2,000-year old **Carloway Broch**; then the folk museum at **Shawbost** and then **Arnol** with its **Black House Museum** which shows how the people of Lewis used to live. A different world unfolds – white versus black – if, just before Callanish, you take the B8011: it leads to **Uig** and its truly wondrous beaches.

Language problem: The official tourist map of the Outer Hebrides is essential for the Uists. Even though only one main road links the three islands of North Uist, Benbecula and South Uist, most signposts are in Gaelic; the map gives them in English too. The Lochmaddy tourist office has a free sheet of English/Gaelic names put out by the Western Isles Islands Council. To help preserve one of Europe's oldest languages, the Council has put up Gaelic-only place names and signposts in the Outer Hebrides. In English-speaking Benbecula and in Stornoway on Lewis, the signs are also in English.

Lochmaddy, where the ferry from Uig in Skye docks, is the only village on **North Uist**, and you're almost through it before you realise it's there. But to show its capital status it has a hotel and a bank. Outside the "Wehaveit" general store, a small boy told us to expect the Uist roads to be different from the map because the constant movement of the bog made them change direction. Certainly at times the causeway road feels as springy as a dance floor.

The Uist archipelago of low bright islands dominated by the glittering sea is 50 miles long and only 8 miles at its widest (80 by 13 km) and is so peppered with lochs that on the map the east coast round Benbecula looks like a sieve.

Rather than setting south on the A865 which runs for 45 miles (72 km) and which, because of causeway and bridge, virtually makes North Uist, Benbecula and South Uist one island, travel around North Uist in a counter-clockwise direction on the A865. On a 45-mile (72-km) trip, you pass superb beaches and antiquarian treasures.

Stornoway: the harbour is the liveliest part of town.

Three miles (5 km) from Lochmaddy are the standing stones of **Blashaval**. Three miles further on, a turn-off on the right (B893) leads to **Newtonferry** and the short ferry trip to the island of **Berneray** where Prince Charles occasionally recharges his batteries. Back on Uist, in the middle of the north shore, is the rocky islet of **Eilean-an-Tighe**, the oldest pottery "factory" in Western Europe: it produced quality items in Stone Age times.

Still on the north coast is the superb beach of **Vallay** (actually an island reached on foot: beware tides). Round on the west coast, green and whiter than in the east, is **Baleshare,** another island with a great beach joined to Uist by a causeway. Before reaching here, you pass the **Balranald Nature Reserve** which was created to protect the breeding habitat of the red-necked phalarope.

At **Clachan** the A865 turns south while the A867 runs east to return to Lochmaddy. Five miles (8 km) along the latter is **Barpa Lanyass**, a 5,000-year-old squashed beehive tomb. Nearby is the **Pobull Fhinn** standing stone circle. Backtrack to the A865; just before the causeway is **Carinish** where Scot-

land's last battle with swords and bows and arrows took place. Nearby is the ruined 12th-century **Trinity Temple**.

Cross the North Ford by the 5-mile (8-km) causeway to reach tiny **Benbecula** whose eastern part is so pitted with lochs that most people live on the west coast. The traveller now has the choice of proceeding due south for 5 miles (8 km) to the southern tip of Benbecula or turning right onto the B892 which makes a 10-mile (16-km) loop around the west of the island before rejoining the A865.

The loop road first passes the small airport (flights to Glasgow, Barra, Stornoway) and a Royal Artillery base before **Culla Beach** – the best of many great beaches – and the ruins of **Borve Castle** with 10-foot (3-metre) thick walls. The castle, one of the most important medieval ruins in the Outer Hebrides, was built in the 14th century and was the home of the MacDonalds of Clanranalad, who once ruled Benbecula.

Flora, that gallant MacDonald who helped Bonnie Prince Charlie escape after his humiliation at Culloden, belonged to this family. Benbecula is ever associated with the wanderings of Charlie who landed at Rossinish at the northwest corner of the island on 27 April, 1746 and, after 60 days dodging the English – this was for ever compounded by his losing his shoes in the peaty bogs – left Benbecula for Skye.

The South Ford, separating Benbecula and **South Uist** is crossed by a half-mile long single-track bridge. Immediately on entering South Uist turn right and drive for a mile along the loch-lined road to **Eochar** and the shell-covered school bus in Flora Johnstone's garden. Flora so enjoyed sticking on shells that, in the 1960s, she then started on her cottage walls. Beyond this is **Loch Bee** with its hundreds of mute swans.

Return to the main road (A865) which runs down the west of the island for 22 miles (35 km) before terminating at Pollachar at the southwest tip. All the time, to the west, are seascapes with yet more splendid beaches and, to the east, mountains and peat bogs dominated by

Sheep shearers at work on South Uist.

Ben Mhor (2,034 feet/610 metres) and Hecla (1,988 feet/587 metres). These names, Celtic and Norse, reveal the dual main stream in the island's population.

First encountered, to the east, after 4 miles (6 km) atop **Rueval Hill,** "hill of miracles", is the modern pencil-like statue of **Madonna and Child** which was paid for by world-wide donations. Just beyond this, still to the east, is the **Loch Druidiberg Nature Reserve** with its corncrakes and greylag geese.

Next, to the west, is **Howmore.** Little here indicates that this was the ancient ecclesiastical centre of the island: now, protected white-washed cottages, one a youth hostel, stand in flowery meadows. Continue beyond Howmore to reach a superb beach.

Another 6 miles (10 km) to the south and, on the right, before the turn-off to **Milton,** is a bronze cairn and plaque honouring the birthplace of Flora MacDonald. Two miles (3 km) further south, the A865 turns left to run for 4 miles (6 km) to tiny **Lochboisdale,** the main village in the south of the island and the terminal for the Oban ferry. The Highlands and Islands Development Board which, along with the EEC, puts a great deal of money into the Western Isles, provided the tourist office in this pleasantly wandering little village, as it did in many other parts of the islands. The general store sells everything.

At **Pollachar** is a 3,000-year-old standing stone surrounded by wild orchids and clover from where you can gaze across to Eriskay and Barra. From **Ludag,** a mile to the east, a car ferry (subject to tides) crosses the 1¾-mile (3-km) stretch of water to **Eriskay.**

The island, famous because of the hauntingly beautiful "Eriskay Love Lilt", is disappointing: just an unimpressive hump. For a fishing island only 2 by 3 miles (3 by 5 km) with a population of around 200, it has had much fame. Bonnie Prince Charlie landed on the long silver beach on the west side on 23 July 1745. Two hundred years later the *Politician,* a cargo ship carrying 24,000 cases of whisky, sank in the Eriskay Sound. Compton Mackenzie's *Whisky Galore* (known in America as *Tight Little Island*) was a hilarious retelling of the redistribution of the cargo.

The timetable for flights to much more gentle **Barra,** the most southerly of the inhabited Hebridean islands, must be the only one in the British Isles to specify that arrivals are subject to tides. The small Logan Air passenger planes servicing the island land on Cockle Strand, a runway that twice a day disappears under the incoming tide.

Fishing dominates Barra, as it always has. In the 1880s, choice Barra cockles were eaten in London. By the 1920s, Barra herring were so important that girls came from as far away as Yarmouth in England to work 17 hours a day in **Castlebay,** the capital, gutting the silver darlings. In the past 20 years, lobster fishing has become important, with about 40 boats operating.

Although the islanders sometimes feel isolated, especially in winter when the boat from the mainland can't always get in, they are resourceful and self-reliant, even producing a weekly bilingual paper, the *Barra Bulletin.*

Coming out of her shell: Flora Johnstone of Eochar, South Uist.

CENTRAL SCOTLAND

Just who recorded that the Romans said "Behold the Tiber" at first sight of the Tay isn't clear, but certainly all roads lead to **Perth**, Scotland's one-time capital, and a superb centre for exploring Central Scotland.

Georgian terraces and imposing civic buildings line the riverside, but principal streets are uncompromisingly Victorian. No dullness, though. "All things bright and beautiful" on the bells of the handsome 15th-century **St John's Kirk** heralds the hour strike in a 36-bell belfry – a contrast to the iconoclastic rantings and ravings when John Knox preached here in the mid-16th century.

Away from the smart shops are surprises like the golden salmon that leaps over Malloch's fishing tackle shop, and the Auto Garden Chain-saw Centre, promising peaceable massacre. Behind **High Street** the near-circular projections of house stairs play at castles, and rushing streams under stone bridges turn wheels for city mills to entertain customers of the Stakis City Mills Hotel.

Behind the imposing portico and dome of the **Museum and Art Gallery** is drama in Sir David Young Cameron's landscape *Shadows of Glencoe*, in the stuffed but still snarling wildcat, its bushy tail black-tipped, and in Perth's link with space, the Strathmore Meteorite of 1917. More art can be enjoyed in the round-house of the old waterworks, now a delightful gallery devoted to the life and works of the Perthshire painter J. D. Ferguson, one of the Scottish colourists. *The Fair Maid of Perth*, Sir Walter Scott's virginal heroine, lived nearby in **Fair Maid's House**, the setting for his novel of the time of the battle of Clans on the meadow of the North Inch nearby. The house is now a contemporary crafts shop.

Those with aesthetic tastes or presents to buy are also catered for at **Caithness Glass**, where the mysteries of paperweight-making are revealed. Others can view blending, bottling and taste the product of **Dewar's**, whose old premises do service for Perth's castle. They can then work off the effects at **Bell's Sports Centre**. History and tradition take the stage in the **Perth Theatre**, the longest established theatre in Scotland.

Splendid views over the city and River Tay can be enjoyed from the top of **Kinnoull Hill** on the outskirts of the city, while **Branklyn Gardens** have been described as "the finest two acres of private gardens in the country."

Perth is ringed with castles, some still family homes, but many are romantic ruins like **Huntingtower**, 3 miles (4 km) west, where the space between two towers is called the Maiden's Leap. Perhaps the resident bat colony frightened her. An intriguing roof-top walk gives glimpses of hidden stairs and dark voids that must have struck terror into James I during his year's imprisonment. How often must he have lifted his eyes to these same printed ceilings?

Scone Palace, 2 miles (3 km) north of Perth, was Scotland's Camelot and home to the much travelled **stone** on which 40 kings of Scotland were crowned.

Preceding pages, taking a dip in Loch Lomond. Left, Scone Palace. Below, a race on the River Tay.

Brought here in the 9th century and taken to London in 1296 by Edward I, it was stolen in 1950 from beneath the Coronation Chair in Westminster Abbey and recovered from Arbroath. The Earl of Mansfield's home offers such diverse charms as six generations of family photographs, Highland cattle, ornamental fowls and giant trees as well as a treasure house of period furniture, elegant porcelain and paintings.

Tickling and curling: A lake for all seasons, **Loch Leven** is heaven for trout anglers and the chosen wintering ground for wild geese and curling enthusiasts. On an island and reached by ferry from the lochside is ruined **Loch Leven Castle**, which keeps open house in summer though it was once prison to the notorious Wolf of Badenoch and Mary Queen of Scots. After nearly a year, during which she suffered a miscarriage, Mary escaped by boat with the help of her jailer's son. The keys he threw in the lake were recovered 400 years later.

Falkland Palace, sitting cosily in the main street of its old Royal Burgh, was the favourite retreat of the Stuart kings. The streets themselves are full of love tokens. Stone lintels that top many doors carry the incised initials of the couples the houses were built for in the 1600s, the date and a heart. On one house front: "Contentment is great riches". Loving care is evident everywhere in the many laundered green spaces and carefully conserved weavers' houses.

Castle Campbell is rather impressively situated at the head of Dollar Glen, southwest of Perth. **Menstrie Castle**, near Stirling, the birthplace of Sir William Alexander, James VI's lieutenant, links Scotland with Nova Scotia. Near Crieff, **Drummond Castle** opens only its gardens and surprisingly they are Italian – statues, trees and shrubs dotting the parterre like chess pieces.

The King of Fife: The M90 motorway that links Perth to Edinburgh does more than by-pass Fife, thrust out into the North Sea between the Firth of Forth and the Tay. It by-passes an area rich in history, architecture and scenery. The kingdom's harbours nudge one another

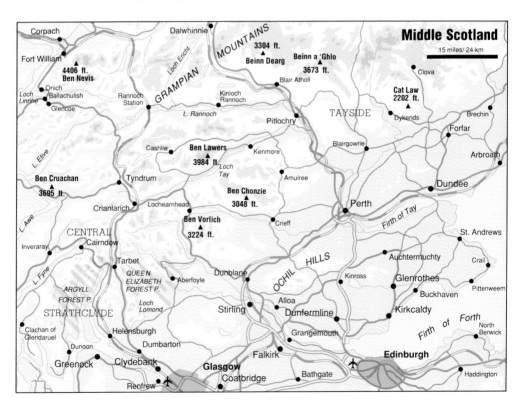

on a coast tilted towards Scandinavia, buildings and customs reflecting the thriving trade it had in the 17th century with the Baltic and the Low Countries.

Culross, where the Firth of Forth narrows, is a unique survival: a 17th and 18th-century town that looks like a film set, and often is. Then it was a smokey, industrial town with coal mines and salt pans, manufacturing griddles and baking plates for oatcakes. Scottish parents often threatened their children with "I'll gar your lugs ring like a Culross griddle." A clip round the ear?

Sir George Bruce, who took over where the mining monks left off in 1575, went on to such success that James VI made Culross a Royal Burgh. Today, the town's wealth of old buildings, with their crow-stepped gables and red pantiled roofs, make it one of Scotland's finest showplaces. The **Town House**'s clock tower dominates the waterfront and the **Mercat Cross**, the tiny market place and oldest house (1577).

Wynds, or pathways, lead past the "**Palace**", the "**Study**", with its 17th-century Norwegian painted ceiling, and **Snuff Cottage** (1673) with the inscription "Wha wad ha thocht it". "Noses wad ha bought it" is the second line. Past the house with the Evil Eyes are the church, the ruined abbey and the magnificent Abbey House. One typical whitewashed cottage contains, of all things, an electricity substation.

Although **Dunfermline** was for 600 years capital of Scotland, burial place of kings, with a fine church and abbey, it owes its international importance to its humblest son, Andrew Carnegie. The great philanthropist opened the first of 3,000 free libraries here in 1881. The tiny cottage where he was born contrasts vividly with **Pittencrieff**, the mansion he left to the town on his death. Both are museums. In mock castellation the cut-out words "King Robert the Bruce" on the church tower advertise his burial here in 1329, "wrapped in a cloth of gold". The columns of the Norman nave, chevroned and diagonalled like Durham, preside over pewless space.

From the sublime to the grotto: at

The gardens at Falkland Palace, a favourite retreat of the Stuarts.

Leven, behind the esplanade and the parked oil rigs, are marvellous shell gardens. Begun in 1914, walls, walks, menagerie and aviary are patterned with shells, broken china and enough Staffordshire figures to make an antique dealer's fingers itch.

Kirkcaldy's all too evident association with coal and floor coverings may not appeal, but Lang Town, as it is often called, made important contributions to architecture, economics and literature. Robert Adam and Adam Smith were born here.

Lower Largo, its tiny harbour and inn stage-set beneath a viaduct, gave birth in 1676 to Alexander Selkirk, Daniel Defoe's "Robinson Crusoe".

The original "Fifie" fishing boats were built at **St Monans**, but the shipyard now builds only pleasure craft. A path leads from the harbour to the 14th-century church, its feet on the rocky shore.

Pittenweem bustles with the business of fish. Above it, the old Royal Burgh snoozes with its memories of Augustinian monks and a tax collector

whose robbery in 1736 led to riots in Edinburgh. Next door, almost, **Anstruther**, with a fisheries museum, and **Crail** end the run of picturesque harbours before Fife Ness is reached. The oldest Royal Burgh in East Neuk, Crail's crow-stepped gables and red-tiled roofs ensure that artists outnumber fishermen.

Sport of kings: There is a nice contrast in leaving the simplicities of Crail for the concentration of learning, religious importance and historical significance that is **St Andrews.** Here, even golf qualifies as "Ancient" as well as "Royal", its Old Course laid out in the 15th century and the Royal and Ancient Golf Club formed in 1754. There are no fewer than six courses. If none of these appeal, then all sorts of interesting memorabilia can be enjoyed at the **British Golf Museum** immediately opposite the "Old" starters' hut.

It is not known whether John Knox played the game, but the damage to the cathedral following his impassioned sermons started neglect that reduced it to ruins. **St Rule** nearby survives as a tower and St Andrews Castle fared little better. Elsewhere, the **West Port** spans a main street and steeples abound, but not for climbing, as Dr Johnson found. The **University**, whose buildings line North Street, is the oldest in Scotland. The most touching connection with the past is a flourishing thorn tree in the quadrangle of St Mary's College. It was planted by Mary Queen of Scots.

A cryptic note for gourmets: Dr Johnson and Boswell, Hebrides bound, had a good supper at Glass's Inn of "Rissered haddocks and mut chops". They had previously had tea at **Cupar**, on the road back to Perth. **Auchtermuchty** has surviving thatched cottages once used by weavers, with straw thatch as thin as a child's Christmas crib. Abernethy's tea shop keeps the key to the Pictish, chimney-like church tower, built when horns, not bells, summoned the faithful. At its base is an incised Pictish stone.

Lochs, rivers and mountains: Westward from Perth, roads follow rivers in the ascent to the lochs and watershed of the Grampians. At **Crieff** good taste demands visits to **Glenturret**, the oldest

Dunfermline Abbey, burial place of kings.

distillery in Scotland, and glass, pottery and textile workshops. What romance attaches to the **Drummond Arms** as the scene of Prince Charles Edward's council of war in 1746 is a little dimmed by its having been rebuilt since. Five miles (8 km) southeast of Crieff, the oldest public library in Scotland, the **Innerpeffray Library**, has a Treacle Bible, so called because "Is there no balm in Gilead?" is translated into "Is there no treacle in Gilead?"

Comrie's situation on the River Earn where two glens meet makes it an attractive walking centre. Earthquakes too! The Highland Boundary Fault divides the Lowlands from Highlands here and earth tremors were bad enough to damage houses in 1839. One of these houses contains the **Museum of Scottish Tartans**, with over 1,300 patterns and a record of every known tartan.

From Comrie the road passes Loch Earn with magnificent mountain scenery until **Lochearnhead** is reached. Beyond here the high peaks have it – **Ben More**, **Ben Lui** and **Ben Bhuidhe** –

until the lochs reach in like fingers from the coast of the Western Isles.

Crianlarich is a popular centre with climbers and walkers. For those on wheels, **Ardlui** is a beautiful introduction to Loch Lomond. The largest body of water in Britain, full of fish and islands, it is best known and loved through the song which one of Prince Charles Edward's followers wrote on the eve of his execution. There are fairies at the end of the Loch in Fairy Glen in the **Balloch Castle Country Park**.

The road back to **Aberfoyle** traverses the Queen Elizabeth forest park and leads to the splendid wooded scenery of the **Trossachs**, best viewed from the summer steamer on **Loch Katrine**. Scott's *Lady of the Lake* and *Rob Roy* attracted flocks of Victorian visitors. **Callander** found fame as the "Tannochbrae" of the BBC TV series *Dr Finlay's Casebook*, and its **Trossachs and Rob Roy Visitor Centre**, in an old kirk, tells you all about this glorified cattle thief.

Doune's 15th-century castle is remarkably complete with two great tow-

Students at St Andrews Castle.

ers and hall between. In Ruskin's judgement – and who would challenge that? – the west front of **Dunblane**'s 13th-century cathedral is a perfect example of Scotland's church architecture. But how did the three Drummond sisters buried here come to meet their deaths, as the tombstone tells us, by poisoning in 1501?

The Scots are so obsessed with golf that Mary Queen of Scots could go off to play when her husband had just been assassinated. At **Gleneagles** the moorland courses are a golfer's paradise.

Follow the mill trail: **Auchterarder**'s situation to the north of the Ochil Hills is a convenient point at which to hit the **Mill Trail**. Thanks to good grazing and soft water, Scotland's world-famous tweeds, tartans and knitwear have been produced here in the Hillfoot's villages since the 16th century. From the Heritage Centre in Auchterarder, with the only surviving steam textile engine and **Tillicoultry**'s handsome Clock Mill powered by waterwheel, to the most modern mills in **Alloa** and **Sauchie**, producing designer knitwear with fa-mous labels, the trail links modern technology with the cottage production of the past in a fascinating way. Amongst so much weaving there is much learning: **Dollar** is home to the Dollar Academy, founded in 1818.

From Perth, the motorway north bypasses **Bankfoot**'s raspberry canes and motor museum. At **Dunkeld**, cross Telford's fine bridge over the Tay's rocky bed for the charm and character of this old ecclesiastical capital of Scotland. Cathedral and town were fought over and the Highlanders defeated in 1689. Dunkeld Little Houses replaced those ruined, but only the choir of the cathedral in its superb setting was restored. A delightful local museum in the **Chapter House** introduces Neil Gow, the celebrated fiddler. For good measure there is an ell, the Scottish yard, fixed to a house in the square. Romantics will feel at home at **The Hermitage**, a mile west of the town. Built in 1758, this is the centrepiece of a woodland trail beside the River Braan on the Duke of Atholl's estate, a folly poised over a

Entertainment: 19th-century style at Pitlochry Theatre...

waterfall. Wordsworth wrote a verse about it and Mendelssohn sketched it. It was a favourite haunt of Beatrix Potter.

At the foot of the Highlands is **Blairgowrie**. Matter-of-fact, it reserves its charm for anglers and lovers of raspberries and strawberries. Buy your bagpipe, kilt, sporran or feather bonnet at Piob Mhor's. At **Meikleour** the road to Perth is bordered by a beech hedge, nearly 99 ft (30 metres) high and 1,980 ft (600 metres) long and planted in 1746.

Aberfeldy and **Loch Tay** are easily achieved from Dunkeld by the stone bridge General Wade built in 1733. Here the world-renowned Black Watch Regiment became part of the British Army in 1740. Picnic in view of the Moness Falls. To the west of Aberfeldy is **Castle Menzies**, a good example of a 16th-century Z-plan tower house. Beyond is glorious **Glen Lyon**, the longest and also one of the most beautiful glens in Scotland, with the attractive thatched-cottage village of **Fortingall**.

Loch Tay, a centre for salmon and salmon fisheries, has **Ben Lawers** 1,214 ft (367 metres) above it and the beginnings of the River Tay at its foot.

Seek out **Pitlochry** for spectacle. The Festival Theatre, famous as the "Theatre in the Hills" and magnificently situated overlooking the River Tummel, is an attraction in itself. But it's upstaged by the dam at the hydro-electric power station where in spring and summer thousands of migrating salmon can be seen through windows in a fish ladder.

The Queen's View, 8 miles (13 km) northwest of Pitlochry, a renowned viewpoint named after Queen Victoria's 1866 visits, provides a truly royal vista up Loch Tummel, dominated by the cone-shaped Schiehallion (3,547 ft/ 1,083 metres).

Beyond the **Pass of Killiecrankie** where Soldier's Leap recalls the battle of 1689, is **Blair Atholl**, key to the Central Highlands. Scottish at its most baronial, Blair Castle's white walls owe too much to Victorian restoration. This much visited house is home to the 10th Duke of Atholl and the Atholl Highlanders, Britain's only private army.

...and medieval style – a pageant at Arbroath.

THE EAST COAST

If the silhouette of mainland Britain resembles "a witch riding on a pig" – with Scotland the witch and England and Wales the pig – then the crone's bony, jutting forehead is to be found in that lean coastline between the firths of Tay and Moray. Scotland's east coast and its hinterland are often neglected by indolent tourists, but reward industrious ones.

The east coast, after all, is probably the most industrious (but not industrial) region of the country. Its ports and coastal villages have given Scotland its fishing industry. Its agriculture, from the rich croplands of Angus to the famous beef farms of Aberdeenshire – the largest stretch of uninterrupted farmland in Britain – has been hard won and hard worked. "Our ancestors imposed their will on Buchan," says the writer John R. Allan of that particularly flinty outcrop buffeted by the North Sea, "...an idea imposed on nature at great expense of labour and endurance, of weariness and suffering."

It is, therefore, the east coast of Scotland which most physically and visibly exemplifies that which is most dogged and determined (and perhaps dour) in the Scottish character; and that which best knows how to exploit its assets. The northeast port of Peterhead, for example, already Europe's busiest fishing harbour, turned itself into a major berth for North Sea oil supply vessels; while the gentle, wooded valley of the River Spey is not only the centre of malt whisky production but with its "Whisky Trail" has made tourist capital out of its celebrated local industry.

For all its pragmatism, for all its gritty devotion to the work ethic, the coast and countryside between the neat and businesslike Firth of Tay and the sunny, sandy, open-mouthed Moray Firth is a region of rare and subtle loveliness. Here you can learn to live without the majestic wilderness and Gothic melodrama of the West Highlands and their archipelago (although you will find echoes of their atmosphere in the Grampian glens of Angus and the outriders of the Cairngorms which reach into Aberdeenshire) and explore the versatility of our dealings with the land and the sea. Here the scale is human and the history consequently dense.

Tale of two cities: The east coast cities are Dundee and Aberdeen. They are of comparable size (about 200,000), separated only by 70 miles (110 km), yet they couldn't be more different. Dundee has been the sad exception to the general rule of east coast energy and enterprise. Despite a vigorous industrial past rooted in textiles, shipbuilding and the jute industry (or perhaps because of it) Dundee, until recently, has long had the feel of a city down on its luck; whereas Aberdeen, the Granite City, is as solid and unyielding as its nickname, a town of such accustomed prosperity and self-confidence that it assumed its new title of oil capital of Europe in the manner of one doing the multinationals a favour.

Topographically, **Dundee** promises more than it fulfills. It has a magnificent

Preceding pages, Aberdeen anglers. Left, making Portsoy marble, obtained from a vein of serpentine.

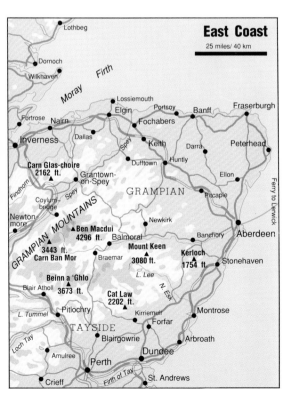

East Coast
25 miles/ 40 km

position on the Tay estuary. It is dominated by an extinct volcano called the Law, and it has been fancifully called (sometimes in a spirit of satire) the Naples of the North. From the south side of the estuary, from the spectacular approaches of its road and rail bridges (look into the waves and see the forlorn piers of the original rail bridge which collapsed below a train, losing all passengers, during a Wagnerian tempest in 1879), you might be persuaded that its setting merits the comparison.

There are other points of similarity. Like Naples, Dundee has had its share of slums and deprivation; like Naples, it is a port with a long maritime history (it was once the centre of the Scottish wine trade, and a leading importer of French claret). Unlike Naples, it has dealt its own history a mortal blow by destroying its past in a series of insensitive, speculative and sometimes shady developments. (In the 1970s the city's local authority was plagued by a succession of corruption scandals.)

"Perhaps no town in Scotland has been oftener sacked, pillaged and destroyed than Dundee," wrote an 18th-century historian, commenting on the fact that since the 11th century Dundee had the habit of picking the losing side in the various internecine and international conflicts which plagued Scotland. The city's own fathers – and the new **University of Dundee** – completed the process in the 20th century. A distinguished Scottish newspaper editor refused to set foot in Dundee after its graceful 17th-century town house was demolished to make way for the mediocre **Caird Hall** (concerts and civic events) in the 1930s.

Little is left of antiquity for the history-conscious tourist: the 15th-century **Old Steeple**; the venerable **Howff graveyard,** which occupies land given to the city by Mary Queen of Scots; the **East Port,** remnant of Dundee's fortified wall. But showing new initiative – and in the spirit of enterprise which is revitalising its economy through sunrise industries – Dundee is now capitalising on its maritime past.

Dundee: Shopping as it used to be.

The central Victoria Dock has long been the home of *HMS Unicorn*, the oldest British warship still afloat and one of the only four frigates left in the world. To this attraction Dundee has recently added *RRS Discovery*, the ship which carried Captain Scott's 1901–04 expedition to the Antarctic. It was, in fact, built in Dundee, which had a high reputation for the building of clippers and whalers around the turn of the century, and which annually sent is own fleet of whalers north to the Arctic. Both ships are now museums and there is a whaling exhibition at the **Broughty Ferry Museum** in the attractive seaside suburb of Broughty Ferry.

Dundee, therefore, is worth a visit – but not a long one. And it's worth the affectionate corner it occupies in the Scottish heart for the one great cultural gift it has bequeathed the nation: the *Sunday Post*. This folksy, idiosyncratic, highly successful newspaper (it goes all over the world) is produced by the long-established Dundee publishing house of D.C. Thomson, which has given Scot-

land its two most enduring comic-strips, "Oor Wullie" and "The Broons", and given Britain the immortal children's comics *The Beano* and *The Dandy*.

And the city's hinterland is reason alone for visiting Dundee. The county of Angus is an eloquent fusion of hill, glen, farmland, beaches and cliffs and its towns and villages reach back into the dawn of Scottish history. The twin hills near **Brechin** (which has a 12th-century cathedral and one of the only two Celtic round towers remaining on the Scottish mainland) are ringed with concentric Iron-Age ramparts. There are Pictish sculptured stones in the churchyard of **Aberlemno**, while the former Royal Burgh of **Arbroath**, a fishing port and holiday resort moving into light industry, had its origins in a Pictish settlement.

Arbroath Abbey, now a handsome ruin, dates back to 1178 and was the scene, in 1320, of a key event in the troubled history of Scotland: the signing of the Declaration of Arbroath. There, the Scottish nobles reaffirmed

The *Discovery* carried Captain Scott to the Antarctic.

their determination to resist the persistent invasions of the English and to preserve the liberty and independence of their country. (The most noble and dignified sentiments of the Declaration are chiselled into the base of the enormous bronze statue of Sir William Wallace, the Scottish patriot, in Aberdeen's Union Terrace.)

Arbroath's red cliffs and harbour at the Fit o' the Toon (*foot of the town*) remain atmospheric, and you will find there the local cottage industry of smoking haddock to produce the celebrated Smokies. The **Signal Tower** complex, built in 1813 to serve the families of the keepers of the lonely Bellrock Lighthouse, now houses a museum. In its heyday, the flagstaff sometimes signalled personal messages to the Bellrock. If a keeper's wife gave birth to a child, trousers or a petticoat would be quickly hoisted to tell him whether the baby was a boy or girl.

Between Arbroath and Dundee is the resort of **Carnoustie**, which has a famous golf course and a lot of sand, while 13 miles (22 km) to the north is the elegant town of **Montrose**, built at the mouth of a vast tidal basin which is the winter home of pink-footed Arctic geese and pink-cheeked ornithologists. Inland, the country town of **Forfar** (where King Malcolm Canmore held his first parliament in 1057) is a striking point for the gloriously underused and somehow secretive glens of Angus and lies close to what must be considered the county's star attraction: **Glamis Castle**, the exquisite fairy-tale home of the Earls of Strathmore and Kinghorne and a royal residence since 1372.

Glamis was the childhood home of Queen Elizabeth and the Queen Mother; Princess Margaret was born there; and it was claimed by Shakespeare for the legendary setting of *Macbeth*. ("Hail Macbeth, Thane of Glamis!") It is now discreetly open to the public and four 17th-century cottages in the village of Glamis have been turned into the **Angus Folk Museum**, indicating the nature of domestic and agricultural life over the past 200 years.

Glamis Castle: interior grandeur and exterior splendour.

A visit to Glamis can easily be combined with a visit to **Kirriemuir,** birthplace of the writer J. M. Barrie and the "Thrums" of his novels. The house in which the author of *Peter Pan* was born is now maintained as a museum by the National Trust for Scotland and you can see there Barrie's very first theatre – the wash-house.

Kirriemuir is also the gateway to **Glen Prossen** and **Glen Clova**, from where the committed walker can penetrate deep into the heart of the Grampians to **Glen Doll** and pick up the old drove roads over to Deeside. These ancient routes were used by armies and rebels as well as cattle drovers and look deceptively easy and appealing walks on the Ordnance Survey map. But the Grampians can be as treacherous as any Scottish hills; the drove roads have claimed the lives of seven walkers, caught in blizzards, over the past two decades.

To the southwest is **Glen Isla** and to the north **Glen Lethnot** (route of a "whisky road" formerly used by smugglers to outwit Revenue men) and grace-ful, meandering **Glen Esk**, which is reached through the pretty village of **Edzell** with its remnants, in the shape of a walled renaissance garden, of the ancestral home of the Lindsay family.

Edzell lies on the Angus boundary with the county of Kincardine, and here the countryside begins to alter subtly. It lies, too, on the western edge of the **Howe of the Mearns**, which means something special to lovers of Scots literature. This is the howe, or vale, which nurtured Lewis Grassic Gibbon, whose brilliant trilogy *A Scots Quair* gave the 20th-century Scottish novel and the Scots language its most distinctive voice: *Sunset Song, Cloud Howe, Grey Granite*. His lilting, limpid prose sings in your ears as you cross these rolling fields of rich red earth and granite boulders to a coast that becomes ever more riven and rugged as you near **Stonehaven** and the big skies, luminous light, spare landscape and chilly challenge of the northeast.

"The Highland Fault meets the sea at Stonehaven, and when you cross it you

Rough seas can confine fishing-boats to port for between three weeks and three months a year.

say goodbye to ease and amplitude," writes John R. Allan, the northeast's most eloquent advocate. "By the stony fields and diffident trees you may guess you have come to a soil very roughly ground through the mills of God." The A92 to Aberdeen now by-passes Stonehaven, but this solid, dignified if plain little fishing port-turned-seaside resort is worth a visit for the drama of its cliffs and **Dunottar Castle**, standing on its own giant rock above the town.

In the dungeons of these spectral ruins Covenanters were left to rot and the Scottish Regalia – the "Honours of Scotland" – were concealed in the 17th century from Cromwell's Roundheads. It's said that, when Dunottar was besieged, the wife of the minister of nearby Kineff Church smuggled the Honours out of the besieged castle with the crown in her lap and the sceptre disguised as a distaff, and hid them in the church.

From Stonehaven to Aberdeen is a clear, high, exhilarating run of 15 miles (24 km) along the cliffs. But why not let the Granite City and the coast be the climax to your northeast tour and take, instead, the A987 to the lower Dee valley? Called the Slug Road for the steepness of its incline from Deeside, it deposits you near the little town of **Banchory**, where you can watch salmon leaping at the **Bridge of Feugh** and visit the late 16th-century tower house of **Crathes** and its renowned gardens. This is *the* complete castle, still furnished with period pieces and wall hangings as it was when the family seat of the Burnetts. (Aberdeenshire is said to have more castles, both standing and ruined, than any other county in Britain.)

The **Dee valley** is justly celebrated for its expansive beauty and the pellucid, peat-brown grace of its river, and at the handsome village of **Aboyne**, between Banchory and Ballater (*see page 288*) you begin to tread on the rougher hem of the Eastern Highlands. Deeside's Royal associations make it the tourist honeypot of Aberdeenshire at the expense, or perhaps the sparing, of Donside. The valley of Aberdeen's second, lesser known river is equally rewarding,

Dunottar Castle: Covenanters were once left there to rot.

and felt by many to be the more subtle and characterful riverway of the two.

Ancient times: From Banchory you can strike over to Donside on the A980, passing through the village of **Lumphanan**, alleged to be the burial place of the doomed King Macbeth whose history has so often been confused with Shakespeare's fiction. But **Macbeth's Cairn** doesn't mark the grave of the king. Not only is it a prehistoric cairn, but is has now been established that Macbeth, like so many of the early Scottish kings, was buried on Iona. You can see at Lumphanan, however, one of Scotland's earliest medieval earthworks, the **Peel of Lumphanan** and, in a circle of trees on the hillside, **Macbeth's Cairn**, said to mark the spot where the dying king supposedly cried: "Lay on Macduff; and damn'd be him that first cries 'Hold, Enough!'"

A few miles farther on **Craigievar Castle**, the most sublime expression of the Aberdeenshire school of castle-building, now in the hands of the National Trust for Scotland but once the 17th-century family home of the Forbes.

Donside's metropolis is the little country town of **Alford**, now promoting itself as a tourist centre. It can offer the **Alford Valley Railway**, a narrow-gauge passenger steam railway which runs during the summer months; **Grampian Transport Museum** and nearby **Kildrummy Castle**, a romantic and extensive 13th-century ruin which featured prominently in the Jacobite Rebellion of 1715 and which now slumbers exotically in a Japanese water garden. Robert Bruce sent his wife and children here for safety but they were betrayed to the English by a blacksmith in return for "as much gold as he could carry". His reward was the metal in molten form, poured down his throat.

Highlight of the Donside summer is the **Lonach Highland Gathering,** traditional games of a kind more authentic than the glitzy gathering at Braemar.

Both Dee and Don have their sources in the foothills of the **Cairngorms**, that lonely, savage massif which dominates the Eastern Highlands. There is no direct route through its lofty bulk, but from Deeside and Donside you can pick up the road which scuttles round it and give yourself a thrilling journey.

At the hamlet of **Cockbridge**, beside the austere, curtain-walled **castle of Corgarff**, the A939 becomes the **Lecht Road** which rises precipitously to some 2,000 ft (600 metres) before careering giddily down into the village of Tomintoul. In winter, the Lecht is almost always the first main road in Scotland to be blocked with snow, encouraging an optimistic ski development at its summit. A mile or so to the north of that summit, look out for the **Well of the Lecht**. Above a small natural spring, a white stone plaque, dated 1745, records that five companies of the 33rd Regiment built the road from here to the Spey. Its straightness testifies to their precision as Government troops extended control over the Highlands after the Jacobite Rebellion of 1745.

Tomintoul, at 1,600 ft (500 metres), is one of the highest villages in Scotland and a pickup point for the "Whisky Trail" which, if you have the energy and

Harvesting the barley: the area is rich in croplands.

the interest, can take you meandering (or perhaps reeling) through eight famous malt whisky distilleries in and around the Spey Valley. The trail (you can get maps in any of the local tour offices) is about 70 miles (110 km) long, and you can spend an hour in each distillery with guides who will admit you to some of the secrets of the Glenlivet, Tamdhu, Glen Grant and Glenfiddich, and offer samples.

Strathspey – *strath* means valley – is one of the loveliest valleys in Scotland, as much celebrated for the excellence of its angling as for its malt whisky industry. When you descend from the grim uplands of the Lecht passage through Tomintoul to the handsome granite town of **Grantown-on-Spey**, you see a land gradually tamed and gentled by natural woodland, open pastures and the clear, comely waters of the River Spey itself. The mountains are never very far away, and you can view them in comfort and style from the **Strathspey Railway** and the steam train which runs through the valley during the summer months.

Grantown, like so many of the small towns and large villages in this area, was an 18th century "new town", planned and built by its local laird. It makes a good centre for exploring Strathspey and it's also within easy striking distance of the Moray Firth, and the leading resort and former spa town of Nairn. The route from Grantown (the A939) takes you past the island castle of **Lochindorb**, once the lair of the Wolf of Badenoch – Alexander Stewart, the notorious outlawed son of Robert II, who sacked the town of Forres and destroyed Elgin Cathedral.

Nairn, when the sun shines – and the Moray Firth claims to have the biggest share of sunshine on the Scottish mainland – is a splendid place, even elegant, with fine hotels and golf courses, glorious beaches and big blue vistas to the distant hills on the north side of the firth. It is also at the heart of this amiable region's most picturesque and interesting attractions. On its doorstep is **Cawdor Castle**, 14th-century home of the Thanes of Cawdor (more Macbeth

Craigievar: a sublime example of local castle building.

associations); up the coast are the ghostly **Culbin Sands**, which in a great sandstorm of 1695 finally overwhelmed the village of Culbin, which lies buried beneath them; and on the Ardesier peninsula is awesome and still occupied **Fort George** – one of the outstanding artillery fortifications of Europe – built to control and intimidate the Highlands after the 1745 Rebellion.

Blasted heath: The most poignant and atmospheric reminder of Charles Edward Stuart's costly adventure, however, is **Culloden Moor**, which lies between Nairn and Inverness, Culloden was the last battle fought on Britain's mainland and here the Jacobite cause was finally lost to internal conflicts and the superior forces of the Hanoverian Army. It is a melancholy, blasted place – in effect, a war graveyard where the Highlanders buried their dead in communal graves marked by rough stones bearing the names of each clan.

It becomes even more melancholy when you learn that, although the battle lasted only 40 minutes, the Prince's army lost 1,200 men to the King's 310, and that "Butcher" Cumberland's Redcoats performed with such enthusiasm that they slaughtered some of the bystanders who had come out from Inverness to watch.

The coast and countryside to the east of Nairn is worth attention – a combination of fishing villages like **Burghead** and **Findhorn** (now famous for the Findhorn Foundation, an international "alternative" community whose life and work, based on meditation and spiritual practice, have turned the sand dunes into flourishing vegetable gardens). And there are pleasing, dignified inland towns built of golden sandstone like **Forres**, **Elgin** and **Fochabers**, the ancient capital of Moray. Elgin's graceful cathedral dates back to 1224 (it was rebuilt after its destruction by the Wolf of Badenoch in 1390) and, although now partially ruined, is undergoing restoration. With its medieval street plan still well preserved, Elgin must be counted one of the loveliest towns in Scotland.

Monks clad in coarse white habits

Blooms in the prosperous heartland of Aberdeenshire.

add a medieval touch to the giant **Pluscarden Abbey**, hidden in a sheltered valley 5 miles (8 km) southwest of Elgin. The abbey, founded in 1230, fell into disrepair until, in 1948, an order of converted Benedictines started to rebuild it.

The **River Spey**, which debouches at Spey Bay (site of the **Tugnet Ice House**, built in 1830 to store ice for packing salmon and now housing an exhibition dedicated to the salmon fishing industry and wildlife of the Spey estuary) marks something of a boundary between the fertile, wooded country and sandy coast of the Moray Firth and that plainer, harsher land which pushes out into the North Sea.

Decision time: Here the motoring tourist, with Aberdeen in his sights, is faced with a choice. You can either cut the coastal corner by driving straight through the prosperous heartland of Aberdeenshire by way of **Keith, Huntly, Inverurie** and yet more Aberdeenshire castles (Huntly, Fyvie and Castle Fraser, to name but three); or you can hug the forbidding littoral of Banffshire and Buchan and see for yourself John R. Allan's "stony fields and diffident trees", and the workmanlike ports of **Buckie, Fraserburgh** and **Peterhead**, and that whole chain of grey grimly-forged fishing villages and harbours which has harnessed this truculent coast into something productive.

You will then discover that there are pockets of prettiness, hollows of warmth to be found among its cliffs and bays, as well as gusty, spectacular seascapes, rich bird life and the enduring fascination of working harbours, fish markets and museums dedicated to maritime history. Still the leading contributor to the British fishing industry, this was also the Herring Coast in the days of the great silver shoals which fed Scotland and beyond, and gave Banffshire and Buchan most of its income. There is even a "Fishing Heritage Trail" which you can follow.

Banff itself is a town of some elegant substance with a Georgian centre, while the 16th-century merchants' houses

Looking for a bargain at Turriff Show.

around **Portsoy** harbour have been agreeably restored. This village is also distinguished for the production and working of Portsoy marble, and a pottery and marble workshop are installed in one of the harbour buildings, while there is beauty and drama to be found in **Cullen** with its striking series of 19th-century railway viaducts and its sweep of sand.

Between Macduff and Fraserburgh, where the coast begins to take a right-angle bend, tortuous minor roads link the precipitous villages of **Gardenstown, Crovie** and **Pennan**, stuck like limpets to the cliffs, and south of Peterhead the sea boils into the **Bullers O'Buchan**, a high circular basin of rock which Dr Johnson described as a "monstrous cauldron" before insisting on sailing into it "through the high arch in the rock which the tempest has driven out".

Close by are the gaunt clifftop ruins of **Slains Castle**, said to have ignited the imagination of Bram Stoker and inspired his novel *Dracula*. It is certainly true that Stoker spent holidays at the golfing resort of **Cruden Bay**, where the craggy shore begins to yield to sand until, at the village of **Newburgh** and the mouth of the River Ythan, you find the dramatic dune system of the Sands of Forvie nature reserve. From there south, an uninterrupted stretch of dune and marram grass reaches all the way to Aberdeen.

Granite city: Aberdeen inspires strong emotions. You are either convinced that it is indeed "the silver city by the golden sands", and that its own conceit of itself is well deserved (the city's Book of Remembrance contains the sentiment, "Aberdeen to Heaven – nae a great step"); or you find its exposed interface with the North Sea and its granite austerity wintry of aspect and chilly of soul.

But if Aberdeen is either loved or loathed, even those who affect to dislike it do so with ambivalence. The northeast's most famous writer, Lewis Grassic Gibbon, had this to say about the city where he worked as a journalist, and about its stone: "It has a flinty shine when new – a grey glimmer like a morn-

THE IMPACT OF BIG OIL

The days when it was assumed that the North Sea's "black gold" would cure all Scotland's social and industrial ailments have long gone. The huge oil revenues (£7.5 billion a year) have disappeared into the maw of the British Treasury, and precious little has come back across the border. As one Scottish nationalist put it: "Scotland must be the only country on Earth to discover oil and become worse off."

Which is not quite true. Scotland may have no access to the revenues, but it has acquired a mature, technologically advanced industry which employs many thousands of people and underwrites a great many other jobs all over the country. The offshore oil industry almost (but not quite) makes up for the thousands of jobs lost in traditional heavy industries like coal, shipbuilding, engineering and steel.

Crude oil is now flowing from 49 oilfields off the east coast of Scotland. The fields range in size from established giants like Forties, Brent and Ninian to barely eco-

nomic mini-fields like Arbroath and Ivanhoe-Rob Roy. Many are in the deep, stormy waters of the East Shetland Basin, while others lie under the shallower seas east of Edinburgh. The North Sea was producing, at its peak, just under 120 million tonnes of oil a year, but the gravy train has already slowed down only 16 years after it started to roll, and by the early 1990s only 100 million tonnes a year was flowing.

The early days between 1972 and 1979, however, were astonishing. Every week new schemes were announced for supply bases, refineries and petrochemical works. Scotland was galvanised. The Scottish National Party (SNP) startled Britain by getting 11 members elected to parliament in 1974 on the crude but effective slogan "It's Scotland's Oil."

Heady days, but they didn't last. When the price of oil slumped in 1985–86 from $40 to less than $10 a barrel, recession struck the east coast, and job losses have continued ever since. But reports of the demise of Aberdeen have been greatly exaggerated. The old Granite City remains the oil capital of Europe, the town which services most of the 25,000 men working offshore and the place where every oil company, exploration firm, oil-tool manufacturer and diving company has a foothold.

The oil comes ashore in Scotland at three points: on the island of Flotta in Orkney, at St Fergus north of Aberdeen, and at Sullom Voe in Shetland. Sullom Voe is the biggest of the three terminals, with a "throughput" of 1.2 million barrels of oil a day from the oilfields of the East Shetland Basin. For more than 16 years the tiny Shetland Island Council argued with the oil giants over the rent for Sullom Voe. The council asked for £100 million a year; the companies initially offered £300,000.

In the early days industrial Scotland had high hopes of "downstream" developments such as oil refineries and petrochemical plants. But not many came about, and those that were built employed very few people. It's a sign of the times that the Cromarty Firth and the Firth of Forth are now heavily used to "stack" redundant drilling rigs and pipe-laying barges. And companies have been scouting the east coast for a site to break up unwanted drilling rigs and platforms into scrap. **North Sea oil rig.** ∎

ing North Sea, a cold steeliness that chills the heart.... Even with weathering it acquires no gracious softness, it is merely starkly grim and uncompromising.... One detests Aberdeen with the detestation of a thwarted lover. It is the one haunting and exasperatingly lovable city in Scotland."

Aberdeen itself is largely indifferent to the opinions of outsiders. Its infuriating complacency, however, has been its strength, and will almost certainly be its salvation when the North Sea oil wells run dry and the city re-focuses on its own considerable resources of sea, land and light industry. Its reverse side is self-reliance.

Of all Britain's cities, Aberdeen is the most isolated. It comes as a shock to drive through miles of empty countryside from the south and, breasting a hill, find revealed below you the great grey settlement clasped between the arms of Dee and Don, as if it were the simple, organic extension of rock and heath and shore instead of a complex human artifice. On the sea's horizon you might see a semi-submersible oil rig on the move; in the harbour, trawlers jostle with supply vessels; and there are raw new ribbon developments of housing and warehousing to the north and south of the city. But otherwise Aberdeen, in its splendid self-sufficiency and glorious solitude, remains curiously untouched by the coming of the oil industry.

Granite endures. Much of historic Aberdeen remains, although most of its imposing city centre dates only from the 19th century with the building of **Union Street**, its main thoroughfare, in the early 1800s and the re-building of **Marischal College**, part of the ancient University of Aberdeen, in 1891. The facade of Marischal College, which stands just off Union Street in Broad Street, is an extraordinary fretwork of pinnacles and gilt flags in which the unyielding substance of white granite is made to seem delicate. The building itself is the second largest granite building in the world – the largest is the Escorial in Madrid.

Union Street's die-straight mile from

Two faces of Aberdeen, the Granite City.

Holborn Junction skirts the arboreal churchyard of St Nicholas, Aberdeen's "mither kirk", and terminates in the **Castlegate**, which is virtually the same square which has occupied that space since the 13th century. Its centrepiece is the 17th-century **Mercat Cross**, with its sculptured portrait gallery of the Stuart monarchs. The cross is the focus of Aberdeen's long history as major market town and import-export centre. For centuries fishwives from **Fittie**, the fishing village at the foot of the Dee, and farmers from the expansive hinterland brought their produce to sell round the cross, while more exotic products from Europe and the New World were hefted up the hill from the harbour by porters from the Shore Porters' Society, Britain's oldest company. (Founded in 1498, Shore Porters now concentrate on furniture removals.)

Aberdeen's oldest quarter and civic origins, however, lie to the northwest of the city centre on the banks of the River Don, whose narrow, sandy estuary was never developed as harbour and port in the manner of its larger twin, the Dee. Although Aberdeen was already a busy port when it was granted a royal charter in the 12th century by King William the Lion, its earliest settlement was to be found clustered around **St Machar's Cathedral** in Old Aberdeen, once an independent burgh.

The cathedral, founded in the 6th century, is one of the oldest granite buildings in the city (although it has a red sandstone arch which is a remnant of an earlier building) and the cobbled streets and lamplit academic houses surrounding it are atmospheric and peaceful. Here, too, is Aberdeen's first university, **King's College** (founded in 1495 by Bishop Elphinstone), with its graceful crown tower, and a nearby bridge, the **Brig o' Balgownie**, which Aberdeen owes to Robert the Bruce.

Aberdeen's history has often been self-protective; the city gave the Duke of Cumberland, later to become infamous as "Butcher" Cumberland, a civic reception as he led his Hanoverian army north to confront Prince Charles Edward

Fittie Village.

Stuart's Jacobites at Culloden. But it is to its credit that it offered protection to Robert the Bruce during Scotland's Wars of Independence in the 14th century. In return, Bruce gave the "Freedom Lands" to the city (which still bring it an income) and ordered the completion of the Brig o' Balgownie, whose building had been interrupted by the wars.

Today, besides all its other activities, Aberdeen confidently promotes itself as a holiday resort, and indeed it is one of the few cities to be recommended for a family holiday with young children. The sands are authentically golden, and there is a vast sweep of them between the mouths of the two rivers and many dunes beyond. But don't expect to sunbathe often or comfortably on them: the northeast gets a major share of Scotland's sunshine, but Aberdeen's beach is open-backed and exposed to every bitter breeze from the North Sea.

Its parks, however, are glorious, wonderfully well kept and celebrated, like many of the other open spaces, for their roses. (Aberdeen has won the "Brit-ain in Bloom" award 10 times and is now officially Britain's Cleanest City.)

Hazelhead, on the city's western perimeter, **Duthie Park**, with its extensive winter gardens, and **Seaton Park** on the River Don are probably the most superior open spaces, but all have above-average play areas and special attractions for children during the summer. There is also a well-run permanent funfair at the beach, and a few miles inland at Maryculter in the Dee Valley one of the country's most attractive small "theme parks": **Story Book Glen**, with its lifesize and giant tableaux of many favourite childhood characters.

A lively theatre, a vigorous art gallery, a well-stocked museum, a succession of festivals and games – you could go on listing the more obvious attractions of Aberdeen. But the real interest for the serious tourist lies in the character of Britain's most northern city, in the rich, robust dialect of its people and their cocky but cautious nature which has had long experience in handling rewards won by their own unremitting industry.

Story Book Glen.

THE NORTHERN HIGHLANDS

Nowhere in Britain is the bloodied hand of the past so heavily laid as it is in the Highlands. The pages of its history read like a film script – and have often served as one. There are starring roles for Bonnie Prince Charlie, Flora Mac-Donald, Mary Queen of Scots, Rob Roy, the Wolf of Badenoch and Macbeth, with a supporting cast of clansmen and crofters, miners and fisher folk, businessmen and sportsmen. On the soundtrack, the skirl of the pipes is heard…

The cameras could find no point better at which to start turning than **Inverness,** the natural "capital" of the Highlands. It is assured of that title by its easily fortified situation on the River Ness where the roads through the glens converge. Shakespeare used it for location shots and sadly maligned the man who was its king for 17 years, Macbeth. His castle has disappeared,

Preceding pages, Suilven, Scotland's Matterhorn. Left, Inverness.

but from Castlehill a successor dominates the city: a pink cardboard cut-out, like a Victorian doll's house, that makes Flora MacDonald in bronze shield her eyes and her dog lift a paw. There are kind words, however, at the foot of the statue from Dr Samuel Johnson.

In the nearby **Museum,** the death mask of Flora's Bonnie Prince shares cases with Mr Punch in his "red Garibaldi coat", and Duncan Morrison's puppet figure that once delighted local children. Traditions are strongly represented in silversmithing, taxidermy and the making of bagpipes and fiddles, but reserve your enthusiasm for a 7th-century Pictish stone depicting a wolf – magic! Inverness is sentimental at heart.

Preserved in front of the **Town House**, on busy High Street, uphill from the river, is the **Clach-na-Cuddain**, a stone on which women rested their tubs of washing. **Abertarff House**, on Church Street, rescued from years of neglect by the National Trust for Scotland, is now its Highland Office, with a chimneypiece marriage lintel of 1691 in the gift shop.

Here be monsters: From an area of Inverness rich in industrial archaeology the **Caledonian Canal** climbs through six locks like a flight of stairs to the "Hill of Yew Trees", **Tomnahurich**. This Highland waterway, which joins the North Sea and the Atlantic Ocean through the Great Glen, was dreamt of by a local seer a century before it was built; he predicted: "Full-rigged ships will be seen sailing at the back of Tomnahurich." Now you can set sail here in summer on the *Scot II* for a trip on **Loch Ness** and enjoy "a wee dram in the lingering twilight". The dram may assist you in spotting the Monster, the lake's supposed ancient occupant.

Another way to find "Nessie" is to board the *Taurus*, a five-person submarine for a one-hour voyage to the depths of Loch Ness, Britain's deepest body of fresh water. The submarine's base is just north of **Castle Urquhart**, a picturesque ruin on the loch's edge (15 miles/24 km south of Inverness on the A82) which bears the scars of having been fought over for two centuries. Across the water, at **Foyers**, Britain's

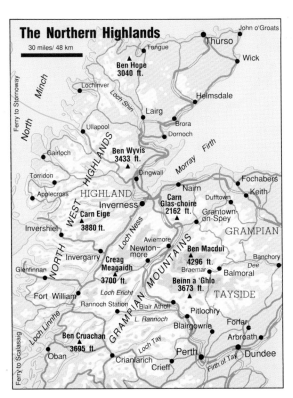

The Northern Highlands

30 miles/ 48 km

John o'Groats
Thurso
Tongue
Wick
Ben Hope 3040 ft.
Lochinver
Loch Shin
Helmsdale
Lairg
Ferry to Stornoway
North Minch
Ullapool
Brora
Dornoch
Gairloch
Ben Wyvis 3433 ft.
Firth
Torridon
Dingwall
Moray
Fochabers
Applecross
HIGHLAND
Nairn
Keith
Inverness
Carn Glas-choire 2162 ft.
Dufftown
Invershiel
Carn Eige 3880 ft.
Grantown-on-Spey
Loch Ness
GRAMPIAN
Aviemore
Newton-more
Ben Macdui 4296 ft.
Banchory
Invergarry
Creag Meagaidh 3700 ft.
Braemar
Dee
Balmoral
Glenfinnan
Beinn a 'Ghlo 3673 ft.
TAYSIDE
Fort William
Loch Ericht
Rannoch Station
Blair Atholl
Pitlochry
Loch Linnhe
L. Rannoch
Blairgowrie
Forfar
Ben Cruachan 3695 ft.
Loch Tay
Arbroath
Ferry to Scalasaig
Oban
Crianlarich
Perth
Dundee
Crieff
Firth of Tay
NORTH WEST HIGHLANDS
GRAMPIAN MOUNTAINS

first hydro-electric scheme, built to provide power for a now defunct aluminium factory, feeds power into the National Grid. Dr Johnson, on horseback, praised the lochside road, which "between birch trees, with the hills above, pleased us much", and took a dram with an old woman who shared her earth hut with her goats. Later, at a public house called the General's Hut, he dined with Boswell off "mutton-chops, a broiled chicken, bacon and eggs and a bottle of Malaga".

At **Fort Augustus** (29 miles/48 km further south), the canal descends in another flight of locks near the Great Glen Heritage Exhibition, which illustrates the glen's history from Pictish to modern times. The garrison, set up after the 1715 Jacobite Rising, became – swords to ploughshares – a Benedictine abbey and is now a Heritage Centre.

Turn right at **Invergarry** onto the A82 for the beauty of glen and mountain on the road to Kyle of Lochalsh and Skye. Still on the A82, seven heads for seven brothers on the "Well of the Heads" monument record the murder of a 17th-century chieftain's two sons and, as reprisal, the deaths of seven brothers, whose heads were washed in the well, then presented to the chief.

The A82 now crosses to the east bank of **Loch Lochy**. Six miles (10 km) before Fort William is **Nevis Range** where gondolas whisk you in 12 minutes to 2,150 ft (645 metres), giving stunning views of Scotland's highest mountains. On the outskirts of Fort William, take the A830 and you'll immediately reach "Neptune's Staircase" (*see page 222*), where eight locks lead the Caledonian Canal into the sea and from where there are grand views of Ben Nevis.

Seaports and spas: Back at the northern end of the Great Glen the A9 crosses the neck of the **Black Isle**, which is neither island nor black but forest and fertile farmland, and is bisected by new roads built to serve the oil centres on the north shore of the Cromarty Firth.

Two plaques can be found at **Fortrose**, on the east shore. One marks where Scotland's last witch was burnt in 1722 – a distinction hotly contested by nearby

Loch Ness: inspiration for monster fantasies.

Dornoch; the other where the Brahan Seer was burnt in an oil barrel in the 17th century after offending his patroness but not before he had successfully foretold the building of the Caledonian Canal, the demise of crofting, and much more. Also in Fortrose are the magnificent ruins of a 14th-century cathedral.

Cromarty, at the extreme tip of the Isle, lost face as a Royal Burgh through declining fortunes as a sea port and trading community, but has earned rightful popularity as a place where visitors can literally step back into history in the unspoilt old town. Taped tours point out some of the most beautiful late 18th-century buildings in Britain: the courthouse, now a prize-winning museum; the thatched cottage where early geologist Hugh Miller, Cromarty's most famous scholarly son, lived; and the East Kirk, with its three wooden lofts.

A road leads to **South Sutor**, one of two precipitous headlands, guarding the narrow entrance to the Firth of Cromarty where numerous oil rigs are moored. Around the rigs swim the North Sea's only resident group of bottlenose dolphins plus innumerable grey and common seals.

Though Scotsmen had long known the local sulphur and chalybeate springs at **Strathpeffer**, it took a doctor who had himself benefited to give substance to "miracle" recoveries and incidentally recognise their profitable potential. Dr Morrison opened his pump room around 1820 and the new railway brought thousands to fill the hotels, attend concerts in the spa pavilion and, if they felt inclined, enjoy "low-pressure subthermal reclining manipulation douche". Strathpeffer had arrived. Given good weather, it might have become another Salzburg. A couple of wars intervened and the spa declined; but, like all things Victorian, this elegant town is enjoying something of a revival as a resort of character that has been likened to an Indian hill station. And you can still taste the waters at the new Water Sampling Pavilion.

On leaving Strathpeffer, join the A832 which, after **Garve**, winds through Strath Ben and **Achnasheen**. From here the

A ploughing contest near Inverness.

southern leg (A890) through Glen Carron is the stuff of photomurals, with Kyle of Lochalsh at the end of the rainbow that leads across the sea to Skye. Achnasheen's northern leg (A832) points for 9 miles (14 km) to **Kinlochewe** at the head of **Loch Maree** and close to the National Nature Reserve of Ben Eighe. The mountain itself is a fascinating pudding of old red sandstone topped with white quartzite. In the pine forests there is a good chance of seeing rare and protected wildlife; deer, wildcat, pine marten and golden eagle. Nature trails begin in the car park.

Eastern promise: From **Dingwall** – was Macbeth really born here? – road (A9) and rail cling to the east coast. Near **Alness**, on a hill, is a replica of the Gate of Negapatam in India, which General Sir Hector Munro, hero of its capture, had built by local men, thus simultaneously alleviating poverty and satisfying pride. Had he lived today instead of in the 18th century, North Sea oil would have solved his unemployment problem. The place is dormitory to **Inver-gordon** on Cromarty Firth, which offered shelter to Britain's navy through two world wars and suffered the closure of its naval base in 1956. For better or worse, certainly for richer or until the oil lake dries up, the choice of Nigg Bay for the construction of oil rig platforms brought dramatic changes to the area.

Tain's memories are older, going back to 1066, when it became a Royal Burgh. Though St Duthac was born and buried here, it didn't save the two chapels dedicated to him from disastrous fires – or guarantee sanctuary.

Wonderland of Sutherland: From Tain, the A836 leads to **Bonar Bridge** and nothing, as Lewis Carroll's Alice would have said, is the same. Motorists adjust to the pace set by single-track roads and the sheep that share them and enjoy spectacular views of heather-covered moor and loch. This is Viking country, more Scandinavian than English.

At **Invershin** is a superbly situated castle without a burden of history. Retainers, some heavy-laden, come and go beneath the towers and battlements with

A crofter's life, near Applecross.

which it is over endowed. It was built as late as 1914 for the Duchess of Sutherland and is now a youth hostel. Each April to November, at the nearby **Falls of Shin**, salmon returning upstream to their spawning grounds provide a heart-rending spectacle.

"All roads meet at Lairg," it's said. Sometimes in August it seems all the sheep in Scotland do as well. **Lairg** is in the heart of Sutherland crofting country and the lamb sales identify it as a major market-place. Mirrored in the quiet waters of Loch Shin, an Iron Age hut circle on the hill above the village keeps company with council houses below.

The eastern spoke (A839) from Lairg's hub reaches the coast at Loch Fleet and **Dornoch**, where some regard Royal Dornoch, opened in 1616, as offering better golf than the Old Course at St Andrews. Not a sporting chance, though, for Janet Horn, who was burnt as a witch for having the Devil shoe her daughter after she had turned her into a pony. Dornoch Castle's surviving tower suffered the indignities of use as a garrison, court-house, jail, school and private residence. Now it's a hotel.

To the north is **Golspie** which lives in the shadow of the Sutherlands. An over-size statue of the First Duke looks down from the mountain; a stone in the old bridge is the clan's rallying point; and nearby is the Duchess's Dunrobin Castle, an improbable confection of pinnacles and turrets trying to be a schloss or a chateau. Formal gardens are a riot of colour in summer. The prehistoric fort at Carn Liath a little further along the coast is a nice antidote.

Havens, harbours, herring: The gold-rush that brought prospectors to the burns of **Helmsdale** in the 1860s was short-lived. More rewarding is the country that lies ahead: **Caithness**, for centuries so remote from the centres of Scottish power that it was ruled by the Vikings. Trade links were entirely by sea and in the boom years of the fishing industry scores of harbours were built. The fleets have gone; the harbours remain.

The A9 to **Berriedale** twists spectacularly past the ravines of the Ord of

Off to a lamb sale at Lairg.

Caithness and on to **Dunbeath**, where a few lobster boats are a reminder of past glories. **Lybster** offers more bustle, but at **Mid Clyth** leave the road at a sign, "Hill o' Many Stanes", for a mystery tour. On a hillside are 22 rows, each with an average of eight small stones, thought to be Bronze Age. For star sightings, perhaps? There are more stones in the Whaligoe Steps at **Thrumster;** fishwives used to carry laden creels up the cliff face's 365 steps and walk the 6 miles (10 km) to Wick market.

Herring were the backbone of **Wick**'s prosperity come to life again in the Wick Heritage Centre. More than 1,000 boats once set sail to catch the "silver darlings". Now the near-deserted quays give the harbour a wistful charm. Maybe the disappearance of herring explains why the fishermen were so superstitious: aboard ship, no-one mentioned salmon by name – they were "red fish". The evasions went further: rabbits were "four footers", pigs were "sandy Campbells" and the minister was "the man in the black coat". Where we "touch wood",

they touched iron, saying "caul iron". What is the most celebrated product of Wick? Caithness glass.

For cross-country record breakers, **John o' Groats**, at the end of the A9, has a natural attraction – although, contrary to popular belief, it is not the northernmost point in Britain. A Dutchman, Jan de Groot, came here in 1500 under orders from James IV to set up a ferry service to Orkney to consolidate his domination over this former Scandinavian territory. Jan's response to requests from his eight sons as to who should succeed him was to build an octagonal house with eight doors and with an octagonal table in the middle so that each sat at the "head". A mound and a flagstaff commemorate the site.

Boat trips run from the harbour to **Duncansby Head**, 2 miles (4 km) to the east, where many species of birds nest on the dramatic towering stacks. From here a road runs to the lighthouse. Across the Pentland Firth the Orkney islands lie "like stranded whales".

West of John o' Groats, on the A836,

Sutherland's hiking country, looking towards Suilven.

286

is **Castle of Mey**, the Queen Mother's home. Further on is **Dunnet Head**, the British mainland's most northerly point.

The approaches to **Thurso** are heralded by the Caithness "hedges" that line the fields, the flagstones that were once shipped from local quarries to every corner of the old Empire. The streets of Calcutta were paved by Caithness. It is hard to find Thurso's harbour attractive. **Fisherbiggins**, the fishermen's old quarter, is a facsimile reproduction from 1940, but elsewhere there is pleasant Victorian town planning. **Scrabster** is Thurso's outport, with a ferry to Orkney. The site of Scotland's first nuclear power station, now defunct, at **Dounreay** was chosen for its remoteness. Besides electricity it generated traffic, spawned housing development and boosted the local economy.

The furthest point: It's an odd feeling: nothing between you and the North Pole except magnificent cliff scenery. At **Tongue** the sea loch pokes deep into the bleak moorland, and near **Durness,** which has some huge expanses of wonderful beach, the Alt Smoo River drops from the cliff into the Caves of Smoo. From Durness, a combined ferry and bus service travels to **Cape Wrath**. From here, the top left-hand corner of Britain, Orkney and the Outer Hebrides can be seen. Look out for cooties, sea cockies, tammies and tommienoories (puffins by another name).

The return to Lairg can be made south from Tongue on the lovely A836 through **Altnaharra**, where crosses, hut circles and Pictish brochs abound. From Durness the A838 joins the western coast at **Scourie**, where mermaids are mistaken for seals and palm trees grow. **Ullapool**, 52 miles (83 km) south of Scourie, is a resort for all seasons, beautifully situated on Loch Broom facing the sunset; it's crowded in summer.

Herring inspired the British Fisheries Society in 1788 to build fisher cottages and improve the harbour. Today, a car ferry serves Stornoway in Lewis and trippers leave for the almost deserted but delightfully named **Summer Isles**. Smoking is good for health at **Achiltibuie**. Fish and game to be cured are "steeped in spicy aromatic brines which gently permeate and cure the raw materials. Treacle, juniper berries, bay leaves and rum add subtlety and character as the flavours develop." What palate can resist such a description?

Downhill racing: It's doubtful if the Clan Grant, whose war cry was "Stand Fast Craigellachie", could have resisted the forces at work in **Aviemore**, below their rallying place. The quiet Speyside halt has been transformed over 25 years into a year-round resort by the opening of roads into the Cairngorms and chairlifts for the skiers. Brewers built the centre; hotels, restaurants, a theatre, ice rink and go-cart tracks followed. In summer, Aviemore goes German for a Beer Fest with oompah music, sauerkraut, bratwurst, and foaming tankards. The Highlands answers with nail hammering, haggis throwing, barrel hurling and the Games. More sober delights can be had in wining and dining on a Highland Railway steam train en route from the town to **Boat of Garten**.

Appropriately enough, **Glenlivet** is

Tartanry again, this time at Aviemore's leisure complex.

at hand. Visiting Speyside in 1822, George IV was told his favourite malt whisky was unobtainable. The honour of Rothiemurchus was saved by Elizabeth Grant, who produced bottles from her own bin "long in wood, mild as milk, and the true contraband gout in it". Grant's father was made a judge.

Six miles (10 km) southwest of Aviemore is the **Kincraig Highland Wildlife Park** (an outpost of the Royal Zoological Society of Scotland), where once indigenous animals, including boar and bison, run free. Part of the park is drive-through, part walk-through.

Further south, duck to enter the Blackhouse in the Highland Folk Museum at **Kingussie**. A peat fire fills this replica of an Isle of Lewis stone house with pungent smoke. You know how the salmon must have felt in the Victorian corrugated-iron smokehouse nearby. In the museum is ideal equipment for a strolling player: a chanter walking-stick and bagpipes from Waterloo.

Royal haunts: Blame **Braemar** on Queen Victoria. She loved it. The village is best enjoyed in September when the Highland Gathering brings people from all over the world to watch cabers tossed, stones put and hammers thrown, as well as the daring intricacies of sword dancing and the Highland fling. Fairytale Braemar Castle's surprising charm and intimacy stem from being lived in.

Eight miles (13 km) west of Braemar on the A93 there's **Balmoral**. If the Gaels called it Bouchmorale ("majestic dwelling") before Prince Albert's rebuilding, what superlatives would they have found for the new baronial palace? Since 1855 it has been a royal residence, though in midsummer the Queen shares her gardens with the public and her prayers with her subjects at nearby **Crathie** church. **Ballater** continues the royal progress down the Dee, and this is where the family pops down to the shops (look for the "By Appointment" signs). Against the backdrop of forest, mountains and castles, what more fitting place to bring down the curtain on an extravaganza which began as melodrama and ends as musical comedy?

Balmoral Castle, the Queen's holiday home in Aberdeenshire.

PEATLAND VERSUS PROFIT

One man's wilderness is another's development potential. This age-old conflict of interests has been a bitter dispute between conservationists and business interests in the Highlands as commercial foresters talk about expanding the 13 percent of Scotland that is tree-covered to 30 percent by the end of the century.

At the centre of the controversy is the Flow Country of Caithness and Sutherland in the far north, so called because the peat bogs which cover it appear to be moving like a slowly advancing glacier. This extraordinary landscape, one of Europe's last remaining wildernesses, is a breeding ground for many of Britain's most important wading-birds such as the rare greenshank, the merlin and the black-throated diver. Yet vast new forests of lodgepole pine and sitka spruce are marching across the peatland, destroying the bird's habitats.

The forestry industry argues that the new plantations help cut Britain's import bill for timber, but the true propulsion for the accelerating afforestation is that it provides generous tax concessions for wealthy investors – such as London-based sportsmen, pop stars and television personalities.

One TV personality, Magnus Magnusson, who is of Icelandic descent, finds himself on the other side of the argument as president of the Royal Society for the Protection of Birds. "This is wanton vandalism of one of our greatest national assets," he says. "My ancestors were accused of rape and pillage, but I think even they would be ashamed of what is going on."

So remote is this vast area of soggy open moorland and low, featureless hills that until recently only a handful of bird-watchers and fishermen realised the extent to which "tax-avoidance forestry" was advancing. Planting in Scotland requires no planning permission and the investment companies behind the schemes kept an understandably low profile. The other major planter, the Forestry Commission, has traditionally possessed such wide powers that it is known in the Highlands as "a state within a state".

The Flow Country, thanks to its magical landscape, provided a potent focus for pressure groups wishing to draw the media's attention to the problem. But elsewhere in Scotland huge numbers of conifers have been planted by forestry companies. About one-fifth of the southwest region of Dumfries and Galloway is now forested, and hill farms in the Borders area have also had to make way for trees. Islanders on Arran, in the Clyde estuary, began calling their island "Little Finland" as more and more of it disappeared under encroaching conifers.

The debate is far from one-sided, however. Many Scots, bemused to find that familiar areas have become "eco-systems", are impatient with the conservationists. The now defunct Highlands and Islands Development Board argued that a ban on forestry and other land uses would kill prospects for up to 2,000 local jobs and would jeopardise the economic future of whole communities. The Highland Regional Council agree: what was the point of having no trees, it asked, if it led to no jobs and no people?

The conservationists had an answer. Forestry employs relatively few people, they said, whereas tourism provides 100,000 jobs in Scotland. And tourists won't want to gaze at a landscape of lodgepole pine. ∎

The unspoilt Highlands.

ORKNEY

Six miles (12 km) of sea separate the northeast corner of Scotland from an archipelago of 70 islands, about one-third of which are inhabited. This is Orkney (the word means "seal islands" in old Icelandic) which extends over 1,200 sq. miles (3,100 sq. km). If you believe there are more islands it may be because you have drunk too well of the products of Orkney's two distilleries or are counting seals – both common and grey – which abound in these waters.

In few places in the world is the marriage of landscape and seascape so harmonious. On halcyon summer days, the blues of the sky and of the sea complement the greens of rolling pastures and the gold of fields of grain. Later, when zephyrs blow, scudding cumulus clouds are matched by the white horses of waves.

The "ey" is Old Norse for islands and one should refer to Orkney and not "the Orkneys" or "the Orkney islands". It also announces an ancient affiliation with Norway, an affiliation historical rather than geographical, for Norway lies 300 miles (480 km) to the east. Orkney was a Norwegian appendage until the end of the 15th century and the true Orcadian is more Norse than Scot. With a rich tradition of sagas, it's no surprise that 20th-century Orkney has produced such distinguished literati as Edwin Muir, Eric Linklater and George Mackay Brown.

To Orcadians, Scotland is the "*sooth*" (south) and never the "mainland" for that is the name of the group's principal island: when inhabitants of the smaller islands visit the largest, therefore, they journey to **Mainland**, and when they travel to the United Kingdom they are off "*sooth*" to Scotland. Not that there are many of them to travel: the population is about 19,000, of whom one-quarter live in the capital, Kirkwall.

Shortest flight: Travel within the archipelago is by ferries and more often by planes. The Loganair flight between Westray and Papa Westray is the shortest commercial flight in the world. In perfect weather conditions, it takes only one minute.

To wander these islands is, for the dedicated lover of archaeology, a taste of paradise: for the uninitiated it is the threshold of a world of wonder. Orkney offers an uninterrupted continuum of mute stones from Neolithic times (about 4500 BC) through the Bronze and Iron Ages to about AD 700, followed by remains from the days when the islands were occupied successively by the Celts and the Vikings.

On average, every square mile (2.6 sq. km) has three recorded items of antiquarian interest. The key to these is often kept at the nearest farmhouse and payment is made by placing money in an honour-box. Anyone interested to scrape away with a toothbrush – after first contacting the appropriate authorities – is almost assured of unearthing some exciting artefact.

One in six of all seabirds that breed in Britain nests in Orkney, which boasts about 30 major seabird cliffs. Every nook, every cranny, every ledge of

The Orkney Islands

10 miles/ 16 km

weathered sandstone is jammed with nesting birds: guillemots and razorbills, shags and storm petrels, gannets and gulls. Puffins pop in and out of their earth burrows while cormorants flap above the water or, after diving, perch on an exposed rock and hoist their wings to dry in caricature of an armorial eagle.

Fishing is excellent and varied. Wild brown trout abound in myriad lochs where, thanks to an ancient Norse law, you don't need a permit to fish. As a bonus, in spring, late summer and autumn, sea trout (similar to salmon) leave the sea to spawn in burns and lochs. In recent years the potential for sea angling has been realised and lucky anglers catch 200-lb (90-kg) skate and halibut and a variety of other species.

City sights: Kirkwall is dominated by the 12th-century **St Magnus Cathedral**. Construction began in the Norman style but a healthy leavening of Gothic features attests to more than 300 years of building. Facing the cathedral is the ruined **Bishop's Palace**, a massive structure with a round tower remi-

niscent of a castle. Here in the 13th century, the great Norwegian king, Haakon Haakonson, lay dying while Norse sagas were read aloud to him. Nearby is a third ancient building, the **Earl's Palace**, a romantic gem of renaissance architecture. It is roofless: in the 17th century its slates were removed to build the town hall.

Other Kirkwall attractions are the **Tankerness House Museum** which presents the complete story of Orkney from prehistory to the present; the **Orkney Library**, the oldest public library in Scotland, and a golf course.

War and peace: South of Kirkwall is the great natural harbour of **Scapa Flow**. Here, the captured German fleet was anchored after World War I and here the fleet was scuttled. Only six of the 74 ships remain on the bed of this deep, spacious bay which is bliss for the scuba-diver, a peaceful cornucopia for the deep sea angler.

The island of **Flotta**, at the south of Scapa Flow, is a North Sea oil terminal through which 12 percent of Britain's

Kirkwall Harbour: familiar to sailors in both world wars.

oil passes. This is the Orcadians' only concession to black gold – and enough is enough. Mining for uranium near Kirkwall has been firmly rejected.

Fifteen miles (24 km) west of Kirkwall is picturesque **Stromness**, Orkney's second town. A well on the main street testifies that, in the 17th century, Stromness was developed by the Hudson Bay Company whose ships made this their last port of call before crossing the Atlantic. Stromness has a good Art Centre, a museum, an indoor swimming pool and a golf course.

Most of Mainland's major archaeological sites are to the north of Stromness. Crawl into awesome **Maeshowe**, the most magnificent chambered tomb in Britain, which dates from 3500 BC. Within is a spacious burial chamber built with enormous megaliths on some of which are incised the world's largest collection of 12th-century runic (Viking) hieroglyphics. One stone, surely the forerunner of today's graffiti, says simply: "Ingigerd is the sweetest woman there is."

Chapel built in Orkney by Italian prisoners during World War II.

Near Maeshowe are the **Ring of Brodgar** and the **Standing Stones of Stenness**, the remains of two of Britain's most spectacular stone circles. When the former (whose name means "Circle of the Sun") was completed, about 1200 BC, it consisted of 60 standing stones set along the circumference of a circle about 340 ft (103 metres) in diameter. Today, 27 stones, the tallest 14 ft (4 metres), still stand. The four giant monoliths of Stenness are all that remain of that particular circle of 12 stones erected about 2300 BC.

Skara Brae, Britain's Pompeii, sits on the Atlantic coast alongside a superb sandy beach. The settlement, remarkably well preserved, consists of several dwelling houses and connecting passages and was engulfed by sand 4,500 years ago after having been occupied for 500 years. Skara Brae is a quintessential Stone Age site; no metal of any kind was found: all furniture – beds, chairs – are made of stone.

Five miles (8 km) north is **Birsay** with the 16-century **Earl's Palace**. Op-

posite is the **Brough of Birsay**, a tiny tidal island (avoid being stranded); it is covered with rich remains of Norse and Christian settlements.

A further 8 miles (13 km) east, and guarding Eynhallow Sound, is the **Broch of Gurness**. Brochs are Iron Age (100 BC to AD 300) strongholds built by the Picts. These structures, unique to Scotland and ubiquitous in Orkney, were circular at their base and their massive walls tapered gently inwards to a height of about 60 ft (18 metres).

Echoes of war: The principal southern islands are South Ronaldsay, Burray, Lamb Holm, Hoy and Flotta. Technically, the first three are no longer islands, being joined to Mainland by the **Churchill Barriers**. These were built by Italian prisoners during World War II after a German submarine penetrated Scapa Flow and sank the battleship *Ark Royal*.

On **Lamb Holm** enter some Nissen huts and be astonished at the beautiful chapel built with scrap metal by these prisoners. An unusual Wireless Museum at St Margaret's Hope on **South Ronaldsay** has its band of devotees.

Hoy, the second largest island of the archipelago, is spectacularly different. The southern part is low-lying but at the north stand the heather-covered Cuilags (1,420 ft/426 metres), from where all Orkney, except Little Rysa, can be viewed. A stroll along the 1,140-ft (367-metre) high **St John's Head**, which teems with seabirds (beware the swooping great skuas) and boasts some rare plants, is sheer delight for the geologist, ornithologist and botanist or for those who just like to ramble. Immediately south of St John's Head is Orkney's most venerable inhabitant, the **Old Man of Hoy**, who, sad to say, appears to be cracking up. This 450-ft (135-metre) perpendicular sandstone column challenges the world's leading rock-climbers and foolish neophytes.

Northward-bound: And so to the northern islands. Fertile **Shapinsay** is so near Mainland that it is called suburbia. Also near Mainland, but further west and readily reached by local ferry are **Rousay** and **Egilsay**. Rich archaeological finds

Ring of Brodgar: 3,000 years ago there were 60 stones.

have earned the former the sobriquet "Egypt of the North". Visit the remarkable 76-ft-long (23-metre) Neolithic **Midhowe** chambered tomb, aptly named the "Great Ship of Death", which has 12 burial compartments on either side of a central passage. Nearby is the magnificent **Midhowe Broch**. Ascend the summit of Mansemass Hill and stroll to Ward Hill for superb views of **Eynhallow**, medieval Orkney's Holy Island, between Rousay and Mainland.

On **Egilsay** an unusual round church, which has affinities with similar buildings in Ireland, marks the 12th-century site of the martyrdom of St Magnus.

Low-lying **Sanday**, with its white beaches, has room for a golf course but not to the exclusion of archaeological remains. Most important is the **Quoyness chambered cairn**, standing 13 ft high (3 metres) and dating from about 2900 BC. It is similar to, but even larger than, Maeshowe. **Stronsay**, another low-lying island with sandy beaches, was formerly the hub of the prosperous Orkney herring industry. **Eday** may be bleak and barren yet is paradise for bird watchers and has the customary complement of archaeological edifices.

Westray, the largest northern island, is unique in that its population is increasing. This is largely because of a successful fishing fleet which contradicts the allegation that the Orcadian is "a farmer with a boat". **Noup Head** is Westray's bird reserve and splendid view point. The island also has a golf course and the ruined renaissance **Notland Castle**. Papa Westray's **North Hill Nature Reserve** is home to arctic terns and skuas. At **Knap of Howar** are considerable remains of the earliest standing dwelling houses in northwest Europe (approximately 3000 BC). Their occupants, archaeologists have found, had "a strong preference for oysters".

On the most northerly island, **North Ronaldsay**, a dyke around the island confines sheep to the shore, leaving better inland pastures for cattle. Seaweed, the sole diet of these sheep, results in dark meat with an unusually rich flavour: an acquired taste.

Orkney boasts the world's shortest commercial flight: it lasts one minute.

SHETLAND

The writer Jan Morris called them "inset islands". In those two words she succinctly defined the mystery of the **Shetland Islands**, whose remoteness (200 miles/320 km to the north of Aberdeen) means that, in maps of Britain, they are usually relegated to a box in the corner of a page. "This has subtly affected our concept of them," wrote Morris. "They are much, much further away than most people suppose. They are much more foreign places, much harder, older and more distinct."

Preceding pages: Lerwick, Shetland's capital. Left, Britain's most northerly lighthouse.

The 20 or so inhabited islands – nearly 80 more are uninhabited – scarcely seem part of Britain at all. The extension of UK road numbering produces peculiarities: what on earth is a small island doing with an A970? The declining population (23,000) doesn't regard itself as British, or even as Scottish, but as Norse. The nearest mainland town is Bergen in Norway. Norwegian is taught in the schools. The heroes of myths have names like Harald Hardrada and King Haakon Haakonsson.

Wildlife wonders: The islands, dotted over 70 miles (112 km) of swelling seas, are a geologist's and bird-watcher's paradise, and appeal to hardy walkers. Spring comes late, with plant growth speeding up only in June. Rainfall is heavy, mists are frequent and gales (record gust: 177 miles/285 km an hour) keep the islands virtually treeless. But conditions change rapidly, hence the islanders' advice: "If you don't like the weather, wait a minute." It's never very cold, even in mid-winter, thanks to the caresses of the North Atlantic Drift; and in mid-summer (the "Simmer Dim") it never quite gets dark. (A game of golf gets under way at midnight on midsummer's eve.)

The late-January festival of Up-Helly-Aa is loosely based on a pagan fire festival intended to herald the impending return of the sun. A procession of *guizers* (men dressed in winged helmets and shining armour) parades through the streets carrying burning torches with which they set fire to a replica of a Viking longship. It is an authentic fiesta and visitors aren't encouraged; for one thing, there's no-one to look after guests since everybody on ths island is much too busy celebrating.

At other times, the Shetlander is exceptionally hospitable and talkative. When he says, "You'll have a dram", it's an instruction rather than an enquiry and you're unlikely ever to be offered a larger glass of whisky. It's worth attending a folk concert, not just for the drink but because the islands are full of astonishingly accomplished fiddlers.

Oil boom: Two check-in counters confront passengers at **Sumburgh Airport** on the main island, **Mainland**: one is for fixed-wing aircraft, the other for helicopters. North Sea oil generates the traffic and at one time threatened to overwhelm the islands. But the oil companies, pushed by a determined local council, made conspicuous efforts to lessen the impact on the environment and, although half of Britain's oil flows through the 1,000-acre (400-hectare)

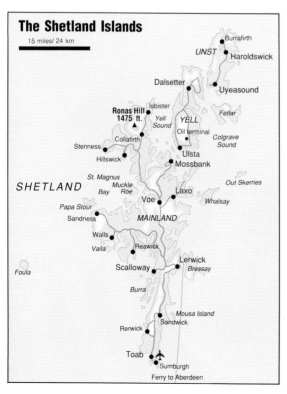

The Shetland Islands

15 miles/ 24 km

Burrafirth
UNST
Haroldswick
Dalsetter
Uyeasound
Isbister
Ronas Hill 1475 ft. ▲ Yell Sound YELL Fetlar
Oil terminal
Collafirth Colgrave Sound
Stenness
Hillswick Ulsta
Mossbank
St. Magnus Muckle Out Skerries
SHETLAND Bay Roe Laxo
Papa Stour Voe Whalsay
Sandness MAINLAND
Walls
Vaila Reawick
Lerwick
Scalloway Bressay
Foula
Burra
Mousa Island
Sandwick
Rerwick
Toab
Sumburgh
Ferry to Aberdeen

Sullom Voe terminal or a strip of land at the northern end of Mainland, they seem to have succeeded beyond most islanders' expectations. The 16 crude oil tanks, each holding 21 million gallons (95 million litres) were painted mistletoe-green, 124 species of birds have been logged within the terminal boundary, and outside the main gates a traffic-sign gives priority to otters.

Sheep outnumber people by eight to one. "They eat everything," says one islander. "The place would be covered in wildflowers if it weren't for the wretched sheep." Shetland ponies are more loved. They were carefully bred to keep their legs short so that they could pull carts through Britain's coal mines, but these days they graze freely, their manes tangled by the wind, or are sold as children's pets.

But it's birds that dominate Shetland. Because of the lack of woodlands there are fewer than 50 breeding species, but no lack of numbers. Filling the sky and the cliff ledges are 30,000 gannets, 140,000 guillemots and 300,000 ful-mars. There are over 3,000 pairs of great skua (known locally as bonxies), piratical birds who will dive-bomb intruders during the breeding season. It's the puffins everyone wants to see, however; they begin to arrive in May and before long there are 250,000 of them. Take a small boat round the islands and, as well as the birds, you can find seal colonies, porpoises and dolphins.

Ancient mound: A concentrated anthropological history of the islands is located at **Jarlshof**, a jumble of buildings near the airport. Waves of settlers from the Stone, Bronze and Iron Ages built dwellings here, each on the ruins of its predecessor. The Vikings built on top of that and medieval farmsteads later buried the Viking traces. At the end of the 19th century the site was just a grassy mound, topped with a medieval ruin. Then a wild storm laid bare massive stones in a bank above the beach and archaeologists moved in. Hearths were found where peat fires burned 3,000 years ago. Today old wheelhouses (so called because of their radial walls) have

A Viking festival sets Lerwick alight every January.

been revealed and an exhibition area fleshes out Jarlshof's history.

En route to the capital, Lerwick, 27 miles (43 km) to the north, the offshore island of **Mousa** is home to sheep and ponies, and also to a spectacularly well-preserved broch, a round dry-stone tower more than 40 ft (13 metres) high.

Lerwick looks no more planned than Jarlshof was. The old town has charm, with intimate stone-paved alleys leading off the main street of granite houses and dignified shops (no chain stores here). But little attempt has been made to blend in newer commercial premises and housing estates; ugly jerry-building predominates. The windows of the baronial-looking **town hall**, presented to the town by Norway, Holland and Germany as thanks for Shetland's kindness to seamen, are a reminder of Lerwick's relationship with the elements. It huddles round the harbour, as if preparing itself for the next gale.

For centuries the miniature metropolis has been a crossroads of the North Atlantic for fishing fleets from Spain, Holland, Norway, Germany and Russia, and a babel of accents can still be heard. One of the town's most famous sons, Arthur Anderson, went on to co-found the P&O shipping line in the 19th century; the **Anderson Educational Institute**, the island's only senior secondary school, was endowed by him.

The sea dominates the **museum**, sited above the library in Hillhead. It has a good collection of harpoons, decorative 19th-century sea chests, and coins found in shipwrecks dating back 400 years. More information would be useful about the purpose of certain implement on display, such as trussing drivers, flensing knives, shivs, pluckers and flinchers. The museum also houses various Victorian trinkets and lace shawls, and a collection of 5,000-year-old beads, pots and pumice stones found when excavating Sumburgh airport.

Six miles (10 km) from Lerwick, in a sheltered bay, is the old fishing port of **Scalloway**, once Shetland's capital. Its main feature is the gaunt ruins of an early 17th-century castle built for Earl Patrick Stewart, a nephew of Mary Queen of Scots. So tyrannical was the earl that he is reputed to have used a mixture of eggs, blood and human hair as building plaster.

Deep voes (inlets) poke into the Shetland Islands like long fingers so that no part of the watery landscape is more than 3 miles (5 km) from the sea. As you drive across Mainland's moors, meadows and hills, dramatic sea views abruptly materialise. Shetlanders were always more sailors than farmers; but at **Tingwall**, north of Lerwick, an **Agricultural Museum** lays out in an old farmyard a rare collection of old peat-cutting tools and cooking pots.

Island-hopping: Small ferries connect a handful of smaller islands to Mainland. **Yell**, a peaty place, has a local museum and craft centre and a knitwear centre selling genuine rather than generic Shetland garments. A minister of the kirk said: "Yell is Hell, but Unst – oh! Unst!" **Unst**, the UK's most northerly island, has an important nature reserve at Hermanness and a Royal Air Force base. From the cliffs at Hermanness gaze out on rocky **Muckle Flugga**, the last land before the Arctic Circle. **Fetlar's** name means "fat island", a reference to its fertile soil. **Whalsay** is prosperous, thanks to its notably energetic fishermen. The **Out Skerries**, a scattered archipelago, has a thriving fishing fleet. The peacefulness and abundant wild flowers of **Papa Stour**, a mile of turbulent sea west of Mainland, once attracted a transient hippy colony.

Foula, 14 miles (23 kn) to the west of Scalloway, must be Britain's remotest inhabited island and, most winters, is cut off for several weeks by awesome seas. The spectacular 1,200-ft (370-metre) cliffs are home to storm petrels, great skuas and a host of other seabirds.

Another staging-post for the birds is provided by **Fair Isle**, 20 miles (32 km) to the south-west, halfway to Orkney. This self-reliant island, now owned by the National Trust for Scotland, has an observatory to monitor the birds' movements and is home of Fair Isle sweaters, whose distinctive geometric patterns can be dated back 2,000 years to Balkan nomads.

INSIGHT GUIDES
Travel Tips

FOR THOSE
WITH MORE THAN
A PASSING INTEREST
IN TIME...

Before you put your name down for a Patek Philippe watch *fig. 1*, there are a few basic things you might like to know, without knowing exactly whom to ask. In addressing such issues as accuracy, reliability and value for money, we would like to demonstrate why the watch we will make for you will be quite unlike any other watch currently produced.

"Punctuality", Louis XVIII was fond of saying, "is the politeness of kings."

We believe that in the matter of punctuality, we can rise to the occasion by making you a mechanical timepiece that will keep its rendezvous with the Gregorian calendar at the end of every century, omitting the leap-years in 2100, 2200 and 2300 and recording them in 2000 and 2400 *fig. 2*. Nevertheless, such a watch does need the occasional adjustment. Every 3333 years and 122 days you should remember to set it forward one day to the true time of the celestial clock. We suspect, however, that you are simply content to observe the politeness of kings. Be assured, therefore, that when you order your watch, we will be exploring for you the physical—if not the metaphysical—limits of precision.

Does everything have to depend on how much?

Consider, if you will, the motives of collectors who set record prices at auction to acquire a Patek Philippe. They may be paying for rarity, for looks or for micromechanical ingenuity. But we believe that behind each $500,000-plus

bid is the conviction that a Patek Philippe, even if 50 years old or older, can be expected to work perfectly for future generations.

In case your ambitions to own a Patek Philippe are somewhat discouraged by the scale of the sacrifice involved, may we hasten to point out that the watch we will make for you today will certainly be a technical improvement on the Pateks bought at auction? In keeping with our tradition of inventing new mechanical solutions for greater reliability and better time-keeping, we will bring to your watch innovations *fig. 3* inconceivable to our watchmakers who created the supreme wristwatches of 50 years ago *fig. 4*. At the same time, we will of course do our utmost to avoid placing undue strain on your financial resources.

Can it really be mine?

May we turn your thoughts to the day you take delivery of your watch? Sealed within its case is your watchmaker's tribute to the mysterious process of time. He has decorated each wheel with a chamfer carved into its hub and polished into a shining circle. Delicate ribbing flows over the plates and bridges of gold and rare alloys. Millimetric surfaces are bevelled and burnished to exactitudes measured in microns. Rubies are transformed into jewels that triumph over friction. And after many months—or even years—of work, your watchmaker stamps a small badge into the mainbridge of your watch. The Geneva Seal—the highest possible attestation of fine watchmaking *fig. 5*.

Looks that speak of inner grace *fig. 6*.

When you order your watch, you will no doubt like its outward appearance to reflect the harmony and elegance of the movement within. You may therefore find it helpful to know that we are uniquely able to cater for any special decorative needs you might like to express. For example, our engravers will delight in conjuring a subtle play of light and shadow on the gold case-back of one of our rare pocket-watches *fig. 7*. If you bring us your favourite picture, our enamellers will reproduce it in a brilliant miniature of hair-breadth detail *fig. 8*. The perfect execution of a double hobnail pattern on the bezel of a wristwatch is the pride of our casemakers and the satisfaction of our designers, while our chainsmiths will weave for you a rich brocade in gold *figs. 9 & 10*. May we also recommend the artistry of our goldsmiths and the experience of our lapidaries in the selection and setting of the finest gemstones? *figs. 11 & 12*.

How to enjoy your watch before you own it.

As you will appreciate, the very nature of our watches imposes a limit on the number we can make available. (The four Calibre 89 time-pieces we are now making will take up to nine years to complete). We cannot therefore promise instant gratification, but while you look forward to the day on which you take delivery of your Patek Philippe *fig. 13*, you will have the pleasure of reflecting that time is a universal and everlasting commodity, freely available to be enjoyed by all.

Should you require information on any particular Patek Philippe watch, or even on watchmaking in general, we would be delighted to reply to your letter of enquiry. And if you send us

fig. 1: The classic face of Patek Philippe.

fig. 4: Complicated wristwatches circa 1930 (left) and 1990. The golden age of watchmaking will always be with us.

fig. 6: Your pleasure in owning a Patek Philippe is the purpose of those who made it for you.

fig. 9: Harmony of design is executed in a work of simplicity and perfection in a lady's Calatrava wristwatch.

fig. 10: The chainsmith's hands impart strength and delicacy to a tracery of gold.

fig. 5: The Geneva Seal is awarded only to watches which achieve the standards of horological purity laid down in the laws of Geneva. These rules define the supreme quality of watchmaking.

fig. 7: Arabesques come to life on a gold case-back.

fig. 11: Circles in gold: symbols of perfection in the making.

fig. 2: One of the 33 complications of the Calibre 89 astronomical clock-watch is a satellite wheel that completes one revolution every 400 years.

fig. 8: An artist working six hours a day takes about four months to complete a miniature in enamel on the case of a pocket-watch.

fig. 12: The test of a master lapidary is his ability to express the splendour of precious gemstones.

fig. 3: Recognized as the most advanced mechanical regulating device to date, Patek Philippe's Gyromax balance wheel demonstrates the equivalence of simplicity and precision.

PATEK PHILIPPE
GENEVE
fig. 13: The discreet sign of those who value their time.

your card marked "book catalogue" we shall post you a catalogue of our publications. Patek Philippe, 41 rue du Rhône, 1204 Geneva, Switzerland, Tel. +41 22/310 03 66.

OYSTER GLX

S Samsonite*

Our Strengths Are Legendary*

*Trademarks of Samsonite Corporation

TRAVEL TIPS

Getting Acquainted

Time Zones

Scotland, like the rest of the UK, follows Greenwich Mean Time (GMT). In spring the clock is moved forward one hour for British Summer Time, and in autumn moved back again to GMT. Especially in the north of Scotland, this means that it is light till 10pm and after in June and early July.

When it is noon GMT, it is:

2am in	Honolulu
4am	Los Angeles and Vancouver
6am	Chicago, Houston and Winnipeg
7am	New York, Toronto, Montreal and Lima
8am	Caracas, Santiago and Halifax
9am	Buenos Aires, Montevideo and Rio de Janeiro
noon	London, Dublin and Accra
1pm	Amsterdam, Belgrade, Copenhagen, Gibraltar, Lagos, Madrid, Malta, Oslo, Rome and Stockholm
2pm	Alexandria, Athens, Cairo, Cape Town, Helsinki, Istanbul, and Leningrad
3pm	Baghdad, Moscow and Nairobi
3.30pm	Tehran
5pm	Karachi
5.30pm	Bombay, Calcutta, Colombo and New Delhi
6pm	Dacca
7pm	Bangkok and Jakarta
8pm	Hong Kong, Manila, Peking, Perth and Singapore
9pm	Tokyo
9.30pm	Adelaide
10pm	Melbourne and Sydney
midnight	Christchurch and Wellington

Climate

No matter what you say about Scottish weather, you are bound to be wrong. There are those who rave about the cloudless fortnight they spent on Skye and those who have spent more than one holiday there and have yet to see the Cuillins.

With this word of warning, it can be said that the west is generally wetter and warmer than the east. Nowhere can the weather be depended upon. Summer is, in Scotland, a somewhat misleading expression.

Nevertheless, there have been occasions when people have been admitted to Aberdeen hospitals suffering from heatstroke. The best place for sunshine in Britain is the Hebridean island of Tiree, while the coldest temperature ever recorded in Britain was at Braemar in the Highlands.

For what it's worth, Edinburgh's highest/lowest daily average temperatures in Celsius (Fahrenheit in brackets) are: January 6/1 (42/34), February 6/1 (43/34), March 8/2 (46/36), April 11/4 (51/39), May 14/6 (56/43), June 17/9 (62/49), July 17/9 (65/52), August 18/11 (64/52), September 16/9 (60/49),October 12/7 (54/44), November 9/4 (48/39), December 7/2 (44/36). April, May and June are usually drier months than July, August and September – but take an umbrella whenever you go.

Planning the Trip

Clothing

Given the climate, it follows that you should never be without a raincoat or a warm sweater. Neither should you be without light clothes in summer. For those attracted to the excellent opportunities for hill-walking and rock-climbing, it is essential to come properly prepared. In the mountains the weather can change very quickly. Each year people suffer serious and needless injury through setting out without adequate equipment; the Highlands is no place to go on a serious hill walk in a T-shirt and tennis shoes.

Electricity

220 volts is standard. Hotels usually have dual 220/110-volt sockets for razors. If you are visiting from abroad, you will probably need an adaptor to link other small electrical appliances to the three-pin sockets universal in Britain; it is usually easier to find these at home before leaving than in Scotland.

It is advisable to have medical insurance. Citizens of European Community countries are entitled to medical treatment under reciprocal arrangements and similar arrangements exist with some other countries. No matter which country you come from, you will receive immediate emergency treatment free at a hospital casualty department.

A Wise Man Never Thinks How Far He's Come. He Thinks How Far He Can Still Travel.

REMY XO BECAUSE LIFE IS WHAT YOU MAKE IT

THOMAS COOK MASTERCARD TRAVELLERS CHEQUES...

...HOLIDAY ESSENTIALS

Travel money from the travel experts

THOMAS COOK MASTERCARD TRAVELLERS CHEQUES ARE
WIDELY AVAILABLE THROUGHOUT THE WORLD.

MONEY MATTERS

Currency: The British pound is divided into 100 pence. The coins used are 1p, 2p, 5p, 10p, 20p, 50p, and £1. One of the minor pleasures of living in Scotland is that the £1 coin is not nearly so common as in England and that £1 notes (issued by the Royal Bank of Scotland) still circulate along with notes of £5, £10, £20, £50 and £100. (Technically, Scottish notes are not legal tender in England and Wales, but many shops will accept them and English banks will readily change them for you.)

Traveller's Cheques: Eurocheques and Eurocard can be used at banks and travellers' cheques can be cashed at banks, *bureaux de change* and many hotels, though the best rates are normally available at banks.

Credit Cards: Access (alias Mastercard) and Visa are the most commonly acceptable credit cards, followed by American Express and Diners' Club. Small guest houses and bed-and-breakfast places will wish payment in cash.

Banks

Scotland has its own banks, the Royal Bank of Scotland, the Bank of Scotland and the Clydesdale. They still issue their own notes – although the Royal Bank is the only one to issue the £1 note – which circulate alongside Bank of England notes.

Don't expect consistent opening hours. The Royal Bank and the TSB (Scotland) are open in the cities Monday–Friday 9.15am–4.45pm and until 5.30pm on Thursday. The Bank of Scotland is open 9.30–4.45pm except on Thursday when it closes at 3.30pm, but re-opens from 4.30–5.30pm. The Clydesdale is slightly different again, opening from 9.15am–4pm each day except Thursday when it remains open until 5.30pm. In rural areas, banks may close between 12.30 and 1.30pm and may not be open later on Thursday.

PUBLIC HOLIDAYS

Local, public and bank holidays can be frustrating for visitors but generally there will be a small shop open somewhere during the major public holidays which are 25 and 26 December, 1 and 2 January and Good Friday.

Other national holidays in Scotland are May Day (first Monday in May); Spring Holiday (Monday in late May); Summer Holiday (first Monday in August).

GETTING THERE

By Air

Scotland is reasonably well served by direct non-stop flights from the North American continent and by direct non-stop flights from parts of Europe. British Airways flies from New York to Glasgow; American Airlines flies from Chicago to Glasgow; Northwest Airlines flies from New York and Boston to Glasgow; United Airlines flies from Washington DC to Glasgow and Air Canada flies from Calgary, Halifax and Toronto to Glasgow. In addition Icelandair flies from Reyjavik (Iceland) and Aer Lingus from Dublin to both Edinburgh and Glasgow.

Air France and British Airways fly from Paris to Glasgow; Air UK flies from Amsterdam to Aberdeen, Edinburgh and Glasgow; Sabena flies from Brussels to both Glasgow and Edinburgh; British Midland flies from Copenhagen to Glasgow; Lufthansa flies from Frankfurt to Glasgow and Air Malta flies from Malta to Glasgow. Air UK and Scandinavian Airlines fly from Stavanger to Aberdeen; Air UK fly from Bergen to Aberdeen and Business Air fly from Esbjerg (Denmark) to Aberdeen.

There are excellent services from London (Heathrow, Gatwick and Stanstead airports) and several English regional airports to Edinburgh, Glasgow, Aberdeen and Inverness. These include no-book shuttle flights on which stand-by tickets are often available at considerable reductions. Airlines flying these routes include British Airways, British Midland and Air UK. Flying time between London and Edinburgh or London and Glasgow is about 70 minutes; roughly 50 percent longer from London to Aberdeen or Inverness.

Edinburgh airport (Tel: 0131-331 1000) is 6 miles (10km) west of the city centre with good road access and a useful airlink bus service to the heart of town. Glasgow airport (Tel: 0141-887 1111) is 8 miles (13km) west of the city centre alongside the M8 motorway at Junction 28. A coach service runs between the airport and Anderston and Buchanan bus stations, both in the heart of the city. Aberdeen airport (Tel: 01224 722331) is 7 miles (11km) west of the city centre with excellent road access (A96). A coach service runs between airport and city centre.

By Rail

There are frequent InterCity services to Scotland from 93 stations in England. On most trains the journey time from London (Euston or Kings Cross) to Edinburgh is slightly more than four hours and from London (Euston or Kings Cross) to Glasgow about five-and-a-half hours. Sleeper and Motorail services run between London (Euston) and Edinburgh, Glasgow, Aberdeen, Inverness and Fort William.

Avoid travel on Sundays when services are often curtailed and journeys take much longer. Tel: London Euston, (0171) 387 7070; London Kings Cross, (0171) 278 2477; Edinburgh, (0131) 556 2451; Glasgow, (0141) 204 2844; Aberdeen, (01224) 594222; Inverness, (01463) 238924; Dundee, (01382) 28046; Perth, (01738) 37117. Information offices are open 8am–9pm daily while London, Edinburgh and Glasgow provide a 24-hour service.

By Road

There are good motorway connections from England and Wales. The M1/M6 is the quickest route, though heavily congested at the southern end. The A1, a more easterly approach, is longer but may be a better bet if you plan to make one or two stopovers on the way. Edinburgh and Glasgow are about 400 miles (650km) from London.

By Bus: Scottish Citylink (Tel: 0171-636 9373) and National Express (Tel: 0171-730 0202) operate daytime and overnight coaches from England to Scotland. The journey takes about 8 hours from London to Edinburgh or to Glasgow. Coach travel may not be as comfortable or as fast as the trains, but it is a good deal cheaper.

Practical Tips

For emergency services such as police, ambulance, the fire service or lifeboat service dial 999.

Although Scotland isn't normally associated with mosquitoes, an aggressive breed of midge exists, especially in warm, humid conditions, in parts of the west coast and calls for a tough repellent.

MEDIA

Newspapers
The Scotsman, printed in Edinburgh, is the national newspaper and, indeed, the only Scottish quality daily. This Thomson-owned paper has good coverage of both Scottish and other UK news and foreign news, as well as material on the arts and business. *The Herald,* printed in Glasgow, has good middle-market coverage and is popular in and around its native city (although it has dropped "Glasgow" from its title in an attempt to widen its appeal). Dundee boasts the quirky *Dundee Courier*. Aberdeen has the *Press and Journal* which has a reputation for excessive parochialism, epitomised by the spurious headline on what proved to be a story about the sinking of the *Titanic*: "Aberdeen man lost at sea".

The most popular is the tabloid *Daily Record*, a stablemate of England's *Daily Mirror*. English dailies circulate widely in Scotland.

The four main cities have evening papers which concentrate on sport and entertainment listings. Scotland's most popular Sunday newspaper is the *Sunday Post*, from the same stable as the *Dundee Courier*. It defies classification: perhaps the most useful comment on it would be that it tries to be useful and inoffensive. The Thomson-owned *Scotland*

on Sunday is the country's only quality Sunday.

Throughout Scotland, there are many local weekly papers which you may find both entertaining and informative if you are interested in a particular region, or interested in newspapers.

Magazines
Scotland is poorly served by magazines. However, the *Scottish Field* and the *Scots Magazine* are good-quality monthly magazines which deal with Scottish topics. The *Edinburgh Review* is a literary review of consistent quality. *The List*, an Edinburgh-based listings magazine which appears every two weeks, provides lively and comprehensive coverage of events in both Edinburgh and Glasgow.

Radio & Television
Radio and TV are excellent, for the most part. Radio Scotland is the main BBC radio service and national BBC radio stations also operate in Scotland; so it is possible to hear excellent Radio 4 (FM 92.4–94.6/LW 198) (a mixture of news, current affairs and light entertainment) as well as the classical music channel on Radio 3 (FM 90.2–92.4). Classic FM (FM 99.9–101.99) serves up the more familiar classics and some intriguing and challenging quiz games. Radio 2 (FM 88–90.2) concentrates on light entertainment and sport. Sports' aficionados will tune in to Radio 5 Live (MW 693/909).

Radio 1 (FM 97.6–99.8), Virgin (MW 1215), Atlantic (LW 252) and local radio stations run by both the BBC and commercial companies offer wall-to-wall pop and light music, interspersed with terse news summaries. Local stations tend to provide an unimaginative diet of pop music but can be useful sources of local traffic news and other important information.

Television services are provided by BBC and commercial companies. BBC1 is a general TV service, mirrored (though with a more down-market emphasis) by the commercial ITV network. BBC2 and its commercial stablemate, Channel 4, recognise the existence of more specialist audiences and minority groups.

Telephone
When dialling from abroad, the international access code for Britain is **44**, followed by the area code (Edinburgh 131, Glasgow 141, Aberdeen 1224, etc).

To reach other countries from Scotland, first dial the international access code **010**, then the country code (e.g. Australia 61, France 33, Germany 49, Japan 81, the Netherlands 31, Spain 34, US and Canada 1). If using a US credit phone card, dial the company's access number: **Sprint** 00 801 15; **AT&T** 00 801 10; **MCI** 00 801 11.

The minimum charge for a call made at a public telephone is 10 pence. Many telephones accept only cardphone cards which can be purchased at post offices and shops displaying the cardphone sign for either £1, £2, £4 or £10, depending on the amount of telephone time they will provide.

Excuse me, where is the nearest toilet please?

Per favore, dov'è la toilette?

Perdone, ¿dónde está e servicio más cercano?

请 问 最 就 近 的 洗 手 间 在 那 里？

Простите, скажите, пожалуйста, где здесь туалет?

Unskyld, men hvor er det nærmeste toilet?

Με συγχωρείτε, ξέρετε αν υπάρχουν τουαλέτες εδώ κοντά;

Alternatively, we offer three ways to clear up diarrhoea.

Delhi belly. Montezuma's revenge. Spanish tummy. Call it what you will, for an acute attack of diarrhoea, you won't find a quicker remedy than Diocalm* Ultra with its loperamide formula.

Or you may prefer the dual action of Diocalm tablets. They help stop those nasty tummy pains, and things going from bad to worse.

Either way you'd be well advised to take Diocalm Replenish as well. It helps replace the essential fluids, minerals and salts you lose when you have diarrhoea. Diocalm Replenish is the only type of diarrhoea treatment recommended by the World Health Organisation, and by doctors for kids under six. Always read the label.

So if you want to send diarrhoea packing, pack Diocalm.

 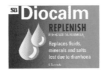 

WHATEVER YOUR SYMPTOMS, WHAT A RELIEF.

He'll take you to paradise and back for just 50 pesos

When you need cash, use the GlobalAccess Card. Local currency from more than 170,000

Cash only, of course.

Swatch. The others just watch.

seahorse/fall winter 94-95

shockproof
splashproof
priceproof
boreproof
swiss made

swatch✚

SCUBA 200

Direct dialling is possible to most parts of the world. Some useful numbers are:
Directory enquiries **192**
International directory enquiries **153**
Assistance in making UK calls **100**
Assistance in making international calls **155**
Emergencies – Police, Fire and Ambulance **999**

Postal Services
Main post offices are open 9am–5.30pm Monday–Friday, and 9am–1pm on Saturday. Sub-post offices (which often form part of another shop) keep similar hours, though they usually close for one half-day during the week.

TOURIST INFORMATION

Scotland
General postal enquiries should be made to the Scottish Tourist Board, 23 Ravelston Terrace, Edinburgh EH4 3EU. Tel: (0131) 332 2433.

The Scottish Tourist Board has its Scottish Travel Centre in South St Andrew Street in the centre of Edinburgh. Other tourist information is provided by local tourist boards throughout Scotland. Their main offices are:

Edinburgh Tourist Office, 3 Princes Street, Waverley Market. Tel: (0131) 557 1700.

Greater Glasgow Tourist Board & Convention Bureau, 35–39 St Vincent Street, Glasgow G1 2ER. Tel: (0141) 204 4400.

Scottish Borders Tourist Board, Murrays Green, Jedburgh, Roxburghshire, TD8 6BE. Tel: (01835) 863435.

Dumfries and Galloway Tourist Board, Campbell House, Bankend Road, Dumfries DG1 4TH. Tel: (01387) 50434.

Ayrshire Tourist Board, Burns House, Burns Statue Square, Ayr KA7 1UP. Tel: (01292) 288688.

Isle of Arran Tourist Board, Brodick Pier, Brodick, Isle of Arran KA27 8AU. Tel: (01770) 302140.

East Lothian Tourist Board, 31 Court Street, Haddington, East Lothian EH41 3AE. Tel: (0162) 082 7422.

Dunfermline District Council, Dalgety House, Viewfield, Dunfermline KY12 7LY. Tel: (01383) 726262.

Forth Valley Tourist Board, Annet House, High Street, Linlithgow, West Lothian EH49 7EJ. Tel: (01506) 844600.

Clyde Valley Tourist Board, Horsemarket, Ladyacre Road, Lanark, Lanarkshire ML11 7QL. Tel: (01555) 662544.

Bute and Cowal Tourist Board, Tourist Information Centre, 7 Alexander Parade, Dunoon, Argyll PA23 8AB. Tel: (01369) 3785. Also at Tourist Information Centre, 15 Victoria Street, Rothesay, Isle of Bute PA20 0AJ. Tel: (01700) 502151.

Loch Lomond, Stirling and Trossachs Tourist Board, 41 Dumbarton Road, Stirling FK8 2QQ. Tel: (01786) 475019.

West Highlands and Islands of Argyll Tourist Board, Albany Street, Oban, Argyll. Tel: (01631) 63122.

Perthshire Tourist Board, 45 High Street, Perth PH1 5TJ. Tel: (01378) 638353.

City of Dundee Tourist Board, Tourist Information Centre, 4 City Square, Dundee DD1 3BA. Tel: (01382) 27723.

Angus Tourist Board, Tourist Information Centre, Market Place, Arbroath DD11 1HR. Tel: (01241) 72609.

St Andrews and NE Fife Tourist Board, 70 Market Street, St Andrews KY16 9NU. Tel: (01334) 72021.

Kircaldy District Council Tourist Information Centre, The Beehive, Dunie Street, Leven KY8 4HE. Tel: (01333) 429464.

Inverness, Loch Ness and Nairn Tourist Board, Castle Wynch, Inverness IV2 3BJ. Tel: (01463) 234353.

Grampian Highlands and Aberdeen Tourist Board, St Nicholas House, Broad Street, Aberdeen AB9 1DE. Tel: (01224) 632727.

Banff and Buchan Tourist Board, Collie Lodge, Banff AB4 1AU. Tel: (012612) 812419.

Moray District Tourist Board, 17 High Street, Elgin IV30 1EG. Tel: (01343) 542666.

Kincardine and Deeside Tourist Board, Bridge Street, Banchory AB31 3SX. Tel: (01330) 822066.

Ross and Cromatory Tourist Board, North Kessock, Black Isle IV1 1XB. Tel: (01463 73) 505.

Sutherland Tourist Board, The Square, Dornoch, Sutherland IV25 3DS. Tel: (01862) 810400.

Fort William and Lochaber Tourist Board, Cameron Centre, Cameron Square, Fort William PH33 6AJ. Tel: (01397) 703781.

Aviemore and Sprey Valley Tourist Board, Grampian Road, Aviemore PH22 1PP. Tel: (01479) 810363.

Isle of Skye and South West Ross Tourist Board, Meall House, Portree, Isle of Skye IV51 9BZ. Tel: (01478) 612137.

Western Isles Tourist Board, 26 Cromwell Street, Stornoway, Isle of Lewis PA87 2XY. Tel: (01851) 703088.

Caithness Tourist Board, Whitechapel Road, Wick, Caithness KW1 4EA. Tel: (01955) 2596.

Orkney Tourist Board, 6 Broad Street, Kirkwall, Orkney KW15 1NX. Tel: (01856) 872856.

Shetland Islands Tourism, Market Cross, Lerwick, Shetland ZE1 0LU. Tel: (01595) 3434.

London
The Scottish Tourist Board runs a Scottish Information Centre at 19 Cockspur Street, London, on the southwest side of Trafalgar Square. Tel: (0171) 930 8661. Information about Scotland is available through the British Tourist Authority offices. (See listing on the following page.)

Europe & North America

Australia, BTA, 8th Floor, University Centre, 210 Clarence Street, Sydney NSW 2000. Tel: (2) 267 4555, Fax: (2) 267 4442.

Belgium, BTA, 306 Avenue Louise, 1050 Brussels. Tel: (2) 646 35 10, Fax: (2) 646 39 86.

Canada, BTA, 111 Avenue Road Suite 450, Toronto, Ontario M5R 3J8. Tel: (416) 925 6326, Fax: (416) 961 2175.

Denmark, BTA, Mønergade 3, 1116 Copenhagen K. Tel: 33 33 91 88.

France, Tourisme de Grande-Bretagne, Maison de la Grande-Bretagne, 19 rue des Mathurins (entrance at les rues Tronchet et Auber), 75009 Paris Tel: (1) 44 515620, Fax: (1) 44 515621.

Germany, BTA, Taunusstrasse 52-60, 60329 Frankfurt. Tel: (69) 2380711, Fax: (69) 2380717.

Ireland, BTA, 123 Lower Baggot Street, Dublin 2. Tel: (01) 661 4188.

Italy, BTA, Corso V. Emanuele 337, 00186 Rome. Tel: (6) 688 06464, Fax: (6) 687 9095.

Japan, BTA, Tokyo Club Building, 3-2-6 Kasumigaseki, Chiyoda-ku, Tokyo 100. Tel: (3) 3581 3603/4, Fax: (3) 3581 5797.

Netherlands, BTA, Stadhouderskade 2 (5e), 1054 ES Amsterdam. Tel: (20) 685 5051.

New Zealand, BTA, Suite 305, 3rd Floor, Dilworth Building, Corner Queen & Customs Streets, Auckland 1. Tel: (9) 303 1446, Fax: (9) 377 6965.

Norway, BTA Postbox 1554 Vika, 0117 Oslo 1. Tel: (95) 468 212444.

Singapore, BTA, 24 Raffles Place, #20–01 Clifford Centre, Singapore 0104. Tel: 535 2966, Fax: 534 4703.

South Africa, BTA, PO Box 41896, Craighall 2024. Tel: (11) 325 0343. (For visitors only: Lancaster Gate, Hyde Lane, Hyde Park).

Spain, BTA Torre de Madrid 6/5, Plaza de España 18, 28008, Madrid. Tel: (91) 541 1396, Fax: (91) 542 8149.

Sweden, BTA, Box 745, S 101, 35 Stockholm. Tel: (8) 212444, Fax (8) 213129. (For visitors only: Klara Norra Kyrkogata 29, S 111, 22 Stockholm.

Switzerland, BTA, Limmatquai 78, CH-8001 Zurich. Tel: (1) 261 4277, Fax (1) 251 4456.

USA: New York, BTA, 551 Fifth Avenue, New York, NY 10176-0799. 1-800-GO-2-BRITAIN, Fax: (212) 986 1188. **Chicago**, BTA, 625 N. Michigan Avenue, Suite 1510, Chicago, IL 60611 (personal callers only).

Australia, Hobart House, Hanover Street, Edinburgh EH2. Tel: (0131) 226 6271.

Belgium, 19 Ainslie Place, Edinburgh EH6 7AS. Tel: (0131) 226 6811.

Denmark, 4 Royal Terrace, Edinburgh EH7 5AB. Tel: (0131) 556 4263

Finland, 53 George Street, Edinburgh EH2 2HT. Tel: (0131) 225 1295.

France, 11 Randolph Crescent, Edinburgh EH3 7TT. Tel: (0131) 225 7954.

Germany, 16 Eglinton Crescent, Edinburgh EH12 5DG. Tel: (0131) 337 2323; James Sellars House, 144 West George Street, Glasgow G2. Tel: (0141) 331 2811.

Greece, 2a Coates Crescent, Edinburgh EH2 1DE. Tel: (0131) 225 6744; 98 Bardonald Drive, Glasgow G12. Tel: (0141) 334 0360.

Iceland, 389 Argyll Street, Glasgow G1. Tel: (0141) 221 6943.

Italy, 32 Melville Street, Edinburgh EH3 7HA. Tel: (0131) 226 3631; 170 Hope Street, Glasgow G2. Tel: (0141) 332 4297.

Japan, 2 Melville Crescent, Edinburgh EH3 7HW. Tel: (0131) 225 4777.

Malawi, 17 York Road, Edinburgh. Tel: (0131) 552 2519.

Malta, 139 Old Dalkeith Road, Edinburgh. Tel: (0131) 664 1070.

Monaco, 39 Castle Street, Edinburgh EH2 3BH. Tel: (0131) 225 1200.

Netherlands, 113 Dundas Street, Edinburgh EH3 5DE. Tel: (0131) 550 5000.

Norway, 86 George Street, Edinburgh EH2 3BU. Tel: (0131) 226 5701; 80 Oswald Street, Glasgow G1. Tel: (0141) 204 1353.

Pakistan, 137 Norfolk Street, Glasgow G5. Tel: (0141) 429 5335.

Philippines, 22 Hill Street, Edinburgh EH2. Tel: (0131) 225 1136.

Poland, 2 Kinnear Road, Edinburgh EH3 5PE. Tel: (0131) 552 0301.

Portugal, 25 Bernard Street, Edinburgh EH6 6SH. Tel: (0131) 555 2080.

South Africa, 69 Nelson Mandela Place, Glasgow G2. Tel: (0141) 221 3114.

Spain, 63 North Castle Street,, Edinburgh EH2 3LJ. Tel: (0131) 220 1843; 389 Argyle Street, Glasgow G1. Tel: (0141) 221 6943.

Sweden, 6 St John's Place, Leith, Edinburgh EH6 7EL. Tel: (0131) 554 6631; 36 Washington Street, Glasgow G2. Tel: (0141) 221 7845.

Switzerland, 66 Hanover Street, Edinburgh EH2. Tel: (0131) 226 5660.

Thailand, 70 Wellington Street, Glasgow G2. Tel: (0141) 248 6677.

United States, 3 Regent Terrace, Edinburgh EH7 5BW. Tel: (0131) 556 8315.

GETTING AROUND

DOMESTIC TRAVEL

By Air

There is a network of air services within Scotland which is especially valuable if going to the islands. Flying to these destinations saves a lot of time and also can give a different perspective on the country-side. The major carriers are Loganair and British Airways.

These are the relevant airport telephone numbers for internal Scottish services:

Loganair:	Aberdeen	(01224) 723 306
	Glasgow	(0141) 889 3181
	Inverness	(01667) 62332
	Orkney	(01856) 3457
	Shetland	(0159) 584 246
British Airways:		
	Aberdeen	(01224) 722 331
	Edinburgh	(0131) 333 1000
	Glasgow	(0141) 887 1111
	Inverness	(01463) 232 471
	Wick	(01955) 2215

By Rail

British Rail is happy to quote the Scottish novelist Robert Louis Stevenson, no stranger to trains in Victorian times: "I travel not to go anywhere, but to go. I travel for travel's sake: the great affair is to move." Certainly, the purpose is splendidly achieved in Scotland, where you can watch spectacular scenery – lochs, glens and forests – from the comfort of a train.

Scotrail offers a wide variety of tickets which permit unlimited travel throughout Scotland. Freedom of Scotland Rovers permit unlimited travel on eight or 15 consecutive days or on four out of eight or 10 out of 15 consecutive days. Area Rovers (choice of North Highlands, West Highlands, Heart of Scotland or Festival Cities) permit unlimited travel in any one of these regions for seven consecutive days or, in the case of Festival Cities for three out of seven consecutive days.

Scottish Travelpasses permit unlimited travel for eight or 15 consecutive days on Scotrail and most of the Caledonian MacBrayne west coast ferries. Together with discounts on the P&O ferries and many buses and postbuses these are truly comprehensive Scottish travel tickets. Details can be obtained from Scotrail information offices in the cities listed.

Aberdeen	(01224) 594222
Dundee	(01382) 28046
Edinburgh	(0131) 556 2451
Glasgow	(0141) 204 2844
Inverness	(01463) 238924
Perth	(01738) 637117
Stirling	(01786) 464754

A few possible routes that you might take are: **Glasgow to Fort William and Mallaig** (164 miles/265km). Train enthusiasts head for the West Highland line, which operates steam locomotives on Tuesday, Thursday and Sunday during the summer months from Fort William to the fishing port of Mallaig, from which a ferry departs for Skye. From Glasgow, the route passes alongside Loch Lomond, across the wild Rannoch Moor and, after Fort William, over the majestic Glenfinnan Viaduct and hillsides dotted with deer. For more details, contact: ScotRail West Highland Transport Centre, Fort William PH33 6AN, (Tel: 01397 703791).

Glasgow to Oban (101 miles/163km). The train branches off the Fort William route at Crianlarich and heads past ruined Kilchurn Castle and the fjord-like scenery of the Pass of Brander to Oban, "gateway to the Inner Hebrides".

Perth to Inverness (118 miles/190km). The route, through forested glens and across the roof of Scotland, takes in Pitlochry, Blair Atholl and Aviemore. As well as being a ski centre, Aviemore is the departure point for steam trains on the 5-mile (8-km) Strathspey Railway line.

Inverness to Kyle of Lochalsh (82 miles/132km). From mid-May until October (no Sunday service) this regular service on a twisting line with breath-taking scenery is enhanced by the Hebridean Heritage train having an observation car while both it and the Atlantic Heritgage train have a dining car service. A commentary is provided. The journey, which takes in lochs, glens and mountains from the North Sea to the Atlantic Ocean, is especially dramatic towards Kyle of Lochalsh from where ferries depart for Skye.

Inverness to Wick or Thurso (161 miles/260km). Passes by castles, across wild moorland and on to Britain's most northerly rail terminals.

Steam Trains

Railway preservation societies, which enable fanatics all over Britain to dirty their hands on steam locomotives, are alive and thriving in Scotland. Apart from the popular West Highland line, half a dozen other lines operate steam trains of one sort or another.

The **"Northern Belle"** (Grampian Railtours. Tel: 01358 6895137) is a steam-pulled excursion train which runs from Aberdeen on Sunday during August and September. The train travels over the Grampians to Speyside, passing Inverurie, Huntly and Keith and on to Elgin for visits to the Glenfiddich and Cardhu distilleries, Baxters' renowned food factory at

Fochabers and the Cashmere Visitor Centre. The **Caledonian Railway** (Brechin), Angus, holds several steam days during the summer and Brechin station is open most weekends. Enquiries to Brechin Station, 2 Park Road, Brechin, Angus DD9 7AF. The **Bo'ness & Kinneil Railway**, West Lothian runs steam trains on summer weekends. A particular attraction is the Scandinavian Vintage Train hauled by a huge Swedish B-class engine. Enquiries to Bo'ness Station. Tel: (0150682) 2298.

Strathspey Railway runs during the summer months for 5 miles (8km) from Aviemore (Speyside) to Boat of Garten, providing good views of Cairngorm Mountains. Enquiries to Boat of Garten Station, Inverness-Shire PH24 3BH. Tel: (01479) 810725.

West Buchan Railway Co, a 15-inch narrow gauge line, mixes steam and diesels and provides public transport as well as sightseeing excursions between Banff Harbour and Swordanes. Enquiries to West Buchan Railway Co., 12 Station Place, Cruden Bay, Peterhead, Grampian AB4 7NF. Tel: (0177981) 2410.

The **Mull & West Highland Railway** has volunteers manning steam and diesel trains on a narrow-gauge track for 1¼ miles (2km) across the Isle of Mull, saving a tiring walk from Craignure to Torosoy Castle. Enquiries can be made at Tel: (01680) 389. The **Lochty Private Railway** is run by the Fife Railway Preservation Group and open to visitors on Sunday afternoons in summer months. Enquiries to FRPG Secretary, 48 Hendry Road, Kirkcaldy, Fife KY2 5JN.

At the top end of the market, the *Royal Scotsman*, the local answer to the *Orient Express*, mixes castles with caviar, carrying no more than 32 pampered passengers, mostly Americans, through the Highlands in wood-panelled but very pricey splendour. Six days in a state cabin costs £2,200. (All-in prices include as much whisky and champagne as you care to imbibe and a champagne reception at Glamis Castle, where the Queen Mother was born.) The train is marketed through the tour operators Abercrombie & Kent, Sloan Square House, Holbein Place, London SW1W 8NS. Tel: (0171) 730 9600.

WATER TRANSPORT

Ferries

A must for the visitor who intends to explore the island-studded west coast – the Hebrides and the islands of the Clyde – is the Caledonian MacBrayne timetable which can be obtained from: Ferry Terminal, Gourock, PA19 1QP, Scotland. Tel: (01475) 650100. This is as incomprehensible to the first-time visitor as a Chinese scroll. Locals whip through it with ease. The rest of us, not knowing Kilchoan from Kyleakin or unaware that there are a trio of Tarbets, take a day to plot a route. Summer booking is vital to avoid the nerve-wracking, time-consuming "standby" queue.

Caledonian MacBrayne, a fusion of two compa-

nies, grew out of the 19th-century passenger steamers and now has a near-monopoly on west coast routes. Its 30 vessels call at 53 ports on the mainland and on 23 islands. They sell island hopscotch tickets and, best value for visitors with cars – rover tickets for driver and one passenger giving 8 or 15 days unlimited travel on most routes.

The ferries are great. On long routes, like the 5-hour Oban to Barra ferry, there are car decks, cabins, comfortable chairs, a restaurant and self-service. On others such as the 7-hour round trip to the tiny island of Eigg, Muck, Rum and Canna, ferries are basic with wooden seats and minimal refreshments. These working boats, carrying goods, mail, as well as passengers, are mainly used by islanders, with some bird-watchers and the occasional curious visitors who take the chilling trip for interest. Take note that unless you specify beforehand, disembarking for sightseeing is not allowed.

There is plenty of small private enterprise on the west coast. There are cruises from Arisaig on the mainland to Skye and Mull as well as to Eigg, Muck, Rum and Canna. Day trips to the National Trust island of Staffa with Fingal's Cave, to the bird island of Lunga and the uninhabited Treshnish islands, start from the Ulva, Dervaig and Fionnphort, all of which are on Mull while Staffa can also be reached from Iona. There is a virtual 10-minute shuttle service from Fionnphort on the southwest tip of Mull to Iona. These trips allow time ashore and there is no difficulty in finding out about such services when you arrive. Tourist information centres and many hotels have brochures.

In northern Scotland, the ferry services to Orkney and Shetland are a great deal easier to grasp than those to the Western Isles; for one thing, there are only two major islands and only two major companies. Once again, summer booking is essential.

Orkney

There is just one vessel for cars to Orkney: the comfortable roll-on/roll-off *St Ola* run by P&O which takes 2 hours to cross from Scrabster on the mainland to Stromness on Orkney. There is one sailing a day except Sunday in January, February, March and two or three sailings a day (only one on Sunday) throughout the rest of the year with extra services during high summer. There is a good car park on Orkney.

A passenger ferry runs from May to September from Gill's Bay, near John o' Groats to Burwick on South Ronaldsay. There are two or three daily departures, including Sunday. The crossing takes around 40 minutes. Buses and coaches can be boarded on Orkney and there are cars for hire. For further information contact: Thomas & Bews Ferry Office, John o' Groats, Caithness. Tel: (0195) 581 353 (summer only).

Once on Orkney, a dozen or so smaller islands can be visited by local ferries. The Kirkwall tourist office has more details.

Shetland

During the summer the P&O service, which takes 14 hours between Aberdeen and Lerwick, Shetland's main port, is doubled from one boat to two. Both ferries are modern roll-on/roll-off vessels with cabins, shops, restaurants and cafeterias. The second ferry makes the round trip, calling at Orkney, where it remains for 2 hours, on both the outward and the return journey. Once again local ferries ply between the tiny islands of Yell, Unst and Fetlar. P&O Ferries brochures can be obtained from PO Box 5, P&O Ferries Terminal, Jamieson's Quay, Aberdeen AB9 8DL. Tel: (01224) 572615.

Pleasure Steamers

On Loch Katrine, which has supplied Glasgow with water since 1859, the *SS Sir Walter Scott*, Scotland's only screw steamer in regular passenger service, makes three daily round-trip voyages between the Trossachs and Stornachlachar piers from mid-April until the end of September. The morning trip permits a 15-minute landing at Stronachlacher while the two one-hour afternoon trips are non-landing. (No morning trip on Saturday). Enquiries to Water Department, Strathclyde Regional Council, 419 Balmore Road, Glasgow G22 6NU. Tel: (0141) 355 5333; or to Callander Tourist Information Office, Leny Road, Callander. Tel: Callander 30342.

From May until October the undistinguished *The Second Snark* and *Rover*, which are based at Greenock, make a variety of half-and full-day cruises visiting renowned beauty spots of the Firth of Clyde and permitting landings of 2–4 hours. Shorter cruises are made by the *MV Kenilworth*. (Clyde Marine Cruises, Princes Pier, Greenock, PA16 8AW. Tel: 01475-721281.) Similar cruises from Gourock, with somewhat longer time ashore, can be enjoyed from the end of April until mid-October on Caledonian MacBrayne craft. Tel: (01475) 650100.

From May to mid-September the *Maid of the Forth* sails from South Queensferry, just outside Edinburgh, to Inchcolm Island with its ruined, medieval abbey. Sailing time on the Firth of Forth (seals are often seen) is 30 minutes and 1½ hours is spent ashore. (Maid of the Forth, Hawes Pier, South Queensferry. Tel: 0131-331 4857.)

At Easter and from May to September the 130-passenger *MV Shearwater* sails each morning from Arisaig for a full day to the small islands (Rum, Eigg, Muck) of the Inner Hebrides or to Skye. Several hours are spent ashore. (Murdo Grant, Arisaig Harbour, Inverness-Shire, PH39 4NH. Tel: 016875-224.)

During the summer months the *TSMV Western Isles*, a converted fishing boat, makes half-and full-day cruises from Mallaig past dramatic scenery to surrounding lochs, or to the Island of Eigg or to Skye with landings. (Bruce Watt Sea Cruises, Mallaig. Tel: 01687-2320.)

From May to September daily sailings (weather permitting) are made from Anstruther to the Isle of

May aboard either the *Sapphire* or *Serenity*. The trip lasts about 5 hours, with 3 hours ashore to explore the island whose cliffs, at least until July, are covered with breeding kittiwakes, razorbills, guillemots and shags. The remains of a 12th-century chapel can also be visited. (Anstruther Pleasure Trips, 30 Dreelside, Anstruther, KY10 3EF. Tel: 01333-310103.)

From Easter until mid-October *Anne of Etive* departs from Taynuilt on 3-hour cruises into Loch Etive and to the mountains of Glencoe. The route covered is inaccessible except by boat. If fortune favours then seals on the rocks, the golden eagle of Ben Starav and deer on the crags will be seen. Morning and afternoon departures except at the start and finish of season. (Contact Donald Kennedy, Taynuilt. Tel: 018662-430.)

Several companies run 2 to 4-hour cruises from Ullapool to the Summer Isles. Some of these are nature cruises, some are sunset cruises and some permit landing on the islands. (MacKenzie Marine, Green Pastures, Ullapool. Tel: 01854-612008.) Summer Isles cruises also depart from Achiltibuie aboard the *Island Lass*. These last about 4 hours and permit landing on the islands. (I. Macleod, Achiltibuie Post Office. Tel: 01854-622200.)

During the summer months the *MV Statesman* departs on 2-hour cruises (11am, 2pm and 4pm) from Kylesku to the head of fjord-like Loch Glencoul where the Eas-coul-Aulin waterfall – four times higher than Niagara – tumbles into the loch. (Statesman Cruises, Heatherbrae, Inver, Lochinver, Sutherland. Tel: 01571-844444.)

The *Hebridean Princess*, more a stately country-house hotel on water than the usual run-of-the-mill luxury liner and accommodating only 40 passengers in elegant staterooms makes a series of cruises from Oban from the beginning of April until the end of October. The region covered is the northwest coast of Scotland, Inner and Outer Hebrides, the Orkney and Shetland Islands and even St Kilda. The route varies from cruise to cruise and voyages last 6, 8, 10 and 15 days. In the words of the Captain Iain Cameron "We are on a cruise: not on an expedition" and so the printed schedule may be altered to avoid bad weather and to prevent passengers suffering the inconvenience of sea-sickness. An unusual feature of this luxurious ship is that automobiles can roll-on and roll-off, thus enabling travellers to explore independently at the various ports of call. (Bookings can be made through Hebridean Island Cruises Ltd., Acorn Park, Skipton North Yorkshire, BD23 2UE. Tel: 01756-701338.)

PUBLIC TRANSPORT

By Bus: Major towns have their own bus services. In addition, there are bus services serving rural communities and linking the various towns. These are fairly good and the visitor who intends to make frequent use of buses should investigate the various tickets which allow unlimited use of buses for specific periods. Details are available from bus stations and tourist offices.

An unusual delight and a superb way to meet the people and learn something of their customs is to board one of the Royal Mail Postbuses which provide an essential 'post-and-passenger service in isolated parts of the country. To people in rural communities the familiar red Postbus is both a welcome friend and a lifeline to the world outside. The buses cover nearly 150 routes stretching from the Borders to the Outer Hebrides.

By Taxi: The major cities have sufficient taxi stands. Outside the cities, it will usually be necessary to telephone for a taxi.

PRIVATE TRANSPORT

Driving: Scotland has an excellent network of roads which, away from the central belt, are usually not congested. Driving on the left is the rule and passengers must wear seat belts. In urban areas, the speed limit is either 30 or 40 mph (48 or 64 kmph), the limit on country roads is 60 mph (97kmph), and on motorways and dual carriageways 70 mph (113 kmph).

In some parts of the Highlands and on many of the islands, roads are single track with passing places. The behaviour of drivers on these roads tends to show that good old-fashioned courtesy is not dead.

Radio Scotland (FM 92.4–94.7/MW 810) broadcasts details of road conditions throughout the day at the following times: Monday–Saturday 06.54, 07.28, 07.52, 08.28, 16.30, 17.30, Sunday 06.55 and 09.00. Details of particular problems, accidents or emergencies are broadcast as appropriate throughout the day. The broadcast travel information includes details of ferry, rail or air travel hold-ups or changes. Local stations also broadcast travel and road information throughout the day.

In the Highlands and on the islands, it is wise to fill up on Saturday if you are planning to drive on Sunday. This is because, in some places, strict Sunday observance means that filling stations will be closed.

CAR RENTALS

Self-drive rental costs £15–£30 a day, depending on the type of car and the duration of the rental. The rates are reduced in the October–April off-season. For more detailed information, apply directly to the car rental companies. A list of car rental companies appears below.

EDINBURGH

(Area code: 0131)
Arnold Clark, Lochrin Place, Tollcross. Tel: 228 4747.
Avis Rent-A-Car, 100 Dalry Road. Tel: 337 6363.
Budget Rent-a-Car, The Royal Scot Hotel, 111 Glasgow Road. Tel: 334 7739

EuroDollar Rent-A-Car, Shrubhill Service Station, Leith Walk. Tel: 555 0565.
Europcar UK Ltd, 24 East London Street. Tel: 661 1252.
Hertz Rent-a-Car, 10 Picardy Place. Tel: 556 8311.
Little's Chauffeur Drive, 33 Corstorphine High Street. Tel: 334 2177.
Mitchell's Self Drive, 32 Torphichen Street. Tel: 229 5384.
W. L. Sleigh Ltd (chauffeur-driven), 6 Devon Place. Tel: 337 3171.
Woods Car Rental, Hilton International, 69 Bedford Road. Tel: (01506) 858660.

• EDINBURGH AIRPORT
Alamo. Tel: 334 3250.
Avis Rent-a-Car. Tel: 333 1866.
Europcar UK Ltd. Tel: 333 2588.
Hertz Rent-a-Car. Tel: 333 1019.
Woods Car Rental. Tel: (01506) 858660.

THE BORDERS

• GALASHIELS
Chalmers McQueen Ltd, Albert Place. Tel: (01896) 753304.

• GULLANE
Fairway Tours, 8 Roseberry Place. Tel: (01620) 842349.

• HAWICK
Guthrie of Hawick (Motors) Ltd, 61 High Street. Tel: (01450) 372287.

THE SOUTHWEST

• AYR
Dalblair of Ayr, 27 Prestwick Road. Tel: (01292) 269123.

• CAMPBELTOWN
Campbeltown Motor Company, Kinloch Road. Tel: (01586) 552030.
Phoenix Motors, Shore Street. Tel: (01586) 552018.

• DUMFRIES
Arnold Clark, New Abbey Road. Tel: (01387) 63000.

• DUNOON
The County Garage, Alexandra Parade, East Bay. Tel: (01369) 3199.
Wilson's Garage Co. (Argyll) Ltd, East Bay. Tel: (01369) 3094.

• PRESTWICK
Godfrey Davis Europcar Ltd, 14 Kirk Street. Tel: (01292) 77218.

- **PRESTWICK AIRPORT**
Avis Rent-a-Car, Terminal Building. Tel: (01292) 77218.
Budget Rent-a-Car, Rosefields Motors (Ayr), 196 Prestwick Road. Tel: (01292) 264087.
EuroDollar Rent-A-Car, Terminal Building. Tel: (01292) 76517.

- **STRANRAER**
E & W Lithgow (Transport) Ltd (Car Hire), Aird Filling Station, London Road. Tel: (01776) 702833.
Rosefield Motors (Ayr) Ltd, West End Garage, Leswalt Road. Tel: (01776) 703636.

GLASGOW

(Area code: 0141)
Arnold Clark, Allison Street (Tel: 423 9559); 40 Hamilton Road (Tel: 778 2979); St Georges Road (Tel: 221 9517); Vinicombe Street (Tel: 334 9501).
Avis Rent-A-Car, 161 North Street. Tel: 221 2827.
Budget Rent-a-Car, Moat House Hotel, Congress Road. Tel: 226 4141.
Charlton Chauffeur Drive, 11 Sherbrook Avenue. Tel: 427 1155.
EuroDollar Rent-A-Car, 76 Lancefield Quay. Tel: 204 1051.
Europcar InterRent, 556 Pollokshaws Road. Tel: 423 5661.
Hertz Rent-a-Car, 106 Waterloo Street. Tel: 248 7736.
Jim Neary (Car and Van Hire) Ltd, 15 Fairley Street. Tel: 427 5475.
Kingston Chauffeur Drive, 197 Reid Street. Tel: 554 6066.
Little's Chauffeur Drive, 1282 Paisley Road West. Tel: 883 2111.
Mitchell's Self-Drive, Multi-Storey Car Park, Mitchell Street. Tel: 221 8461.
Woods Car Rental, Unit 9, Airlink Ind. Est., Inchinnan Road, Paisley. Tel: 848 1559.

- **GLASGOW AIRPORT**
Alamo, Terminal Building. Tel: 848 6488.
Arnold Clark, Phoenix Park, Winwood. Tel: 848 0202.
Avis Rent-a-Car, Terminal Building. Tel: 887 2261.
Budget Rent-a-Car, Phoenix House, Inchinnan Road, Paisley. Tel: 887 0501.
Eurodollar Rent-A-Car, Terminal Building. Tel: 887 7915.
Europcar InterRent, Terminal Building. Tel: 887 0414.
Hertz Rent-a-Car, Terminal Building. Tel: 887 2451.
Woods Car Rental, Unit 9, Airlink Ind. Est., Inchinnan Road, Paisley. Tel: 848 1559.

FORTH & CLYDE

- **BROXBURN**
Broxburn Chauffeur Drive, 112 Forest Walk, Uphall. Tel: (01506) 855496.
Woods Car Rental, Unit 16 Tartraven Place, East Mains Ind. Est. Tel: (01506) 858660.

- **HAMILTON**
EuroDollar Rent-A-Car, Limetree Garage, Glasgow Road, Burnbank. Tel: (01698) 828281.
Mitchell's Self Drive, Miller Street. Tel: (01698) 285744.

- **MOTHERWELL**
Europcar UK Ltd, 477 Windhill Street, Knowetop. Tel: (01698) 266354.

- **STIRLING**
Arnold Clark Automobiles Ltd, Kerse Road. Tel: (01786) 478686.
EuroDollar Rent-A-Car, Borentone Crescent, St. Ninians. Tel: (01786) 470123.
Europcar UK Ltd, Mogil Motors Ltd, Drip Road. Tel: (01786) 472164.
T. M. Templeton (Vehicle Hire) Ltd, 11 Whitehouse Road. Tel: (01786) 463137.

THE WEST COAST

- **FORT WILLIAM**
Budget Rent-a-Car, MacRae & Dick Ltd, Gordon Square. Tel: (01397) 702500.
Foss Self Drive, Ben Service Station, Lochy Bridge. Tel: (01397) 2903.
J & L Self Drive, 15 Lanark Place, Lochview Estate. Tel: (01397) 3348.

- **LOCH CARRON**
Ross Rentals, Loch Garage. Tel: (015202) 205.

- **OBAN**
Argyll Motor Services (Oban) Ltd, Shore Street. Tel: (01631) 63519.
Foss Self Drive, Combie Street. Tel: (01631) 63565.
Fiat Rental, Hazelbank Motors Ltd, Stevenson Street. Tel: (01631) 66476.
Hazelbank Motors Ltd, Lynn Road. Tel: (01631) 66476.
Milford Motors, Mill Lane. Tel: (01631) 66476.
West End Car Rentals, Dairach Road. Tel: (01631) 63237.

INNER HEBRIDES

- **ARINGAGOUR, ISLE OF COLL**
Isle of Coll Hotel. Tel: (018793) 334.

- **ISLAY**
Bowmore Engineering, Jamieson Street, Bowmore. Tel: (01496) 810206 (day) 810207 (night).

- **SKYE**
Ewen MacRae, West End Garage, Portree.
Tel: (01478) 612334.
Sutherland's Garage, Broadford. Tel: (01471) 822225.
- **TIREE**
Maclennan, Pier Head, Scarnish. Tel: (018992) 555.

OUTER HEBRIDES

- **LEWIS**
Arnol Motors, Arnol. Tel: (01851) 710548.
Lewis Car Rentals, 52 Bayhead Street, Stornoway.
Tel: (01851) 703760.
Lochs Motor Transport, 33 South Beach, Stornoway. Tel: (01851) 705857.
Mackinnon, 18 Inaclete Road, Stornoway.
Tel: (01851) 702948.
Mitchell's, Bayhead Street, Stornoway. Tel: (01851) 702888.
Stornway Car Hire, Airport. Tel: (01851) 702658.

- **BENBECULA**
Ask Car Hire, 1A Vachdar. Tel: (01870) 602818.
MacLennan Bros. (Motors) Ltd, Balivanich.
Tel: (01870) 602191.

- **SOUTH UIST**
Laing Motors, Lochboisdale. Tel: (01878) 700267.

CENTRAL SCOTLAND

- **AUCHTERARDER**
Europcar UK Ltd, Gleneagles Hotel. Tel: (01738) 631322.

- **DUNFERMLINE**
Laidlaw (Dunfermline) Ltd, Halbeath Road.
Tel: (01383) 721536.

- **KIRKCALDY**
Arnold Clark, Abbotshall Road. Tel: (01592) 262141.
Europcar UK Ltd, Drummond Motor Co, Ferrard Road. Tel: (01592) 268497.

- **PERTH**
Arnold Clark, St. Leonard's Bank. Tel: (01738) 442202.
Europcar UK Ltd, 26 Glasgow Road. Tel: (01738) 636888.
Hertz Rent-a-Car, 405 High Street. Tel: (01738) 624108.
Practical Car & Van Rental, 97 Crieff Road.
Tel: (01738) 620804.

- **PITLOCHRY**
Oakfield Self Drive Hire Cars, 12 Higher Oakfield, Rosemount Hotel. Tel: (01796) 472302.

THE EAST COAST

- **ABERDEEN**
Arnold Clark, Girdleness Road. Tel: (01224) 248842 and Seaforth Road. Tel: (01224) 640433.
Avis Rent-a-Car, 16 Broomhill Road. Tel: (01224) 57452.
Budget Rent-a-Car, 2 Canal Road, Mount Hooly.
Tel: (01224) 639922.
EuroDollar Rent-A-Car, 46 Summer Street.
Tel: (01224) 626955.
Europcar UK Ltd., 121 Causewayend. Tel: (01224) 631199.
Hertz Rent-a-Car, Railway Station. Tel: (01224) 210748.
Kenning Car Hire, 238 Market Street. Tel: (01224) 571445.
Valentine Chauffeur Drive, Arch 23, South College Street. Tel: (01224) 213066.

- **ABERDEEN AIRPORT**
Avis Rent-A-Car, Dyce. Tel: (01224) 722282.
Budget Rent-a-Car, Terminal Building. Tel: (01224) 725067.
Europcar UK Ltd, Terminal Building. Tel: (01224) 725080.
Hertz Rent-a-Car, Terminal Building Dyce.
Tel: (01224) 722373.

- **ARBROATH**
Keptie Self Drive, 74 Keptie Street. Tel: (01241) 77637.
Kerr Self Drive, 41 Lindsay Road. Tel: (01241) 77990.
Ritchie's Self Drive, 2 Montrose Street.
Tel: (01241) 76617.

- **BRECHIN**
Deys Self Drive, Forfar Road. Tel: (013562) 624886.
Fisken Motors, 3 Crookston Road. Tel: (0856) 622146.
Ritchie's Self Drive, Car & Van Rentals, 2 Montrose Street. Tel: (01356) 623558.

- **DUNDEE**
Albany Chauffeur Travel, 164 Arbroath Road.
Tel: (01382) 459004.
Arnold Clark, Trades Lane. Tel: (01382) 25382.
Avis Rent-A-Car, 411 Clepington Road. Tel: (01382) 832264.
Budget Rent-a-Car, Tayford Motor Co., Balfield Road. Tel: (01382) 644664.
EuroDollar Rent-A-Car, 45–53 Gellalty Street.
Tel: (01382) 24073.
Europcar UK Ltd, 135 Marketgate. Tel: (01382) 21281.
Hertz Rent-a-Car, 19 Roseangle. Tel: (01382) 23711.
Mitchell's Self Drive, 90 Marketgate. Tel: (01382) 23484.
Playfair Private (Chauffeur driven) Hire, Playfair

Terrace. Tel: (01382) 826477.
Practical Car & Van Rental, 102/108 Logie Street.
Tel: (01382) 645124.

● **ELGIN**
Budget Rent-a-Car, East Road. Tel: (01343) 545281.
B & J Hire, Sandy Road. Tel: (01343) 542625.
● **FORRES**
Forres Self Drive, St Leonards Road. Tel: (01309)
673312.

● **PETERHEAD**
Budget Rent-a-Car, MacRae and Dick Ltd, 43–45
Windmill Street. Tel: (01779) 479191.

● **STONEHAVEN**
Mitchell's Garage, 72 Barclay Street. Tel: (01569)
762077.

THE NORTHERN HIGHLANDS

● **AVIEMORE**
Grants of Aviemore, 115 Grampain Road.
Tel: (01479) 810232.
MacDonald's Self Drive Car Hire, Tiga Beag, 13
Muirton Avenue. Tel: (01479) 811444.

● **AVOCH**
Daimler Chauffeur Hire, Avoch Filling Station.
Tel: (01381) 620247.

● **DINGWALL**
Budget Rent-a-Car, MacRae & Dick Ltd, Station
Road. Tel: (01349) 862151/863223.
Cross Country Hire, Rootfield. Tel: (01349) 863299.

● **DORNOCH**
Gordon's Coaches, Masonic Buildings. Tel: (01862)
810503.

● **INVERNESS**
Budget Rent-a-Car, Railway Terrace. Tel: (01463)
713333.
Cordiners Inverness Ltd, Harbour Road.
Tel: (01463) 224466.
EuroDollar Rent-A-Car, Shope Street. Tel: (01463)
238084.
Europcar UK Ltd, Highlander Service Station,
Millburn Road. Tel: (01463) 234886.
Hertz Rent-a-Car, Mercury Hotel and Railway
Station. Tel: (01463) 224475/511479.
H.W. Jack (Car Hire) Ltd, Diriebught Road.
Tel: (01463) 236572.
Kenning Car Rental, c/o Ness Motors, 16 Telford
Street. Tel: (01463) 242400.
Peugeot Rental, Ferries of Inverness, Harbour
Road. Tel: (01463) 231536.
Sharps Reliable Wrecks, 1st Floor, Highland Rail
House, Station Square, Academy Street. Tel: (01463)
236684.

● **INVERGORDON**
Ken's Garage, Kildary. Tel: (01862) 842266.

● **INVERNESS AIRPORT**
Avis Rent-A-Car, Dalcross. Tel: (01667) 62787.
Europcar UK Ltd, Dalcross. Tel: (01667) 462374.

● **THURSO**
W. M. Dunnea & Co Ltd, 20 Trail Street.
Tel: (01847) 63101.
Practical Car Hire, Park Lane Motors, Bridgend.
Tel: (01847) 62924.
Richard's Garage. Tel: (01847) 66226.

● **WICK**
Peugot Rental, Mowatts Garage, George Street.
Tel: (01955) 2321.
Practical Car Hire and Van Rental, Airport.
Tel: (01995) 4125.
Richard's Garage, Francis Street. Tel: (01955)
4123.

ORKNEY

● **KIRKWALL**
Dolphin Private Car Hire, The Depot Burnmouth
Road. Tel: (01856) 872290.
Europcar UK Ltd, Scarth Hire Ltd, Great Western
Road. Tel: (01856) 872601.
W. R. Tullock & Sons Ltd, Castle Garage, Castle
Street. Tel: (01856) 876262.

● **KIRKWALL AIRPORT**
Europcar UK Ltd, Terminal Building. Tel: (01856)
872125.

SHETLAND

● **LERWICK**
Bolt's Car Hire, 26 North Road. Tel: (01595) 2855.
John Leask & Son, Esplanade. Tel: (01595) 3162.
McLeod & McLean, Commercial Road. Tel: (01595)
3162.
Star Rent A Car, 22 Commercial Street.
Tel: (01595) 2075.
Stronach Gordon, Garthspool. Tel: (01595) 3718.

● **SCATSA AIRPORT**
Bolt's Car Hire, Terminal Building. Tel: (0180622)
311.

● **SUMBURGH AIRPORT**
John Leask & Son. Tel: (01950) 60209.

● **TINGWALL AIRPORT**
Godfrey Davis Europcar Ltd, Terminal Building.
Tel: (01595) 2855.
Bolt's Car Hire, Terminal Building.. Tel: (01595)
2855.

WHERE TO STAY

A wide range of accommodation is available in Scotland, from hotels of international standard to simple bed-and-breakfast (B&B) accommodation. Prices vary as well, from under £10 a night for bed-and-breakfast to over £100 at the most expensive hotel.

How does one select a suitable place at which to stay? The Scottish Tourist Board has a somewhat complicated assessment scheme. Their approved accommodation will display an oval sign with the Tourist Board logo. This will tell you two things about the hotel. First, how extensive its facilities are; this is indicated by the word "listed" for the most basic facilities to five crowns for those with the most facilities. In addition, the accommodation is graded for quality into three categories to include: "Approved", "Commended" or "Highly Commended".

The intention is to give an idea not just of the quantity of facilities but of the quality of the place. It would be possible for a hotel to have five crowns indicating an excellent range of facilities, but to be awarded only the "Approved" quality grade because the Tourist Board's inspectors didn't think much of the ambience.

If planning a caravan holiday, look out for the Thistle logo. The "Thistle Commendation" is awarded by the industry and the Tourist Board to parks which meet the highest standards of excellence in environment, facilities and the caravans.

If you decide to go for a self-catering holiday, the Association of Scotland's Self Caterers has a quality scheme indicated by their triangular logo.

Staying in bed-and-breakfast accommodation is not only economical, it is also a flexible and potentially interesting way to see the country. Local tourist offices operate booking schemes and, except at the height of the tourist season in July and August, it is not necessary to book in advance. Bed-and-breakfasts in the Scottish Tourist Board scheme will, at a minimum, be clean and comfortable. With luck you may find the proprietor friendly and a mine of local information with suggestions about the route to take or the things to see and do. Most of the better bed-and-breakfast establishments serve dinner on request, which is usually excellent and modestly priced.

Particularly good value are Campus Hotels, the name given to bed-and-breakfasts and self-catering facilities offered by the Scottish Universities in Aberdeen, St Andrews, Dundee, Edinburgh, Glasgow and Stirling. These are available during vacations. In addition to accommodation, they offer the use of university facilities such as tennis courts and swimming pools.

Information on all types of accommodation is available at the Scottish Tourist Board and local tourist offices.

Except for the more expensive city hotels, prices quoted include breakfast. Approximate guides to prices per person per night in a hotel double room are: £ = below £30; ££ = £30–£50; £££ = £50–£70; ££££ = above £70. For guest houses, private hotels, farms and B&B establishments: £ = less than £15; ££ = £15–£30. On occasions, the distinction between bed-and-breakfast establishments, guest houses and private hotels becomes blurred especially when the former have en suite facilities and serve dinner.

HOTELS

EDINBURGH

(Area code: 0131)

Balmoral Hotel, Princes Street. Tel: 556 2414. 189 rooms. Edinburgh's premier hotel reopened in 1991 after a £23 million facelift. Many rooms with view of the castle. ££££

Bank Hotel, 1 South Bridge Road. Tel: 556 9043. 9 rooms. Former bank in midst of Royal Mile and recently converted into cafe-bar with bedrooms above. ££

Bruntsfield Hotel, 69–74 Bruntsfield Place. Tel: 229 1393. 50 rooms. Well-established hotel 3 miles (5km) from city centre. ££

Channings, South Learmont Gardens. Tel: 315 2226. 48 rooms. A series of splendid Edwardian adjoining houses a few minutes from city centre. Bedrooms individually furnished in a somewhat contemporary manner. £££

Caledonian Hotel, Princes Street. Tel: 225 2433. 239 rooms. The "Grande Dame" of Edinburgh hotels is constantly being upgraded. Many rooms with view of the castle. ££££

George Hotel Inter-Continental, 19–21 George Street. Tel: 225 1251. 195 rooms. Very central, well-established, grand old hotel, recently refurbished. ££££

Howard Hotel, 32–36 Great King Street. Tel: 557 3500. 16 rooms. Three inter-connected 18th-century town houses in the New Town result in a magnificent classical hotel, made all the more comfortable by contemporary bathrooms. Garden. ££££

Inner Sanctum, 351 Castlehill, Royal Mile. Tel: 225 5613. One suite adjacent to Witchery restaurant. The place – completely over the top – for that once-in-a-lifetime occasion. £££

Roxburghe Hotel, 38 Charlotte Square. Tel: 225 3921. 75 rooms. Country house hotel situated close to Princes Street. Recently refurbished. £££

Royal Terrace Hotel, 18 Royal Terrace. Tel: 557 3222. 97 rooms. Georgian terrace building on a cobbled street, minutes from east end of Princes Street, constitute this handsome chintzy hotel. Complete leisure club and large private garden. £££–££££

Scandic Crown Hotel, 80 High Street. Tel: 557 9797. 238 rooms. A recently opened property situated on the Royal Mile between the Castle and Holyrood Palace. Well equipped leisure centre and undercover car park. ££££

Sheraton Grand Edinburgh Hotel, 1 Festival Square. Tel: 229 9131. 261 rooms. Set back from busy Lothian Road and close to city centre. Complete leisure club. ££££

Thrums Private Hotel, 14/15 Minto Street, Newington. Tel: 667 5545. 14 rooms. Detached Georgian house with garden, five minutes from city centre. ££

Ashlyn Guest House, 42 Inverleith Row. Tel: 552 2954. 8 rooms (5 en suite). Listed Georgian house. Close to Botanic Garden and five minutes from city centre. ££

Galloway Guest House, 22 Dean Park Crescent. Tel: 332 3672. 10 rooms (6 en suite) In a residential area close to Princes Street. ££

Joppa Turrets, 1 Lower Joppa. Tel: 669 5806. 5 rooms (1 en suite). For those who must be by the seaside. On the beach at Joppa but close to bus routes and 5 miles (8km) from city centre. Parking no problem. £–££

Mayfield Guest House, 12–14 Mayfield Gardens. Tel: 662 1518. 11 rooms (all en suite). On main route into city (10 minutes). ££

Meadows Guest House, 12–14 Mayfield Gardens. Tel: 662 2528. 11 en suite rooms. On main bus route 2 miles (3km) south of city. Dinner served. ££

Newington Guest House, 18 Newington Road. Tel: 667 3356. 8 rooms (5 en suite). Lovely period furnishings in a Victorian house on the main road into the city from the south. ££

Salisbury Guest House, 45 Salisbury Road. Tel: 667 1264. 12 rooms (9 en suite). Georgian listed building, near Holyrood Palace and Royal Mile. ££

Sibbet (Mrs) Aurora, 26 Northumberland Street. Tel: 556 1078. 4 rooms. Stay with the "Auld Alliance" (Scotland-France) in a home filled with antiques and family photographs in heart of New Town. Sumptuous breakfasts to the sound of Mr Sibbet playing the bagpipes. ££

Smith (Mrs) Eirlys, Advocate, 28 Northumberland Street. 3 rooms (2 en suite). Before rushing off to her legal duties Mrs. Smith will see that you enjoy a hearty breakfast in her handsome Georgian town house in heart of New Town. ££

Stuart House, 12 East Claremont Street. Tel: 557 9030. 7 rooms (6 en suite). Refurbished Georgian house close to city centre. Non-smoking. ££

THE BORDERS

Arran
Kinloch Hotel, Blackwaterfoot. Tel: (01770) 860444. 47 rooms. Superb views of Mull of Kintyre. Leisure facilities include indoor pool and squash court. ££

Hawick
Kirklands Hotel, West Stewart Place. Tel: (01450) 372263. 12 rooms. Charming Victorian house with large garden. ££

Mansfield House Hotel, Weensland Road. Tel: (01450) 373988. 10 rooms. Victorian country house hotel in 10 acres (4 hectares). Glorious public rooms. ££

Innerleithen
The Ley. Tel: (01896) 830240. 4 rooms (all en suite). A Victorian home full of antiques set in 30 acres (12 hectares) of pretty woodland. Beautifully furnished bedrooms. Although a B&B establishment the McVicars serve superb dinners accompanied by a good wine card. ££

Kelso
Sunlaws House Hotel. Tel: (01573) 450331. 22 bedrooms. An 18th-century country house, owned by the Duke of Roxburghe, 3 miles (5km) from Kelso. Superb public rooms. 200 acres (81 hectares) of beautiful grounds through which flows the River Teviot: great opportunities for fishing. Also clay-pigeon shooting, croquet, tennis. £££

Melrose
Burts Hotel, Market Square. Tel: (0189682) 2285. 21 rooms. Tastefully modernised old townhouse in main square. ££

Moffat
Auchen Castle Hotel, Beattock. Tel: (01683) 407. 25 rooms of which 10 are in modern wing. Set in 54 acres (22 hectares) with spectacular views over upper Annandale. A truly gracious Scottish home. ££

Beechwood Country House Hotel. Tel: (01683) 20210. 7 rooms. Elegant country house on a hill overlooking Moffat. ££

Moffat House Hotel, High Street. Tel: (01683) 20039. 20 rooms. An 18th-century Adam mansion set in own grounds. ££

Corehead Farm, Annanwater. Tel: (01683) 20973. 3 rooms (2 en suite). Five miles (8km) from Moffat, the grounds include Hart Fell (2,600ft/800m) one of the highest peaks in southern Scotland. ££

Peebles
Cringletie House Hotel. Tel: (01721) 720233. 13 rooms. Turreted baronial mansion 2 miles (3km) from Peebles set in 30 acres (12 hectares) of garden and woodland. Comfortable and with luxurious bathrooms. ££

Kingsmuir Hotel. Tel: (01721) 720151. 10 rooms. In quiet area on south side of Peebles overlooking parkland running down to the River Tweed. £

Peebles Hotel Hydro. Tel: (01721) 720602. 137 rooms. Large imposing château-style hotel set in 34 acres (14 hectares) overlooking the River Tweed valley and Border hills. Leisure centre and excellent tennis and riding. ££

St Boswells

Dryburgh Abbey Hotel. Tel: (01835) 822261. 26 rooms. This newly renovated Victorian building is beautifully situated and stands immediately next to Dryburgh Abbey and the River Tweed. £££

Selkirk

Philipburn House Hotel. Tel: (01750) 20747. 17 rooms. Georgian house from 1751 with bright bedrooms. Outdoor swimming pool and 5 acres (2 hectares) of beautiful grounds. ££

THE SOUTHWEST

Gatehouse of Fleet

Cally Palace. Tel: (01557) 814341. 56 rooms. Magnificent public rooms and comfortable bedrooms in this Georgian mansion set in 100 acres (40 hectares) of forest and parkland. Extensive leisure facilities including indoor swimming pool and 18-hole golf course. ££

Murray Arms Inn, Anne Street. Tel: (01557) 814207. 13 rooms. Attractive 18th-century Posting inn where Robert Burns wrote *Scots Wha Hae*. Modest but comfortable bedrooms. Free golf and fishing. ££

Girvan

Turnberry Hotel, Golf Courses & Spa, Turnberry. Tel: (01655) 31000. 132 rooms. For nearly 100 years a hotel of choice. Recent completion of a country club and spa incorporating 17 deluxe bedrooms has further enhanced the hotel's image. Elegance and gracious service obvious throughout especially in the restaurants which provide superb views of the islands of Ailsa Craig and Arran. Horse-riding, squash, tennis and, of course, golf. ££££

Newton Stewart

Kirroughtree Hotel. Tel: (01671) 2141. 22 rooms. Cheerful, colourful Georgian mansion in 7 acres (3 hectares) of landscaped gardens. Strong Burns' associations. Clay pigeon shooting, croquet and free golf. Renowned for Scottish food. £££

Stranraer

North West Castle Hotel. Tel: (01776) 704413. 70 rooms. Comfortable hotel on seafront. Indoor curling rink and full leisure centre with indoor pool. ££

Troon

Piersland House Hotel, Craigend Road. Tel: (01292) 314747. 19 rooms. Built for Sir Alexander Walker of whisky fame, the hotel is adjacent to the golf courses. ££

GLASGOW

(All phone numbers carry the code 0141)

Boswell Hotel, 27 Mansionhouse Road. Tel: 632 9812. 13 rooms. Small bustling hotel on south side of city with three busy bars. Near public transport. Family suites. £

Central, 99 Gordon Street. Tel: 221 9860. 221 rooms. The city's oldest hotel is part of Central Station. During the 1980s it enjoyed a facelift in an attempt to regain former glories. Leisure centre. ££

Copthorne, George Square. Tel: 332 6711. 140 rooms. Situated in the heart of George Square next to Queen Street Station. £££

Ewington, 132 Queens Drive. Tel: 423 1152. 42 rooms. Well-appointed terrace hotel in leafy street beside Queen's Park. About 2 miles (3km) from the city centre. ££

Forte Crest, Bothwell Street. Tel: 248 2656. 251 rooms. Five-minute walk from Central Station. £££

Hilton Hotel, 1 William Street. Tel: 204 5004. 319 rooms. Glasgow's newest hotel, a 20-floor sliver, stands in the centre of the city, just off the motorway. Extensive health and leisure club. ££££

Hospitality Inn, 33 Cambridge Street. Tel: 332 3311. 307 rooms. First-class hotel in heart of the city. £££

Marriot, 500 Argyle Street. Tel: 226 5577. 298 rooms. Standard modern hotel just off the motorway. Excellent health club with pool and two squash courts. ££££

Moat House, Congress Road. Tel: 204 0733. 264 rooms. One of the city's newest hotel. Stands next to the Scottish Exhibition Centre. £££

One Devonshire Gardens, 1 Devonshire Gardens. Tel: 339 2001. 27 rooms. An exquisite West End hotel in residential district. Each room different, service deluxe and old-fashioned. ££££

Sherbrooke Castle, 11 Sherbrooke Avenue. Tel: 427 4227. 25 rooms. Scottish baronial castle in own grounds in southside, about 3 miles (5km) from city centre. Handy for the Burrell and Pollok Country Park. ££

Stakis Grosvenor, Grosvenor Terrace. Tel: 339 8811. 95 rooms. Hotel with striking facade near Botanic Gardens, University of Glasgow and trendy Byres Road. ££

Town House Hotel, Nelson Mandela Place. Tel: 332 3320. 34 rooms. Grand new lavishly furnished hotel in the heart of the city. £££

Alamo Guest House, 46 Gray Street. Tel: 339 2395. 7 rooms (none en suite). Situated on pleasant, quiet road alongside Kelvingrove Park. £

Iona Guest House, 39 Hillhead Street. Tel: 334 2346. 9 rooms (none en suite). Well-established and comfortable. Close to Botanic Gardens. ££

Dalmeny, 62 St Andrews Drive. Tel: 427 1106. 8 rooms (2 en suite). More a guest house than hotel, situated in its own large garden. About 3 miles from the city centre. £

Divers (Mrs) C, Kirkland House, 42 St Vincent Crescent. Tel: 248 3458. 5 rooms (all en suite). In the quieter part of a beautiful crescent. Close to the city centre. ££

McClays Guest House, 268 Renfrew Street. Tel: 332 4796. 62 rooms (39 en suite). Well appointed, comfortable guest house only a few minutes from city centre. ££

The Town House, 4 Hughenden Terrace. Tel: 357 0862. 10 rooms (all en suite). Elegantly refurbished Victorian townhouse in quiet conservation area in West End. ££

FORTH & CLYDE

Stirling
Garfield Hotel, 12 Victoria Square. Tel: (01786) 473730. 8 rooms (5 en suite). Large Victorian house overlooking quiet square and close to city centre. £
Golden Lion Hotel, 8 King Street. Tel: (01786) 475351. 71 rooms. A recently refurbished hotel in city centre. ££
The Heritage, 16 Allan Park. Tel: (01786) 473660. 4 rooms. An elegant hotel with a French ambience. Bedrooms large but bathrooms somewhat small. Superb restaurant with excellent wine list. £
Forth Guest House, 23 Forth Place. Tel: (01786) 471020. 3 rooms (all en suite). Terraced house close to railway station. £
Park Lodge Hotel, 32 Park Terrace. Tel: (01786) 474862. 10 rooms. Part Victorian, part Georgian hotel in heart of city filled with antiques, original paintings and sumptuous furnishings. Some rooms with 4-poster beds. £–££
Stirling Highland Hotel, Spittal Street. Tel: (01786) 475444. 76 rooms. A newly restored, listed, former school with complete leisure centre in city centre. £££
Stirling Management Centre, University of Stirling. Tel: (01786) 451666. 74 rooms (all en suite). Purpose-built conference centre/hotel on bucolic university campus 5 miles (8km) from Stirling. University leisure/entertainment facilities available. Not mere "college" accommodation. £
The Topps Farm, Fintry Road, Denny. Tel: (01324) 822471. 8 rooms (all en suite). A working sheep farm in lovely location, 11 miles (18km) south of Stirling. Non-smokers only. Superb cuisine. ££

THE WEST COAST

Appin
Invercreran Country House Hotel, Glen Creran. Tel: (0163272) 414. 9 rooms. An isolated, most unusual country house hotel with superb views from public rooms and individually designed bedrooms. Painted ceiling in dining room will get all talking. Situated in 25 acres (10 hectares) of woodlands. £££

Arisaig
Arisaig House. Tel: (016875) 622. 13 rooms. A handsome Victorian house with a relaxed atmosphere set in 20 acres (8 hectares) of magnificent grounds which stretch down to the sea. Each bedroom is distinct and extremely comfortable although some are on the small side. Beautiful walled garden. Half-board only. Highly regarded contemporary cuisine in non-smoking dining room. (Room rate puts hotel in the ££££ category.)

Crinan
Crinan Hotel. Tel: (0154683) 261. 22 rooms. Rooms are individually designed; some have private balconies; all have stunning sea views. Dine in Lock 16, the rooftop restaurant, with the yachting fraternity, and admire the seascapes while delighting in the food landed from these waters only hours before dinner. £££

Eriska
Isle of Eriska, Ledaig by Oban. Tel: (01631) 72371. 17 rooms. A welcoming hotel on a private island far away from it all and joined to the mainland by a short bridge. Bedrooms vary in size and each has its own character. Breakfast from bygone days. Lovely grounds with tennis, croquet. ££££

Glenelg
Glenelg Inn. Tel: (0159982) 273. 6 rooms. A lively pub with restaurant is the focal point of this waterfront inn. Bedrooms, which are individually and tastefully decorated – especially the "master bedroom" – have grand views of Skye. ££

Kilchrenan
Ardanaiseig Hotel, by Taynuilt. Tel: (0186) 63333. 14 rooms. An elegant country house hotel far away from it all on the shores of Loch Awe. Beautiful public rooms. Immaculate woodland garden. Hotel boats suitable for fishing, solarium, tennis, snooker. Half-board only. A restricted menu with imaginative dishes served with panache in the very pleasant restaurant. Wine list strong in Californian labels. (Room rate puts hotel in the £££ category.)
Taychreggan Hotel, by Taynuilt. Tel: (0186) 63211. 15 rooms. Delightful hotel around a cobbled courtyard on a secluded part of Loch Awe. Game and course fishing, clay-pigeon shooting, boating. Local products well presented. ££

Kyle of Lochalsh
Lochalsh Hotel, Ferry Road. Tel: (01599) 4202. 40 rooms. Magnificently situated comfortable hotel on the water's edge with superb views of Skye and the Cuillins. ££

Oban
Alexandra Hotel, Esplanade. Tel: (01631) 62381. 60 rooms. A grand old hotel, on the waterfront. ££
Caledonian Hotel, Station Square. Tel: (01631) 63133. 70 rooms. An imposing, recently modernised hotel. Close to the ferries to the islands. ££
Columba Hotel, Esplanade. Tel: (01631) 62183. 49 rooms. Well-established hotel on waterfront. ££
Knipoch Hotel, 6 miles (10km) south of Oban. Tel: (018526) 251. 17 rooms. A peaceful, elegant paradise with delightful public rooms in which log fires burn. Well appointed bedrooms including those in the purpose-built extension. The hotel has its own smokery which contributes to the superb meals in which local produce features. Excellent wine list. £££

Loch Melfort Hotel, by Oban. Tel: (018522) 233. 26 rooms. A relaxed atmosphere prevails in this splendid hotel which looks out on magnificent scenery. Bedrooms have either a balcony or patio. ££
Manor House Hotel, Gallanach Road. Tel: (01631) 62087. 11 rooms. Situated in own grounds on commanding promontory above Oban Bay. ££ (includes dinner).
Soroba House Hotel, Soroba Road. Tel: (01631) 62628. 25 rooms. Situated in 10 acres (4 hectares) of ground above the town. £
Willowburn Hotel, Clachan Seil, Island of Seil. Tel: (018523) 276. 6 rooms. A delightful small hotel with rather small bedrooms 10 miles (16km) south of Oban, reached only by a single-span bridge over the Atlantic. £

Ardblair Guest House, Dalriach Road. Tel: (01631) 62668. 15 rooms (12 en suite). Situated close to city centre. £
Old Clachan Farmhouse, by Oban. Tel: (018523) 493. 4 rooms (3 en suite). A traditional 18th-century farmhouse, formerly a drovers' inn next to "the bridge across the Atlantic". Excellent accommodation with large public and bedrooms. Place your dinner order in the morning – seafood a speciality – and dine in elegance. £

Talladale
Loch Maree Hotel, Talladale, By Achnasheen. Tel: (0144 584) 271. 17 rooms. This recently refurbished hotel situated on Loch Maree has a wonderful atmosphere and is a fishermen's haven. Bedrooms somewhat small except for the one in which Queen Victoria stayed. ££

Tarbert (Loch Fyne)
Stonefield Castle Hotel. Tel: (01880) 820836. 33 rooms. Baronial mansion set in 56 acres (20 hectares) with magnificent views over Loch Fyne. Better bedrooms are in main building. Glorious gardens. Outdoor heated pool, sauna, solarium, snooker. Includes dinner. £££

Ullapool
Ceilidh Place, 14 West Argyle Street. Tel: (01854) 612103. 24 rooms (only 10 are en suite). With bookshop, café, restaurant and concert hall, this is not only an excellent hotel but is also the cultural centre of Ullapool. The Bunk House with 11 rooms is somewhat spartan but immaculate and great for families. £–££
Glendhu Guest House, Garve Road. Tel: (01854) 612560. 4 rooms (none en suite). Delightful, comfortable modern home on the edge of the town with views of Loch Broome. £
Royal Hotel, Garve Road. Tel: (01854) 612181. 52 rooms. Stands in own grounds with several balcony rooms overlooking harbour and Loch Broom. ££
Strathmore Guest House, Lochinver Road. Tel: (01854) 612423. 7 rooms (4 en suite). The upstairs en suite rooms with a private lounge are very pleasant and have commanding views of Loch Broome. ££

INNER HEBRIDES

Muck
Port Mor House. Tel: (01687) 2365. 8 rooms (none en suite). Friendly house with imaginative cooking and home baking. £ (includes evening dinner which is quite splendid).

Mull
Ardfenaig House, by Bunessan. Tel: (06817) 210. 5 rooms (3 en suite). Isolated spot simply perfect for relaxing and close to ferry for Island of Iona. Set in 15 acres (6 hectares) of woodland and gardens. £££ (includes dinner).
Druimard Country House Hotel, Dervaig. Tel: (016884) 345. 6 rooms. (4 en suite). Beautifully restored small Victorian country house hotel widely known for interesting cuisine. Pleasant conservatory and informal atmosphere. Adjacent to Mull Little Theatre. ££
Tiroran House, Tiroran. Tel: (06815) 232. 9 rooms. A remote and enchanting country house hotel on Loch Scridain set in 15 acres (6 hectares) of grounds which slope down to the loch. Accommodation is either in the house which is filled with chintz and *objects d'art* or in the no-less comfortable annex. Dining room renowned for its roasts – stuffed or marinated – and other excellent local produce. ££££ (includes dinner).
Western Isles Hotel, Tobermory. Tel: (0688) 2012. 28 rooms. Gothic-style building magnificently situated above Tobermory Bay. ££

Ardrioch Farm, Dervaig. Tel: (06884) 264. 4 rooms (1 en suite). A cedar farmhouse with great views of sea, loch and hills. No smoking. ££

Rum
Kinloch Castle. Tel: (0687) 2037. 9 rooms. Step back in time and savour the Edwardian lifestyle. Built by an English industrialist in 1901, this is possibly Scotland's most unusual hotel. In 1957 it was sold to the nation by Sir George's widow and is now owned by Scottish Natural Heritage with virtually all the original fittings and furnishings – grand piano, priceless antiques – intact. Rooms are enormous and each is different. Guests dine *en famille*. Billiards. ££££ (includes mandatory dinner).

Skye
Ardvasar Hotel, Ardvasar. Tel: (014714) 223. 10 rooms. Traditional white-washed hotel overlooks Sound of Sleat and Mallaig. One mile from Mallaig–Armdale ferry. ££
Atholl House Hotel, Dunvegan. Tel: (01470) 521219. 9 rooms. Formerly a manse on the outskirts of village with superb views of Loch Dunvegan. £

Cuillin Hills Hotel, Portree. Tel: (01478) 612003. 26 rooms. Situated just outside Portree with views over Portree Bay to the Cuillins. ££

Eilean Iarmain (Isle of Ornsay) Hotel, Sleat. Tel: (014713) 332. 12 rooms. A very friendly 19th-century inn by the sea featuring Gaelic hospitality. Six of the individually furnished rooms are in the inn and six across the drive in the Garden House. Spectacular views. Renowned for its cuisine featuring the world's best scallops. ££

Flodigarry Country House Hotel, Staffin. Tel: (01470) 552223. 24 rooms (16 en suite). Historic mansion beneath the Quiraing mountains and offering glorious views. Variety of rooms. In the grounds the house where Flora MacDonald lived after her marriage has been tastefully converted into en suite rooms. £–££

Glendrynoch Lodge, Carbost. Tel: (01478) 640218. 3 rooms. A sporting lodge in superb setting. ££

Glenview Inn, near Portree. Tel: (01470) 562248. 6 rooms. Small, friendly inn in one of the loveliest areas of Skye. ££

Harlosh House, near Dunvegan. Tel: (01470) 521367. 6 rooms. Perfectly positioned on shores of Loch Caroy with superb view of the Cuillins. Elegant, yet homely, atmosphere, with emphasis on peace and tranquillity. ££

Rosedale Hotel, Beaumont Crescent, Portree. Tel: (01478) 613131. 24 rooms. Very comfortable privately-owned hotel converted from former fishermen's houses situated on the waterfront. Some bedrooms are very small and hotel is a regular warren. ££

Skeabost House Hotel, Skeabost Bridge. Tel: (01470) 532202. 26 rooms. This former hunting lodge with a cosy ambience stands in 12 acres (5 hectares) of secluded woodlands and garden on the shore of Loch Snizort. Delightful bedrooms in 4-room annexe. Famous Sunday buffet lunch in sunny conservatory. The hotel owns 8 miles (13km) of the River Snizort (sea trout and salmon) and has boat on nearby loch. Also 9-hole golf course, bowling green, snooker. ££

Viewfield House, Portree. Tel: (01478) 612217. 10 rooms (8 en suite). A most idiosyncratic country house hotel in extensive wooded grounds overlooking the bay. Each room different: all large. Something of a time warp although bathrooms modern. An experience. ££

Almondbank Guest House, Viewfield Road, Portree. Tel: (01478) 612696. 6 rooms (4 en suite). Beautiful modern home with excellent bedrooms and large public rooms. Dinner, most enjoyable, served. ££

Clan Donald Centre, Armadale. Tel: (014714) 305. 2 large suites. Superb self-catering accommodation next to Visitor's Centre (where there is restaurant) and overlooking Sound of Sleat. De-luxe furnishings and facilities. Minimum let 3 nights. £

Craiglockhart Guest House, Beaumont Terrace, Portree. Tel: (01478) 612233. 9 rooms (3 en suite). Centrally situated and overlooking the harbour. £

MacFarlane (Mrs), Quiraing, Viewfield Road, Portree. Tel: (01478) 612870. 4 rooms (all en suite). Overlooking the bay. ££

Ptarmigan, Broadford. Tel: (01471) 822744. 3 rooms (all en suite). Delightful accommodation 8 miles (13km) from the ferry with grand views across Broadford Bay. Binoculars in bedrooms are boon for bird-watchers. ££

OUTER HEBRIDES

Barra
Castlebay Hotel, Castlebay. Tel: (08714) 223. 12 rooms. Overlooks the bay with its castle. Easy access to ferry terminal. £

Harris
Scarista House, Scarista. Tel: (085985) 238. 7 rooms. Former manse with superb views of beach and sea. Bedrooms, including those in the annexe, individually designed. No credit cards. ££

North Uist
Lochmaddy Hotel, Lochmaddy. Tel: (08763) 331. 15 rooms. £

CENTRAL SCOTLAND

Aberfeldy
Farleyer House, Aberfeldy. Tel: (01877) 820332. 11 rooms. A spot of luxury in the middle of the Perthshire highlands. A former dower-house dating back to the 16th century. ££

Anstruther
The Spindrift, Pittenweem Road. Tel: (01333) 310573. 8 rooms (all en suite). A Victorian house B&B establishment. Non-smoking. ££

Auchterarder
Gleneagles Hotel. Tel: (01764) 662231. 236 rooms. Elegance is the name of the game here. Public rooms, including the ballroom, are grand. Bedrooms vary considerably but all are tastefully furnished and comfortable. Nightly dancing to live band in drawing room. Health spa and leisure centre. Activities abound and include acres of tennis and croquet courts, squash, clay-pigeon shooting, coarse and game fishing, horse riding and, of course, golf. ££££

Auchtermuchty
Ardchoille Farm Guest House, Dunshalt. Tel: (01337) 28414. 3 rooms (all en suite). Elegant, modern farmhouse with superb views of Lomond Hills. Attractive dining room with elegant china and crystal: excellent food. ££

Callander
Bridgend House Private Hotel, Bridgend. Tel: (01877) 330130. 6 rooms (5 en suite). 18th-century family-run hotel with magnificent views of Ben Ledi. ££

323

Highland House Private Hotel, South Church Street. Tel: (01877) 330269. 9 rooms (7 en suite). Non-smoking Georgian house. £

Roman Camp Hotel, Callander. Tel: (01877) 330003. 14 rooms. Hunting lodge from 1625 set in beautiful gardens that sweep down to the River Teith in which fishing is available. Although secluded the town is just beyond the garden. Renowned for its cuisine. £££

Arden House Guest House, Bracklinn Road. Tel: (01877) 330235. 6 rooms (all en suite). A non-smoking house with superb views of the Trossachs. Renowned as the setting for the vintage BBC TV series *Dr Finlay's Casebook*. ££

Crianlarach
Allt-Chaorain Country House. Tel: (018383) 300283. 8 rooms. A pleasant house near the main road with commanding views of the glorious mountains. Tastefully furnished. Restricted smoking. ££

Dunblane
Cromlix Hotel, Kinbuck, Dunblane. Tel: (01786) 822125. 14 rooms. One of Scotland's great country house hotels stands in 5,000 acres (2,000 hectares). Antiques abound in this hotel which oozes gracious living. All rooms are large and antiques abound. Magnificent conservatory. Most bedrooms, over half of which are suites, are also magnificent. Noted for its dining room and superb food (die for the desserts) and extensive wine list. Four private lochs available for fishing. Also riding, clay-pigeon shooting, tennis and croquet. £££–££££

Stakis Dunblane Hydro. Tel: (01786) 822551. 219 rooms. Hotel with Victorian facade in 44 acres (18 hectares) grounds. Excellent sports and leisure facilities. ££

Dunkeld
Kinnaird Estate. Tel: (01796) 82440. 9 rooms. Be petted and pampered in elegant, warm surroundings in this country house hotel 4 miles (6km) northwest of Dunkeld. Everything is luxurious. Renowned for its cuisine and service. ££££

Stakis Dunkeld House. Tel: (01350) 727771. 92 rooms. A splendid hotel, formerly the home of the Duke of Atholl, standing on the banks of the River Tay in 280 acres (112 hectares) of woodland. Extensive leisure facilities, clay-pigeon shooting and tennis. £££

Falkland
Templelands Farm. Tel: (01337) 57383. 2 rooms (not en suite). Set on Lomond Hills with superb views. Spacious attractively furnished bedrooms. £

Perth
Ballathie House Hotel, Kinclaven by Stanley. Tel: (01250) 883268. 27 rooms plus a ground floor suite. Relaxing and civilized baronial shooting lodge. Graciously proportioned public rooms and splen-

didly comfortable bedrooms. Lawns roll down to banks of River Tay. £££

Huntingtower Hotel, Crieff Road. Tel: (01738) 683771. 22 rooms. Country house hotel 3 miles (5km) west of Perth, standing in its own beautiful grounds. ££

Lovat Hotel, Glasgow Road. Tel: (01738) 636555. 30 rooms. Privately-owned, friendly hotel. ££

Murrayshall Country House Hotel, Scone, Perth. Tel: (01738) 651171. 19 rooms. Sumptuously appointed, elegant country house in 290 acres (120 hectares) of parkland. 4 miles (7km) north of Perth. Better bedrooms are in original part of house. Superb food accompanied by equally superb wine list with numerous half-bottles is served in a luxurious dining room. Hotel has its own challenging 18-hole golf course. Also tennis. £££

Parklands, St Leonards Bank. Tel: (01738) 622451. 14 rooms. Classical Georgian town house, newly refurbished, overlooking the South Inch. ££££

Queens Hotel, Leonard Street. Tel: (01738) 625471. 51 rooms. Recently modernised and with new leisure complex added. In city centre. £££

Salutation Hotel, 34 South Street. Tel: (01738) 630066. 69 rooms. One of Scotland's oldest hotels where Bonnie Prince Charlie is said to have stayed. ££

Stakis City Mills Hotel, West Mill Street. Tel: (01738) 628281. 76 rooms. Comfortable hotel overlooking a 15th-century water-mill, in the city centre. ££

Station Hotel, Leonard Street. Tel: (01738) 624141. 70 rooms (not all en suite). Solid, old-fashioned hotel adjacent to station and situated close to city centre. ££

Sunbank House Hotel, 50 Dundee Road. Tel: (01738) 624882. 9 rooms. Elegant Victorian house in large garden with views of the River Tay and the city. ££

Iona Guest House, 2 Pitcullen Crescent. Tel: (01738) 627261. 5 rooms (2 en suite). Comfortable, semi-detached house with private parking close to town centre. £

Kinnaird Guest House, 5 Marshall Place. Tel: (01738) 628021. 7 rooms (5 en suite). Comfortable, friendly guest house which is part of an 1806 Georgian terrace. Overlooks South Inch. Private parking. ££

Lochiel House, Pitcullen Crescent. Tel: (01738) 633183. 3 rooms (none en suite). Comfortable, semi-detached house with private parking close to town centre. ££

Pitlochry
Atholl Palace Hotel, Atholl Road. Tel: (01796) 472400. 84 rooms. A majestic building set in 50 acres (20 hectares) and with health club. ££

Balrobin Hotel, Higher Oakfield. Tel: (01796) 472901. 15 rooms. Victorian house in own grounds somewhat out of town. £

Dunfallandy Country House Hotel, Logierait Road.

Tel: (01796) 472648. 9 rooms. A Georgian mansion set above the town and with glorious views of Tummel valley. £

Fishers Hotel, 75–79 Atholl Road. Tel: (01796) 472000. 139 rooms. Well established hotel popular for many years. Own bowling and putting greens. ££

Killiecrankie Hotel. Tel: (01796) 473220. 11 rooms. Personally run country house hotel set in 5 acres (2 hectares) of ground overlooking the Pass of Killiecrankie, 3 miles (5km) north of Pitlochry. ££

Knockendarroch House Hotel, Higher Oakfield. Tel: (01796) 473473. 12 rooms. A Victorian mansion overlooking the village and Tummel valley. Two rooms have four-poster beds. £

Pitlochry Hydro Hotel, Knockard Road. Tel: (01796) 472666. 64 rooms. Recently refurbished hotel with health club stands in own grounds overlooking town. £££

Scotlands Hotel, 32–46 Bonnethill Road. Tel: (01796) 472292. 60 rooms. Traditional family-run hotel with health and leisure club near centre of town. £££

Westlands of Pitlochry, 160 Atholl Road. Tel: (01796) 472266. 15 rooms. A recently refurbished hotel on the edge of town. ££

Strathtummel

Port-an-Eilean Hotel, Strathtummel, 9 miles (14km) west of Pitlochry. Tel: (01882) 634233. 8 rooms. Built as a hunting lodge in 1865 this delightful homely hotel stands on the lochside. Large bedrooms furnished with antique objects. No credit cards. £

St Andrews

Argyle House Hotel, 127 North Street. Tel: (01334) 473387. 19 rooms. Late Victorian building 400 yards from Old Course and beaches. £

Rufflets Country House Hotel, Strathkinness Low Road. Tel: (01334) 472594. 25 rooms. Country house set in 10 acres (4 hectares) of beautiful gardens 2 miles (3km) from golf course and beaches. Rose Cottage situated in the grounds has 3 charming bedrooms each decorated with a different floral theme. One of the rooms has a queen-sized four poster. Cooking is light with emphasis on fresh Scottish produce (includes dinner). £££–££££

Rusacks Hotel, Pilmour Links. Tel: (01334) 474321. 50 rooms. A grand recently refurbished Victorian hotel overlooking the 18th hole of the Old Course. Excellent service. £££–££££

St Andrews Old Course Hotel. Tel: (01334) 474731. 125 rooms. Reopened in 1990 after a major transformation which resulted in elegance. Overlooks the famous 17th Road Hole of Old Course. Well equipped health club. ££££

Cleveden Guest House, 3 Murray Place. Tel: (01334) 474212. 6 rooms (4 en suite). Five minutes walk from Old Course, beach and town centre. ££

West Park House, 5 St Mary's Place. Tel: (01334) 475933. 4 rooms (3 en suite). Listed Georgian house close to all activities. ££

St Fillans

Four Seasons Hotel. Tel: (01764) 685333. 18 rooms. Comfortable, unpretentious Scandinavian type hotel at eastern end of Loch Earn, with open fires in the library. ££

Achray House Hotel. Tel: (01764) 685231. 10 rooms. A cosy hotel at the side of Loch Earn serving excellent food. ££

THE EAST COAST

Aberdeen

Atholl Hotel, 54 Kings Gate. Tel: (01224) 323505. 35 rooms. Victorian hotel in the west end. Recent major refurbishment. £–££.

Caledonian Thistle Hotel, Union Terrace. Tel: (01224) 640233. 80 rooms. Recently refurbished hotel in city centre. £££

Copthorne Aberdeen, 122 Huntly Street. Tel: (01224) 630404. 89 rooms. City centre hotel with all facilities. ££–£££

Craiglynn Private Hotel, 36 Fonthill Road. Tel: (01224) 584050. 9 rooms (7 en suite). Victorian elegance wth modern comforts. ££

Imperial Hotel, Stirling Street. Tel: (01224) 589101. 110 rooms. City centre hotel with easy access to main shopping areas and public transport terminals. ££

Palm Court Hotel, 81 Seafield Road. Tel: (01224) 310351. 24 rooms. Privately-owned recently refurbished hotel in quiet residential area in west end of city. £–££

Westhill Hotel, Westhill. Tel: (01224) 740388. 52 rooms. Modern style, in the city suburbs, 7 miles (11km) from city centre. ££

Aboyne

Hazlehurst Lodge, Ballater Road. Tel: (03398) 86921. 3 rooms. Standing in a large garden, this was formerly the coachman's lodge to Aboyne castle. Comfortable bedrooms. £

Alford

Kildrummy Castle Hotel, Kildrummy. Tel: (019755) 71288. 15 rooms. Baronial mansion built in 1901 with lots of wood panelling, tapestries and grand staircase overlooks ruined 13th-century castle. Mixture of modern and Victorian furniture. Glorious gardens. Excellent food accompanied by splendid wine list with two score half-bottle labels. £££

Banchory

Invery House Hotel, Bridge of Feugh. Tel: (01330) 824782. 14 rooms. Antique furnished bedrooms in this magnificent Georgian mansion are named after the novels of Sir Walter Scott, a frequent visitor to the house. Hot food can be provided 24 hours. Excellent restaurant with superb wine list and armchairs rather than conventional dining room chairs. Tennis, croquet, snooker and fishing in the river that runs through the grounds. £££

Boat of Garten

Avingormack Guest House. Tel: (01479) 831614. 4 rooms (2 en suite). Great conversion of a former croft provides superb views of Cairngorms through picture windows. Excellent cooking specializing in vegetarian and traditional meals. Non-smoking house. Mountain bicycles for hire. £

Dundee

Invercarse Hotel, 371 Perth Road. Tel: (01382) 69231. 38 rooms. Victorian house with modern bedroom extension set in own grounds in quiet residential area close to city centre. Single rooms not very attractive. £–££
Old Mansion House, Auchterhouse by Dundee. Tel: (0182626) 366. 6 rooms. A 16th-century baronial house 7 miles (11km) north of Dundee in 10 acres (4 hectares) of delightful gardens and woodland. Spacious bedrooms with excellent bathrooms; splendid service and views. Garden, outdoor heated pool, tennis, croquet. ££.
Shaftesbury Hotel, 1 Hyndford Street. Tel: (01382) 69216. 12 rooms. Refurbished Victorian mansion in peaceful residential area yet close to city and University. ££
Stakis Dundee Earl Grey Hotel, Earl Grey Place. Tel: (01382) 29271. 104 rooms. Modern hotel with leisure facilities. Situated on the banks of the River Tay with a view of the Kingdom of Fife. ££

Elgin

Mansion House Hotel, The Haugh. Tel: (01343) 548811. 20 rooms. A tastefully restored and decorated baronial mansion with castellated tower overlooking River Lossie. Many rooms have four-poster beds. Leisure centre with indoor pool. £££

Grantown-on-Spey

Culdearn House, Woodlands Terrace. Tel: (01479) 872106. 9 rooms (all en suite). Elegant Victorian house which is more like a hotel than a B&B. Great selection of malt whiskies and moderately priced wine list. ££
Dar-il-Hena Guest House, Grant Road. Tel: (01479) 873097. 7 rooms (none en suite). £

Huntly

Old Manse of Marnoch, Bridge of Marnoch. Tel: (01466) 780873. 5 rooms. A charming 1805 historical manse with all mod cons in ground through which River Deveron flows. Great attention to detail. Rooms large and individually furnished. Excellent food and possibly the world's most extensive breakfast menu. ££

Nairn

Carnach House Hotel, Inverness Road. Tel: (01667) 452094. 14 rooms. Edwardian house 2 miles (3km) west of Nairn in 8 acres (3.5 hectares) of wooded grounds. ££
Clifton Hotel, Viewfield Street. Tel: (01667) 453119.

26 rooms. The owner's theatrical interests are evident in this unusual tastefully decorated town house hotel. Most rooms enjoy a sea views. Bedrooms are highly individualist. Excellent restaurant with French cuisine and a wine list with 75 champagnes. ££
Golf View Hotel, Seabank Road. Tel: (01667) 452301. 48 rooms. Imposing Victorian hotel overlooking the sea and the Black Isle. New leisure centre, tennis and near golf course. Nearly half the bedrooms suitable for family occupation. ££–£££
Invernairne Hotel, Thurlow Road. Tel: (01667) 452039. 9 rooms. Former mansion house, now a family-run hotel. Private path to safe beach. £.
Links Hotel, 1 Seafield Street. Tel: (01667) 453321. 10 rooms. Elegant Victorian building with sea views. Log fires. Inclusive golf packages utilising 30 courses. £

Newburgh

Udny Arms Hotel, Main Street. Tel: (01358) 789444. 26 rooms. Village pub with great food and character. Rooms tastefully and individually furnished with period furniture. Close to renowned Cruden Bay golf course. ££

THE NORTHERN HIGHLANDS

Achiltibuie

Summer Isles Hotel. Tel: (085482) 282. 13 rooms. A simple, but delightful hotel with glorious views over the Summer Isles. ££

Aviemore

Stakis Aviemore Coylumbridge Resort Hotel. Tel: (0479) 810661. 175 rooms. In the heart of the Grampians and an ideal centre for outdoor leisure. Complete leisure centre. ££
Stakis Aviemore Four Seasons Hotel. Tel: (0479) 810681. 89 rooms. Luxury hotel with leisure centre in heart of highlands. £££

Ballater

Darroch Learg Hotel, Braemar Road. Tel: (013397) 55443. 20 rooms. Superb views from this granite pile set in 5 acres (2 hectares) of grounds. Comfortable rooms. £–££.
Tullich Lodge. Tel: (013397) 55406. 10 rooms. An elegant, granite, Victorian baronial house set in its own grounds. Spacious rooms filled with chintz and antiques. Bedrooms individually decorated. Delicious Scottish cuisine served in non-smoking dining room. £££

Dee Valley Guest House, 26 Viewfield Road. Tel: (013397) 55408. 3 rooms (1 en suite). Detached house in quiet residential area close to village centre. ££
Netherley Guest House, 2 Netherley Place. (03397) 55792. 9 rooms (4 en suite). Family-run guest house in centre of village. ££

Beauly

Lovat Arms Hotel, The Square. Tel: (01463) 782313. 22 rooms. All rooms in this recently refurbished comfortable family hotel feature a clan tartan and many have canopied or half-tester beds. Produce from family farm served in dining room. ££
Priory Hotel, The Square. Tel: (01463) 782309. 21 rooms. A comfortable privately-owned hotel in an attractive village square next to priory ruins. Scrumptious afternoon tea. £

Cromarty

Royal Hotel, Marine Terrace. Tel: (01381) 600217. 10 rooms. Comfortable, welcoming family hotel with great view of the Cromarty Firth where dolphins swim among parked oil rigs. £

DORNOCH

Royal Golf Hotel, Grange Road. Tel: (01862) 810283. 24 rooms. A mansion overlooking Dornoch Firth and playful dolphins. New leisure centre, two tennis courts and adjacent to championship golf course. ££

Drumnadrochit (on Loch Ness)

Borlum Farmhouse. Tel: (0456) 450358. 6 rooms (3 en suite). Extremely comfortable B&B accommodation in an 18th-century homely farmhouse with antique furnishings. The summer sitting room in the glass conservatory offers superb views of Loch and Glen. Large horse-riding school next door. ££

Fort William

Innseagan House Hotel, Achintore Road. Tel: (01397) 702452. 24 rooms (21 en suite). Pleasant views of loch. £
Inverlochy Castle Hotel, Torlundy. Tel: (01397) 702177. 16 rooms. Possibly the grandest hotel in Scotland with imposing public rooms such as the Great Hall. Impeccable service. Set in glorious grounds with views of Ben Nevis. Wonderful contemporary cuisine and outstanding expensive wine list rich in Californian labels. Snooker, tennis and game fishing. ££££
Moorings Hotel, Banavie. Tel: (01397) 772797. 24 rooms. 3 miles (5km) from town at Neptune's Staircase at the start of the Caledonian Canal with superb views of Ben Nevis. ££

Foyers

Foyers Bay House. Tel: (01456) 486624. 3 rooms (all en suite). Delightful Victorian villa standing on wooded slopes overlooking Loch Ness and 500 yards from Falls of Foyers. ££

Glenmoriston

Cluanie Inn. Tel: (01320) 340238. 11 rooms. A traditional Scottish Inn, now fully modernised, far away from it all on the main road to Skye. Roaring fires in public rooms. £–££

Invermoriston (near Loch Ness)

Glenmoriston Arms Hotel. Tel: (01320) 451206. 8 rooms. This 200-year-old coaching inn nestles in lovely glen close to Loch Ness. £

Inverness

Brae Ness Hotel, Ness Bank. Tel: (01463) 712266. 10 rooms. A non-smoking family-run hotel on the River Ness. Close to town. £
Bunchrew House Hotel, Bunchrew. Tel: (01463) 234917. 11 rooms. Every inch a 17th-century Scottish baronial home yet very laid-back. Stands in 15 acres (6 hectares) of grounds on the shores of the Beauly Firth. 5 miles (8km) west of Inverness. Large rooms. £££
Caledonian Hotel, Church Street. Tel: (01463) 235181. 100 rooms. Elegant city hotel alongside the River Ness with all facilities. ££–£££
Columba Hotel, Ness Walk. Tel: (01463) 231391. 86 rooms. Refurbished hotel on banks of River Ness. Close to town. ££
Culduthel Lodge, 14 Culduthel Road. Tel: (01463) 240089. 12 rooms. A non-smoking splendid 19th-century house overlooking the Moray Firth, Inverness and the Black Island. The circular drawing room is unusual. £
Culloden House Hotel, Culloden. Tel: (01463) 790461. 23 rooms. An architectural gem 3 miles (5km) east of Inverness which is associated with Bonnie Prince Charlie and the Battle of Culloden. Magnificent public rooms including an Adam dining room. Four-poster curtain-framed beds. Dine in the Adam Room to local produce cooked in the French manner. 40 acres (17 hectares) of lovely grounds. Tennis, sauna, solarium, snooker. ££££
Dunain Park, 1 mile from Inverness on A82. Tel: (01463) 230512. 14 rooms. Georgian country house set in 6 acres (2.5 hectares) of gardens and grounds. A wide variety of bedrooms, some with 4-poster beds. Two cottages. Elegant public rooms. Auld Alliance (marriage of French and Scottish produce and skills) is served in the non-smoking dining room accompanied by a fair selection of wines. Indoor swimming pool, sauna, croquet. £££.
Glen Mhor Hotel, 10 Ness Bank. Tel: (01463) 234308. 30 rooms. In quiet, residential area overlooking the River Ness. ££
Station Hotel, Academy Street. Tel: (01463) 231926. 67 rooms (not all en suite). Distinctive Victorian city centre hotel adjacent to railway station. ££
Whinpark Hotel, 17 Ardross Street. Tel: (01463) 232549. 8 rooms (4 en suite). Victorian house situated in quiet area close to the River Ness. £

Chisholm (Mrs) Elizabeth, 43 Charles Street. Tel: (01463) 225689. 3 rooms (none en suite). Family-run Victorian house 3 minutes from town centre. £
Emslie (Mrs) J. R., 7 Harris Road. Tel: (01463) 237059. 3 rooms (1 en suite). Comfortable, non-smoking, friendly home with lovely garden. Attractive area. £

Kingussie
Osprey Hotel. Tel: (0540) 661510. 8 rooms. A pleasant, small Highland hotel just off the main road providing friendly service. Vegetarian meals. £

Lochinver
Inver Lodge Hotel. Tel: (01571) 844496. 20 rooms. A modern hotel with superb views of the loch. £££

The Albannach, Baddidarroch. Tel: (01571) 844407. 6 rooms (3 en suite). A delightful 19th-century house set in a walled garden. All comforts for those who enjoy the outdoors. Good home cooking and vegetarians welcomed. Log fires in lounge and centrally heated bedrooms. £
Veyatie, 66 Baddidarroch. Tel: (01571) 844424. 3 rooms (2 en suite). Beautifully located and very comfortable. ££

Newtonmore
Ard-Na-Coille. Tel: (0540) 673214. 7 rooms. A former Edwardian shooting lodge set "high in the woods" with glorious views of the Cairngorms. A comfortable homely atmosphere with many Edwardian features retained. An exquisite no-choice 5-course menu is accompanied by moderately priced wines with informative notes from an extensive and varied wine cellar. ££

Scourie
Eddrachilles Hotel, Badcall Bay, Scourie. Tel: (01971) 502080 11 rooms. Beautifully maintained hotel on 320 acres (133 hectares) of waterfront property with stunning sea views. Spotless, well maintained, functional bedrooms. ££
Scourie Lodge. Tel: (01971) 502148. 4 rooms (2 en suite). Large house set in beautiful gardens. Large, comfortable rooms with all facilities and some with 4-poster bed. Superb breakfast. £

ORKNEY

Albert Hotel, Kirkwall. Tel: (01856) 876000. 19 rooms. Traditional hotel in centre of town; recently refurbished. ££
Foveran Hotel, St Ola, Kirkwall. Tel: (01856) 872389. 8 rooms. Family-run hotel set in 35 acres (14 hectares) overlooking Scapa Flow. ££
Lynfield Hotel, Holm Road, Kirkwall. Tel: (01856) 872505. 8 rooms. Formerly the residence of the distillery manager: you can still sniff the "guid stuff" – and it's free. £

SHETLAND

Grand Hotel, Commercial Street, Lerwick. Tel: (01595) 2826. 22 rooms. Oldest purpose-built hotel in Shetland and has recently been refurbished. Close to harbour and town centre. ££
Busta House Hotel, Busta, North Mainland. Tel: (0180622) 506. 20 rooms. A country house hotel 23 miles (37km) north of Lerwick with the building dating from 1588 and a private harbour and slipway. ££
Shetland Hotel, Holmsgarth Road, Lerwick. Tel: (01595) 5515. 65 rooms. Modern with leisure complex. Views of harbour and Isle of Bressay. ££

Broch House Guest House, Upper Scalloway, Scalloway. Tel: (0159588) 767. 3 rooms (all en suite). Modern house in elevated position with excellent view over Scalloway. £

CAMPUS HOTELS

Excellent accommodation is available during summer and easter vacations and, on several campuses throughout the year, at eight universities. In total, more than 14,000 bedrooms, many but not all en suite and with no single supplement, are available while self-catering accommodation in units suitable for 4–8 persons is also offered. The standard of accommodation gets better and better, e.g., the Chancellor's Hall at Strathclyde has 231 rooms all with television and tea and coffee making facilities and a lounge area while Dundee's West Park Centre is specifically designed to meet the needs of the disabled. At Dundee, Glasgow, Heriot-Watt (in Edinburgh), St Andrews, Strathclyde (in Glasgow) and Stirling accommodation is under £20 while at Aberdeen and Edinburgh it is between £20 and £25. These rates include breakfast. Contacts are:

Aberdeen	(01224) 272664
Dundee	(01382) 23181 ext 4038
Edinburgh	(0131) 677 1971
Glasgow	(0141) 3305385
Heriot-Watt	(0131) 451 315
St Andrews	(01334) 476161 ext 474
Stirling	(01786) 467140/1
Strathclyde	(0141) 553 4148

YOUTH HOSTELS

There are about 80 youth hostels, many of them in the Highlands. These hostels provide very cheap accommodation, usually with dormitory-type bedrooms. To join the Youth Hostels Association costs from £2.50–£6 and accommodation is between £3.15 and £7.25 a night depending on the facilities at the hostel. For details contact the Scottish Youth Hostels Association, 7 Glebe Crescent, Stirling, FK8 2JA. Tel: (01786) 451181.

EATING OUT

More than 50 years have elapsed since that distinguished travel writer H.V. Morton wrote: "Scotland is the best place in the world to take an appetite." The country has long been renowned for its produce from river and sea, from farm and moor. Fish is something of a speciality, with salmon being particularly good: kippers and Arbroath Smokies (haddock smoked over wood) are delicious too. Shellfish – lobsters, prawns, oysters, mussels – are unsurpassed and exported all over the world, while Aberdeen Angus beef and Border lamb are both renowned. Various dishes are distinctly Scottish, such as haggis – which is probably more enjoyable if you don't know what should be in it (the heart, lungs and liver of a sheep, suet, oatmeal and onion).

Over the past decade culinary skills have matched the quality of the produce and today it is possible to enjoy superb meals in Scotland served in the most elegant of restaurants as well as in simple small spaces with scarcely more than half-a-dozen tables. The hours at which restaurants, especially smaller ones away from the main cities, serve meals tend to be less flexible than in many other countries. High tea, usually served from 5 to 7pm, is an interesting meal consisting usually of fish and chips or an egg dish followed by lashings of scones and pancakes and all accompanied by gallons of tea.

Dr Johnson remarked that "If an epicure could remove by a wish, in quest of sensual gratifications, wherever he had supped he would breakfast in Scotland." No doubt he would say the same today. There is surely no better way to start the day than porridge, Loch Fyne kippers and Scottish oatcakes.

On a more mundane level, there is no shortage of fast food outlets of one sort or another throughout Scotland. For a cheap and enjoyable takeaway meal, you could do a lot worse than try the humble "chippie" (fish and chip shop).

The symbols at the end of each entry provide a rough guide to prices, based on the average cost of a three-course evening meal, excluding wine. £ = under £10; ££ = £10–£20 per head; and £££ = £20–£30 per head. Lunch is almost invariably considerably less expensive and nearly all restaurants serve table d'hôte meals which are about half the price of an à la carte dinner.

WHERE TO EAT

EDINBURGH

(All phone numbers begin with the code 0131)

French

Chez Jules, 29 Cockburn Street. Tel: 225 7007. Also in New Town at 61 Frederick Street. Tel: 225 7983. Closed Sunday. Classic food served with no frills at bargain prices. £

L'Auberge, 56-58 St Mary's Street. Tel: 556 5888. Successful marriage of Scottish produce and French culinary skills. Excellent fish dishes and wide selection of desserts. 600 wines, almost exclusively French, with numerous half-bottles. £££

La Cuisine l'Odile, 13 Randolph Crescent. Tel: 225 5366. Monday–Saturday noon–2pm. A simple bistro (no alcohol) in the basement of L'Institut Français d'Écosse. Serves a limited menu of delightful, inexpensive dishes. £

Le Café Saint-Honoré, 34 N.W. Thistle Street Lane. Tel: 226 2211. Step into this pleasant bistro, leave Scotland behind and enter France. Good value lunch. Some imaginative dishes. Decent wine list. ££

Marché Noir, 2-4 Eyre Place. Tel: 558 1608. Closed Sunday. Provençal menus served with excellent wines in pleasant ambience. £££

Merchants Restaurant, 17 Merchant Street. Tel: 225 4009. Innovative and varied French cuisine in smart surroundings. £££

Pierre Victoire, 38 Grassmarket. Tel: 226 2422. Also 8 Union Street. Tel: 557 8451, 10 Victoria Street. Tel: 225 1721 and 5 Dock Place, Leith. Tel: 555 6178 and Queensferry. Tel: 331 5006. Closed Sunday or Monday. All five restaurants have limited menus yet serve excellent dishes. Decent, moderately priced wines. Train yourself to breath in unison. £

Pompadour, Caledonian Hotel, Princes Street. Tel: 225 2433. Possibly Edinburgh's most elegant and formal dining room. Lunchtime features *Legends of the Scottish Table* while in the evening the other member of the *Auld Alliance* (France) holds sway. Classic wines, impeccable service and soothing piano music. £££+

A simpler menu with, nevertheless, a good range of classic and some international dishes is served in **The Carriage**, the Caledonian's second restaurant. ££

Italian

Ferri's Pizzeria, 1 Antigua Street, Leith Walk. Tel: 556 5592. Looking for a meal at 4am: this is the place. Good, reasonably priced food in a cheerful environment. £

Mr V's, 7 Charlotte Street. Tel: 220 0176. Upmarket restaurant with good wine list. Situated in quiet courtyard. Pleasant ambience. ££

Tinelli, 139 Easter Road. Tel: 652 1392. Small, unpretentious restaurant with a limited menu of superb north Italian food. Splendid cheese selection. ££

Indian

Indian Cavalry Club, 3 Atholl Place. Tel: 228 3282. Also 8 Eyre Place, New Town. Tel: 556 2404. The paramilitary uniforms – some ill-fitting – of the staff should not be off-putting. This up-market Indian restaurant with an emphasis on steaming attempts, with a fair amount of success, to blend brasserie and Indian restaurant. Better than average wine list at reasonable prices. ££

Kalpna, 2 St Patrick square. Tel: 667 9890. Gujerati and southern Indian vegetarian food in a non-smoking restaurant. Decent, moderately priced wine list. £

Lancers Brasserie, 5 Hamilton Place. Tel: 332 3444. Rather elegant space with three rooms serving Bengali and north Indian cuisine. Renowned for curries. Modest wine list. ££

Shamiana, 14 Brougham Street. Tel: 228 2265. North Indian dishes served in this rather elegant Indian restaurant. Excellent Tandoori and curry. ££

Chinese

Chinese Home Cooking, 21 Argyle Place. Tel: 229 4404. Straightforward Cantonese cooking in a minuscule converted shop. Bring your own bottle. £

Kweilin, 19 Dundas Street. Tel: 557 1875. Large space serving authentic Cantonese dishes, especially strong on seafood. Many swear the best Chinese in town. £

Szechuan House, 95 Gilmore Place. Tel: 229 4655. For those who like it hot and spicy. Basic surroundings, near the King's Theatre, serving authentic Szechuan dishes. £

Thai

Siam Erawan, 48 Howe Street. Tel: 226 3675. The city's top Thai restaurant with authentic Thai food and laid-back waiters. Good wine list. ££

Mexican

Tex Mex, 47 Hanover Street. Tel: 225 1796. Exactly what the name suggests: reasonably priced and authentic. £

Viva Mexico, 10 Anchor Close. Tel: 226 5145. Also at 50 East Fountainbridge. Tel: 228 4005. Cosy restaurant that transfers diner back to atmosphere of old Mexico. Food (for some) on spicy side. Good selection for veggies. Great margeritas. £

Scottish

Jackson's, 209-213 High Street. Tel: 225 1793. Atmospheric basement restaurant on the Royal Mile serving imaginative Scottish cooking in somewhat cramped space. Very popular with tourists. Set lunch an excellent bargain. £££

Contemporary & International

Martins, 70 Rose St North Lane. Tel: 225 3016. Difficult to find this small, well established restaurant but well worth the trouble. Limited but confident contemporary menu with best cheeseboard in town. Excellent discrete service. £££

The Abbotsford Restaurant and Bar, 3 Rose Street. Tel: 225 5276. Upstairs restaurant, separate from pub, serves splendid pub food in Victorian old-world charm. £

The Atrium, 10 Cambridge Street. Tel: 228 8882. Located in the foyer of the Traverse Theatre, this is the most stylish place in town and currently the "in" place. Sophisticated, imaginative menu served in mellow, contemporary ambience with excellent service. £££

The Witchery, 325 Castlehill, Royal Mile. Tel: 225 5613. New-wave cooking served in two restaurants, each with unusual atmosphere. Upstairs is dark and atmospheric – beams and oil lamps – while downstairs is bright with lots of greenery and small outdoor terrace. Wine list with 300 bin numbers including many halves make excellent reading. £££

Vintner's Rooms, The Vaults, 87 Giles Street, Leith. Tel: 554 6767. Dine either in a unique candelit restaurant in old wine merchants' auction room or in a high functional space with a fire at one end and a bar down one side. In either case, the creative cooking of fresh produce, especially fish, is robust. Everything from the bread to the fudge with coffee is home-made. Single dishes from menu available in wine bar. Naturally, wine list is excellent and not too pricey. £££

Seafood

Café Royal Oyster Bar, 17 West Register Street. Tel: 556 4124. An Edinburgh institution where the ambience is everything. Stained glass and polished wood Victorian ambience which is always bustling and where seafood is preferred. £££

Marinette, 52 Coburg Street, Leith. Tel: 555 0922. Fish and chips as they should be but rarely are: cooked with Gallic flair: simply the best. ££

Skippers, 1A Dock Place, Leith. Tel: 554 1018. "Very fishy, very quayside, very French" with a somewhat nautical atmosphere. £££

The Shore, 3 The Shore, Leith. Tel: 554 5080. Naturally on the waterfront where, in non-smoking dining room and bar (smoking alright) seafood with a Scottish flair is served. £££

Food in bar where prices are much less than in main restaurant is posted on blackboard. £–££

Vegetarian

Helios Fountain, 7 Grassmarket. Tel: 229 7884. A self-service non-smoking bookshop serving mostly organic and proper vegan food in the back. Well established; excellent bread. £

Henderson's Salad Table, 94 Hanover Street. Tel: 225 2131. Basement self-service eatery always busy, especially at lunch, with a mainly young clientele enjoying excellent vegetarian cookery. Real ale, wine and separate wine bar. Live music in evenings. £

Pierre Lapin, 32 W. Nicholson Street. Tel: 668 4332. This is the vegetarian off-shoot of Pierre Victoire and follows that restaurant's highly successful philosophy: cram them in and serve good food in a friendly atmosphere at reasonable prices. Set menus an attraction. £

Two of Britain's top restaurants on the outskirts of Edinburgh are:
Champany Inn, Linlithgow, Lothian EH49 7LU. (17 miles/25km from Edinburgh). Tel: (050683) 4532. Meat is the name of the game in what has been called "the best steakhouse in Britain". The Davidsons' avowed intent is to purchase the best and to cook it magnificently. Aberdeen Angus is the speciality and from the grill come entrecôte, pope's eye, porterhouse, sirloin and rib eye. The inn has its own smokehouse and the seafood is as excellent as the meat. A superb wine list, the majority of whose bottles are reasonably priced, with the largest selection of South African wines this side of the Cape. £££+.
The Champany Inn Chop and Ale House is an informal sister restaurant serving the same excellent – but smaller – steaks and consequently more easy on the pocket. Hamburgers are made from the best ground beef and Boerwors sausages are mixed with lamb. £££
La Potiniere, Main Street, Gullane, Lothian EH31 2AA (17 miles/25km from Edinburgh). Tel: (0620) 843214. A small, unpretentious shopfront exterior belies the joys, both of decor and of food, within. Imaginative, French cooking beyond compare – no choice – served on delicate Limoges china. The wine list, especially the French bottles, is first-rate and reasonably priced. No credit cards: no smoking: booking essential and best to book this year for next. Limited hours of opening. £££+

Bistros
Granary of Shawlands, 42 Queensferry Street. Tel: 220 0550. Large, lively space at the west end of Princes Street with views onto the street. Good for breakfast as well as all day dining. £
La Cuisine d' Odile, 13 Randolph Crescent. Tel: 225 5366. A simple bistro (no alcohol) in the basement of L'Institut Français d'Écosse serves a limited menu of delightful, inexpensive lunches (Monday to Saturday, noon–2pm). £
Ryan's Bistro, 2-4 Hope Street. Tel: 226 7005. A pleasant, relatively small space below a pub at the west end of Princes Street. Small but imaginative menu and courteous staff. **The Doric**, 15 Market Street. Tel: 225 1084. A brash upstairs bistro, a long term favourite, with reasonable wine. Strong on vegetarian dishes. Pleasant at lunch and trendy in the evenings. £
Waterfront Wine Bar & Bistro, 1C Dock Place. Tel: 554 7427. Moderately priced fish dishes and good choice of vegetarian dishes served in a conservatory on the dock. Excellent wine selection on blackboards. ££

Cafés
Buffalo Grill, 14 Chapel Street. Tel: 667 7427. A

hamburger joint serving great inexpensive food. No license. £
Clarinda's, 69 Canongate, Royal Mile. Tel: 557 1888. A small crowded old-fashioned tea-room at the bottom of the Royal Mile which serves delightful home cooked snacks. Great cakes. £
Gallery of Modern Art Coffee Shop, Belford Road. Tel: 332 8600. Delightful self-service café opening out into garden, serves delicious home-cooked lunches. Attracts many locals. Licensed.
Laigh Kitchen, 117a Hanover Street. Tel: 225 1552. An old world stone-flagged basement kitchen which serves (self-service) glorious salads and cakes for which you would kill. Very popular. £
Queen Street Café, National Portrait Gallery, Queen Street. Tel: 556 8921. Delightful home-cooked food and excellent cakes served (self-service) in a somewhat cramped space. Strong on vegetarian dishes. £

PUBS & BARS

Most pubs in Edinburgh now sell "real ale", cask-conditioned beer in various strengths (60°, 70°and 80°) made by Scottish brewers, large and small. Ask for 80/- rather than "heavy" or you'll get the nasty, fizzy stuff. Connoisseurs should look out for Caledonian 70/- and 80/-, which are made using traditional methods in a Victorian brewery in the city. Most pubs have a reasonable selection of malt whiskies.

Licensing hours in Edinburgh are liberal. If you try hard enough, so they say, you can drink for 22 out of 24 hours. Certainly, there is no shortage of pubs which are "open all day", which usually means from about 11am until 11pm or midnight. Sunday afternoons can be more difficult, but the desperate can always try a hotel bar. Most bars are bearable, and some of the traditional drinking haunts shouldn't be missed.

Café Royal, 17 Register Street.
Fiddler's Arms, 9-11 Grassmarket.
The Canny Man's (The Volunteer Arms), 237 Morningside Road.
The Abbotsford, 3 Rose Street.
Bennets, 8 Leven Street.
Sandy Bell's (The Forrest), 25 Forrest Road.
Diggers (The Athletic Arms), 1 Angle Park Terrace.
Leslie's Bar, 45 Ratcliffe Terrace.

THE BORDERS

Kailzie Garden Restaurant, Kailzie, Peebles. Tel: (01721) 722807. An unpretentious restaurant housed in the old stable square and carefully converted to retain as many original features as possible. Limited menu of good home cooking and baking with fruit and vegetables from the gardens. Homely atmosphere. Dinner on Saturday only. Before or after lunch visit the extensive gardens. £–££.

Le Provençale, Monksford Road, Newton St Boswells. Tel: (01835) 823284. The Auld Alliance has got together here (René in the kitchen and Elizabeth in the front of the house) and the result is no nonsense French cooking of the highest standard. No credit cards. £–££

Riverside Inn, Canobie. Tel: (03873) 71512. An old white-painted inn overlooking the River Esk houses a jolly, idiosyncratic bar and restaurant. Both serve unusual – leek and parsnip soup, poached bantam egg in madeira jelly – dishes. Extensive, international and moderately priced wine list. £££. The inn has 8 bedrooms.

Sunflower, 4 Bridgegate, Peebles. Tel: (01721) 722420. A tiny quality food-store has a few tables and serves interesting vegetarian and non-vegetarian snacks throughout the day. Some wines. Credit cards not accepted. £

THE SOUTHWEST

Chapelton House, Stewarton-Irvine Road, Stewarton. Tel: (01560) 482696. An elegant turn-of-the century mansion with panelled dining room. Ambitious contemporary cooking and wine list with nearly 200 bin numbers including many half-bottles. Smart dress preferred. £££. There are 8 bedrooms.

GLASGOW

(Area code: 0141)

Ashoka Tandoori, 108 Elderslie Street. Tel: 221 1761. The touchstone by which all other Glasgow Indian restaurants are measured. Seating upstairs is not as dark and gloomy as the large room below. ££

Baby Grand, 3 Elmbank Gardens, Charing Cross. Tel: 248 4942. Crowded café-bar with continental atmosphere and grand piano. Especially popular after theatre. ££

Belfry, 652 Argyle Street. Tel: 221 0630. Very comfortable and restful restaurant serving Scottish cuisine. Upstairs is its big brother, The Buttery, which is not such a good buy. ££

Café Gandolfi, 64 Albion Street. Tel: 552 6813. The grandfather of modern Glasgow café life. Tasty dishes mean it is busy at lunchtime. Half-a-dozen inexpensive wines are offered by glass or bottle. £

Cantinetta, The Italian Centre, 17 John Street. Tel: 552 6099. A cleverly designed atmospheric basement restaurant serving decent Italian food. This is part of one of Glasgow's newest and most splendid complexes. ££. Other "eateries" in the complex are Qui, a splendid Italian café which serves light meals (£) and Pasticerria, an attractive French tea room which also serves excellent light meals.(£). Both Qui and Pasticerria have tables in attractive courtyards.

De Quinceys, 71 Renfield Streeet. Tel: 333 0633. The decor of this former bank, now a bistro, with coloured tiles on walls and ceiling is most attractive. Reasonable meals at reasonable prices. £

Granary, 82 Howard Street. Tel: 226 3770. Veg-etarian food and excellent baking in a comfortable and friendly atmosphere in city centre. £

Il Pescatore, 148 Woodlands Road. Tel: 333 7239. Small restaurant serving Italian fish dishes. ££

John Street Jam, 8 John Street. Tel: 552 3081. Superb conversion of part of a church into a swinging bar with food, featuring cajun. Especially popular with young crowd. £

La Parmigiana, 447 Great Western Road. Tel: 334 0686. Light modern ambience in a fairly formal, popular restaurant in the west end. Interesting food should be rounded off with crème brûlée alla Strega. Must book at lunchtime. ££

Loon Fung, 417 Sauchiehall Street. Tel: 332 1240. Cavernous room in which Cantonese dishes and a selection of *dim sum* are served throughout the day. Also vegetarian set dinner. Pleasant staff and good menu. ££

Maxaluna, 410 Sauchiehall Street. Tel: 332 1003. From morning to night this chic, contemporary restaurant serves light meals. ££

October Café, The Rooftop, Princes Square, Buchanan Street. Tel: 221 0303. A bright cheery brasserie, the offshoot of the renowned October, where modestly priced food combines east and west cuisines. ££

Peking Inn, 191 Hope Street. Tel: 332 8971. Delightful Cantonese/Pekinese restaurant serving tasty seafood and the best duck in town. ££

Pierre Victoire, 91 Miller Street. Tel: 221 7565. Also at 16 Byres Road. Tel: 357 0994. Just what one expects from Pierre Victoire restaurants: a Gallic ambience; no frills and good limited inexpensive French cuisine. £

Puppet Theatre, Ruthven Lane, off Byres Road. A series of small rooms in which great contemporary dishes are served. £££

Ristorante Caprese, 217 Buchanan Street. Tel: 332 3070. Cheerful, small, well-established family restaurant. Good standard cooking with Neapolitan influence and few surprises. £–££

Ristorante la Fiorentina, 2–20 Paisley Road West, Paisley Road Toll. Tel: 420 1585. Up-market Italain restaurant south of the river but close to the city centre. £££

Rogano, 11 Exchange Place. Tel: 248 4055. A Glasgow institution which is the place for a special occasion. The 1930s Art Deco appearance gives a slightly austere feel. When the fish is good (other food also served) it is superb. Less formal, bistro-style restaurant downstairs and an oyster bar behind the main restaurant for lighter, more reasonably priced, rapidly served meals. £££

Shish Mahal, 45 Gibson Street. Tel: 334 7899. Well-established comfortable restaurant with good service. £

The Brasserie, 176 West Regent Street. Tel: 248 3801. Imposing pillared entrance leads to a dining area that suggests an exclusive club. Excellent food with a slightly *nouvelle* presentation. ££

Two Fat Ladies, 88 Dumbarton Road. Tel: 339 1944. A fairly simple tiny restaurant serving large portions of excellent contemporary food mainly fish and game. A very small, practically exclusively New World, wine list indicating the owner-chef's origins. Advisable to book. ££

Ubiquitous Chip, 12 Ashton Lane. Tel: 334 5007. Long popular Glasgow restaurant in an attractive covered garden courtyard which suggests a hot-house. Traditional and original Scottish recipes make for a most enjoyable cuisine in a delightful atmosphere. Outstanding, competitively priced wine list. Upstairs is a more modestly priced separate restaurant. ££–£££

Willow Tearoom, 217 Sauchiehall Street. Tel: 332 1521. The only Mackintosh tea room still function-ing. A feast for the eyes if not for the stomach. Invariably extremely busy at lunch. Not open for dinner. £

Two excellent restaurants on the outskirts of Glasgow are:

Gleddoch House Hotel, Langbank, Renfrewshire (near Glasgow airport). Tel: (01475) 540711. Elegant restaurant featuring Scottish dishes in a small hotel which has first-class 18-hole golf course and a host of other facilities. Booking essential. £££. The hotel has 33 bedrooms some with view of Loch Lomond.

FORTH & CLYDE

Houston House, Uphall. Tel: (01506) 853831. Excellent Scottish food from local products served in the handsome dining room of a 16th-century house. A prodigious wine list with labels from around the world and a splendid selection of malts. ££–£££. The hotel has 30 rooms, some with four-posters and stands in 20 acres (8 hectares) of grounds next to a golf course.

Old Howgate Inn, Wester Howgate. Tel: (01968) 674244. Danish restaurant in a cosy 18th-century inn serving a wide choice of open sandwiches. A Danish speciality is offered each evening. Decent wine list at reasonable prices. £

Open Arms Hotel, Dirleton. Tel: (0162) 085241. Pleasant restaurant overlooking village green and ruined 16th-century castle. Interesting, well-pre-sented menu concentrating on local produce. ££. Hotel has 7 pleasant rooms.

Kiplings, Mine Road, Bridge of Allan (near Stir-ling). Tel: (01786) 833617. An old Victorian building which was the pump room when Bridge of Allan was a spa. An imaginative menu served in a tastefully furnished semi-circular dining room. ££

WEST COAST

Airds Hotel, Port Appin. Tel: (0163173) 236. A charming old inn on edge of Loch Linnhe. Serves what many claim to be the best food in all Scotland. Excellent wine list. 12 comfortable and chintzy bedrooms for those who wish to stay over.

Loch Fyne Oyster Bar, Clachan Farm, Cairndow. Tel: (04996) 217. Simply the finest of oysters served in this simple café-cum-restaurant, smokehouse and produce shop at the head of Loch Fyne. Those who can tear themselves away from the oysters will enjoy the langoustines and the products – eel, mussels, etc – of the smokehouse. Leave room for excellent Scottish cheese-board. Short good, inexpensive wine list. ££

Lock 16-Rooftop Seafood Restaurant, Crinan Hotel. Tel: (0154683) 261. (This must be distin-guished from the hotel's main dining room on the ground floor.) A simple room with spectacular views especially when the sunset puts on a show. A closer view is of the locks at the end of the Crinan canal and the fishing fleet unloading its catch prior to it becoming the hotel's 5-course dinner (time of delivery noted on menu). Wordy wine list. Booking essential. Jacket and tie. £££. 22 bedrooms, each with a sea view and some with private balconies.

SKYE

Three Chimneys Restaurant, Colbost, by Dunvegan, Skye. Tel: (01470) 511258. Seafood platter and lobster feast are two of the most popular dishes served during a candlelit dinner in this atmospheric restaurant in what was formerly a croft. But do leave room for the scrumptious desserts. No smoking. ££

Lochbay Seafood Restaurant, Stein, Waternish, Skye. Tel: (01470) 592235. Halibut, shark, skate and ling may well be the specials in the atmospheric informal restaurant which consists of two cottages, built in 1740. And if this be a wee bit too esoteric then there are always lobster, crab, scallops, oyster, wild salmon and... Peter Greenhalgh believes that the freshness of his fish would be diminished by elaborate saucing. No credit cards. ££

CENTRAL SCOTLAND

Brambles, 5 College Street, St Andrews. Tel: (01334) 475380. Open: 8.30am–5.30pm. Good for snacks. £

Kind Kyttocks Kitchen, Cross Wynd, Falkland. Tel: (01337) 857477. Just opposite the castle this small tearoom serves home cured ham, free-range eggs, freshly baked bread and scones Separate room for non-smokers. Open only February–December. No credit cards. £

New Victoria, 2 Bruce Street, Dunfermline. Tel: (0138) 3724175. A large upstairs room overlooking the abbey serving tasty inexpensive traditional food. Delicious sweets and puddings. No credit cards. £

Number Thirty Three Seafood Restaurant, 33 George Street, Perth. Tel: (01738) 633771. Every-thing from mussels and a cup of coffee to an à la carte meal available at both lunch and dinner. Main restaurant has a fashionable Art Deco theme while light meals are served in the Oyster Bar. £–££

Ostlers Close Restaurant, 25 Bonnygate, Cupar.

Tel: (01334) 455574. Delights in the use of local produce as far as possible. It is the food that counts rather than the ambience. ££

Peat Inn, Peat Inn by Cupar, Fife. Tel: (01334) 484206. An 18th-century village inn, only 6 miles (10km) from St Andrews with an international reputation. A limited menu lists the very best of Scottish produce cooked imaginatively and served stylishly in beautifully furnished dining rooms. Indecision may be resolved by opting for the tasting menu. There is a superb wine list which includes many half-bottles. £££+.

The Residence has 8 luxury units (7 split-level) which maintain the excellence of the restaurant. £££.

Pepitas, 11 Crails Lane, St Andrews. Tel: (01334) 474084. Good for snacks during the day and serves dinner in the evening. £

Perth Theatre. High Street Perth. Tel: (01738) 621031. A lively place for lunch and pre-and post-theatre dinner. Good coffee bar. £

The Cellar, 24 East Green, Anstruther. Tel: (01333) 310378. Just off the harbour a walled courtyard leads to an atmospheric restaurant serving some of the most splendid seafood around. Excellent wine list – French and New World bins – complements the food. Booking essential. £££

The Hollies, Low Road, Auchtermuchty, Fife. Tel: (01337) 828279. Pleasant atmosphere and a chance to discover that the unlikely sounding Auchtermuchty is a real location. ££

Timothy's, 24 John Street, Perth. Tel: (01738) 626641. This simple well-established restaurant specialises in Danish open sandwiches which are served all day. Come mealtime and excellent daily specials appear on the menu. Naturally, aquavit is in the fridge. ££

THE EAST COAST

Ashvale Fish Restaurant, 44–48 Great Western Road, Aberdeen. Tel: (01224) 596981. A chance to visit a sit-down "chippie" serving not only great fish and chips but other fresh local dishes. ££

But'n'ben, Arbroath. Tel: (01241) 877223. Lunch, high tea and dinner are served in a traditional cottage with quarry tile floors and open fires in this out-of-the-way coastal village. The produce is local, the cooking is traditional and the fish fresh from the Arbroath fleet. Arbroath smokies are served as they should be – hot and buttered. Vegetarian meals. Moderately priced wine. ££

Cornerstone Café, Nethergate, Dundee. Tel: (01382) 202121. Plain cooking with no pretensions. Clean, pleasant café where a square inexpensive meal can be enjoyed. Open: Monday–Saturday, 10am–4pm. £

Megna Tandoori, 11 Dee Street, Aberdeen. Tel: (01224) 572065. Handsome curry house serving good food. £

Old Monastery, Drybridge, Buckie. Tel: (01542) 832660. The Grays food is fit for the gods with the bar in the cloisters and the restaurant in the chapel with original pitch pine ceiling and monk stencils. Extensive wine list. Scottish produce is the order of the day. £££

Raffles Café Restaurant, 18 Perth Road, Dundee. Tel: (01382) 26344. Raffles, which overlooks the River Tay, serves pleasant, moderately price meals – coffee to dinner – in a relaxed atmosphere. Vegetarians welcome. Credit cards not accepted. £

Repertory Theatre Restaurant, Tay Street, Dundee. Tel: (01382) 27684. Casual place to have a drink, a snack or a meal. £

Silver Darling, Pocra Quay, North Pier, Aberdeen. Tel: (01224) 576229. Wonderful ambience just across from the fleet landing its catch. Soon it will be on your table, often cooked in the style of Didier Dejean's native Provence. £££

THE NORTHERN HIGHLANDS

Achin's Bookshop, Inverkirkaig, Lochinver. Tel: (01571) 844262. Simple, excellent home-coooking in Scotland's immaculate and well-stocked most northerly bookshop. Quality craft goods also on sale. £

Altnaharrie Inn, Ullapool. Tel: (085483) 230. Diners gather on the quay at Ullapool to be taken by boat to what has become an institution. Gunn Eriksen is the superb, imaginative chef in this tiny restaurant with 16 covers: Fred Brown is the host. Dinner is set except for a choice of desserts. Wines, which include French, Italian and Californian labels, can be pricey. For that special occasion. Closed: early November–Easter. £££. Sufficiently sated, stay the night in one of the inn's 8 bedrooms.

Anchor & Chain Restaurant, Coulmore Bay, North Kessock, nr. Inverness. Tel: (01463) 731313. Pleasant restaurant on the water's edge uses fresh produce. £

Applecross Hotel, Applecross. Tel: (015204) 262. Excellent local food in tiny restaurant with outside tables offering grand view of Skye. Reservations a must. ££

Badachro Inn, by Gairloch. Tel: (0144583) 255. Tiny, idiosyncratic very popular pub on a sheltered bay with a garden by the sea. Wonderful prawns if available, and colourful hosts. £

Bayview Hotel, Russell Street, Lybster. Tel: (015932) 346. A cosy bar and dining room popular with locals who enthuse over 100 malt whiskies. Very friendly. ££

Brooke's Wine Bar and Restaurant, 75 Castle Street, Inverness. Tel: (01463) 225662. Licensed café opposite the castle. ££

Bunillidh Restaurant and Tea Shop, Helmsdale. Tel: (01431) 821457. Lobsters and langoustines, home-made scones and shortbread. Full wine list. £

Dornoch Castle, Dornoch. Tel: (01862) 810216. Specialises in good Scottish food. ££

Dower House, Muir of Ord. Tel: (01463) 870090. An 18th-century house with an ornate dining room. The food, cooked in the modern style, is renowned not only for taste but also for its presentation. Wine list with many half-bottles. £££. 5 bedrooms all with

Victorian-type bathrooms.

Green Inn, 9 Victoria Road, Ballater. Tel: (013397) 55701. In a village well-served with excellent, yet expensive, restaurants (Craigendarroch, Tullich Lodge) this granite building on the village green houses a more modestly priced restaurant serving imaginative dishes – baked crab with a chive and cheese sauce – prepared with local produce. ££. The inn has 3 bedrooms.

Kishorn Seafood and Snack Bar. Tel: (015203) 240. An immaculate roadside snack shack which serves the freshest of shellfish prepared while you wait. £

Kylesku Hotel, Kylesku. Tel: (01971) 502231. Beautifully situated small restaurant with own smokery serves delicious moderately priced meals. ££. The hotel also has 7 (none en suite) rooms.

Pierre Victoire, 75 Castle Street. Tel: (01463) 225662. Just what one expects from a Pierre Victoire restaurant: Gallic ambiemce; no frills and good, inexpensive limited French cuisine. £

Theatre Restaurant at Eden Court, Bishops Road, Inverness. Tel: (01463) 239841. The restaurant and bar in three glass hexagons overlook lawns, the River Ness and the castle. Traditional, whole food home cooking. £

The Cross, Tweed Mill Brae, Kingussie. Tel: (01540) 661166. Superb Scottish cuisine served in an old tweed mill recently converted into a delightful space. Superb wine list – clarets, half-bottles, dessert wines. Great cheese board. For those too sated to travel The Cross has 9 somewhat small and stark but pleasant rooms. £££

Tigh an Eilean, Shieldaig. Tel: (05205) 251. Excellent, traditional country cooking in a small restaurant in a small hotel on the shores of beautiful Loch Carron. ££. There are 12 (9 en suite) rather small bedrooms.

ORKNEY

Ferry Inn, John Street, Stromness. Tel: (0856) 850280. Interior decor is that of a sailing ship while the bar food ranges from marinated herring to Orkney pâté and Orkney cheese. £

SHETLAND

Burrastow House, Walls. Tel: (0159571) 307. This peaceful remote 18th-century house serves all local produce. Vegetarian choice available. Credit cards not accepted. £££

"De Peerie Fisk" Restaurant, Busta. Tel: (0180622) 679. Probably the most northerly restaurant in the land "The Little Fish" restaurant, which occupies shorefront buildings that have been used as a trading post since Hanseatic times, is devoted to seafoods. No smoking. ££

THINGS TO DO

CULTURE

EDINBURGH

(Area code: 0131)

Brass Rubbing Centre, Chalmers Close, off Royal Mile. Tel: 556 4364. A fascinating collection of replica brasses moulded from ancient Pictish stones, rare Scottish brasses and medieval church brasses. Open: May–October Monday–Saturday 10am–6pm; rest of year 10am–5pm. During festival also Sunday noon–5pm. Admission: free.

Camera Obscura, Outlook Tower, Castlehill, Royal Mile. Tel: 226 3709 Fascinating 19th-century version of TV projects a moving picture onto a screen. Very popular with children. Open: April–October 9.30am–6pm (7pm in July and August); rest of year 10am–5pm.

Castle, Castle Rock, top of Royal Mile. Tel: 244 3101. Open April–September daily 9.30am–6pm, rest of year 9.30am–5pm.

Edinburgh Experience, City Observatory, Calton Hill. Tel: 556 4365. 20-minute slide show explores city in 3-dimensional colour photography. Open: April–October Monday–Friday 2–5pm, Saturday and Sunday 10.30am–5pm; July–mid-September daily 10.30–5pm.

Edinburgh Zoo, Corstorphine Road. Tel: 334 9171. Open April–September Monday–Saturday 9am–6pm Sunday 9.30am–6pm; rest of year Monday–Saturday 9am–4.30pm, Sunday 9.30am–dusk. Don't miss daily 2pm penguin parade March–October.

Georgian House, 7 Charlotte Square. Tel: 225 2160. Town house furnished as a New Town House would have been in the period 1760–1820. Open: April–October Monday–Saturday 10am–5pm, Sunday 2–5pm.

Gladstone's Land, 477b Lawnmarket. Tel: 226 5856. A 17th-century tenement with one floor furnished as the home of a merchant and the ground floor reconstructed as a 17th-century shop. Open: April–October Monday–Saturday 10am–5pm, Sunday 2–5pm.

Hillend, Biggar Road, S. outskirts. Tel: 445 4433. Largest artificial ski slope in Europe. Splendid views from top of chairlift (available to non-skiers). Open daily 9.30am–9pm.

John Knox's House and Netherbow Theatre, 43–45 High Street. Tel: 556 9579 ext. 6593. Recently upgraded museum featuring Knox's Library, and his meeting with Mary Queen of Scots. Open: Monday–Saturday 10am–4.30pm.

Lady Stair's House, off Lawnmarket, Royal Mile. Tel: 225 2424. Built in 1622 and now a museum devoted to Burns, Scott and Stevenson. Open: June–September Monday–Saturday 10am–6pm; rest of year 10am–5pm; Sunday during Festival 2–5pm.

Museum of Childhood, 42 High Street, Royal Mile. 225 2424, ext: 6645. Open: June–September Monday–Saturday 10am–6pm; rest of year 10am–5pm; Sunday during Festival 2–5pm.

National Gallery of Scotland, at the foot of the Mound. Tel: 556 8921. Houses a collection of 1,000 paintings with works by virtually all the Old Masters. Open: Monday–Friday 10am–5pm (extended hours during festival), Sunday 2–5pm. Admission: free.

Nelson's Monument, Calton Hill. Tel: 556 2716. Open April–September Monday 1–6pm Tuesday–Saturday 10am–6pm; rest of year Monday–Saturday 10am–3pm.

Palace of Holyroodhouse, foot of Royal Mile. Tel: 556 7371. Open: April–October Monday–Saturday 9.30am–5.15pm, Sunday 10.30am–4.30pm; November–March Monday–Saturday 9.30am–4.15pm. Closed for occasional State visits in May, June and July.

People's Story, Canongate Tolbooth, Royal Mile. Tel: 225 2424 ext 4057. The museum tells of the lives, work and leisure of the ordinary people from the 18th century to the present. Open: June–September Monday–Saturday 10am–6pm; rest of year 10am–5pm; Sunday during festival 2–5pm.

Royal Botanic Garden, Inverleith Row. Tel: 552 7171. Rare and exotic plants from around the world. Extensive rhododendron collection etc. May–August 10am–8pm; April–September. October 10am–6pm; rest of year. 10am–4pm. Admission: free.

Royal Museum of Scotland, Chambers Street. Tel: 225 7534. National collection of decorative arts, ethnography, natural sciences and technology. Often has special exhibitions and lectures. Open: Monday–Saturday 10am–5pm, Sunday 2–5pm. Admission: free.

Royal Museum of Scotland (Antiquities), Queen Street. Tel: 225 7534. A diverse and fascinating archaeological collection dating from pre-history to the present. Open Monday–Saturday 10–5pm. Sunday 2–5pm. Admission: free.

Royal Scottish Academy, The Mound, Princes Street. Tel: 225 6671. Houses the work of academicians and invited artists with annual summer exhibition held from end of April to early July. Open: Monday–Saturday 10am–7pm, Sunday 2–5pm.

St Giles Cathedral, High Street, Royal Mile. Tel: 225 9442. Open: Daily 9am–5pm. Admission free except to Thistle Chapel.

Scottish Agricultural Museum, Ingliston, near Edinburgh. Tel: (0131) 333 2674. Life and work of Scotland's countryside over the last 200 years. Tape-slide presentations. Open: April–September daily 10am–5pm, October–March Monday–Friday 10am–4pm.

Scottish Mining Museum, Lady Victoria Colliery, Newtongrange. Tel: (0131) 663 7519. Splendid guided tours of living history. Call "Busline" on (0131) 225 3858 for bus services. Open: April–September daily 10am–4pm.

Scott Monument, Princes Street. Tel: 529 4068. Open April–September 9am–6pm; rest of year 9am–3pm.

Scottish National Gallery of Modern Art, Belford Road. Tel: 556 8921. Collection illustrates development of painting over past 100 years with works by Picasso, Magrite, Hockney to name but a few. Open: Monday–Saturday 10am–5pm, Sunday 2–5pm. Until 6pm during festival. Admission: free.

Scottish National Portrait Gallery, Queen Street. Tel: 556 8921. Portraits of all major figures in Scottish history from mid-16th century. Scottish Photography Archive is also here. Open: Monday–Saturday 10am–5pm, Sunday 2–5pm. Admission: free.

Scotch Whisky Heritage Centre, 354 Castlehill, Royal Mile. Tel: 220 0441. Travel in whisky barrel through history of the "guid stuff": audio-visual show. Open: June–September daily 9am–6.30pm; rest of year 10am–5pm.

THE BORDERS

Abbotsford House, Melrose. Tel: (01896) 752043. This 19th-century mansion built by Sir Walter Scott has many relics associated with famous characters in Scotland's history as well as Scott's library. Open: late March–October Monday–Saturday 10am–5pm, Sunday 2–5pm.

Bowhill, Selkirk. Tel: (01750) 20732. Magnificent home with outstanding collection of Old Masters, portrait miniatures, porcelain and furniture. Extensive grounds with riding centre. House open July daily noon–5pm, Sunday 2–6pm. Country Park open May–September daily except Friday noon–5pm, Sunday 2–6pm.

Coldstream Museum, Coldstream. Tel: (01890) 882486. Small museum in original headquarters of Coldstream Guards. Open: Easter–October Monday–Friday 10am–1pm and 2–5pm, Saturday 10am–1pm and 2–5.30pm, Sunday 2–5.30pm.

Dawyck Botanic Garden, 8 miles (13km) southwest of Peebles. Tel: (01721) 760254. Outstation of Edinburgh's Royal Botanic Garden with splendid collection of mature specimen trees, rhododendrons and narcissi. Open: mid-March–end of October Daily 10am–6pm.

Drumlanrig Castle and Country Park, off A76 3 miles (5km) north of Thornhill. Tel: (01848) 30248. Unique example of 17th-century Renaissance architecture filled with Louis XIV furniture and including paintings by Rembrandt, Leonardo and Murillo. Splendid gardens, woodland walks and daily free-flying demonstrations in Bird of Prey Centre. Open: First Saturday May–late August Monday–Saturday except Thursday 11am–5pm, Sunday 1–5pm.

Dryburgh Abbey, 6 miles (10km) southeast of

Melrose. Tel: (0131) 244 2903. One of the four famous Border abbeys. Open: April–October Monday–Saturday 9.30am–6pm, Sunday 2–6pm; rest of year 9.30am–4pm, Sunday 2–4pm.

Floors Castle, Kelso. Tel: (01573) 223333. Impressive mansion built in 1721. Holly tree in ground said to mark spot where James II was killed. Open: April, May, June, September Sunday–Thursday 10.30am–5.30pm; July, August daily 10.30am–5.30pm; October Sunday and Wednesday 10.30am–4pm.

Halliwell's House Museum and Robson Gallery, Selkirk. Tel: (01750) 20096. Row of 18th-century houses contains living museum dealing with Selkirk's history and long connecton with ironmongery trade. Open: April–October Monday–Saturday 10am–5pm, Sunday 2–4pm; July–August daily until 6pm; November–December daily 2–4pm. Admission: free.

Hawick Museum and the Art Gallery, Wilton Lodge Park, Hawick. Tel: (01450) 373457. Open: April–September Monday–Saturday 10am–noon and 1–5pm, Sunday 2–5pm; rest of year Monday–Friday 1–4pm, Sunday 2–4pm.

Jedburgh Abbey and Visitor Centre, Jedburgh. Tel: (0131) 244 3101. One of the four famous Border abbeys. Open: April–September Monday–Saturday 9.30am–6pm, Sunday 2–6pm; rest of year Monday–Saturday 9.30am–4pm, Sunday 2–4pm.

John Buchan Centre, Broughton, Biggar. Tel: (01899) 21050. Centre tells story of John Buchan, Governor-General of Canada, author of *The 39 Steps* and lawyer. Open: Easter–September daily 2–5pm.

Kelso Abbey, Bridge Street, Kelso. Tel: (0131) 244 3101. One of the four famous Border abbeys. Open: All reasonable times. Admission: free.

Manderston House, Duns. Tel: (01361) 883450. Superb Edwardian house renowned for its silver staircase. Delightful grounds noted for rhododendrons. Open: mid-May–September Thursday and Sunday 2–5.30pm.

Mary, Queen of Scots House, Queen Street, Jedburgh. Tel: (01835) 863331. A 16th-century house where Mary Queen of Scots is said to have stayed in 1566. Thought-provoking visitor centre. Open: Easter–mid-November daily 10am–5pm.

Mellerstain House, 7 miles (11km) northwest of Kelso. Tel: (01573) 410381. Glorious house, especially the interiors, begun by William Adam and completed by his son Robert. Attractive terraced gardens. Open: May–September Sunday–Friday 12.30pm–4.30pm.

Neidpath Castle, Peebles. Tel: (01721) 720333. Medieval castle with walls nearly 12-ft (4-metres) thick. Superb views. Open: Easter–September Monday–Saturday 11am–5pm, Sunday 1–5pm; October Tuesday 11am–4pm.

Peter Anderson of Scotland Cashmere Woolen Mill and Museum, Nether Mill, Huddersfield Street, Galashiels. Tel: (01896) 2091. View the entire process of tweed manufacture. Water-wheel runs weaving loom in museum. Open: Monday–Saturday

9am–5pm; June–September Sunday noon–5pm; Tours: Monday–Friday (except Friday pm) 10.30am, 11.30am, 1.30 and 3.30pm.

St Abb's Head Nature Reserve. Tel: (018907) 71443. Rocky cliffs home to a wide variety of seabirds. April–July. Admission free (donations).

Smailholm Tower, 6 miles (10km) north of Kelso. Tel: (0131) 244 3101. Outstanding example of 16th-century Border peel tower. Houses exhibition of dolls and tapestries based on theme of Scott's *Minstrelsy of the Scottish Border*. Open: April–September Monday–Saturday 9.30am–6pm, Sunday 2–6pm.

Thirlestane Castle, Lauder. Tel: (01578) 722430. Castle steeped in Scottish history housing huge toy collection and Border Life Exhibiton. Open Easter week, May, June September Wednesday Thursday and Sunday 2–5pm (grounds noon–6pm); July, August, daily except Saturday same hours.

Traquair House, Innerleithen. Tel: (01896) 830323. House rich in associations with Mary Queen of Scots, the Jacobites and Catholic persecution. Ale is still brewed in and sold from the 18th-century brewhouse. House open: Easter week and May–September daily 1.30–5.30pm except July and August when opens 10.30am. Grounds open May–September daily 10.30am–5.30pm.

THE SOUTHWEST

Bachelors' Club, Sandgate, Tarbolton. Tel: (01292) 541940. Robert Burns helped found this club now filled with Burns memorabilia while lower rooms are set up as a typical cottage interior of his time. Open: April–November daily noon–5pm. Other times by arrangement.

Brodick Castle, Garden and Country Park, Isle of Arran. Tel: (01770) 302202. Superbly furnished castle standing in glorious grounds with nature trail. One of Britain's great rhododendron gardens and walled garden from 1710. Castle open: May–October daily 1–5pm; Easter–May and first three weeks of October on Monday, Wednesday and Saturday 1–5pm. Gardens open: daily 9.30am–sunset.

Burns Cottage and Museum, Alloway, near Ayr. Tel: (01292) 441215. Birthplace of the poet. Adjoining the cottage is a leading museum of Burnsiana. Start of the Burns Heritage Trail. Open: June–August daily 9am–6pm; April May September October Monday–Saturday 10am–5pm, Sunday 2–5pm; rest of year Monday–Saturday 10am–4pm.

Burns House, Burns Street, Dumfries. Tel: (01387) 55297. The house where Burns spent the last days of his life. Open: all year Monday–Saturday 10am–1pm and 2–5pm, Sunday 2–5pm. Closed: Sunday and Monday October–March.

Burns House Museum, Castle Street, Mauchline. Tel: (01290) 550045. Room which Burns took for Jean Armour in 1788 and much Burnsiana. Also exhibition devoted to curling and curling stones that are made in village. Nearby churchyard contains graves of four of Burns's daughters. Open: Easter–

October Monday–Saturday 11am–12.30 and 1.30–5.30pm, Sunday 2–5pm or by arrangement.

Caerlaverock Castle, 9 miles (14km) south of Dumfries. Tel: (0131) 244 3101. Medieval castle with interior reconstructed in the 17th-century as a Renaissance mansion with fine carving. Open: April–September Monday–Saturday 9.30am–6pm, Sunday 2–6pm; rest of year Monday–Saturday 9.30am–4pm, Sunday 2–4pm.

Caerlaverock National Nature Reserve, 9 miles (14km) south of Dumfries. Tel: (0138777) 275. A noted winter haunt of wildfowl, including barnacle geese. Open: always but contact warden for advise on safety. Admission: free.

Carlyle's Birthplace, Eccledechan, Dumfriesshire. Tel: (01576) 300666. Open: April–October daily noon–5pm.

Castle Kennedy Gardens, Stranraer. Tel: (0776) 2024. Superb magnolias, azaleas and rhododendrons and renowned for "Monkey Puzzle Avenue". Open: April–September daily 10am–5pm.

Craignethan Castle, 5 miles (8km) northwest of Lanark. Tel: (0131) 244 3101. A 15th-century castle with later additions illustrating outstanding examples of military fortification. Open: April–September Monday–Saturday 9.30am–6pm, Sunday 2–6pm.

Culzean Castle and Country Park, 12 miles (19km) south of Ayr. Tel: (016556) 274. One of Robert Adam's finest creations. Scotland's first country park. Ranger naturalist service with guided walks, talks and films. Castle open April–October daily 10.30am–5.30pm. Country Park open: daily throughout the year 9am–sunset.

Dundrennan Abbey, 7 miles (11km) southeast of Kircudbright. Tel: (0131) 244 3101. Cistercian house founded in 1142 where Mary Queen of Scots is believed to have spent her last night in Scotland. Open: April–September Monday–Saturday 9.30am–6pm, Sunday 2–6pm.

Galloway Deer Museum, 6 miles (10km) west of New Galloway. Tel: (016442) 285. Museum featuring deer and other aspects of Galloway wildlife. Bruce's Stone is a short walk away. Open: April–September daily 10am–5pm. Admission: free.

Gladstone Court Museum, Biggar. Tel: (01899) 21050. Interesting re-creation of 19th/early 20th-century street. Open: Easter–October Monday–Saturday 10am–12.30pm and 2–5pm; Sunday 2–5pm. Also by arrangement.

Glenluce Abbey, Glenluce. Tel: (0131) 244 3101. Founded in 1192 by the Earl of Galloway for the Cistercian order. Open: April–September Monday–Saturday 9.30am–6pm, Sunday 2–6pm; rest of year weekends only.

Hill House, Upper Colquhoun Stret, Helensburgh. Tel: (01436) 673900. The most splendid example of the domestic architecture of Charles Rennie Mackintosh. Open: Daily 1–5pm.

Land o' Burns Centre, Murdoch's Lane, Alloway, near Ayr. Tel: (01292) 443700. Open: all year daily 10am–5pm except July, August until 5.30pm.

Admission: free.

Logan Botanic Garden, 14 miles (22km) south of Stranraer. Tel: (01776) 860231. Outpost of Edinburgh's Royal Botanic Garden. Profusion of plants from warm and temperate regions flourishing in some of mildest conditions in Scotland. Open: mid-March–October daily 10am–6pm.

Museum of Scottish Lead Mining, Wanlockhead. Tel: (0165974) 387. Visit lead mine and open-air museum with paraphernalia of lead mining. Local gold, silver and mineral collection. Open: Easter–November daily 11am–4.30pm.

Old Blacksmith's Shop Visitors Centre, Gretna Green. Tel: (01461) 338441. Reminder of the days when young couples eloped from England to take advantage of Scotland's marriage laws. Open: all year daily.

Paisley Abbey, Paisley. Tel: (0141) 889 7654. Splendid Cluniac Abbey church founded in 1163. Birthplace of the Stewart dynasty. Open: Monday–Saturday 10am–3.30pm.

Paisley Museum and Art Galleries, High Street. Tel: (0141) 889 3151. Superb collection of Paisley shawls. Open: Monday–Saturday 10am–5pm

Poosie Nansie's, Mauchline. Open: Normal pub hours. An ale-house in Burns's days which inspired part of his *The Jolly Beggars*. Still in use.

Robert Burns Centre, Mill Road, Dumfries. Tel: (01387) 64808. This old mill on the banks of the River Nith is now the major centre of the Burns Heritage Trail. AV show. Open: April–September Monday–Saturday 10am–8pm, Sunday 2–5pm; rest of year Tuesday–Saturday.10am–1pm and 2–5pm.

Scottish Maritime Museum, Harbourside, Irvine. Tel: (01294) 278283. Several historical craft which may be visited. Indoor museum. Open: occasionally.

Souter Johnnie's Cottage, Main Street, Kirkoswald. Tel: (016556) 274. Thatched cottage whose owner and friends were immortalised by Burns in *Tam o' Shanter*. Open: April–October daily noon–5pm. Also by arrangement.

Sweetheart Abbey, New Abbey, near Dumfries. Tel: (0131) 244 3101. Beautiful, romantic 13th-century ruin. Open: April–September Monday–Saturday 9.30am–6pm, Sunday 2–6pm; rest of year Monday, Tuesday, Wednesday, Saturday 9.30am–4pm, Thursday 9.30am–noon, Sunday 2–4pm.

Threave Castle, Castle Douglas. Tel: (0131) 244 3101. Early stronghold of the Black Douglases on an island in the Dee. Open: April–September Monday–Saturday 9.30am–6pm, Sunday 2–6pm.

Torhouse Stone Circle, 4 miles (6km) west of Wigtown. Tel: (0131) 244 3101. A circle of 19 boulders, probably Bronze Age. Open: All reasonable times. Admission: free.

Whithorn Dig and Visitor Centre, 45–47 George Street, Whithorn. Tel: (01988) 500508. Observe archaeologists at work at the site of Scotland's first Christian community. Open: April–October daily 10.30am–5pm.

GLASGOW

(Area code: 0141)

Burrell Collection, Pollok Country Park. Tel: 649 7151. Magnificent collection of paintings and artefacts of the ancient world and the Orient collected by a Glasgow shipowner, a Scottish version of William Randolph Hearst. A fitting gallery has been constructed in Pollok Country Park. Open: all year Monday–Saturday 10am–5pm, Sunday 11am–5pm. Admission: free.

Centre for Contemporary Arts, 350 Sauchiehall Centre. Tel: 332 7521. Multi-purpose arts centre promoting the visual arts through a programme of regular exhibitions. Open: all year Monday–Saturday 11am–6pm (7pm Thursday, Friday). Admission: free.

Charles Rennie Mackintosh Society, Queen's Cross, 870 Garscube Road. Tel: 946 6600. Exhibitions and library in a church designed by Mackintosh, an architect who went largely unrecognised in his own land. Open: Tuesday, Thursday and Friday noon–5pm, Sunday 2.30–5pm. Admission: free.

Glasgow School of Art, 167 Renfrew Street. Tel: 353 4500. The supreme achievement of Mackintosh. Escorted tours Monday–Friday 11am and 2pm, Saturday 10.30am. (Additional tours may operate during summer months.)

Hunterian Art Gallery, University of Glasgow. Tel: 330 5431. Open: Monday–Saturday 9.30am–5pm. Excellent collection of 19th- and 20th-century French and Scottish works plus substantial print collection including many Whistlers. Superb recreation of the house once occupied by Mackintosh. Admission free except to Mackintosh house.

Hunterian Museum, University of Glasgow. Tel: 330 5431. Includes extensive coin and medal collection dating back to ancient Greece. Open: Monday–Saturday 9.30am–5pm. Admission: free.

Kelvingrove Art Gallery and Museum, Kelvingrove Park. Tel: 357 3929. Britain's best civic collection of British and European paintings. Also displays of arms and armours, the Glasgow style, porcelain, silver, pottery and natural history, archaeology, history and ethnography. Open: Monday–Saturday 10am–5pm, Sunday 11am–5pm. Admission: free.

Museum of Transport, Kelvin Hall. Tel: 357 3929. Fascinating exhibits with a fine collection of tramcars and railway locomotives. The Clyde Room has an outstanding collection of model ships. Open: Monday–Saturday 10am–5pm, Sunday 11am–5pm. Admission: free.

People's Palace, Glasgow Green. Tel: 554 0223. Social history of Glasgow is explained through exhibits. Open: Monday–Saturday 10am–5pm, Sunday 11am–5pm. Admission: free.

Pollok House, Pollok Country Park. Tel: 632 0274. Beautiful 18th-century building containing superb collection of Spanish paintings and works of others including William Blake. Open: Monday–Saturday 10am–5pm, Sunday 11am–5pm. Admission: free.

Provand's Lordship, 3 Castle Street. Tel: 552 8819. Only surviving medieval house in city. Open: Monday–Saturday 10am–5pm, Sunday 11am–5pm. Admission: free.

St Mungo Museum of Religious Life and Art, 2 Castle Street. Tel: 553 2557. A delightful small new museum which explores different faiths of the world. Here, too, is the largest Japanese Zen garden in Britain. Open: Monday–Saturday 10am–5pm, Sunday 11am–5pm.

Scotland Street School Museum, 225 Scotland Street. Tel: 429 1202. Mackintosh building from 1904 with impressive north facade. Open: Monday–Saturday 10am–5pm, Sunday 2–5pm. Admission: free.

The Tenement House, 145 Buccleuch Street. Tel: 333 0183. Built in 1892, this house is furnished as it was in its heyday. Open: March–November daily 1.30pm–5pm.

FORTH & CLYDE

Bannockburn Heritage Centre, Bannockburn, near Stirling. Tel: (01786) 812664. AV presentation tells story of events leading up to Battle of Bannockburn (1314). Open: April–November daily 10am–6pm.

Bo'ness and Kinneil Railway, Union Street, Bo'ness. Tel: (01506) 822298. Steam trains run on Easter weekend and during May–September on Saturday and Sunday.

Bothwell Castle, near Uddingston Cross. Tel: (0131) 244 3101 Imposing red sandstone castle on the banks of the Clyde considered best surviving 13th-century castle in Scotland. Open: April–September Monday–Saturday 9.30am–6pm, Sunday 2–6pm.

Chatelherault, 1 mile south of Hamilton. Tel: (01698) 426213. Magnificent hunting lodge and kennels built in 1732 by William Adam for the Duke of Hamilton. House open: All year 11am–4pm. Visitor Centre open: April–October daily 10.30am–6pm; rest of year daily 10.30am–5pm.

Dalmeny House, by South Queensferry. Tel: (0131) 331 1888. Most unusual in this stately home is the Napoleon collection. Open: May–September Monday, Tuesday noon–5.30pm, Sunday 1–5.30pm.

Deep Sea World, North Queensferry, Fife. Tel: (01383) 411411. Experience a "diver's eye view" of myriad fish as they swim along transparent tunnels in the largest aquarium in the northern hemisphere. Open: daily 9am–6pm.

Hopetoun House, west of South Queensferry. Tel: (0131) 331 2451. Home of the Hope family since 1703, this Adam house is set in magnificent parkland. Open: Easter–September daily 10am–5pm.

House of the Binns, Linlithgow. Tel: (0150683) 4255. Earliest part of the house dates from 1478 with major 17th-century additions. House open: Easter Saturday and Sunday and May–September daily except Friday 2–5pm. Park open from 10am–7pm.

Inchcolm Abbey, On Inchcolm Island in Firth of Forth and reached from South Queensferry. Tel:

(0131) 244 3101. The monastic buildings, dating from the 13th century, are the best preserved in Scotland. Pleasant 30-minute boat trip. Open: March–September Monday–Saturday 9.30am–7pm, Sunday 2–7pm.

Linlithgow Palace, Linlithgow. Tel: (0131) 244 3101. The ruined palace where Mary Queen of Scots was born. Open: April–September Monday–Saturday 9.30am–6pm, Sunday 2–6pm; rest of year Monday–Saturday 9.30am–4pm, Sunday 2–4pm.

Livingstone David Centre, Blantyre. Tel: (01698) 823140. Shuttle Row, an 18th-century block of mill tenements where the missionary-doctor was born is now a museum rich with memorabilia. The Africa Pavilion illustrates modern Africa and a social history museum deals with agriculture, etc in Blantyre and district. Open: all year Monday–Saturday 10am–5pm, Sunday 2–5pm.

New Lanark, Lanark. Tel: (01555) 661345. A superb example of an industrial village, the product of the Industrial Revolution in the late 18th and 19th centuries. Reconstruction of the mill and imaginative Visitor Centre Open: Daily all year 10am–5pm.

Stirling Castle. Tel: (0131) 244 3101. Situated atop a 250-ft (75-m) high rock this castle has dominated much of Scotland's history. Open: April–September daily 9.30am–5.15pm; rest of year 9.30am–4.15pm.

Wallace Monument, immediately north of Stirling. Tel: (01786) 475019. 246 steps lead to the top of a 220-ft (73-metre) high monument commemorating Wallace who defeated the English at Battle of Stirling Bridge. AV displays and woodland walks. Open: April–October 10am–5pm (July, August 6pm).

THE WEST COAST

Argyll Wildlife Park, Dalchenna, Inverary. Tel: (01499) 2264. One of Europe's largest collection of wildfowl and large owl collection. Open: Daily 9.30am–6pm/dusk.

Easdale Island Folk Museum, Easdale Island, off Seil Island, by Oban. Tel: (018523) 300370 (evenings only.) Pictorial history of life on the Slate islands in the 1800s. Open: April–October Monday–Saturday 10.30am–5.30pm, Sunday 10.30–4.30pm.

Eilean Donan Castle, 9 miles (14km) east of Kyle of Lochalsh. Tel: (01599) 85202. This, the most romantic and most photographed castle in Scotland, stands on an islet connected to the mainland by a short causeway. Open: Easter–September daily 10am–6pm.

Glenfinnan Monument and Visitor Centre. Glenfinnan, Inverness-Shire. Tel: (01397) 722250. Commemorates 19 August 1745, when on this spot Bonnie Prince Charlie raised his standard. Open: April–end of May and end of September–mid-October 10am–1pm, 2–5pm, daily summer months, daily 9am–6pm.

Inverary Castle, Argyll. Tel: (01499) 2203. Seat of the chiefs of Clan Campbell, Dukes of Argyll, for centuries. Splendid portraits by Gainsborough Ramsay and Raeburn. Open: July, August Monday–Saturday 10am–5pm Sunday 1–5pm; April–June, September–mid-October Monday–Saturday (except Friday) 10am–noon and 2–5pm, Sunday 1–5pm.

Inverary Jail, Inverary. Tel: (01499) 2381. Story of Scottish crime and punishment in 1820 courtroom and jail cells. Open: daily 9.30am–6pm.

Oban Rare Breeds Farm Park, 2 miles (3km) southeast of Oban. Tel: (0163177) 608. Rare breeds from throughout the world. Open: Easter–end of September daily 10am–dusk.

Oban Sea Life Centre, Barcaldine, Argyll. Tel: (0163172) 386. Situated on the shores of an inland loch a major feature is the orphanage for abandoned seal pups. Open: mid-February–November daily 9am–6pm and July, August until 7pm.

INNER HEBRIDES

Achamore House Gardens, Isle of Gigha. Tel: (015835) 254. Beautiful gardens featuring rhododendrons. Open daily 10am–dusk.

Duart Castle, on east point of Isle of Mull. Tel: (016802) 309. A 13th-century keep dominating the Sound of Mull. Open May–September daily 10.30am–6pm.

Iona Abbey, Isle of Iona. Tel: (0141) 552 8391. Home of the Iona community. Open: always. Admission: free.

Mull Museum, Main Street, Tobermory, Isle of Mull. Local history museum. Open: Easter–mid-October Monday–Friday 10.30am–4.30pm, Saturday 10.30am–1.30pm.

The Old Byre, Dervaig, Isle of Mull. Tel: (016884) 229. An audio-visual museum and visitor centre with displays of bird and animal life of Mull. Open: Easter–October daily 10.30am–6.30pm.

Torosay Castle and Gardens, Craignure, Isle of Mull. Tel: (016802) 421. Baronial Victorian castle in 12 acres (5 hectares) of Italian terraced gardens. Served by 10.25"-gauge steam railway from Craignure Old Pier. House open: mid-April–mid-October daily 10.30am–5.30pm. Gardens open all year sunrise to sunset.

SKYE

Clan Donald Centre and Armadale Gardens, Armadale. Tel: (014714) 305. Museum of the Isles, nature trails, woodland gardens, ranger service. Open: April–October Daily 9.30am–5.30pm. Gardens open at all times.

Colbost Folk Museum, Dunvegan. Tel: (01470) 521296. Museum contains implements and furniture from bygone days and has peat fire burning throughout the day. Replica of illicit whisky still can also be seen. Open: Daily 10am–6pm.

Dunvegan Castle and Gardens, Dunvegan. Tel: (01470) 521206. Historic stronghold of the Clan Macleod and still home, after 700 years, of the chiefs of Macleod. Memorabilia traces history of family and clan through 30 generations to the present. Open:

mid-March–October Monday–Saturday 10am–5.30pm.

Skye Museum of Island Life, Hungladder, Kilmuir, 20 miles (32km) NNW of Portree. Tel: (01470) 552279. Seven thatched cottages portraying life in a crofting township in the mid-19th century. Nearby are Flora MacDonald's grave and memorial. Open: April–October Monday–Saturday 9am–5.30pm.

The Old Skye Crofter's House Folk Museum, Luib. Tel: (0147022) 296. Depicts living conditions at the start of the 20th century. Open: Daily 9am–6pm.

The Piping Centre, Borreraig, Dunvegan. Tel: (01470) 521369. Museum of the Bagpipe and the family MacCrimmon, hereditary pipers to the chiefs of the clan Macleod. Open: Easter–mid-October daily 10am–6pm.

OUTER HEBRIDES

Callanish Standing Stones, 12 miles (19km) west of Stornoway. Lewis. Tel: (0131) 244 3101. Megaliths second in importance only to Stonehenge. Open: All times. Admission: free.

Lewis Black House, Arnol, Isle of Lewis. Tel: (0131) 244 3101. Traditional Hebridean dwelling built without mortar and with thatched roof. House retains many original furnishings. Open: April–September Monday–Saturday 9.30am–6pm; rest of year Monday–Saturday 9.30am–4pm.

St Clement's Church, Rodel, Harris. Tel: (0131) 244 3101. The most important ancient church (*circa* 1500) on Outer Islands. Open: all reasonable times. Admission: free.

Shawbost School Museum, 19 miles (32km) northwest of Stornway, Lewis. Tel: (01851) 710213. Schoolchildren have created this museum which shows the old way of life in Lewis. Open: April–November Monday–Saturday 10am–6pm. Donation box.

CENTRAL SCOTLAND

Andrew Carnegie Birthplace Museum, Moodie Street, Dunfermline. Tel: (01383) 724302. Open: April–October Monday–Saturday 11am–5pm, Sunday 2–5pm; rest of the year daily 2–4pm. Admission: free.

Aberdour Castle, Aberdour. Tel: (0131) 244 3101. Beautiful gardens surround an 11th–17th-century castle which overlooks the harbour. Open: April–September Monday–Saturday 9.30am–6pm, Sunday 2–6pm; October–March Monday–Wednesday, Saturday 9.30am–4pm, Thursday 9.30am–noon, Sunday 2–4pm.

Blair Drummond Safari and Leisure Park, Exit 10 off M9 north of Stirling. Tel: (01786) 841456. Only conventional safari park in Scotland. Open: April–early October daily 10am–5.30pm.

British Golf Museum, Opposite R & A Golf Club, St. Andrews. Tel: (01334) 478880. A multitude of golfing memorabilia which will intrigue even if not interested in golf. Open: May–October daily 10am–5pm; November Tuesday–Sunday 10am–5pm; De-

cember Tuesday–Saturday 10am–4pm.

Castle Campbell, Dollar. Tel: (0131) 244 3101. A 15th-century castle set in glorious woodlands with magnificent views. Open: April–September Monday–Saturday 9.30am–6pm, Sunday 2–6pm; rest of year Monday–Wednesday, Saturday 9.30am–4pm, Thursday 9.30am–noon, Sunday 2–4 pm.

Castle Menzies, Aberfeldy. Tel: (01887) 820982. Clasical example of Z-plan fortified tower house which contains Clan Menzies Museum. Open: April–mid-October Monday–Saturday 10.30am–5pm, Sunday 2–5pm.

Crawford Arts Centre, 93 North Street, St Andrews. Tel: (01334) 474610. University arts centre with various exhibitions and performances, including some excellent children's shows. Open: all year Monday–Saturday 10am–5pm, Sunday 2–5pm. Admission: free.

Doune Castle, Doune. Perthshire. Tel: (0131) 244 3101. Splendid ruins of one of the best preserved medieval castles in Scotland. Open: April–September Monday–Saturday 9.30am–6pm, Sunday 2–6pm; October–March Monday–Wednesday, Saturday 9.30am–4pm, Thursday noon–4pm, Sunday 2–4pm.

Doune Motor Museum, Doune, Perthshire. Tel: (01786) 841203. Great collection of vintage automobiles. Open: April–October daily 10am–5pm.

Drummond Castle Gardens, Crieff. Tel: (01764) 681257. Beautiful gardens with statuary. Open: May–September daily 2–6pm.

Dunblane Cathedral Museum, Dunblane, Perthshire. Tel: (0131) 244 3101. Beautifully situated 13th-century cathedral. Open: all reasonable times.

Dunfermline Abbey and Palace, Monsatery Street, Dunfermline. Tel: (0131) 224 3101. Abbey is splendid example of late Norman work and is burial place of Robert the Bruce. Monastic guest-house was converted into royal palace where Charles I was born. Open: April–September Monday–Saturday 9.30am–6pm, Sunday 2–6pm; October–March Monday–Wednesday, Saturday 9.30am–4pm, Thursday 9.30am–noon, Sunday 2–4pm.

Dunkeld Cathedral, High Street, Dunkeld. Tel: (0131) 224 3101. 12th-century cathedral beautifully situated on River Tay. Choir restored and used as parish church. Open: April–September Monday–Saturday 9.30am–6pm, Sunday 2–6pm; October–March Monday–Saturday 9.30am–4pm, Sunday 2–4pm.

Fairways Heavy Horse Centre, Walnut Grove, by Perth. Tel: (01738) 632561. Working and breeding centre for Clydesdale horses which can be seen at work. Open: April–September daily 10am–6pm.

Falkland Palace and Gardens, 11 miles (18km) north of Kircaldy. Tel: (01337) 578397. Glorious Royal Palace in Renaissance style with Real Tennis Court (oldest in Britain and still in use) in picturesque small town. Open: April–September Monday–Saturday 10am–6pm, Sunday 2–6pm; October Monday–Saturday 10am–5pm, Sunday 2–5pm.

Fife Folk Museum, The Weigh House, Ceres, near Cupar. Tel: (0133482) 380. Domestic and agricultural past of Fife shown in an attractive village. Open: April–October Monday–Saturday (closed Friday) 2.15–5pm.

Hill of Tarvit, A916, 2 miles (3km) south of Cupar, Angus. Tel: (01334) 453127. A gloriously furnished Edwardian country house with lovely gardens, hilltop viewpoint. Open: April Saturday, Sunday 2–6pm; May–September daily 2–6pm. Garden open all year 10am–sunset.

Loch Leven Castle, Kinross. Access by boat from Kinross. Tel: (0131) 244 3101. Mary, Queen of Scots was imprisoned in and escaped from this castle. Open: April–September Monday–Saturday 9.30am–6pm, Sunday 2–6pm.

Perth Art Gallery and Museum, George Street. Tel: (01738) 632488. Collections of local history, fine and applied art, natural history, archaeology and ethnography. Open Monday–Saturday 10am–5pm. Admission: free.

Scone Palace, near Perth. Tel: (01738) 652300. Splendid house with magnificent collection of 18th-century clocks, 16th-century needlework, porcelain and ivories. Lovely grounds. Famous for the Stone of Scone. Open: Easter–mid-October Monday–Saturday 9.30am–5pm, Sunday 1.30–5pm but July and August 10am–5pm.

Scottish Centre for Falconry, Turfhills, Kinross. Tel: (01577) 862010. All there is to learn about falconry including flying displays. Open: March–December daily 10am–5.30pm.

Scottish Deer Centre, A91, 3 miles (5km) west of Cupar, Angus. Tel: (01337) 810391. Feed and stroke many species of deer; falconry demonstrations; treetop canopy walk; maze. Open: all year 10am–variable.

Scottish Fisheries Museum, Harbourhead, Anstruther. Tel: (01333) 310628. 16th to 19th-century buildings house excellent exhibition including actual fishing boats. Open: April–October Monday–Saturday 10am–5.30pm, Sunday 11am–5pm; rest of year Monday–Saturday 10am–4.30pm, Sunday 2–4.30pm.

Scottish Tartans Museum, Davidson House, Drummond Street, Comrie. Tel: (01764) 670779. Open: all year April–October Monday–Saturday 10am–6pm, Sunday 11am–5pm; rest of year check times with office.

Scottish Wool Centre, off Main Street, Aberfoyle. Tel: (01877) 382850. Custom-built centre presents story of scottish wool; daily "Sheep Spectacular" in ampitheatre. Open: all year daily 10am–6pm.

THE EAST COAST

Aberdeen Art Gallery and Museums, Schoolhill. Tel: (01224) 646333. Permanent collection of 18th to 20th-century art with emphasis on contemporary works. Open: Monday–Saturday 10am–5pm (Thursday until 8pm), Sunday 2–5pm. Admission: free.

Angus Folk Museum, Glamis. Tel: (01307) 840288. A row of 19th-century cottages contain exhibition of life in the19th century and earlier. Open: mid-

April–September daily 11am–5pm.

Arbroath Abbey, Arboath. Tel: (0131) 244 3101 Splendid red sandstone abbey founded in 1178 which played important role in Scottish history. Open: April–September Monday–Saturday 9.30am–6pm, Sunday 2–6pm; rest of year Monday–Saturday 9.30am–4pm, Sunday 2–4pm.

Arbuthnot Museum, St Peter Street, Peterhead. Tel: (01779) 477778. Open: all year (closed Sunday) Monday–Saturday 10am–noon and 2–5pm. Admission: free.

Barrack Street Museum, Dundee. Tel: (01382) 23141, ext. 65152. The city's museum of natural history. Open: Monday–Saturday 10am–5pm. Admission: free.

Barrie's Birthplace, 9 Brechin Road, Kirriemuir, Angus. Tel: (01575) 572646. Museum devoted to the creator of Peter Pan. Open: Easter and May–September Monday–Saturday 11am–5.30pm, Sunday 2–5.30pm.

Blair Castle, Blair Atholl, Pitlochry. Tel: (01796) 481207. Mary, Queen of Scots, Prince Charles Edward Stuart and Queen Victoria all stayed – not at the same time – in this splendid baronial castle. Open: April–late October daily 10am–6pm.

Brander Museum, The Square, Huntly. Open: all year Tuesday–Saturday 10am–noon and 2–4pm. Admission: free.

Brodie Castle and Gardens, 4 miles (6km) west of Forres. Tel: (01309) 641371. Castle dates from 17th century and contains fine French furniture and a major collection of paintings. Open: Easter and April–September Monday–Saturday 11am–6pm, Sunday 2–6pm.

Broughty Castle Museum, Broughty Ferry, Dundee. Tel: (01382) 76121. Particularly interesting on whaling. Open: daily Monday–Thursday and Saturday 10am–1pm and 2–5pm; July–September also Sunday 2–5pm. Admission: free.

Buckie Maritime Museum, Townhouse, West Cluny Place, Buckie. Tel: (01309) 673701. Open: all year Monday–Friday 10am–8pm, Saturday 10am–noon. Admission: free.

Carnegie Museum, Town Hall, The Square, Inverurie. Tel: (01779) 477778. Open: all year Monday–Friday 2–5pm, Saturday 10am–1pm. Admission: free.

Cawdor Castle and Gardens, Cawdor, 5 miles (8km) southwest of Nairn. Tel: (01667) 404615. A family home for more than 600 years set in glorious, extensive grounds. Macbeth was "Thane of Cawdor". Open: May–October daily 10am–5.30pm.

Craigievar Castle, 6 miles (10km) south of Alford. Tel: (013398) 83635. The gem of Scottish baronial architecture set in 100 acres (40 ha) of parkland. Open: May–September daily 1.30pm– 4.30pm.

Crathes Castle and Gardens, Banchory. Tel: (01330) 844525. A 16th-century home of the Burnetts of Leys, with remarkable painted ceilings and some original Scottish vernacular furniture. Open: mid-Easter–October daily 11am–6pm.

Culloden Visitor Centre, Culloden Moor, near Inverness. Tel: (01463) 790607. Excellent displays and multi-lingual audio-visual programmes on the site of the Battle of Culloden (1746). Open: late May–September 9am–6pm; April, May early September–late October 9.30am–5.30pm.

Discovery Point, Discovery Quay, close to Tay Bridge, Dundee. Tel: (01382) 201245. Visit the *Discovery* which took Captain Scott on his ill-fated voyage to the Antarctic and thrill to an audio-visual which recounts the rescue of the *Discovery* from the ice. Open: March–October Monday–Saturday 10am–5pm, Sunday 11am–5pm; November–February Monday–Saturday 10am–4pm, Sunday 11am–4pm.

Elgin Cathedral, Elgin. Tel: (0131) 244 3101. The "Lantern of the North" when intact was probably the most lovely of all Scottish cathedrals. Much remains to be admired. Open: April–September Monday–Saturday 9.30am–6pm, Sunday 2–6pm; rest of year Monday–Saturday 9.30am–4pm, Sunday 2–4pm.

Fochabers Folk Museum, Fochabers. Tel: (01343) 820362. History of Fochabers over past 200 years. Open: Summer daily 9.30am–1pm and 2–6pm; winter daily 9.30am–1pm and 2–5pm.

Fort George, B9039, off A96 west of Nairn. Tel: (0131) 224 3101. Begun in 1748 as a result of Jacobite rebellion this is one of Europe's most splendid late artillery fortifications. Open: April–Septembr Monday–Saturday 9.30am–6pm, Sunday 2–6pm; October–March Monday–Saturday 9.30am–4pm, Sunday 2–4pm.

Frigate Unicorn, Victoria Dock, Dundee. Tel: (01382) 200900. Oldest British warship afloat and fourth oldest ship afloat in the world. Open: daily 10am–5pm.

Glamis Castle, Glamis. Tel: (01307) 840242. Childhood home of Queen Elizabeth and the Queen Mother. Oldest part of castle is Duncan's Hall, legendary setting for *Macbeth*. Open: Easter and mid-April–mid-October daily 10.30–5.30pm

Grampian Transport Museum, Alford, Aberdeenshire. Tel: (019755) 62292. Extensive collection of historic road vehicles and much, much more. Open: April–November daily 10am–5pm.

McManus Galleries, Albert Square, Dundee. Tel: (01382) 23141 ext. 65136. The city's principal museum and art gallery. Important collection of Scottish and Victorian paintings. Open: all year Monday–Saturday 10am–5pm. Admission: free.

Meigle Museum, Meigle, Perthshire. Tel: (0131) 244 3101. Remarkable collection of sculptured monuments of the Celtic church said to be one of the most notable in Western Europe. Open: April–September, Monday–Saturday 9.30am–6pm, Sunday 2–6pm.

North East of Scotland Agricultural Heritage Centre, Aden Country Park, Mintlaw near Peterhead. Tel: (01771) 622857. Open: Easter and May–September daily 11am–5pm; April, October Saturday, Sunday noon–5pm. Admission: free.

Pluscarden Abbey, 6 miles (10km) southeast of Elgin. Tel: (0134389) 257 (9–11am and 2.30–5pm). Since 1948 Benedictine monks have been restoring this giant abbey. Monastic church services open to public. Archaeological exploration. Open: daily 5am–8.30pm. Admission: free.

Queen's Own Highlanders Regimental Museum, Fort George, Ardersier, Inverness-Shire. Tel: (01463) 224380. Open: April–September Monday–Friday 10am–6pm, Sunday 2–6pm; October–March Monday–Friday 10am–4pm. Admission: free.

Tomintoul Museum, The Square, Tomintoul. Tel: (01309) 673701. Displays of local history, reconstructed farm kitchen and blacksmith's shop. Open: Monday–Saturday 9.30am–6pm, Sunday 2–6pm. Admission: free.

Tugnet Ice House, Spey Bay, 5 miles (8km) west of Buckie. Tel: (01309) 673701. This is a permanent exhibition, about the River Spey, located in large old ice house building. Open: May–September daily 10am–4pm. Admission: free.

THE NORTHERN HIGHLANDS

Balmoral Castle, 8 miles (13km) west of Ballater. Tel: (013397) 42334 – Royalty will not answer. The August/September Royal family home for more than a century. The public can explore the grounds and view exhibition of paintings in the castle Ballroom. Open: May June July Monday–Saturday 10am–5pm.

Cairngorm Reindeer Centre, Reindeer House, Glenmore. Tel: (01479) 861228. Britain's only herd of reindeer. Join guide for walk to reindeers' hillside grazing. Open: all year daily 10am–5pm. Herd visits 11am departure.

Cromarty Courthouse, Cromarty. Tel: (0381) 600418. Computer controlled animated figures. Entrance includes tape-tour of Cromarty available in English, French or German. Open: Easter–October daily 10am–6pm; winter daily noon–4pm.

Dunrobin Castle and Gardens, Golspie, Sutherland. Tel: (01408) 633177. Seat of the Duke of Sutherland set in great park and formal gardens overlooking the sea. Fine paintings and furnishings. Open: May Monday–Thursday 10.30am–12..30pm; June–September Monday–Saturday 10.30am–5.30pm, Sunday 1–5.30pm; 1–15 October Monday–Saturday 10.30am–4.30pm, Sunday 1–4.30pm.

Fortrose Cathedral, Fortrose. Tel: (0131) 224 3101. Magnificant red sandstone ruins of a 14th century cathedral. Open: all reasonable times.

Gairloch Heritage Museum, Gairloch, Ross-shire. Tel: (01445) 2287. All aspects of past life of typical West Highland area from prehistoric times to the present. Open: Easter–September Monday–Saturday 10am–5pm.

Highland Folk Museum, Duke Street, Kingussie. Tel: (01540) 661307. Open-air museum partly housed in an 18th-century shooting lodge splendidly reveals how Highlanders lived in the "good old days" and features a "Black House" from Lewis, a Clack Mill and farming equipment. Indoors are farming museum and exhibition of Highland tinkers. Open: April–October Monday–Saturday 10am–6pm, Sunday 2–6pm; rest of year Monday–Friday 10am–3pm.

Highland Wildlife Park, Kincraig, Inverness-Shire. Tel: (01540) 651270. An outdoor branch of the Royal Zoological Society of Edinburgh featuring breeding groups of Scottish mammals and birds of past and present in natural surroundings. Open: daily 10am–4pm (June–August until 5pm).

Hugh Miller's Cottage, Cromarty. Tel: (01381) 600245. This small thatched cottage built about 1711 was birthplace of the 19th-century stonemason turned eminent geologist and writer. Small museum. Open: April–September Monday–Saturday 10am–1pm and 2–5pm, Sunday 2–5pm.

Inverewe Gardens, 6 miles (10km) northeast of Gairloch. Tel: (0144586) 200. Plants from throughout the world flourish in this renowned garden. Open: All year 9.30am–sunset.

Landmark Visitor Centre, Carrbridge. Tel: (01479) 841613. The first of its kind in Europe. Turbulent Highland history is presented in an audio-visual show. Many outdoor attractions include steam-powered sawmill and 65-ft (20-metre) high viewing tower. Open: Summer daily 9.30am–6pm (July, August until 8pm); Winter daily 9.30am–5pm.

Loch Ness Monster Exhibition Centre, Drumnadrochit, Inverness-Shire. Tel: (01450) 450342. Has 40-minute multi-media presentation of the search for the monster. Open: all year daily 9am–6pm (June–September until 9pm).

Loch Ness Submarine, Clansman Marina, Drumnadrochit. Tel: (01456) 450706. Dive to over 700 feet (210 m) in this 5-man submarine in search of "Nessie".

Strathnaver Museum, Bettyhill, near Thurso. Tel: (016412) 421. Museum of local (Clan MacKay) history. Open: April–October Monday–Saturday 10–5pm.

Urquhart Castle, Drumnadrochit. Tel: (0131) 244 3101. It is from this ruined castle situated on the west shore of Loch Ness that most "sightings" of the "monster" have been made. Open: April–September daily 9.30am–6.30pm; rest of year Monday–Saturday 9.30am–4.30pm, Sunday 11.30–4.30pm.

ORKNEY

(OPEN: STANDARD HOURS – April–September Monday–Saturday 9.30am–6pm, Sunday 2–6pm; rest of year Monday–Saturday 9.30am–4pm, Sunday 2–4pm.)

Brough of Birsay, Birsay. Tel: (0131) 244 3101. Remains of Romanesque church and Norse settlement on island accessible only at low tides. Open: all reasonable times. Admission: free.

Earl's Palace, Birsay. Tel: (0131) 224 3101. Impressive remains of palace built in 16th century for Earls of Orkney. Open: all reasonable times. Admission: free.

Earl Patrick's Palace and Bishop's Palace, Kirkwall. Tel: (0131) 244 3101. The former has been described as the most mature and accomplished piece of Renaissance architecture left in Scotland. The latter dates to the 13th-century with a 16th-century round tower. Open: Standard hours, except October–March when closed.

Eynhallow Church, on Island of Eynhallow. Tel: (0131) 233 3101. A 12th-century church largely in ruins. Open: all reasonable times. Admission: free.

Gurness Broch, 4 miles (6km) northwest of Kirkwall. Tel: (0131) 244 3101. An Iron Age broch surrounded by stone huts. Open: standard hours, except October–March when closed.

Italian Chapel, Lambholm. Using a Nissen hut Italian prisoners-of-war in 1943 created this beautiful little chapel from scrap. Open: all reasonable times. Admission: free.

Knap of Howar, west side of Island of Papray. Tel: (0131) 224 3101. Two 5,000-year-old dwellings constitute one of the oldest sites in Europe. Open: all reasonable times. Admission: free.

Maes Howe, 9 miles (14km) west of Kirkwall. Tel: (0131) 244 3101. Enormous burial ground dating from 2500 BC. Open: all reasonable times.

Midhowe Broch and Cairns, On west coast of Island of Rousay. Iron Age broch and walled enclosure. Open: all reasonable times. Admission: free.

Noltland Castle, Isle of Westray. Tel: (0131) 244 3101 Impressive remains of castle originating in 1520. Open: all reasonable times.

Pier Arts Centre, Victoria Street, Stromness. Tel: (01856) 850209. Former merchant's house from about 1800 houses collection of 20th-century paintings and sculpture. Open: All year Tuesday–Saturday 10.30am–12.30pm and 1.30–5pm. Admission: free.

Quoyness Chambered Tomb, South coast of Island of Sanday. Tel: (0131) 244 3101. Spectacular tomb from *circa* 2900 BC. Open: all reasonable times. Admission: free.

Ring of Brogar, 5 miles (8km) northeast of Stromness. Tel: (031) 224 3101. Magnificent circle of 36 stones. Open: all reasonable times. Admission: free.

St Magnus Cathedral, Kirkwall. One of the best examples of Norman architecture in Scotland. Open: May–August Monday–Saturday 9am–5pm; September–April Monday–Saturday 9am–1pm, 2–5pm. Closed Sunday (except for services). Admission: free.

Skara Brae, 19 miles (32km) northwest of Kirkwall. Tel: (0131) 244 3101. Dwellings dating from 3000 to 2700 BC. Open: standard hours.

Stenness Standing Stones, 5 miles (8km) northeast of Stromness. Tel: (0131) 224 3101. 4 large upright stones from a 3,000 BC stone circle. Open: all reasonable times. Admission: free.

Stromness Museum, 52 Alfred Street, Stromness. Tel: (01856) 850025. Natural history exhibits, selection of ship models and feature on scuttling of German Fleet at Scapa Flow. Open: all year Monday–Saturday 10.30am–12.30pm and 1.30–5pm.

Tankerness House Museum, Broad Street, Kirkwall. Tel: (01856) 873191. Museum of life in Orkney through 5,000 years housed in a 1574 merchant-laird's mansion. Open: all year Monday–Saturday 10.30am–12.30pm and 1.30–5pm; also May–September Sunday 2–5pm.
Unstan Chambered Tomb, near Stromness. Tel: (0131) 144 3101. Cairn with chambered tomb divided by large stone slabs. Site of largest collection of Stone Age pottery found in Scotland. Open: all reasonable hours. Admission: free.

SHETLAND

Clickhimin Broch, Lerwick. Tel: (0131) 224 3101. A broch stands within an Iron Age fort. Open: all reasonable times. Admission: free.
Jarlshof, Sumburgh Head. Tel: (0131) 224 3101. One of the most remarkable archaeological sites in Britain, containing the remains of three villages occupied from Bronze Age to Viking times. Open: April–September Monday–Saturday 9.30am–6pm, Sunday 2–6pm.
Mousa Broch, Island of Mousa (accessible by boat from Sandwick). Tel: (0131) 244 3101. Best preserved example of broch from the Iron Age. Tower rises more than 40ft (12m). Open: all reasonable times.
Scalloway Castle, 6 miles (10km) west of Lerwick. Tel: (0131) 244 3101. Disused castle from early 17th century. Open: all reasonable times.
Shetland Croft House Museum, Voe, Dunrossness. Tel: (01595) 5057. Typical, furnished, mid 19th-century thatched Shetland croft complete with working water mill. Open: May–October Tuesday–Sunday 10am–1pm and 2–5pm.
Shetland Museum, Lower Hillhead, Lerwick. Tel: (01595) 5057. Theme is history of man in Shetland from pre-history to present. Open: All year Monday, Wednesday, Friday 10am–7pm; Tuesday, Thursday, Saturday 10am–5pm. Admission: free.

NIGHTLIFE

Although scarcely a swinging country – other than when dancing the Highland Fling – Scotland has its fair share of after-dark activites. The Scottish National Orchestra and the Scottish Symphony Orchestra give regular concerts in both Glasgow and Edinburgh as well as travelling to other parts of the country. Scottish Opera and Scottish Ballet have similar schedules.

THEATRE

Theatre flourishes with Glasgow's Citizens' Theatre and Edinburgh's Traverse Theatre being internationally renowned for their mounting of new plays and experimental works. Aberdeen, Dundee, Perth and Inverness are home to first-class repertory theatres while during the summer months the Pitlochry

Festival Theatre mounts professional performances.
Commercial theatre is still alive and kicking in the major cities – the Lyceum in Edinburgh and the King's in Glasgow.

• **ABERDEEN**
Aberdeen Arts Centre, 33 King Street. Tel: (01224) 641122.
• **DUNDEE**
Dundee Rep Theatre, Tay Square. Tel: (013820) 23530.
• **EDINBURGH**
Edinburgh Playhouse, 18–22 Greenside Place. Tel: (0131) 557 2590.
Festival Theatre, 13–29 Nicholson Street. Tel: (0131) 529 6000.
King's Theatre, 2 Leven Street. Tel: (0131) 229 4840.
Royal Lyceum, 30b Grindlay Street. Tel: (0131) 229 9697.
Theatre Workshop, 34 Hamilton Place. Tel: (0131) 225 7942.
Traverse Theatre, Cambridge Street. Tel: (0131) 228 1404.
• **GLASGOW**
Citizens' Theatre, Gorbals. Tel: (0141) 429 0022.
Kings Theatre, 297 Bath Street. Tel: (0141) 227 5511.
Tron Theatre, 63 Trongate. Tel: (0141) 552 4267.
• **INVERNESS**
Eden Court Theatre, Bishops Road. Tel: (01463) 221718.
• **MULL**
Mull Little Theatre, Dervaig, Mull. Tel: (016884) 245. The smallest theatre in Britain (43 seats).
• **PERTH**
Perth Repertory Theatre Limited, 185 High Street. Tel: (01738) 621031.
• **PITLOCHRY**
Pitlochry Festival Theatre. Tel: (01796) 472680.
• **ST ANDREWS**
Byre Theatre, Abbey Street. Tel: (01334) 762888.
• **STIRLING**
MacRobert Arts Centre, University of Stirling. Tel: (01786) 61081.

CASINOS

Both Edinburgh and Glasgow provide opportunities for you to lose your money. The law requires you become a member of a casino about 48 hours before you play. Membership is free. Men are expected to wear a jacket and tie.
• **EDINBURGH**
Berkeley Casino Club, 2 Rutland Place. Tel: (0131) 228 4446.
Casino Martell, 7–11 Newington Road. Tel: (0131) 667 7763.
Stakis Regency Club, 14 Picardy Place. Tel: (0131) 557 3585.

Stanley Edinburgh Casino Club, 14 Picardy Place. Tel: (0131) 556 1055.
• GLASGOW
Berkeley Casino Club, Berkeley Street. Tel: (0141) 332 0992.
Chevalier Casino, 95 Hope Street. Tel: (0141) 226 3856.
Princes Casino, 528 Sauchiehall Street. Tel: (0141) 332 8171.
Regency Casino, 15 Waterloo Street. Tel: (0141) 221 4141.

SCOTTISH ENTERTAINMENT

In the Highlands and Islands, especially in isolated villages, the inhabitants hold occasional *ceilidhs*, which might be defined as informal social gatherings with folk music, singing and dancing. Details of such "happenings" can be obtained from local tourist boards.

Some regular and more commerical *ceilidhs*, which are tailored for tourists, are:
• EDINBURGH
Carlton Highland Hotel, North Bridge. Tel: (0131) 556 7277. May–September. Nightly at 7pm.
George Hotel Intercontinental, 19–21 George Street. Tel: (0131) 225 1251. Mid-April–November. Nightly, except Tuesday and Saturday, at 7pm.
King James Thistle Hotel, St. James Centre. Tel: (0131) 556 0111. Mid-April–October. Nightly at 7pm.
Prestonfield House, Priestfield Road. Tel: (0131) 668 3346. Mid-April–October. Sunday–Friday at 7pm.
• GLASGOW
Glasgow Royal Concert Hall, 2 Sauchiehall Street. Tel: (0141) 353-4134. The *Flavour of Scotland*. A Scottish dinner accompanied by Highland entertainment. Summer months, Friday and Saturday, 8pm.
The Renfrew Ferry, Clyde Place. Tel: (0141) 227 5511. Friday only at 9pm–2am.
• INVERNESS
Cummings Hotel, Church Street. Tel: (01463) 233246. *Scottish Showtime*, June–September, Monday–Saturday, 8.30pm.
• LERAGS/OBAN
The Barn, Cologins, Lerags (3 miles/5km)south of Oban. Tel: (01631) 64501. Thursday only. 9pm.
MacTavish's Kitchens, George Street. Oban. Tel: (01631) 63064. Mid-May–September daily 8.30–10.30pm.

Other *ceilidhs*, attended by locals but where tourists are welcome and where audience participation is practically *de rigeur* are:
• BALLATER
Victoria Hall, Ballater. Tel: (013397) 55865. Late June–September, Friday until midnight.
• EDINBURGH
Tron Ceilidh House, Hunter Square. Tel: (0131) 220 1550. Behind the Tron church at the corner of High Street and "The Bridges". Most nights.

• GLASGOW
The Riverside, Fox Street (off Clyde Street). Tel: (0141) 248 3144. Friday and Saturday from 8pm. The place that started the *ceildih* revival in Glasgow.
• SKYE
Flodigarry Country House Hotel, Staffin, Skye. Tel: (0147052) 203. Saturday (and other nights) until 11.30pm (officially).

NIGHTCLUBS

Minus One, Carlton Highland Hotel, North Bridge, Edinburgh. Tel: (0131) 556 7277. Thursday–Saturday 10pm–late.

GAY BARS

• ABERDEEN
Flannies Bar, Stirling Street. Tel: (01224) 571266. Daily till midnight.
The Caberfeidh, (pronounced *caberfay*), Hadden Street. Tel: (01224) 212181. Thursday–Sunday 10pm–2am.
• DUNDEE
The Gauger, (pronounced *gay-ger*), 75 Seagate. Tel: (01382) 26840. Daily until 11pm–midnight.
• EDINBURGH
Chapps Club Bar, 22 Greenside Place. Tel: (0131) 558 1270. Nightly 9pm–4am. Discos Wednesday–Sunday. Leather in lower bar.
Laughing Duck, 24 Howe Street. Tel: (0131) 225 6711. Monday–Wednesday 11am–midnight, Thursday–Saturday 11am–2am, Sunday 6.30.–11pm. Disco Friday and Saturday.
New Town Bar, 26 Dublin Street. Tel: (0131) 556 3971. Newest place in town. Open daily until 12.30am. Cruisy, yet for the older crowd especially downstairs snooker room.
Star Tavern, 1 Northumberland Place. Tel: (0131) 439 8070. Open daily until 2.30am. Mixed at lunch but not so much in evenings. Very friendly.
• GLASGOW
Austin's, 183 Hope Street. Tel: (0141) 332 2707. Basement bar. Monday–Friday 11–1am, Saturday till midnight, Sunday 7.30–11pm.
Bennets, 80 Glassford Street. Tel: (0141) 552 5761. Wednesday, Friday–Sunday until 2am.
Club Xchange, 25 Royal Exchange Square. Tel:(0141) 204 4599. Thursday and Sunday 11.30pm–5am, Friday and Saturday 11.30pm–7.30am.
Squires Lounge, 106 West Campbell Street. Tel: (0141) 221 9184. Monday–Thurday noon–midnight, Friday noon–1am, Saturday noon–2.30pm and 7pm–midnight. Lunch Monday–Saturday, Sunday brunch.

Most shops stay open 9am–5.30pm with some shops in the larger cities opening until late on Thursday evenings. In the smaller towns, there is often an early closing day, though few towns are without a "wee shoppie" which stays open at all hours and can provide food and drink and assorted necessities.

VAT refunds: Visitors to Scotland from non-EC countries can obtain a refund of value-added tax (currently 17.5 percent), which is normally added to most purchases. Many large stores will deduct the VAT from purchases at time of sale when the goods are being shipped abroad directly from the store. In other cases, visitors should obtain a receipt which can be stamped by Customs officers who will inspect the goods at ports or airports of exit; the receipt can then be sent to the store, which will mail a VAT refund cheque.

SPORTS & LEISURE

PARTICIPANT SPORTS

Hill-walking, climbing, skiing, golf and fishing are some of the most obvious sports available, and are the subject of organised special interest holidays. The Scottish Tourist Board has a useful free booklet, *Adventure and Special Interest Holidays in Scotland.* This includes details of various holidays, including not only the activities already mentioned, but also such diverse pursuits as leathercraft courses near Loch Ness and summer painting holidays in Perthshire.

Golf

Scotland is the home of golf and the game can claim to be the national sport. There are hundreds of courses, most of them open to the public. Even the most famous courses such as St Andrews, Carnoustie and Turnberry are public courses and anyone prepared to pay the appropriate fee and who can produce a handicap certificate (usually about 20 for men; 30 for ladies) is entitled to play on these courses. It is advisable to book ahead at the "name" courses, although at St Andrews two-thirds of all start times on the Old Course (closed on Sunday) are allocated by ballot. To be included, contact the starter before 2pm on the day before you wish to play.

Walking

Scotland has 279 mountains over 3,000ft (900m) – these are called Munros – and provides a wide range of climbs and walks suitable for the expert or the novice. The mountains, although not that high, should not be treated lightly. A peak which, when bathed in brilliant sunshine looks an easy stroll can, a few minutes later, be covered by swirling mist, and becomes a death trap. The importance of proper equipment (compass and maps a must) and dress cannot be over-emphasised. The Scottish Tourist Board publishes *Scotland for Hill-Walking* and the

Countryside Commission has a free leaflet on the *West Highland Way*, one of the best long walks (95 miles/152km) in Scotland.

The British Mountaineering Council (Crawford House, Precinct Centre, Booth Street East, Manchester M13 9RZ. Tel: 0161-273 5835) can provide information about mountaineering clubs.

Fishing

Some of Britain's best fishing is found in Scotland. Rivers and lochs of all shapes and sizes can be fished for salmon and trout. Salmon fishing need not be as expensive as most people believe and trout fishing is avaialble in far greater supply than is ever utilised. Local permits must be obtained; details of where to get these are available from tourist offices. The salmon fishing season varies from river to river, starting from January in some places and as late as March in others and running until October. The trout season is from mid-March to early October. Fishing for migratory fish (salmon and sea trout) is forbidden on Sunday. A useful address for general information is the Scottish Anglers National Assocation, 307 West George Street, Glasgow (Tel: 0141-221 7206).

Sea fishing is found around the entire coast with the Orkney and the Shetland islands being a mecca. Shark, halibut, cod, bass, hake and turbot are just a few of the species that can be caught.

Skiing

Skiing has become increasingly popular as facilities have improved. The main centres are at Aviemore, Glencoe, Glenshee and the Lecht. There is also the largest artificial ski slope in Europe at Hillend in the Pentland hills on the outskirts of Edinburgh.

Surfing

Few associate surfing with Scotland and yet enthusiasts claim that some of the world's best surfing is found around the Scottish coast. The North coast, especially the eastern half (between Bettyhill and John o' Groats) has the most consistent of swells and variety of breaks, and Thurso has been the scene of European champioships. Other popular areas are the islands of the Inner Hebrides (Coll and Tiree).

Bird Watching

More than 450 species of birds have been recorded and the country's birdlife is unsurpassed. Some regions attract the rarest of species. Enormous seabird colonies can be seen on coastal cliffs and the islands. Outstanding are Shetland, Orkney, Handa island, Isle of May. Birds of prey, from the buzzard to the merlin, are often seen in the Highlands where golden eagles and the osprey can also be spotted.

Ornithological information can be obtained from the RSPB Scottish Office, 17 Regent Terrace, Edinburgh (Tel: 0141-556 5624). The Scottish Ornithologists's Club is at 21 Regent Terrace, Edinburgh. (Tel: 0131-556 6042).

Diving

Those who wish not only to go down to the sea but also under the sea won't be disappointed when they visit Scotland. Fish and plants abound in the clear waters which bathe the coast. Outstanding sub-aqua areas with good facilities and experienced locals are the waters around Oban, the Summer Isles near Ullapool, Scapa Flow in Orkney and St Abbs Head on the southern part of the east coast. Information can be obtained from Scottish Sub-aqua Club, 16 Royal Crescent, Glasgow (Tel: 0141-332 9291).

LANGUAGE

English in one form or another is spoken in Scotland. There are various regional dialects and local expressions used. Glaswegians appear to assume that anyone whose name they do not know is called "Jimmy". In most parts of Scotland, the uninitiated could be forgiven that the name "Ken" was unusually popular; in fact, the Scots use "ken" at the end of sentences as the English are wont to use "do you know". The Scots have a tendency towards understatement which is well illustrated by the phrase "it's not bad" – for which there is no greater compliment.

In the Highlands and the Islands, Gaelic is still spoken and is the first language to some of the older people. However, nowhere is it anyone's only language.

FURTHER READING

History

Fraser, A. *Mary Queen of Scots.*
MacLean, Fitzroy. *Bonnie Prince Charlie.* Canongate.
MacLean,Fitzroy. *A Concise History of Scotland.* Thames and Hudson.
Prebble, John. *Culloden and The Highland Clearances.*
Smout, T.C. *A History of the Scottish People 1560–1830.* Fontana.
Smout, T.C. *A Century of the Scottish People 1830–1950.* Fontana.
Steel, Tom. *Scotland's Story.* Fontana.

Poetry

Burns, Robert. Many editions available.
McGonagall, William. *Last Poetic Gems.* Winter/ Duckworths. Scotland's (and perhaps the world's) worst poet, who has become something of a cult.

Miscellaneous

Allan, John R. *The Northeast Lowlands of Scotland.* Robert Hale.
Berry, Simon and Hamish Whyte. *Glasgow Observed.* John Donald Publishers.
Brogden, W.A. *Aberdeen, An Illustrated Architectural Guide.* Scottish Academic Press.
Cooper, Derek. *Road to the Isles.* Futura.
Cooper, Derek. *Hebridean Connection.* Futura.
Daiches, David. *A Companion to Scottish Culture.* Arnold.
Daiches, David (ed.). *Edinburgh: A Travellers' Companion.* Arnold.
Daiches, David. *Glasgow.* Andre Deutsch.
Dunn, Douglas. *Scotland: An anthology.* Fontana.
Eames, Andrew. *Four Scottish Journeys.* Hodder & Stoughton.
Graham, Cuthbert. *Portrait of Aberdeen and Deeside.* Robert Hale.
House, Jack. *The Heart of Glasgow.* Richard Drew Publishing.
Johnson, Dr Samuel. *A Journey to the Western Isles*; and James Boswell's *Journal of a Tour to the Hebrides*. Two accounts of the same trip made in the 18th century by the great lexicographer and his biographer. Oxford University Paperbacks.
Morton, H.V. *In Search of Scotland.* Methuen.
Munro, Michael. *The Patter: A Guide to Current Glasgow Usage.* Glasgow District Libraries.
Exploring Scotland's Heritage. Her Majesty's Stationery Office.

Among Apa Publications' range of more than 280 Insight and Pocket Guides are these titles giving information about destinations in the region:

Insight Guide: Wales traces the principality's turbulent history, profiles its people, and provides a full guide to what is (and isn't) worth seeing.

Insight CityGuide: Edinburgh contains more than 250 pages of photography and witty, hard-hitting text about Scotland's majestic capital.

Insight Guide: Great Britain brings together, in more than 400 pages, the diversity of England, Scotland and Wales.

Insight CityGuide: Glasgow reveals, in more than 280 information-packed pages, the least British of Britain's cities.

Insight Guide: Ireland provides an insightful guide to this enduringly popular destination.

ART/PHOTO CREDITS

INDEX

D

E